Vergil

Aeneid Book 10

The Focus Vergil Aeneid Commentaries

For intermediate students
  Aeneid 1 • Randall Ganiban, editor: Available now
  Aeneid 2 • Randall Ganiban, editor: Available now
  Aeneid 3 • Christine Perkell, editor: Available now
  Aeneid 4 • James O'Hara, editor: Available now
  Aeneid 5 • Joseph Farrell, editor: Available now
  Aeneid 6 • Patricia A. Johnston, editor: Available now
  Aeneid 7 • Randall Ganiban, editor: Available now
  Aeneid 8 • James O'Hara, editor: Available now
  Aeneid 9 • Joseph Farrell, editor: In preparation
  Aeneid 10 • Andreola Rossi, editor: Available now
  Aeneid 11 • Charles McNelis, editor: In preparation
  Aeneid 12 • Christine Perkell, editor: In preparation

For advanced students
  Aeneid 1-6 • Ganiban, general editor; Perkell, O'Hara, Farrell, Johnston, editors: Available now
  Aeneid 7-12 • Ganiban and O'Hara, co-general editors; Farrell, Rossi, McNelis, Perkell, editors: In preparation

VERGIL
Aeneid Book 10

Adapted from the
Commentary of T. E. Page

Andreola Rossi
Tufts University

focus an imprint of
Hackett Publishing Company, Inc.
Indianapolis/Cambridge

A Focus book

Focus an imprint of
Hackett Publishing Company

Copyright © 2023 by Hackett Publishing Company, Inc.

All rights reserved
Printed in the United States of America

26 25 24 23   1 2 3 4 5 6 7

For further information, please address
   Hackett Publishing Company, Inc.
   P.O. Box 44937
   Indianapolis, Indiana 46244-0937

   www.hackettpublishing.com

Library of Congress Control Number: 2023932560

ISBN-13: 978-1-64793-016-5 (pbk.)
ISBN-13: 978-1-64793-017-2 (PDF ebook)

The paper used in this publication meets the minimum requirements of American National Standard for Information Sciences—Permanence of Paper for Printed Library Materials, ANSI Z39.48–1984.

Table of Contents

Preface	vii
General Introduction to Vergil's *Aeneid*	1
Introduction to Book 10: Its Role in the *Aeneid*	11
Map	18
Latin Text and Commentary	19
Appendix 1: Vergil's Meter	146
Appendix 2: Stylistic Terms	151
Bibliography	159
List of Abbreviations	169
Vocabulary	170
Index	206

Preface

Book 10 is one of the most significant books of the *Aeneid* as it offers a study of the moral complexities of war and presents episodes which are key to the understanding of the moral economy of the poem as a whole. Taken up almost entirely by battle scenes, it has often been recognized as one of the most Iliadic books of the *Aeneid*. Unfortunately, it is also one of the least-read books of the poem as readers usually favor the "Odyssean" first half. This volume is intended for use at the intermediate level or higher and provides a generous amount of basic information about grammar and syntax so that students of varying experience will have what they need to translate the Latin. At the same time, it addresses issues of interpretation and style so that students at all levels will have a richer experience of the poem. Extensive bibliographic notes have been added to help readers pursue special areas of interest.

This commentary is part of a series of commentaries on the *Aeneid*, with individual volumes for each book; a briefer and differently focused version will also appear in a forthcoming single-volume collection of the last six books (Hackett). The starting point for these volumes was the commentary by T. E. Page of *Aeneid* 7-12 (1900). Page's commentary notes have been modified, updated, and expanded throughout. In addition, the general introduction, appendices on meter and style, and an index of grammatical, stylistic, and metrical items are all new. The vocabulary for *Aeneid* 10 is adapted from that of Jordan's commentary on *Aeneid* 10 (Bristol Classical Press, 1990). I have also consulted a wide range of commentaries on the *Aeneid*, particularly for Book 10 that of S. J. Harrison (1991). The General Introduction is by Randall Ganiban and my appendices on meter and on stylistic terms are adapted from those in his 2008 *Aeneid* 2 commentary. Also this Preface draws upon his as a model. The Latin text used here is that of F. A. Hirtzel (Oxford 1900) with several changes in punctuation and the following differences in readings: *fossae* for *fossas* (24), *nostra* for *nostri* (72), *Astur* for *Astyr* (180 and 181), *Cunere* for *Cynire* (186), *horrentis* for *ardentis* (237), *tristisque* for *cristisque* (270), *referto* for *referte* (281), *spirant* for *sperat*

(291), *vadis* for *vadi* (303), *tres* for *tris* (350), *aquis* for *quis* (366), *petamus* for *petemus* (378), *gnati* for *nati* (470), *tempus versis* for *versis tempus* (512), *gnatoque* for *natoque* (525), *gnatis* for *natis* (531), *terrae* for *ferro* (546), *Achillis* for *Achilli* (581), *mucroni* for *mucrone* (681), *genitore* for *genitori* (704), *pascit* for *pastus* (710), *incumbens* for *accumbens* (727), *ad quem* for *ad quae* (742), *hunc* for *huic* (769), *longe* for *longo* (769), *minaci* for *minacis* (817).

It is with great pleasure that I offer thanks to a number of people who have read various portions of this edition and have given insightful advice: the anonymous readers from Focus Publishing; my colleagues in the Classical Studies Department at Tufts University; my students in 2018, 2020, who tested the commentary and gave me valuable feedback. Finally, I would like to thank Randall Ganiban and James O'Hara for their enormous patience and many helpful suggestions. They have read multiple drafts of the commentary and have saved me from numberless errors. I dedicate this volume to my daughter Caterina and to all my Latin students. I hope that this new generation of Latinists will find the same pleasure in reading Vergil as I did.

Andreola Rossi
Tufts University

General Introduction to Vergil's *Aeneid*

Vergil's lifetime and poetry

Publius Vergilius Maro (i.e., Vergil)[1] was born on October 15, 70 BCE, near the town of Mantua (modern Mantova) in what was then still Cisalpine Gaul.[2] Little else about his life can be stated with certainty, because our main source, the ancient biography by the grammarian Donatus (fourth century CE),[3] is of questionable value.[4] The historical and political background to Vergil's life (by contrast) is amply documented and provides a useful framework for understanding his career. Indeed, his poetic development displays an increasing engagement with the politics of contemporary Rome, an engagement that culminates in the *Aeneid*.

Vergil lived and wrote in a time of political strife and uncertainty. In his early twenties the Roman Republic was torn apart by the civil wars of 49-45 BCE, when Julius Caesar fought and defeated Pompey and his supporters.[5] Caesar was declared *dictator perpetuo* ("Dictator for Life") early in 44 BCE but was assassinated on the Ides of March by a group of senators led

---

1 The spelling "Virgil" (Virgilius) is also used by convention. It developed early and has been explained by its similarity to two words: *virgo* ("maiden") and *virga* ("wand"). For discussion of the origins and potential meanings of these connections, see Jackson Knight (1944) 36-7 and Putnam (1993) 127-8 with notes.
2 Cisalpine Gaul, the northern part of what we now think of as Italy, was incorporated into Roman Italy in 42 BCE. Mantua is located ca. 520 kilometers north of Rome.
3 This biography drew heavily from the *De poetis* of Suetonius (born ca. 70 CE).
4 Horsfall (1995: 1-25; 2006: xxii-xxiv) argues that nearly every detail is unreliable.
5 The Social (or Marsic) War of 91-88 BCE, which took place two decades before Vergil's birth, also looms large in the second half of the *Aeneid*. See Barchiesi (2008), Marincola (2010), and Goldschmidt (2013) 127-31.

by Brutus[6] and Cassius. They sought to restore the Republic which, they believed, was being destroyed by Caesar's domination and intimations of kingship.[7]

The assassination initiated a new round of turmoil that profoundly shaped the course of Roman history. In his will, Caesar adopted and named as his primary heir his great-nephew Octavian (63 BCE-14 CE), the man who would later be called "Augustus."[8] Though only eighteen years old, Octavian boldly accepted and used this inheritance. Through a combination of shrewd calculation and luck, he managed to attain the consulship in 43 BCE, though he was merely nineteen years of age.[9] He then joined forces with two of Caesar's lieutenants, Marc Antony (initially Octavian's rival) and Lepidus. Together they demanded recognition as a Board of Three (*triumviri* or "triumvirs") to reconstitute the state as they saw fit, and were granted extraordinary powers to do so by the Roman senate and people. In 42 BCE they avenged Caesar's murder by defeating his assassins commanded by Brutus and Cassius at the battle of Philippi in Macedonia, but their alliance gradually began to deteriorate as a result of further civil strife and interpersonal rivalries.

Vergil composed the *Eclogues*, his first major work, during this tumultuous period.[10] Published ca. 39 BCE,[11] the *Eclogues* comprise a sophisticated collection of ten pastoral poems that treat the experiences of

---

6   Kingship was hateful to the Romans ever since Brutus' own ancestor Lucius Junius Brutus led the expulsion of Rome's last king, Tarquin the Proud, in ca. 509 BCE, an act that ended the regal period of Rome and initiated the Republic (cf. *Aeneid* 6.817-18, 8.646-48 with notes below). In killing Caesar, Brutus claimed that he was following the example of his great ancestor—an important concept for the Romans.

7   For the reasons behind Caesar's assassination and the fall of the Republic, see the brief accounts in Scullard (1982) 126-53 and Shotter (2005) 4-19.

8   See below.

9   By the *Lex Villia annalis* of 180 BCE, a consul had to be at least forty-two years of age.

10 Other works have been attributed to Vergil: *Aetna, Catalepton, Ciris, Copa, Culex, Dirae, Elegiae in Maecenatem, Moretum,* and *Priapea*. They are collected in what is called the *Appendix Vergiliana* and are generally believed not to have been written by Vergil.

11 This traditional dating, however, has been called into question by some through reevaluation of *Eclogue* 8, which may very well refer to events in 35 BCE. See Clausen (1994) 23-27.

shepherds.¹² The poems were modeled on the *Idylls* of Theocritus, a Hellenistic Greek poet of the third century BCE (see below). But whereas Theocritus' poetry created a world that was largely timeless, Vergil sets his pastoral world against the backdrop of contemporary Rome and the disruption caused by the civil wars. *Eclogues* 1 and 9, for example, deal with the differing fortunes of shepherds during a time of land confiscations that resonate with historical events in 41-40 BCE.¹³ *Eclogue* 4 describes the birth of a child during the consulship of Asinius Pollio (40 BCE) who will bring a new golden age to Rome.¹⁴ By interjecting the Roman world into his poetic landscape,¹⁵ Vergil allows readers to sense how political developments both threaten and give promise to the very possibility of pastoral existence.

The *Eclogues* established Vergil as a new and important poetic voice, and led him to the cultural circle of the great literary patron Maecenas, an influential supporter and confidant of Octavian. Their association grew throughout the 30s.¹⁶ The political situation, however, remained precarious. Lepidus was ousted from the triumvirate in 36 BCE because of his treacherous behavior. Tensions between Octavian and Antony that were simmering over Antony's collaboration and affair with the Egyptian queen Cleopatra

---

12   Coleman (1977) and Clausen (1994) are excellent commentaries on the *Eclogues*. For a discussion of the pastoral genre at Rome, see Heyworth (2005). For general interpretation of the *Eclogues*, see Hardie (1998) 5-27 with extensive bibliography in the notes, Volk (2008a), and Smith (2011).

13   Octavian rewarded veterans with land that was already occupied.

14   This is sometimes called the "Messianic Eclogue" because later ages read it as foreseeing the birth of Christ, which occurred nearly four decades later. The identity of the child is debated, but the poem may celebrate the marriage between Marc Antony and Octavian's sister Octavia that resulted from the treaty of Brundisium in 40 BCE; this union helped stave off the immediate outbreak of war between the two triumvirs. For more on this poem, see Van Sickle (1992) and Petrini (1997) 111-21, as well as the commentaries by Coleman (1977) and Clausen (1994).

15   In addition to the contemporary themes that Vergil treats, he also mentions or dedicates individual poems to a number of his contemporaries, including Asinius Pollio, Alfenus Varus, Cornelius Gallus, and probably Octavian, who is likely the *iuvenis* ("young man") mentioned at 1.42 and perhaps also the patron addressed at 8.6-13.

16   For the relationship between Augustus and the poets, see White (2005). White (1993) is a book-length study of this topic. For an overview of literature of the Augustan period from 40 BCE to 14 CE, see Farrell (2005).

eventually exploded.¹⁷ In 32 BCE, Octavian had Antony's powers revoked, and war was declared against Cleopatra (and thus in effect against Antony as well). During a naval confrontation off Actium on the coast of western Greece in September of 31 BCE, Octavian's fleet decisively routed the forces of Marc Antony and Cleopatra, who both fled to Egypt and committed suicide in the following year to avoid capture.¹⁸ This momentous victory solidified Octavian's claim of being the protector of traditional Roman values against the detrimental influence of Antony, Cleopatra, and the East.¹⁹

Vergil began his next work, the *Georgics*, sometime in the 30s, completed it ca. 29 BCE in the aftermath of Actium, and dedicated it to Maecenas. Like the *Eclogues*, the *Georgics* was heavily influenced by Greek models—particularly the work of Hesiod (eighth century BCE) and of Hellenistic poets such as Callimachus, Aratus, and Nicander (third-second centuries BCE). On the surface, it purports to be a poetic farming guide.²⁰ Each of its four books examines a different aspect or sphere of agricultural life: crops and weather signs (Book 1), trees and vines (Book 2), livestock (Book 3), and bees (Book 4). Its actual scope, however, is much more ambitious. The poem explores the nature of humankind's struggle with the beauty and difficulties of the agricultural world, but it does so within the context of contemporary war-torn Italy. It bears witness to the strife following Caesar's assassination, and sets the chaos and disorder inherent in nature against the upheaval caused by civil war (1.461-514). Moreover, Octavian's success and victories are commemorated both in the introduction (1.24-42) and conclusion (4.559-62) of the poem, as well as in the beginning of the third book (3.139).

---

17   In addition to the political conflicts, there were also familial tensions: Antony conducted a decade-long affair with Cleopatra, even though he had married Octavia, Octavian's (Augustus') sister, as a result of the treaty of Brundisium in 40 BCE (see n. 14 above). Antony divorced Octavia in 32 BCE.

18   For the history of the triumviral period, see the brief accounts in Scullard (1982) 154-71 and Shotter (2005) 20-27; for more detailed treatments, see Syme (1939) 187-312, Pelling (1996), and Osgood (2006). For discussion of the contemporary artistic representations of Actium, see Gurval (1995).

19   This ideological interpretation is suggested in Vergil's depiction of the battle on Aeneas' shield (8.671-713). See Book 8 commentary, notes 8.626-728.

20   Recent commentaries on the *Georgics* include Thomas (1988) and Mynors (1990). For interpretation, see the introduction to the *Georgics* in Hardie (1998) 28-52 with extensive bibliography in the notes, and Volk (2008b). Individual studies include Wilkinson (1969), Putnam (1979), Johnston (1980), Ross (1987), Perkell (1989), Nappa (2005), and Thibodeau (2011). For allusion in the *Georgics*, see Thomas (1986), Farrell (1991), and Gale (2000).

Thus once again, the political world is juxtaposed against Vergil's poetic landscape, but the relationship between the two is not fully addressed.[21]

Octavian's victory represented a turning point for Rome's development. Over the next decade, he centralized political and military control in his hands. He claimed to have returned the state (*res publica*) to the senate and Roman people in 27 BCE.[22] His powers were redefined, and he was granted the name "Augustus" ("Revered One") by the senate. It is true that he maintained many traditional Republican institutions, but in reality he was transforming the state into a monarchy. So effective was his stabilization and control of Rome after decades of civil war that he reigned as *Princeps* ("First Citizen") from 27 BCE to 14 CE, creating a political framework (the Principate) that served the Roman state for centuries.[23]

Vergil wrote his final poem, the *Aeneid*, largely in the 20s, during the first years of Augustus' reign, when the Roman people presumably hoped that the civil wars were behind them but feared that the Augustan peace would not last. The *Aeneid* tells the story of the Trojan hero Aeneas. He fought the Greeks at Troy and saw his city destroyed, but with the guidance of the gods and fate he led his surviving people across the Mediterranean to a new homeland in Italy.[24] As in the *Eclogues* and *Georgics*, Vergil interjects his contemporary world into his poetic world. In the *Aeneid*, however, the thematic connections between these two realms are developed still more

---

21   The overall meaning of the *Georgics* is contested. Interpretation of the *Georgics*, like that of the *Aeneid* (see below), has optimistic and pessimistic poles. Otis (1964) is an example of the former; Ross (1987) the latter. Other scholars, such as Perkell (1989), fall in between by discerning inherent ambivalence. For discussion of these interpretive trends, see Hardie (1998) 50-52.

22   Augustus, *Res Gestae* 34.

23   For general political and historical narratives of Augustus' reign, see the relatively brief account in Shotter (2005); longer, more detailed treatments can be found in A. H. M. Jones (1970), Crook (1996), and Southern (1998). A classic and influential book by Syme (1939) paints Augustus in extremely dark colors. For broader considerations of the Augustan age, see the short but interesting volume by Wallace-Hadrill (1993) and the more comprehensive treatments by Galinsky (1996, 2005) and Wallace-Hadrill (2008). For the interaction of art and ideology in the Augustan Age, see Zanker (1988).

24   For general interpretation of the *Aeneid*, see the recent overviews provided by Hardie (1998) 53-101, Perkell (1999), Anderson (2005), Johnson (2005), Fratantuono (2007), and Ross (2007). For the literary and cultural backgrounds, see Mac Góráin and Martindale (2019), Farrell (2005), Galinsky (2005), and Lowrie (2010).

explicitly, with Aeneas' actions shown to be necessary for and to lead ultimately to the reign of Augustus.

Vergil was still finishing the *Aeneid* when he was stricken by a fatal illness in 19 BCE. The ancient biographical tradition claims that he traveled to Greece, intending to spend three years editing his epic there and in Asia, but that early on he encountered Augustus, who was returning to Rome from the East, and decided to accompany him. Vergil, however, fell ill during the journey and died in Brundisium (in southern Italy) in September of 19 BCE. The *Aeneid* was largely complete but had not yet received its final revision. We are told that Vergil asked that it be burned, but that Augustus ultimately had it published. While such details regarding Vergil's death are doubted, the poem clearly needed final editing.[25] However, its present shape, including its sudden ending, is generally accepted to be as Vergil had planned.

Vergil and his predecessors

By writing an epic about the Trojan War, Vergil was rivaling Homer, the greatest of all the Greek poets. The *Aeneid* was therefore a bold undertaking, but its success makes it arguably the quintessential Roman work because it accomplishes what Latin poetry had always striven to do: to appropriate the Greek tradition and transform it into something that was both equally impressive and distinctly "Roman."

Homer's *Iliad* tells the story of the Trojan War by focusing on Achilles' strife with the Greek leader Agamemnon and consequent rage in the tenth and final year of the conflict, while the *Odyssey* treats the war's aftermath by relating Odysseus' struggle to return home. These were the earliest and most revered works of Greek literature, and they exerted a defining influence on both the overall framework of the *Aeneid* and the close details of its poetry. In general terms, *Aeneid* 1-6, like the *Odyssey*, describes a hero's return (to a new) home after the Trojan War, while *Aeneid* 7-12, like the *Iliad*, tells the story of a war. But throughout the *Aeneid*, Vergil reworks ideas, language, characters, and scenes from both poems. Some ancient critics faulted Vergil for his use of Homer, calling his appropriations "thefts." Vergil, however, is said to have responded that it is "easier to steal his club from Hercules than

---

25 We can be sure that the poem had not received its final revision for a number of reasons, including the presence of roughly fifty-eight incomplete or "half" lines. See commentary note on 10.17.

a line from Homer."²⁶ Indeed, Vergil does much more than simply quote material from Homer. His creative use and transformation of Homeric language and theme are central not only to his artistry but also to the meaning of the *Aeneid*.

Though Homer is the primary model, Vergil was also influenced significantly by the Hellenistic Greek tradition of poetry that originated in Alexandria, Egypt, in the third century BCE. There scholar-poets such as Apollonius, Callimachus, and Theocritus reacted against the earlier literary tradition (particularly epic which by their time had become largely derivative). They developed a poetic aesthetic that valued small-scale poems, esoteric subjects, and highly polished style. Hellenistic poetry was introduced into the mainstream of Latin poetry a generation before Vergil by the so-called "neoterics" or "new poets," of whom Catullus (ca. 84-ca. 54 BCE) was the most influential for Vergil and for the later literary tradition.²⁷

Vergil's earlier works, the *Eclogues* and *Georgics*, had been modeled to a significant extent on Hellenistic poems,²⁸ so it was perhaps a surprise that Vergil would then have turned to a large-scale epic concerning the Trojan War.²⁹ However, one of his great feats was the incorporation of the Hellenistic and neoteric sensibilities into the *Aeneid*. Two models were particularly important in this regard: the *Argonautica* by Apollonius of Rhodes, an epic retelling of the hero Jason's quest for the Golden Fleece,³⁰ and Catullus 64, a poem on the wedding of Peleus and Thetis. Both works brought the great and elevated heroes of the past down to the human level, thereby offering new insights into their strengths, passions, and flaws, and both greatly influenced Vergil's presentation of Aeneas.

---

26 *facilius esse Herculi clavam quam Homeri versum subripere* (Donatus/Suetonius, *Life of Vergil* 46).

27 Clausen (1987, 2002), George (1974), Briggs (1981), Thomas (1988, 1999), and Hunter (2006) display these influences, while O'Hara (1996, expanded reprint 2017) provides a thorough examination of wordplay (important to the Alexandrian poets) in Vergil.

28 The *Eclogues* were modeled on Theocritus' *Idylls*; the *Georgics* had numerous models, though the Hellenistic poets Callimachus, Nicander, and Aratus were particularly important influences.

29 For example, at *Eclogue* 6.3-5, Vergil explains in highly programmatic language his decision to compose poetry in the refined Callimachean or Hellenistic manner rather than traditional epic. See Clausen (1994) 174-5.

30 On the influence of Apollonius on Vergil, see the important book by Nelis (2001).

Of Vergil's other predecessors in Latin literature, the most important was Ennius (239-169 BCE), often called the father of Roman poetry.[31] His *Annales*, which survives only in fragments, was a historical epic about Rome that traced the city's origins back to Aeneas and Troy. It remained the most influential Latin poem until the *Aeneid* was composed, and provided a model not only for Vergil's poetic language and themes but also for his integration of Homer and Roman history. In addition, the *De Rerum Natura* of Lucretius (ca. 94-55/51 BCE), a hexameter poem on Epicurean philosophy, profoundly influenced Vergil with its forceful language and philosophical ideas.[32]

Finally, Vergil drew much from Greek and Roman[33] tragedy. Many episodes in the *Aeneid* share tragedy's well-known dramatic patterns (such as reversal of fortune), and explore the suffering that befalls mortals often as a result of the immense and incomprehensible power of the gods and fate.[34] As a recent critic has written, "The influence of tragedy on the *Aeneid* is

---

31 Ennius introduced the dactylic hexameter as the meter of Latin epic. Two earlier epic writers were Livius Andronicus who composed a translation of Homer's *Odyssey* into Latin, and Naevius who composed the *Bellum Punicum*, an epic on the First Punic War. Both Naevius and Livius wrote their epics in a meter called Saturnian that is not fully understood. For the influence of the early Latin poets on the *Aeneid*, see Wigodsky (1972), and on Ennius, Goldschmidt (2013).

32 See Hardie (1986) 157-240 and Adler (2003). The influence of the Epicurean Philodemus on Vergil (and the Augustans more generally) is explored in the collection edited by Armstrong, Fish, Johnston, and Skinner (2004). For Lucretius' influence on Vergil's *Georgics*, see especially Farrell (1991) and Gale (2000).

33 The earliest epic writers (Livius, Naevius, and Ennius; see above) also wrote tragedy, and so it is not surprising that epic and tragedy would influence one another. Latin tragic writing continued into the first century through the work of, e.g., Pacuvius (220-ca. 130 BCE) and Accius (170-ca. 86 BCE). Their tragedies, which included Homeric and Trojan War themes, were important for Vergil. However, since only meager fragments of them have survived, their precise influence is difficult to gauge.

34 Cf., e.g., Heinze (1915, trans. 1993: 251-8). Wlosok (1999) offers a reading of the Dido episode as tragedy, and Pavlock (1985) examines Euripidean influence in the Nisus and Euryalus episode. Hardie (1991, 2019), Panoussi (2002, 2009), and Galinsky (2003) examine the influence of tragedy, particularly in light of French theories of Greek tragedy (e.g., Vernant and Vidal-Naquet 1988), and draw important parallels between the political and cultural milieus of fifth-century Athens and Augustan Rome. On tragedy and conflicting viewpoints, see Conte (1999), revised now in Conte (2007), and Galinsky (2003).

pervasive, and arguably the single most important factor in Virgil's successful revitalization of the genre of epic."[35]

The *Aeneid* is thus indebted to these and many other sources, the study of which can enrich our appreciation of Vergil's artistry and our interpretation of his epic.[36] However, no source study can fully account for the creative, aesthetic, and moral achievement of the *Aeneid*, which is a work unto itself.

The *Aeneid*, Rome, and Augustus

While Aeneas' story takes place in the distant, mythological past of the Trojan War era, it had a special relevance for Vergil's contemporaries. Not only did the Romans draw their descent from the Trojans, but the emperor Augustus believed that Aeneas was his own ancestor.[37] Vergil makes these national and familial connections major thematic concerns of his epic.

As a result, the *Aeneid* is about more than the Trojan War and its aftermath. It is also about the foundation of Rome and its flourishing under Augustus. To incorporate these themes into his epic, Vergil connects mythological and historical time by associating three leaders and city foundations: the founding of Lavinium by Aeneas, the actual founding of Rome by Romulus, and the "refounding" of Rome by Augustus. These events are prominent in the most important prophecies of the epic: Jupiter's speech to Venus (1.257-96), Anchises' revelation to his son Aeneas (6.756-853), and the scenes on the shield Vulcan makes for Aeneas, discussed in the commentary on Book 8 (8.626-728). Together these passages provide what may be called

---

[35] Hardie (1998) 62. See also Hardie (2019).

[36] See Farrell (2019) for a full and insightful introduction to the interpretive possibilities that the study of intertextuality in Vergil can offer readers. For a general introduction to intertextuality, see Allen (2000). For the study of intertextuality in Latin literature, see Conte (1986), Farrell (1991) 1-25, Hardie (1993), D. Fowler (1997), Hinds (1998), and Edmunds (2001). For Vergil's use of Homer, see Knauer (1964b), Barchiesi (1984, in Italian; trans. 2015), Gransden (1984), Cairns (1989) 177-248, and Dekel (2012). Knauer (1964a), written in German, is a standard work on this topic; those without German can still benefit from its detailed citations and lists of parallels. For Vergil's use of Homer and Apollonius, see Nelis (2001).

[37] Augustus' clan, the Julian gens, claimed its descent from Iulus (another name for Aeneas' son Ascanius) and thus also from Aeneas and Venus. Julius Caesar in particular emphasized this ancestry; Augustus made these connections central to his political self-presentation as well. See, e.g., Zanker (1988) 193-210, and Galinsky (1996) 141-224.

an Augustan reading of Roman history, one that is shaped by the deeds of these three men and that views Augustus as the culmination of the processes of fate and history.[38]

This is not to say that the associations among Aeneas, Romulus, and Augustus are always positive or unproblematic, particularly given the ways that Aeneas is portrayed and can be interpreted.[39] To some, Vergil's Aeneas represents an idealized Roman hero, who thus reflects positively on Augustus by association.[40] In general this type of reading sees a positive imperial ideology in the epic and is referred to as "optimistic" or "Augustan." Others are more troubled by Vergil's Aeneas, and advocate interpretations that challenge the moral and spiritual value of his actions, as well as of the role of the gods and fate. Such readings perceive a much darker poetic world[41] and have been called "pessimistic" or "ambivalent."[42] Vergil's portrayal of Aeneas is thus a major element in debates over the epic's meaning.[43]

Randall Ganiban, *Series Coeditor*

---

38 See O'Hara (1990), however, for the deceptiveness of prophecies in the *Aeneid*, as well as the notes in the commentary on Book 8 to *Aen.* 8.40-1, 341, 533, 626-728, 629, 652, 720-8.

39 For general interpretation of the *Aeneid*, see n. 24 (above).

40 This type of reading is represented especially by Heinze (1915, trans. 1993), Pöschl (1950, trans. 1962), and Otis (1964). More recent and complex Augustan interpretations can be found in Hardie (1986) and Cairns (1989).

41 See, e.g., Putnam (1965), Johnson (1976), Lyne (1987), and Thomas (2001). Putnam's reading of the *Aeneid* has been particularly influential. Of the ending of the poem he writes: "By giving himself over with such suddenness to the private wrath which the sight of the belt of Pallas arouses, Aeneas becomes himself *impius Furor*, as rage wins the day over moderation, disintegration defeats order, and the achievements of history through heroism fall victim to the human frailty of one man" (1965) 193-4. For a different understanding of Aeneas' wrath, see Galinsky (1988). For *furor* and violence in Book 8, see Book 8 commentary, notes to 8.184-279, 196, 219-20, 494.

42 For a general treatment of the optimism/pessimism debate, see Kennedy (1992). For a critique of the "pessimistic" view, see Martindale (1993); for critique of the "optimistic" stance and its rejection of "pessimism," see Thomas (2001), and for brief historical perspective on both sides, see Schmidt (2001). For the continuing debate over the politics of the *Aeneid* and over the Augustan age more generally, see the collections of Powell (1992) and Stahl (1998).

43 Indeed some readers also question whether it is even possible to resolve this interpretive debate because of Vergil's inherent ambiguity. See Johnson (1976), Perkell (1994), O'Hara (2007) 77-103, and Conte (2007). Martindale (1993) offers a critique of ambiguous readings.

Introduction to Book 10:
Its Role in the *Aeneid*

Plot and structure of *Aeneid* 10

Like other books of the poem, *Aeneid* 10 is neatly divided into distinct narrative units. The book opens with a divine assembly (1-117), with Venus and Juno angrily quarrelling over the fate of their protégés, the Trojans and the Latins respectively, and with Jupiter shrewdly claiming impartiality. From heavenly Olympus, the narrative next switches back to earth and resumes from where it broke off at the end of Book 9. While the Trojans are still besieged in the Trojan camp by the Latins, Aeneas, at night, sails down the Tiber and, after an unexpected encounter with the ships of his fleet, now turned into nymphs (cf. 9.77-122), he and his Etruscan allies land on the shore of Latium (118-307). The besieged Trojans welcome back their leader with cries of joy, and, thus, with renewed confidence and alacrity, start the third day of battle (308-908).

This last section of the book, by far the longest, describes the pitched battle between the two sides, and in Homeric fashion alternates between wide-angle views of the movements of the two armies and close-ups of the individual feats of the major heroes. Aeneas' *aristeia** opens the section, establishing the martial valor of the Trojan leader who, after a long absence, finally returns to the battlefield. Two short and balanced *aristeiai* of the Etruscan Pallas (380-425) and of the Italian Lausus (426-38) follow. A fair match for each other, the two young and equally valorous heroes are, however, prevented by fate from meeting in combat. Both Pallas and Lausus, as the narrator sadly foreshadows, are doomed to meet their untimely deaths at the hands of greater heroes: the former is immediately dispatched by a cruel and overly contemptuous Turnus (439-509); the latter will be killed toward the end of the book by Aeneas, who, in stark contrast with Turnus, shows restraint and deep compassion for the fallen youth (789-832). Like Pallas and Lausus, Aeneas and Turnus are also prevented from meeting on this day of battle. Maddened by the news of Pallas' death, Aeneas rages through the field, butchering his opponents and searching for Turnus, but in vain (510-605). Juno creates a phantom Aeneas that diverts her protégé Turnus from the battle (606-89) and thus prevents the real Aeneas from immediately fighting (and killing) him. With Turnus gone, Mezentius, spurred to action by Jupiter, leads the front ranks of the Latins (690-788) and will, ultimately, face Aeneas. Thus, the expected duel between Aeneas and Turnus is postponed and replaced by that between Aeneas and Mezentius, the once ruthless tyrant of Caere who, surprisingly, in his final hour evokes the sympathy of readers for his deep love toward his son Lausus and for his dignified acceptance of death (832-908).

This last section is masterfully articulated with symmetrical duel scenes that artistically contrast the behavior of the two main heroes of the war books of the poem: Turnus and Aeneas. In the first duel (439-509), Turnus kills the young Pallas, Aeneas' closest ally and the only son of Evander; in the second (794-832), Aeneas kills the young Lausus, the only son of Mezentius. Both Pallas and Lausus are the beloved sons of fathers who wish to save them but are unable. Both characters engage in a duel with a stronger and older adversary, and, in both cases, the text emphasizes the uneven character of the conflict. The precise list of narrative parallels invites the reader to connect the two scenes and is a most effective means to call attention to the significant differences in the behavior of Turnus and Aeneas: urged by his sister Juturna to come to the rescue of Lausus and his troops who are fighting against Pallas and the Arcadians, Turnus seeks the young Pallas and an unequal fight, while Aeneas is attacked by Lausus and even attempts to stop Lausus from challenging him; Turnus wishes that Evander were there to witness his own son's death, while Aeneas is moved by Lausus' filial love for his father; Turnus boasts over the body of his beaten enemy and strips him of his armor (his baldric in particular), an action that will bring on his downfall, while Aeneas praises the fallen youth and allows Lausus to keep the weapons that made him happy. But these contrasting parallels and actions not only bring out defining characteristics of each hero. They also, as noted by Barchiesi (2015) 42, have immediate relevance for deciphering the overall plot of the epic: after the pair of duels (Turnus with Pallas and Aeneas with Lausus), Mezentius, Lausus' father, attacks Aeneas, Lausus' killer. The duel between Turnus and Pallas, however, is not followed by the duel between Aeneas (Pallas' "surrogate" father, to whom Evander had entrusted his son) and Turnus. Repetitions and parallels thus trace an empty space that will be filled only at the end of the poem when the two heroes, Turnus and Aeneas, will finally meet.

Heroes at war in *Aeneid* 10

Book 10, taken up almost entirely by battle scenes, has been often recognized as one of the most Iliadic books of the poem. Vergil employs the Homeric model in two different but equally important ways.

First, Vergil uses the *Iliad* as a "code model," to use Gian Biagio Conte's terminology. Vergil, that is, closely follows in his own battle narrative the formulas*, topoi*, and type-scenes* that define Homeric battle scenes in the *Iliad* (for detailed discussion on Vergilian use of Homeric type-scenes and topoi, see 308-908 n.). But these conventions of Homeric narrative are not just passively reproduced by Vergil but often acquire a new connotative meaning. Vergil, that is, does not "imitate" Homer in any mechanical sense, but uses Homer to create new interpretative perspectives. For example: the planting of one's foot on the corpse of a conquered enemy is a functional action in the *Iliad*, for this action allows the hero to retrieve the spear from the enemy's corpse. Yet, this very same action, devoid of special meaning in the *Iliad*, acquires a problematic significance in the *Aeneid*. When Turnus plants his foot on the corpse of the lifeless Pallas, the gesture is completely gratuitous and is meant to highlight Turnus' vain arrogance which is pointedly contrasted with Aeneas' merciful attitude toward the corpse of Lausus. Turnus' action is further problematized by the fact that in Roman (and, especially, in Augustan) culture the gratuitously spiteful behavior toward a beaten foe is invested with a clearly negative resonance as Anchises' famous warning to the Romans (*Romane, memento*) to spare the defeated (*parcere subiectis*) in Book 6.853 reminds the reader all too well (see Barchiesi (2015) 50-1).

Second, Vergil uses the *Iliad* as a "source" model (again, to use Conte's terminology). Vergil, that is, rewrites within his own text important episodes of the Homeric poem, thereby assimilating the heroes of the *Aeneid* to the heroes of the *Iliad*. It is this narrative strategy that allows Vergil to present his reader with complex characters who defy simplistic and one-dimensional interpretations. The representation of Aeneas in *Aeneid* 10 is a good case study. Throughout the poem, Aeneas is presented as the paradigm of a new (Roman) type of heroism; he is a sort of proto-Roman hero who incarnates quintessentially Roman (and, specifically, Augustan) virtues like *pietas* and *clementia*. This reading of his character seems to be further underscored in Book 10. As Aeneas sails back from Etruria to Latium with his allies, we find him standing tall on the ship-stern (*Aen.* 8.680 *stans celsa in puppi*), with flames streaming from the top, holding up with his left arm his glowing new shield. In the center of his shield is Augustus himself who, just like Aeneas, stands tall on a ship-stern (*Aen.* 10.261 *stans celsa in puppi*), twin flames appearing over his head while he leads his army in the battle of Actium which sealed his own triumph over the forces of Cleopatra and Antony. Never is the analogy between Aeneas and Augustus more marked in the poem than in this scene. Never is Aeneas more indissolubly conflated with his most illustrious descendant. And yet, this straightforward reading of the character of Aeneas as a proto-Augustus is soon challenged as Vergil pointedly models Aeneas' behavior after the death of Pallas on that of Achilles who, in his darkest hour, maddened by a ruthless rage (ruthless even by Achilles' standards) after the death of Patroclus, mercilessly slaughters one suppliant after the other (*Il.* 20-1) and sacrifices victims to the shade of his companion (*Il.* 21.26-33). Why does Vergil mold Aeneas in this episode into a savage Achilles? What does this reveal about Aeneas? Is he a proto-Augustus, promoter of a new (and improved) world order, or is he a vicious new Achilles *redivivus*? And perhaps, more importantly, what does this tell us about what Aeneas and Augustus stand for? What ideals and values do they represent?

By contrast, his archenemy, Turnus who, in many ways, embodies the irrational, dark, and chaotic forces of the cosmos, plays, in his duel with Pallas, the role of the Homeric Hector, one of the most sympathetic Homeric characters. Just as Hector had sealed his fate by killing Patroclus, Achilles' dearest companion, and stripping him of his armor, so, too, Turnus kills Pallas, Aeneas' companion and protégé, strips him of his belt, and consigns himself to a premature death at the hands of a furious (and Achilles-like) Aeneas at the end of the poem. Likewise, Mezentius, the great *contemptor divum* (7.648) and ruthless tyrant of Caere (at least in Evander's account, 8.481-95), in Book 10 is assimilated to the quintessential Homeric monster, Polyphemus, the savage man-eater of the *Odyssey* (*Od.* 9.105-566) and of the *Aeneid* (3.655-91), only to undergo a dramatic transformation at the end of the book. The deep pain he experiences at Lausus' death and the unwavering way he meets his fate after his son's death cast him in the role of Priam, the quintessential father of epic who in the *Iliad* had witnessed the death of his son Hector (*Il.* 22) and who, in *Aeneid* 2 (506-58), courageously meets his fate after watching the death of his own son Polites. Vergil's usage of the

Homeric subtexts allows him therefore to create multilayered characters rich in complexity and interpretative depth. The *Aeneid*, at every level, challenges the simplistic notions of "good guys" and "bad guys," "right" and "wrong."

And in this book, just as in all the war books of the *Aeneid*, the very business of war is put to the test. In Homer war is the central activity that defines a hero's life; war is a dire but accepted necessity of the heroic environment, bringing its triumphs and tragedies as parts of the human condition. Vergilian battle scenes are, instead, colored by intense pathos and a deep sense of futility. The deaths of the young Pallas and Lausus, both, like so many young heroes of the poem, victims of their youthful enthusiasm and almost childish heroism, are narrated with deep sympathy as Vergil himself mourns their untimely deaths in war (10.433-8). And further, as Conte (2007) and Bonfanti (1985), among others, have shown, Vergil, somewhat differently from Homer, often allows the reader to experience the realities of war from the viewpoint of the defeated. In this way, multiple perspectives on an event are often dramatically allowed to coexist in the *Aeneid* without authorial resolution.

But it is, above all, the nature of the war between Trojans and Latins that informs Vergil's battle narrative, for war, in this poem, is always tainted with the troubling associations of civil war. The Trojans' journey to Latium is, after all, presented as a "return" to the homeland. Dardanus, the Trojans' ancestor, is an Italian (cf. *Aen.* 3.165-71). Trojans and Latins are kindred *gentes* even before being eventually united into that one race at peace announced at the end of the poem (cf. *Aen.* 12.504 *aeterna gentis in pace futuras*). This very notion informs Vergil's narrative strategy in *Aeneid* 10 and, again, the Homeric subtext is meaningfully adapted by Vergil into the narrative of the *Aeneid* to underscore this idea. As noted by Quint (2018) 150-79, for example, all the major characters in *Aeneid* 10—Pallas, Turnus, Lausus, Aeneas, and Mezentius—are cast, at some point in the book, in the role of Sarpedon, the Iliadic hero eventually killed by Patroclus in *Iliad* 16 and in the role of his opponent, the victorious Patroclus. The major heroes of *Aeneid* 10 flip constantly between these two important Homeric models, Sarpedon and Patroclus. In this way, their intertextual identity becomes somewhat blurred. Each of them becomes, at some level, a mirror image of the other and each of them is, therefore, forced, at some level, to fight a mirror image of his own self. As a result, the war they fight against each other takes on the connotation of an internecine war which may ultimately be read as a somber reflection and commentary on the series of more recent fratricidal wars that plagued Rome and Italy in the first century BCE, wars many of which, in many cases, Vergil and Vergil's contemporary audience had witnessed and experienced firsthand.

Works consulted, additional reading

On the structure of the book, see Benario (1967), Barchiesi (2015) 35-52 (translation of *La traccia del modello* (1984), for a review of which in English, see S. J. Harrison (1986)).

On Vergilian battle narrative, see Heinze (1993) 142-94, Krischer (1979), Willcock (1983), Horsfall (1987), S. J. Harrison (1988), S. J. Harrison (1991) xxxi-xxxiii, Rossi (2004), Barchiesi (2015).

On Vergil and the Homeric model, see Anderson (1957), Knauer (1964a) (though in German, Knauer's extensive list of Vergilian borrowings is useful for non-German-speakers), Knauer (1981) (a summary in English of his arguments), Gransden (1984) 126-54, Putnam (2011) 19-65, Barchiesi (2015) 1-52, Quint (2018) 150-79.

On Vergil and focalization*, see Bonfanti (1985) especially 31-84 (in Italian; reviewed in English by S. J. Harrison (1987)), Fowler (1990), Rossi (2004) 84-104, Conte (2007).

On Vergil's war narrative as reflective of the Roman civil wars, see Rossi (2004) 150-68, Rijser (2011), Newman (2015). On Vergil's war narrative as resonating with the divisions between Romans and Italians in the Social Wars, see Barchiesi (2008, in Italian), Marincola (2010), Goldschmidt (2013) 127-31.

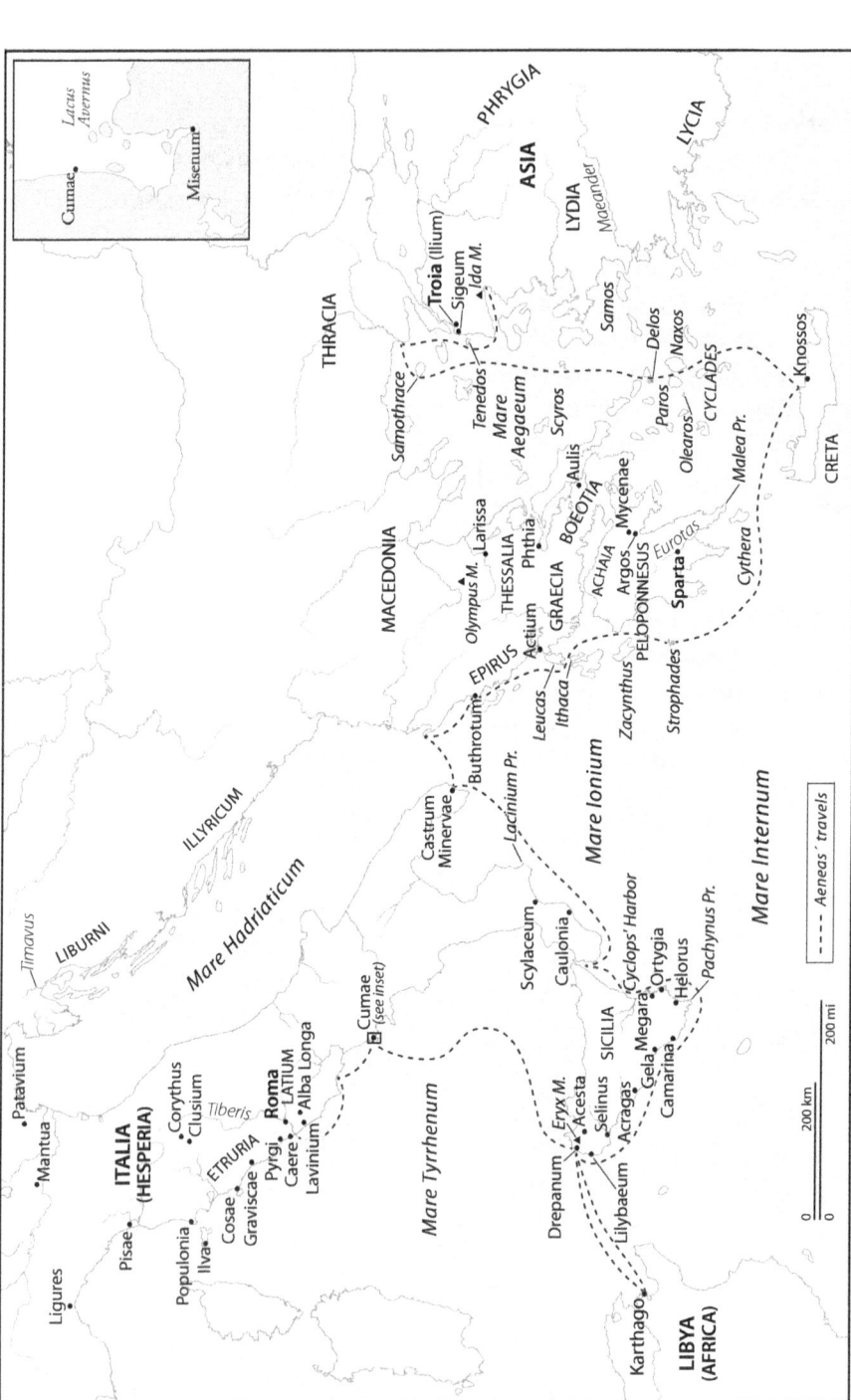

LIBER DECIMUS[1]

1-117: The assembly of the gods

Book 10 opens with Jupiter summoning a council of the gods and expressing his displeasure at their instigation of war. Jupiter claims that the gods had voted on a course of action that he had approved but have, instead, done what he forbade. A time for strife will come, he promises, when Juno's Carthage will attack Venus' Rome (6-15). After both Venus and Juno appeal their cases (16-95), Jupiter issues his final verdict: he refuses to take sides and, apparently abandoning his original plea for peace, states that he will allow the fates to find their way (96-117).

The three speeches are all very different in tone and are in line with Vergil's characterization of the three gods. Jupiter's speech is solemn and, like his other speeches in the poem, highly disingenuous, if not outright false in some of his assertions (see notes on 12-13, 15, and 107-8). Juno's and Venus' are bitter and ironic as both goddesses draw selective and misleading parallels between the present

---

1 *Please note:* When reference is made to a passage from *Aeneid* 10, the line number alone is given, without the book number (e.g., "cf. 110"), along with reference to the note on that passage, if relevant (e.g., "cf. 110 n."). When reference is made to another book of the *Aeneid*, the number of that book is given as well (e.g., "cf. 6.203"). Reference to notes in other commentaries is made by using the last name of the commentator (details of the editions cited can be found in the bibliography). References will also be made to the commentary of the fourth-century CE grammarian and commentator Servius. This commentary exists in both long and short form. The long form (to be referred to throughout as "Servius *auctus*") is believed to incorporate work of Aelius Donatus, a grammarian of the fourth century CE. References to *Allen and Greenough's New Latin Grammar* (see Mahoney (2001) in the bibliography) are provided by abbreviation and section number (e.g., AG §471c). *OLD* refers to the *Oxford Latin Dictionary* (2nd ed. 2012) with s.v. (*sub verbo*) indicating the dictionary headword, and *VE* to *The Virgil Encyclopedia* (Thomas and Ziolkowski (2014)), an invaluable resource. *FRL* refers to *Fragmentary Republican Latin* (Goldberg and Manuwald (2018)). Terms marked with an asterisk (e.g., chiasmus*) are defined in Appendix 2 on stylistic terms; for metrical features, see Appendix 1 on meter. The fundamental debt of the volumes in this series to the commentary of Page (1894, 1900) has been described in the series Introduction.

situation and aspects of the Trojan War. Venus focuses on the fate of the besieged Trojan camp now experiencing what once had been the fate of the besieged (and eventually sacked) Troy. Juno instead concentrates on the causes of the war and draws an implicit comparison between Paris and Aeneas, both guilty, in her opinion, of having stolen a bride from her legitimate spouse/fiancé and having started the war (Paris, the Trojan War; Aeneas, the present one).

Divine assemblies are a set piece of classical epic. The divine assembly in *Aeneid* 10, the only such assembly in the poem, has different models. From a structural point of view, it recalls closely the assembly of the gods in *Iliad* 20: in both cases the assembly opens the book and marks the return of the greatest hero to combat: Achilles in the *Iliad*, Aeneas in the *Aeneid*. This assembly, however, also presents verbal parallels with the divine councils at the beginning of *Iliad* 4 and 8 (with Jupiter's indignation at Juno in the former matching closely that of Zeus at Hera at *Il.* 4.30-3). Vergil, however, seems to have "Romanized" the divine assembly as the scene borrows both language and elements of Roman senatorial procedures, with Jupiter taking the role of the presiding magistrate calling the meeting and making the *relatio* (a report of the matter at hand), and Venus and Juno presenting the views of opposing senators (the *interrogatio sententiae*). The equation of the divine assembly with the Roman senate will be fully exploited by Ovid (*Met.* 1.167-76) to link Augustus to Jupiter and problematize the nature of the *princeps*' supreme power.

For an overview of the role of the gods in Greek and Roman epic, see Feeney (1991); for the *Aeneid*, see Feeney (1991) 129-87, Hardie (1998) 94-101. For a convincing article on the ambivalent role of Jupiter in this assembly (and, overall, in the poem), see Hejduk (2009). On the various models for this *concilium deorum*, see S. J. Harrison *ad* 1-117, Bretzigheimer (1993) 26-36 (in German). Goldschmidt (2013) 127-31 draws important parallels between Vergil's divine assembly and that of Ennius, an archaic Roman poet, who had a divine assembly in Book 1 of his epic poem titled *Annales*. On the inconclusiveness of the Vergilian council, see Morgan (2019).

On fate in the *Aeneid*, see Hejduk (2013).

LIBER DECIMUS 21

    PANDITVR interea domus omnipotentis Olympi
    conciliumque vocat divum pater atque hominum rex
    sideream in sedem, terras unde arduus omnis
    castraque Dardanidum aspectat populosque Latinos.
    considunt tectis bipatentibus, incipit ipse: 5

1-15. Jupiter summons a council of the gods and bids them cease their strife for or against the Trojans until the day when Carthage will make war on Rome.

    Although highly dignified in tone, Jupiter's speech shows his cunning ability to adapt his words to different situations. It is difficult, for example, to reconcile his words to Venus in *Aeneid* 1 "[Aeneas] will wage a huge war in Italy" (*bellum ingens geret Italia* 1.263) with his statement at 10.8 that "I had forbidden Italy to meet the Teucrians in war," as readers since Servius have complained. On Jupiter's speech and its ambivalence, see especially Lyne (1987) 88-90, O'Hara (1990) 123-7, and Hejduk (2009).

1. **panditur:** "is opened." Historical present tenses are common in poetry. See also *aspectat* (4) and *considunt* (5). The verb, in emphatic initial position, indicates the physical opening of the "palace of all-powerful Olympus" (*domus omnipotentis Olympi*; cf. *Aen*. 8.262) but is also suggestive of the mysteries inside the palace which are about to be revealed (cf. 7.641 and 10.163). Some commentators take the verb to indicate the beginning of a new day: the "palace of Olympus" is opened at dawn just as it is closed at nightfall (1.374). But, if this were the case, the new (and third) day of battle of the *Aeneid* would be extremely short, ending at 145. It is better to follow S. J. Harrison (1991, xxxiii) and understand that the council takes place on the day which began at 9.459-60, as also suggested by the following *interea* ("meanwhile") in line 118. For a chronology of events, see also 118-307 n. Conte (1993) 209 calls attention to a similar chronological problem present in *Iliad* 8 which, too, opens with a divine council and is one of the main models for the Vergilian divine assembly. **omnipotentis:** most often used of Jupiter (but also of other gods and *Fortuna*), the epithet* here and at 12.791 is transferred to Olympus, the council-chamber of omnipotence.

2. **conciliumque vocat:** recalls the expression used to convene the assembly of the gods at *Iliad* 20.4 (*agorēnde kalessai*), but *vocare* is also used for calling a meeting of the senate, see 1-117 n. **divum...rex:** i.e., Jupiter. The archaic* form *divum* (for *divorum*) and the monosyllabic ending both add solemnity to the verse (for monosyllabic endings, cf. also 107-8, 361, 734-5, 802, and 843). The line is a borrowing from Ennius, an archaic poet who lived in the second century BCE and wrote the first Latin epic in hexameters, the *Annales*. Cf. fr. 203-4 in Skutsch and in *FRL* 1 *tum cum corde suo **divom** pater atque hominum **rex** | effatur*. The line appears also at 743, 1.65, and 2.648.

3. **sideream in sedem:** "into (his) starry dwelling"; cf. Hom. *Il*. 19.128. **arduus:** "on high." Jupiter, just like Zeus in the *Iliad* (5.753-4), has a high vantage point. **omnis:** accusative agreeing with *terras*.

4. **Dardanidum:** archaic* for *Dardanidarum*. On the patronymic*, see 92 n. Note how the names of the opposing parties flank the central point of the hexameter.

5. **tectis bipatentibus:** ablative of place without a preposition (common in poetry). *Tectum* ("roof") is used by synecdoche* for "house." The literal meaning of *bipatens* is

'caelicolae magni, quianam sententia vobis
versa retro tantumque animis certatis iniquis?
abnueram bello Italiam concurrere Teucris.
quae contra vetitum discordia? quis metus aut hos
aut hos arma sequi ferrumque lacessere suasit?   10

"double-opening" and here the adjective seems to indicate that the building has a door at either end as some temples do. *Bipatens* is rare. Servius (*ad loc.*) reports that it was found in Ennius and Skutsch believes that the term may have been used in the divine assembly of *Annales* 1 (see 1-117 n.). It is used only once elsewhere by Vergil of "folding doors" (2.330), and it is not attested in any other author in classical Latin. **ipse:** "he himself," i.e., Jupiter. The intensive pronoun emphasizes his supreme position.

6. **caelicolae:** the epic compound (literally meaning "inhabitants of the sky") is a masculine noun of the first declension and agrees with *magni*. The term is archaic* and found already in Ennius (fr. 445 Skutsch and *FRL* 1) in his assembly of the gods in *Annales* 1 (see 1-117 n.). Jupiter's archaic* language marks his speech as formal and solemn. **quianam:** archaic* for *cur* (cf. also 5.13). **sententia:** "decision," is also the technical term used of senatorial resolutions. **vobis:** a dative of reference with *sententia* or a dative of agent after *versa* (*est*), "by you."

7. **versa retro:** sc. *est*, "has been reversed" (lit. "has been turned back"). As he clarifies in the following lines, Jupiter claims that the gods are no longer obeying his will, since he forbade a war in Latium. They have changed their mind and are now divided into two rival factions headed by Juno and Venus. His claim does not seem altogether accurate, see 8 n.

8. **abnueram:** "I had forbidden," governs the accusative-infinitive construction *Italiam concurrere*. *Abnuo* is the opposite of *adnuo* and, when used of Jupiter, indicates his prohibiting nod. **bello:** "in war." **Italiam:** the first syllable, naturally short, is here long for convenience (see Austin at *Aen.* 1.2; cf. also 32-3). Jupiter's claim to have forbidden war in Italy openly contradicts what he foretold to Venus at 1.263 (*bellum ingens* (i.e., Aeneas) *geret Italia*). Contrary to what Jupiter states, it is he who has undergone a reversal of *sententia*. Vergil draws attention to this contradiction via the intratextual marker *sententia versa* which recalls his declaration *neque me sententia vertit* of his speech to Venus (1.260). See Thomas (2004-5) 145. **Teucris:** dative after the compound *concurrere*. Cf. *Aen.* 1.493 *viris concurrere*.

9-10. **quae:** interrogative adjective with *discordia*. Supply *est*. **contra vetitum:** "against my prohibition." **discordia:** either the internal dissension of the gods or the strife between Latins and Trojans, or, likely, both. The term is, tellingly, used by Roman contemporary authors to describe civil wars. See Breed, Damon, and Rossi (2010) 4-8; cf. also 8.702, where *Discordia* is represented on the shield of Aeneas as rejoicing at the battle of Actium. **quis metus:** subject of *suasit*. The interrogative pronoun *quis* is often used where we would expect an interrogative adjective (in this instance *qui*). **aut hos...lacessere:** the infinitive of purpose (here with subject acc. *aut hos aut hos*) after *suadeo* (and after verbs of advising, commanding, urging, etc.) is common in Vergil instead of the more prosaic construction *ut* + subjunctive. Cf. also AG §563. Again, Jupiter's language is vague. *Aut hos aut hos* could be referring to the two divisions of deities (see 7 n.) or to the two factions (Trojans vs. Latins) on earth. In the first instance, *metus* would mean "fear" such as, for example, Juno had for Carthage (1.23, 280) or Venus for Aeneas (8.370). In the second, *metus* should be taken as the "mutual suspicion or terror" of the

adveniet iustum pugnae, ne arcessite, tempus,
cum fera Karthago Romanis arcibus olim
exitium magnum atque Alpis immittet apertas:
tum certare odiis, tum res rapuisse licebit.
nunc sinite et placitum laeti componite foedus.' 15

---

opposing factions on earth. The rough ending with two monosyllables reflects Jupiter's indignation (Williams *ad loc.*). **ferrumque lacessere**: "to provoke the sword" (i.e., to provoke war). *Ferrum* ("iron") is a metonymy* for sword, since swords were made of iron. For similar expressions, cf. 5.429 *pugnamque lacessunt* and 11.254 *ignota lacessere bella*. The phrase restates the same essential idea expressed in *arma sequi* ("to pursue war") and is an example of *dicolon abundans**, the restatement of an initial phrase in different language. For *dicolon abundans* in Vergil, see Conte (1993) 208 and Conte (2007) 101.

11. **pugnae**: gen. after *iustum tempus*, "for battle" (lit. "of battle"). **ne arcessite**: the construction *ne* + present imperative to express prohibition (instead of the more common perfect subjunctive) is poetic. Short parenthetical imperatives are commonly used by Vergil in speeches. Cf. 6.399 (*absiste moveri*).

12-13. **cum...immittet**: temporal clause, "when Carthage will unleash." **Romanis arcibus**: dative after the compound verb *immittet*. **olim**: in connection with a future tense (*immittet*) is used with a future meaning "in the future," cf. 1.203 *forsan et haec olim meminisse iuvabit*. **immittet**: comprehensible with *magnum exitium*, "will unleash a great destruction," but less so with *Alpis apertas* ("the opened Alps"). An example of zeugma*. With rhetorical boldness Carthage will unleash the "opened Alps" on Rome because the opened Alps will unleash the invaders through their passes. The reference is to Hannibal's crossing of the Alps in 218 BCE. Jupiter predicts Roman debacles in the war but calculatingly omits Hannibal's final defeat at Zama (202 BCE) and the destruction of Carthage (146 BCE). For Jupiter's seeming deception of Juno, see E. L. Harrison (1984).

14. **certare odiis**: the infinitive (together with *rapuisse*) is governed by *licebit*. Notably, the expression seems to recall that of Dido when, endowed with prophetic powers on the point of death, she calls on the Carthaginians and one great avenger in particular to pursue the descendants of Aeneas (*Aen.* 4.623 *exercete odiis*). See Goldschmidt (2013) 130 n. 94. **res rapuisse**: "to have seized plunder." The perfect emphasizes the idea of completed action (AG §486b). According to Servius, *res rapere* is a formal phrase used by the *fetiales* (a college of Roman priests devoted to Jupiter as a protector of good faith) in the so-called *clarigatio*, a solemn demand for redress for some injury received, without which there would be a declaration of war. **licebit**: sc. *vobis*.

15. **sinite**: "allow (it)," imperative plural; i.e., cease your strife. **placitum**: agrees with *foedus*. The language is again ambiguous: *placitum* (from *placeo*) can mean either (1) *quod fato placuit*, lit. "that which has pleased destiny," i.e., that which was decreed by destiny over which I, Jupiter, have little control, as also suggested at 109-13 or (2) *quod mihi placuit*, lit. "that which has pleased me," i.e., that which I have decreed (since I, Jupiter, rule over destiny), as Jupiter clearly suggests in the prophecy to Venus in *Aeneid* 1 (see especially 278-83). The ambiguity of this phrase reflects the ambiguous relationship between Jupiter and fate throughout the poem. See Feeney (1991) 153-4, Hejduk (2013).

Iuppiter haec paucis; at non Venus aurea contra
pauca refert:
'o pater, o hominum rerumque aeterna potestas
(namque aliud quid sit quod iam implorare queamus?),
cernis ut insultent Rutuli, Turnusque feratur   20
per medios insignis equis tumidusque secundo
Marte ruat? non clausa tegunt iam moenia Teucros:

16-95. As soon as Jupiter finishes his speech, Venus and Juno, in turn, perorate their causes, with two indignant speeches.

The angry speeches of the two goddesses stand in stark contrast with Jupiter's dignified opening speech and contain many devices of formal rhetoric. Servius states that these two speeches were cited by ancient rhetorical theorists as examples of *controversiae* (speeches of defense or prosecution in fictitious court cases). Particularly noticeable is their use of irony* (29-30, 42-3, 53-5, 61-2, 75, 89) and the way in which Juno turns Venus' own language against her (65, 67, 73, 74, 75, 76, 81, 85, 86, 89).

For the two speeches, see also 1-117 n.

16-62. Venus complains bitterly about the Trojans' great sufferings and Juno's intervention. As all else is lost, she asks her father to let Aeneas bear his fate but begs him to save at least the life of little Ascanius.

16-17. **paucis…:** sc. *verbis*. The omission of the verb of speech (e.g., *dixit* vel sim.) and of *verbis* reflects Jupiter's authoritative brevity (cf. 621); by contrast *non…pauca* (used of Venus' speech) suggests the stereotypical loquacity of women and conveys the passion of Venus' response. **aurea:** Venus' epithet* is Homeric, cf. *Il.* 3.64. **contra:** adv. "in reply."

17. Vergil introduces a speech with a half-line in this book also at 490, 580, but probably meant to revise the poem so that no half-lines remained. Overall, there are fifty-eight half-lines in the poem, but the number is disputed because some original half-lines may have been completed by scribes. For the poem left unfinished at the time of Vergil's death, see O'Hara (2010).

18. **rerumque:** "and of the things" (i.e., of the world). **potestas:** the abstract *potestas* ("power") is used here for the concrete ("ruler"), cf. Juv. 10.100 *Gabiorumque esse potestas*. The hiatus* after the interjection *o* is not uncommon in poetry, cf. *Geo.* 2.486 *o ubi campi*, Hor., *Carm.* 1.1.2. *o et praesidium*. Venus opens with a *captatio benevolentiae* (a rhetorical technique aimed at capturing the audience's goodwill at the beginning of a speech), appealing both to Jupiter's affection and authority. For a similar appeal to Zeus, cf. Aphrodite's speech in the assembly of the gods (*Il.* 8.31).

19. **namque…sit:** "(I appeal to you) for what (*quid*) other (thing) (*aliud*) is there that (*quod*) we can now appeal to?" **sit:** potential subjunctive. **quod…queamus:** relative clause of purpose.

20-2. **ut:** "how," introduces the three following indirect questions (*insultent, feratur, ruat*). **insultent:** the verb suggests malicious exultation. Translate "triumph." **feratur:** the verb ("is borne"), together with *ruat* ("rushes") and the adjective *tumidus* ("swollen"), points to Turnus' out-of-control passion. For the expression *feratur per medios*, cf. 12.477-8 (*similis medios Iuturna per hostis | fertur*). **equis:** abl. of specification after *insignis*. **secundo | Marte:** abl. of

quin intra portas atque ipsis proelia miscent
aggeribus murorum et inundant sanguine fossae.
Aeneas ignarus abest. numquamne levari 25
obsidione sines? muris iterum imminet hostis
nascentis Troiae nec non exercitus alter,
atque iterum in Teucros Aetolis surgit ab Arpis
Tydides. equidem credo, mea vulnera restant
et tua progenies mortalia demoror arma. 30

---

cause explaining *tumidus*. *Marte* is a metonymy* for "war"; the expression appears again at 11.899 and 12.497. *Secundo* here means "favorable."

23-4. **quin:** "in fact"; when used with the indicative (*miscent, inundant*) *quin* creates a strong emphasis. Cf. also 470 and 570. **intra portas:** "inside the gates," a reference to Turnus' incursion inside the Trojan camp at 9.672-818 and to his slaughtering of many Trojans. **ipsis...aggeribus:** abl. of place (see 5 n.). *Agger* is the mound at the base of the defensive walls. The same expression occurs at 144 and 11.382. **inundant...fossae:** "the ditches overflow." Manuscripts vary between this reading and *fossas*. *Fossae* should be preferred since the same phrase is found at 11.382. For discussion, see Horsfall (2003) *ad loc.* and Conte (2007) 212-14.

25. **ignarus abest:** Aeneas had left the Trojan camp in Book 8 (80-100) to seek the help of Evander and is, therefore, unaware that the Trojan camp is under siege. **numquamne:** when the enclitic *-ne* is added to a negative word, an affirmative answer is expected (AG §332b). **levari:** infinitive passive after *sines*. Its subject is an understood *eos* (i.e., the Trojans). For infinitives after a verb of "permitting," see AG §563 c.

26-7. **obsidione:** abl. of separation after *levari*. **muris:** dative with the compound verb *imminet* (AG §370). **nascentis Troiae:** i.e., the Trojan camp. Venus laments that the Trojans are, once more, defending the walls of the new "Troy being born." However, the Iliadic subtext allows also for a different identification: the Trojan camp recalls not Troy but the Greek camp in the *Iliad*, the beachhead built on the shore by the Greek invaders for a successful assault on the enemy land. For a fuller discussion, see Quint (1993) 67, Hardie (1994) 11. **nec:** combined with another negative produces a strong positive statement.

28-9. **atque iterum...:** note the emphatic repetition of *iterum* ("again") from line 26. **Aetolis... Tydides:** i.e., Diomedes. Diomedes, "the son of Tydeus" (*Tydides*), was a Greek warrior who fought at Troy but emigrated from Aetolia to Southern Italy after the Trojan War. There he founded the town of Arpi which is therefore described as *Aetolis...Arpis* (similarly at 11.239 *Aetola ex urbe*). Latins have sent him an embassy to ask for his aid (8.9-17) and Venus seems to assume that this embassy will be successful, but instead Diomedes will refuse his aid (11.225-30). Note how *Tydides* is placed at the end of the sentence, in single-word enjambment*. **mea vulnera restant:** "my wounds (i.e., wounds inflicted on me) remain (to be completed)." Venus envisages a repetition of what had happened to her at Troy when she was wounded by Diomedes (*Il.* 5.336).

30. **demoror:** "I cause delay," i.e., Venus (*tua progenies*) presents herself as a mere hindrance to the progress of mortal arms (Harrison *ad loc.*).

si sine pace tua atque invito numine Troes
Italiam petiere, luant peccata neque illos
iuveris auxilio; sin tot responsa secuti
quae superi manesque dabant, cur nunc tua quisquam
vertere iussa potest aut cur nova condere fata? 35
quid repetam exustas Erycino in litore classis,
quid tempestatum regem ventosque furentis
Aeolia excitos aut actam nubibus Irim?

---

31. **pace:** from *pax* ("peace") but here "approval"; cf. the common *pace tua dixerim*. **invito numine:** sc. *tuo*, lit. "with (your) divine power unwilling"; abl. of attendant circumstance. *Sine pace tua* and *invito numine* express similar ideas in different language (*dicolon abundans**, see 9-10 n.). Venus knows that Aeneas has reached Italy with Jupiter's approval but wants to force Jupiter to disclose publicly what he had revealed to her (1.227-60).

32-3. **Italiam:** see 8 n. **petiere:** shortened perfect for *petierunt*. **luant:** jussive subjunctive. **neque...| iuveris:** from *iuvo* (1); *ne* followed by the perfect subjunctive expresses prohibition (AG §450).

33. **sin:** "but if"; here introduces the preferred alternative. **tot:** "so many (as you know)"; the word assumes that the oracles and their number are known to the person addressed. **secuti:** sc. *sunt*. The Trojans are the subject of the verb.

34-5. **cur nunc tua quisquam...fata:** "why can anyone now overturn your bidding and why (can anyone) make new fates?" As noted by Harrison (*ad loc.*), the question is rhetorically loaded: *nunc* contrasts with Jupiter's promise of Aeneas' success at 1.263-6, *tua* appeals to Jupiter's vanity by implying that his orders should be immutable, and the pronoun *quisquam* generally used in negative sentences implying "surely nobody can," stresses the universality of his rule. For *quisquam*, cf. also 65 and 11.392. Venus, differently from Jupiter (15 n.), construes an all too perfect equation between Jupiter's *iussa* and *fata*.

36-7. **quid repetam:** *repetam* is a deliberative subjunctive. Translate "why should I recall?" For *quid* = "why," see 611 n. This is a formula* of rhetorical *praeteritio**. **exustas...classis:** "the ships incinerated." In Book 5 Iris (see 38 n.), at Juno's command, had convinced the Trojan matrons to set fire to the ships, while the Trojan men were celebrating the funeral games for Aeneas' father Anchises on the shore of Mt. Eryx (hence *Erycino in litore*) in Sicily (5.604-63). Venus' claim is exaggerated for only four ships were burned (5.699). **quid tempestatum regem:** construe as *quid repetam tempestatum regem*. The anaphora* *quid...quid* suggests indignation. Aeolus was the king of winds, which he ruled in his kingdom in Aeolia (an island off the NE coast of Sicily). In Book 1 Juno persuades Aeolus to release raging winds from Aeolia upon the Trojan fleet (1.52-91).

38. **Aeolia:** the abl. expresses place from which with *ex* omitted (cf. also the following *nubibus*). **actam nubibus Irim:** Iris is the goddess of the rainbow and often messenger of Juno. In the *Aeneid*, Iris was sent twice by Juno to advance her plan among humans, the first time to cause the burning of the ships (5.606, see 36-7 n.), the second (9.2) to arouse Turnus to attack the Trojans.

LIBER DECIMUS

nunc etiam manis (haec intemptata manebat
sors rerum) movet et superis immissa repente   40
Allecto medias Italum bacchata per urbes.
nil super imperio moveor; speravimus ista,
dum fortuna fuit; vincant, quos vincere mavis.
si nulla est regio Teucris quam det tua coniunx
dura, per eversae, genitor, fumantia Troiae   45

39-41. **nunc:** picks up the *nunc* at 34 and turns the discussion back to the present. **manis:** acc. plural; "spirits of the dead," but here, by metonymy* "Underworld." **haec intemptata manebat | sors rerum…:** "this (*haec*) portion assigned by lot (*sors*) of the universe (*rerum*) (still) remained untried." The term *sors* here alludes to the partition of the universe by lot among the sons of Cronus (Zeus received the heavens, Poseidon the sea, and Hades the Underworld) but its use here possibly also reflects the phrase "sortiri provinciam" used of a Roman magistrate obtaining his province by lot. Juno, having tried all the powers of the upper world, had at last summoned the Fury Allecto from Acheron (7.312 *Acheronta movebo*) to stir up the Latins against Aeneas. **movet:** subject is Juno. In this speech, Venus intentionally never calls Juno by name (cf. *quisquam* above). **superis immissa…| Allecto:** Allecto is the subject. *Superis* (dative after a compound verb) is "the world above" (i.e., earth) as juxtaposed with the Underworld where the Fury Allecto lives. Allecto (from the Greek *allēktos* "unceasing one") is a fury who serves primarily as Juno's agent of discord in the second part of the poem. **bacchata:** sc. *est*. "Has raged as a Bacchante." *Bacchor* is deponent. The verb is pointed: Allecto had indeed inspired Bacchic frenzy in Amata, who (together with her followers) was described as roaming the woods in a kind of counterfeit worship of Bacchus in *Aeneid* 7 (385-91, 405). Cf. also 4.301-2 where another queen, Dido, about to be abandoned by Aeneas, is compared to a raging worshipper of Bacchus as she roams through Carthage in her fury.

42. **nil…:** *nil* (= *nihil*) is emphatic and used adverbially, "not at all." **super:** here preposition meaning "concerning" (instead of *de*). This usage is colloquial and common in Plautus, an archaic* Roman comic playwright. Venus' use of the term *imperium* shrewdly recalls Jupiter's previous promise to her of an endless empire for the Romans (1.279 *imperium sine fine dedi*). **speravimus:** "we hoped" (though we no longer do). The perfect underscores that Venus' hope has been irrevocably lost. **ista:** acc. plural neuter. Refers loosely to *imperio* above.

43. **dum fortuna fuit:** *dum* ("while") regularly takes a present indicative when it describes an action taking place at the same time as some other action (cf. 58). When length of time has to be emphasized, so that *dum* means "as long as," it takes a past tense as here (AG §556a). Aeneas uses the same expression at 3.16 when he tells Dido, during his flashback narrative at Carthage, how the Thracian allies betrayed the Trojans after the fall of Troy. **vincant:** jussive subjunctive. Note the emphatic repetition of *vincere*. **quos:** antecedent is *illi*, the understood subject of *vincant*. **mavis:** subject is "you" (i.e., Jupiter).

44-5. **det:** is subjunctive in a relative clause of characteristic. **tua coniunx | dura:** the possessive maliciously implies that, although Juno is his *coniunx* ("wife"), Jupiter has lost control over her.

45-6. **per…obtestor:** "by the…I entreat you." *Per* + accusative (*fumantia…excidia*) is typical of the language of prayers and oaths. The present participle *fumantia* creates a pathetic and vivid

excidia obtestor: liceat dimittere ab armis
incolumem Ascanium, liceat superesse nepotem.
Aeneas sane ignotis iactetur in undis
et quacumque viam dederit Fortuna sequatur:
hunc tegere et dirae valeam subducere pugnae.   50
est Amathus, est celsa mihi Paphus atque Cythera
Idaliaeque domus: positis inglorius armis

---

image. **eversae...Troiae:** genitive after *excidia*. **genitor:** recalls *pater* (18) at the opening of the speech.

46. **liceat:** sc. *mihi*; jussive subjunctive, "let it be allowed" (cf. also *liceat, iactetur, sequatur, exigat* at 47-53). Note the pathetic anaphora* (*liceat...liceat*, 47) and asyndeton*. **ab armis:** "from battle/war" by metonymy*.

47. **Ascanium:** direct object of *dimittere*. **nepotem:** "grandson"; the term is used pointedly. Ascanius is Venus' grandson and, therefore, Jupiter's descendant and the one who, at least in Jupiter's words to Venus in *Aeneid* 1, will be the founder of Alba Longa (267-71). *Liceat superesse nepotem* restates (with different words) what was said in the previous clause (*liceat dimittere incolumem Ascanium*) and is another example of the *dicolon abundans*∗ (see 9-10 n.). Petrini (1997) 103-10 notes how Aeneas' son in the *Aeneid* is trapped in the role of *puer*, who is, thus, unable to deliver on the promises of the future, and suggests a connection between him and the historical Marcellus, Augustus' designated heir, another young man who remained trapped in a similar role, unable to fulfill his potential because of his untimely death (*Aen.* 6.861-86).

48. **Aeneas...iactetur:** for the subjunctive *iactetur* see 46 n. Note the emphatic initial position of *Aeneas* and *hunc* (50). **sane:** has a concessive force "by all means." **ignotis...in undis:** the phrase represents Aeneas tossed (*iactetur*) on stormy and unknown seas (*ignotis in undis*) and grossly misrepresents his progress up a calm river Tiber (8.57-8; 86-96). Note how the phrase *iactetur in undis* is metrically equivalent to and recalls *iactatus et alto* of the proem which describes the many trials of Aeneas' journey before he was able to arrive in Italy.

49. **et quacumque...Fortuna:** lit. "where(ever) Fortune will have given a way." Vergilian parallels support the reading *quacumque* over *quamcumque*. Cf. 12.368 *sic Turno, quacumque viam secat, agmina cedunt*. **dederit:** the future perfect expresses indefinite remoteness (Venus is professing not to care). **sequatur:** for the subjunctive, see 46 n.

50. **hunc:** i.e., Ascanius. **dirae...pugnae:** the dative of separation is frequent after verbs of taking away (*subducere*). **valeam:** optative subjunctive expressing a wish and governing the two infinitives *tegere* and *subducere*.

51. **Amathus:** third declension noun (*Amathūs, -ūntis*, f.); the *-us* is long for it represents the Greek diphthong *-ous*. Like *Paphus* and *Idalium* (or *Idalia*), Amathus was a city of Cyprus, celebrated for the worship of Venus. **celsa:** nominative feminine agreeing with Paphus (*Paphus, -ī*, f.). **Cythera:** an island off the coast of Laconia, near which Venus rose from the sea.

52. **Idaliae:** gen. singular. *Idalia* is a feminine variant (cf. 51 n.) of the more usual *Idalium* and is first found in Vergil. Cf. 1.693. **domus:** here "temple." Venus had a temple at Idalium. Venus once before brought Ascanius there, after she had Cupid take on the appearance of Ascanius

exigat hic aevum. magna dicione iubeto
Karthago premat Ausoniam: nihil urbibus inde
obstabit Tyriis. quid pestem evadere belli 55
iuvit et Argolicos medium fugisse per ignis
totque maris vastaeque exhausta pericula terrae,
dum Latium Teucri recidivaque Pergama quaerunt?
non satius cineres patriae insedisse supremos

(1.691-4). **positis...armis:** abl. abs. **inglorius:** "without glory"; the term corresponds to the Homeric *akleēs*. The Greek term is connected to the verb "to hear" and literally means "not to be heard about by others." A Homeric hero earns *kleos* ("glory" or literally "what others hear about you") by accomplishing great (martial) deeds. Since Venus plans to hide Ascanius in one of her sanctuaries and remove him from the action of war (*positis armis*), he is condemned to be "not heard about" and, therefore, will live an inglorious (and, therefore, un-epic) life of obscurity.

53. **exigat:** see 46 n. **hic:** "here," i.e., in one of the places mentioned above. **iubeto:** second person future imperative. The archaic* future imperative conveys solemnity.

54-6. **Karthago:** subject of *premat.* **premat:** subjunctive in indirect command after *iubeto* with *ut* omitted (see AG §565a and *OLD* s.v. *iubeo* 3b). **urbibus...Tyriis:** dat. after *obstabit*; i.e., Carthage; it is so called because it was a Phoenician colony, founded from Tyre. The plural is used to exaggerate Carthage's power. **inde:** "from there"; it refers to *Ausoniam*, i.e., from Italy (see 267-8 n.), which, with Aeneas gone and Ascanius "spending his days inglorious," will never prove a rival to Carthage. **quid...| iuvit:** "what benefit was it?" *iuvit* governs the infinitives *evadere*, *fugisse*, and *exhausta* (sc. *esse*). **pestem...belli:** direct object of *evadere*. For the "plague of war," cf. *Il* 15.736. **evadere:** the accusative subject of the infinitive is an understood Aeneas or Ascanius. **Argolicos...per ignis:** "(that he) had fled through the middle of the Greek fires," i.e., the fires of Troy kindled by the Greeks. **medium:** acc. subject of *fugisse*. It is an adjective modifying an understood Ascanius or Aeneas but can be translated adverbially. Cf. 1.348 *quos inter medius venit furor* (with Austin *ad loc.*). For the adjective *Argolicus* used as a collective designation of the Greeks in the Trojan War, see also *Aen.* 8.374 *dum bello Argolici vastabant Pergama reges*. The account of the escape from Troy is given at 2.632-804.

57. **totque...exhausta pericula:** sc. *esse*; lit. "and so many dangers had been drained to the end." For the metaphor* "draining the cup of danger," cf. 4.14 *quae bella exhausta canebat!*

58. **dum...quaerunt:** for *dum*, cf. 43 n. **recidivaque:** "grown again"; the metaphor* is derived from arboriculture. For Venus describing the Trojan camp as a new Troy, see 26-7 n. **Pergama:** the citadel of Troy in poetry often stands for Troy itself. For Juno's and Jupiter's agreement (12.808-41) preventing the "refounding" of Troy, see Feeney (1984)

59. **non satius:** sc. *fuit*, "had it not been (= would it not have been) better"; cf. *Ecl.* 2.14-15 *nonne fuit satius...| pati?* The expression is colloquial and often found in comedies. Cf. Plaut., *Epid.* 60 *plus scire satiust quam loqui servom hominem. ea sapientia est.* **cineres patriae insedisse supremos:** "to have settled on the last ashes of their fatherland." *Insedo* with the accusative (*cineres supremos*) is first found in Augustan authors.

atque solum quo Troia fuit? Xanthum et Simoenta 60
redde, oro, miseris iterumque revolvere casus
da, pater, Iliacos Teucris.' tum regia Iuno
acta furore gravi: 'quid me alta silentia cogis
rumpere et obductum verbis vulgare dolorem?
Aenean hominum quisquam divumque subegit 65

---

60. **fuit:** as often, emphatic "was, but is no longer." Cf. 42 n. **Xanthum et Simoenta:** Xanthus and Simois are the two rivers of Troy and are evocative of the sufferings of the Trojans. Cf. 6.88-9 *non Simois tibi nec Xanthus nec Dorica castra | defuerint.*

61-2. **revolvere...| da:** the imperative *da* means "allow" and takes the infinitive (of purpose) *revolvere*. For this construction, see AG §460. **revolvere:** "to unroll again"; the metaphor* of *volvo* is that of unrolling a rolled-up scroll of papyrus or parchment. For a similar metaphor*, cf. 1.262 *volvens fatorum arcana movebo* (Jupiter's speech to Venus). **casus |...Iliacos:** "the misfortunes of Ilium" were proverbial; cf. Cic., *Att.* 8.11.3 *tanta malorum impendet Ilias.* **pater:** Venus ends her speech as she had begun it (see 18 n.)—by addressing Jupiter as *pater*. With this ring composition, Venus plays on Jupiter's paternal feelings. Her abrupt conclusion at mid-line denotes passion. **Teucris:** dat. after *da*. Venus' speech ends in a paradox. She prays for what might seem the extreme of calamity, but which would be a relief in comparison with the Trojans' present sufferings.

62-95. Juno answers Venus reminding her that Aeneas chose to make Turnus his enemy by bringing war to a peaceful land. Turnus has every right to defend himself and any assistance she may give the Rutulians is justified. She asks Venus not to interfere in the war.

62-6. **tum...Latino:** Juno's speech opens with a dramatic sequence of rhetorical questions resembling the opening of an invective. Note also the omission of the verb of speech (e.g., *dixit* vel sim.), a sign of Juno's excitement.

62. **regia:** recalls the Roman cult title of *Iuno Regina*.

63. **furore:** in the poem, *furor* and *ira* are often associated with Juno who becomes, in many ways, the embodiment of these (female) destructive powers. Hershkowitz (1998) 95-128 suggests that the struggle between Jupiter and Juno takes on also a metanarrative dimension, as Juno attempts to transform Jupiter's poem of *fata* into a poem of *furor*. For the victors problematically achieving *pietas* and *imperium* through *furor* at the end of the poem, see Perkell (1999) 38-9. **alta silentia:** "deep silence" (i.e., "long silence").

64. **rumpere...vulgare:** for the infinitives, see 9-10 n. **obductum...dolorem:** Servius suggests that *obductum* means "skinned over," a reference to the scar over a wound (cf. Cic., *Leg. Agr.* 3.4 *refricare obductam iam reipublicae cicatricem*). *Dolor* is, above all, the painful wound caused by the judgment of Paris (cf. 1.26-7).

65. **Aenean:** Greek acc., direct object of *subegit*. **hominum quisquam divumque:** for the archaic* form *divum*, see 2 n. This is a reply to Venus' assertion at 34 (*superi manesque*) with *quisquam* pointedly echoing Venus' *quisquam* at 34. For Juno, Aeneas (note his emphatic position at the opening of the line) is the sole aggressor.

bella sequi aut hostem regi se inferre Latino?
Italiam petiit fatis auctoribus (esto)
Cassandrae impulsus furiis: num linquere castra
hortati sumus aut vitam committere ventis?
num puero summam belli, num credere muros?   70
Tyrrhenamque fidem aut gentis agitare quietas?
quis deus in fraudem, quae dura potentia nostra
egit? ubi hic Iuno demissave nubibus Iris?

---

66. **sequi...inferre:** the infinitives (with subject acc. *Aenean*) are dependent on *subegit*. See 9-10 n. **hostem:** is in apposition to *se*. **regi...Latino:** dat. after compound verb *inferre*.

67-8. **Italiam...:** the wording again echoes Venus' at 32 (*Italiam petiere*). Juno sarcastically allows (*esto* = "so be it"; future imperative) Venus' claim that Aeneas had only "sought Italy by the authority of fate" (lit. "with the fates (being) the authors"), but gives it a different meaning by associating fate with "the mad ravings of Cassandra" (*Cassandrae furiis*). It is ironic* for Juno to mention "the furies of Cassandra" but to leave unmentioned the real Fury which she has unleashed to stir war (7.324-40). For Cassandra's prophecy, see 3.182-8. **num:** the particle *num* suggests a negative answer. Note the rhetorically effective triple anaphora* of *num*. **linquere:** as with *committere*, *credere*, *agitare*, the infinitive is governed by *hortati sumus* (see 9-10 n.). The accusative subject of the infinitives is an understood Aeneas. Juno picks up Venus' *Aeneas ignarus abest* (25) but implies that Aeneas' absence is the result of his desertion of the camp (*linquere*).

69. **hortati sumus:** "did we advise?" By using the plural, Juno usurps the collective authority of the assembled gods. Juno's statement is mendacious for, in *Aeneid* 8, the god Tiberinus had indeed advised Aeneas to go to Pallanteum to seek an alliance with Evander, the king of the city (8.51-8).

70. **puero:** dat. after *credere*, "to entrust to a boy (i.e., Ascanius)." **summam belli:** "the highest administration of the war." **muros:** the "walls" of the camp. The claim is exaggerated, see 9.172-3.

71. **Tyrrhenamque...quietas:** *agitare*, "to disturb," governs the accusatives *Tyrrhenamque fidem* and *gentis quietas*. **Tyrrhenamque fidem:** "the loyalty of the Etruscans." Juno is, of course, exaggerating. In *Aeneid* 8.470-95 we learn that the Etruscans had already broken their oath of loyalty to their king Mezentius before Aeneas' alliance with them and had threatened war against Turnus who had offered refuge to the exiled Etruscan tyrant. **gentis...quietas:** "people at peace."

72. **quis:** see 9-10 n. **in fraudem:** "to (suffer) harm." **dura potentia nostra:** replies to Venus' *coniunx | dura* (44-5). The reading *nostra* (instead of *nostri*) should be preferred since the nom. plur. adjective succeeding its noun at line end is common in Vergil.

73. **egit:** the object is an understood Aeneas. **ubi hic...Iuno?:** i.e., "where in all this (lit. *hic* = here) (is the intervention of) Juno?" Juno finally voices the name which Venus had never openly uttered. See 39-41 n. For a character using his/her own name, cf. 825-6, 830. **demissave nubibus Iris:** is a direct reply to Venus' *actam nubibus Irim* (see 38 n.), but the language is also reminiscent of Juno's action at 9.2 (= 5.606) *Irim de caelo **misit** Saturnia Iuno*.

> indignum est Italos Troiam circumdare flammis
> nascentem et patria Turnum consistere terra, 75
> cui Pilumnus avus, cui diva Venilia mater:
> quid face Troianos atra vim ferre Latinis,
> arva aliena iugo premere atque avertere praedas?
> quid soceros legere et gremiis abducere pactas,

74-5. **indignum:** "unfitting." **Italos...| nascentem:** the accusative subject *Italos* and infinitive *circumdare* (just as *Turnum consistere*, below) are governed by *indignum est*. *Troiam... nascentem* is the object of *circumdare*. The expression picks up Venus' *muris iterum imminet hostis | nascentis Troiae* (26-7). For Juno, however, such an aggression on the newly born Troy in Latium is a legitimate attempt by Turnus to make a stand (*consistere*) against the Trojans on his native soil, here emphatically labeled *patria...terra*. Goldschmidt (2013) 180 notes that Juno sets Turnus up as acting out the proto-Roman role of the one man staking (and then sacrificing) his life in the service of the state. On newborn Troy, see 26-7 n.

76. **cui Pilumnus avus:** sc. *est*. *Cui* is dative of possession. Pilumnus was an ancient Italian deity of agriculture and fertility. **avus:** "ancestor." At 619 he is called *quartus pater* ("great-great grandfather") of Turnus and *parens* ("ancestor") at 9.3. **cui diva Venilia mater:** sc. *est*. Venilia was a goddess/nymph and possibly Amata's sister, cf. 7.366 (with Servius and Horsfall (2000) *ad loc.*). The phrase is meant both to irritate Venus by implicitly equating Turnus and his "goddess-mother Venilia" with Aeneas and his goddess-mother Venus and to boast about Turnus' Italian genealogy.

77. **quid:** "what?"; implies *dignum est vel sim.* after it, "what (is it fitting?)" **Troianos...ferre:** the accusative subject and infinitive construction is dependent on the understood *dignum est* vel sim. (just as the infinitives *premere...avertere, legere, abducere, orare* and *praefigere*, below). **face...atra:** cf. 9.74 *facibus...atris* (said of Turnus' men arming themselves with fire-torches). For *ater* see, 603 n.

78. **iugo:** instrumental ablative; the yoke of ploughing oxen, but also, metaphorically*, the yoke of captivity.

79. **quid soceros...pactas:** for the construction, see 77 n. Aeneas is understood as the accusative subject of *legere, abducere, orare,* and *praefigere*. The plurals *soceros* and *pactas* (both direct objects) are rhetorical exaggerations (cf. 7.98, 270). Juno accuses Aeneas of subverting the (Roman) laws of marriage according to which it was the father-in-law who chose (*legere*) the groom and turns Aeneas into a new Paris, who infamously abducted (note the verb *abducere*) Helen (see also 89 n.). The charges misinterpret the events (Lavinia was freely offered by Latinus to Aeneas, 7.259-73) and are quite damning. **gremiis:** i.e., the lap of her mother. For the plural, see above. **pactas:** from *pango* (3), "betrothed (women)"; the perfect participle is here used as a substantive. The term is tendentious and reflects Amata's (7.365-6) and Turnus' idea (12.17) that Turnus and Lavinia were formally engaged, an idea neither supported nor refuted by the narrator who allows for different perspectives to stand.

> pacem orare manu, praefigere puppibus arma? 80
> tu potes Aenean manibus subducere Graium
> proque viro nebulam et ventos obtendere inanis,
> et potes in totidem classem convertere nymphas:
> nos aliquid Rutulos contra iuvisse nefandum est?
> "Aeneas ignarus abest": ignarus et absit. 85
> est Paphus Idaliumque tibi, sunt alta Cythera:

80. **pacem...arma?**: the two clauses are placed side by side in an example of paratactic style (the juxtaposition of sequential main clauses without a subordinating conjunction, see parataxis*). Cf. 48-50 *Aeneas...hunc*. **manu:** i.e., carrying boughs as a sign that they were suppliants. The reference is to the embassy sent by Aeneas to Latinus (7.153-5). For the arms on the ship of Aeneas, see 8.92-3. **puppibus:** dative after a compound verb.

81-4. **tu potes...| nos...nefandum est:** the contrasted clauses conveying adversative ideas are marked by the initial position of the two personal pronouns—"You have the power... (but) is it a crime that I...?"

81-2. **Aenean:** see 65 n. **manibus:** dative of separation (cf. 50 n.). **subducere:** means "to carry off by stealth" (with echo of Venus' *subducere* at 50), while *abducere* (79) suggests violence. **Graium:** see 333-4 n. **proque viro:** *pro* here means "in place of," see AG §221.19a; *viro* = Aeneas. **obtendere:** "stretch out as a barrier." These lines refer to two events from the *Iliad*: Aphrodite's rescue of Aeneas from Diomedes (*Il.* 5.312-18) and Apollo's use of a phantom of Aeneas to distract Diomedes (5.444-53). Juno, however, alters the latter Homeric episode by ascribing the divine help solely to Venus. Juno's complaint about Venus' unlimited ability to rescue her son is somewhat ironic* for Juno will be able to do exactly the same for Turnus in the new day of battle (10.633-88).

83. **in totidem...nymphas:** a reference to the transformation of Aeneas' ships into nymphs narrated at 9.80-122. Juno assumes that the metamorphosis of the Trojan ships was an act of Venus (it was actually an act of Cybele). **classem:** "fleet."

84. **nos...iuvisse:** the accusative subject (*nos*) and the infinitive are dependent on *nefandum est*. *Aliquid* is a cognate accusative (AG §390c) after *iuvisse*, "to have helped in some way the Rutulians (*Rutulos*)." **nos:** note the royal "we" in contrast with *tu* (81). Juno emphasizes Venus' help to the Trojans and is quick to minimize her role in starting the war. **contra:** is used adverbially, "in reply."

85. The verse is a direct answer to Venus' complaint at 25 with Juno repeating verbatim Venus' *Aeneas ignarus abest* and then contemptuously dismissing her plea with, "and in ignorance let him stay away" (*absit* is jussive subjunctive).

86. **tibi:** dative of possession. **Cythera:** nom. plural (from *Cythēra, ōrum*). The list of cities with sanctuaries to Venus virtually repeats Venus' list at 51-2, leaving out only Amathus. The sequence of thought should be the following —Aeneas is away and let him stay away (85), Venus, the goddess of love, too, should follow his example by staying away in her sanctuaries (86), instead of meddling with war, which is not her area of competence (87). For the idea that war is the business of men cf. 7.444 (Turnus to Allecto) and *Il.* 6.492 and 20.137. More generally, for love as not belonging to the epic genre but always present in it, see Hinds (2000).

quid gravidam bellis urbem et corda aspera temptas?
nosne tibi fluxas Phrygiae res vertere fundo
conamur? nos? an miseros qui Troas Achivis
obiecit? quae causa fuit consurgere in arma 90
Europamque Asiamque et foedera solvere furto?

87. **quid:** see 611 n. **bellis:** ablative of specification. The metaphor* *gravidam bellis* is of a pregnant animal. Cf also *gravidam imperiis* (4.229). **urbem:** i.e., Laurentum, the city of Latinus. The city is mentioned in the *Aeneid* with various periphrases (involving the epithet* *Laurens* but is never given the specific name *Laurentum*). **corda aspera:** "the warlike (lit. "rough") spirits" of the inhabitants of the land (cf. also 9.603-13). Note, however, that in the proem of Book 7 (45-6), these same Italians are said to have long lived in a peaceful state before Aeneas' arrival. On Vergil's ambivalent representation of the Italian people, see Horsfall (2000) *ad* 7.183 and O'Hara (2007) 96-8. **temptas:** zeugma*; the verb means "try to influence" with *corda* but "try to capture" with *urbem*.

88. **nosne:** i.e., Juno. For *nos*, see 84 n. **tibi:** ethical dative (AG §380). Translate "I ask you." **fluxas...res:** lit. "flowing fortunes," hence "frail fortunes." Cf. Sall., *Jug.* 104.2 *scilicet ignari humanarum rerum, quae fluxae et mobiles semper in adversa mutantur*. **Phrygiae:** see 582 n. **fundo:** the ablative from *fundus, -i* ("bottom, foundation") is here used almost adverbially "from the bottom." The metaphor* may be from water dribbling away from a vessel partly overturned, which someone at last tilts over (Conington and Nettleship *ad loc.*).

89. **conamur:** isolated in enjambment* for emphasis. **nos?:** (sc. *conamur*), the pronoun is repeated for emphasis (i.e., "was it we who did this?"). For *nos*, see 84 n. **qui:** i.e., Paris (*Dardanius adulter* 92). Juno blames Paris for the Trojan War (note the masculine pronoun), but Paris' abduction of Helen resulted from Venus promising Paris the love of Helen, the most beautiful woman in the world, in return for his favorable judgment in the beauty contest between her, Juno, and Athena. Juno is, therefore, also indirectly blaming Venus for the war. See also 92 n. **miseros...Troas:** Juno mockingly picks up Venus' language at 61-2 (*miseris...Teucris*). *Troas* is a Greek acc. with short final syllable.

90-1. **quae:** interrogative adjective in agreement with *causa*. **consurgere...| Europamque Asiamque:** the construction (accusative subjects and infinitive) is dependent on *quae causa fuit*. **foedera:** lit. "compacts"; the reference here is probably to the ties of hospitality broken by Paris because of his theft (*furto*, abl. cause) of Helen (cf. *Il.* 3.354). The term, however, is also suggestive of the marriage contract (Ov., *Met.* 11.743 *coniugale foedus*) between Helen and Menelaus which Paris broke by stealing away Helen. For Aeneas' Paris-type behavior in Latium, according to Juno, see 79 n.

LIBER DECIMUS

    me duce Dardanius Spartam expugnavit adulter,
    aut ego tela dedi fovive Cupidine bella?
    tum decuit metuisse tuis: nunc sera querelis
    haud iustis adsurgis et inrita iurgia iactas.'   95
      Talibus orabat Iuno, cunctique fremebant

---

92. **me duce:** is emphatic and sarcastic, for Juno's rhetorical question points to (what she sees as) the guilty role that Venus played in Paris' affairs when he abducted Helen from Sparta. See also *ego* (93) implying that the truth requires *tu*. **Dardanius...adulter:** Dardanus was the mythical ancestor of the Trojans, hence "Dardanian adulter," i.e., Paris. **expugnavit:** lit. "to capture by storm a fortified position"; the military terminology picks up *me duce*. According to Servius, the verb should be taken literally as a reference to the story (believed by Servius) that Paris stormed Sparta to carry off Helen, but the verb could also be suggestive of the fact that Paris "conquered" the chastity of Helen, queen of Sparta. Cf. Cic., *Cael.* 49 *expugnare pudicitiam*.

93. **tela:** is also suggestive of the darts of Cupid who is mentioned immediately afterward. **fovi... Cupidine bella:** "I fostered (lit. "heated up") wars by means of Cupid (i.e., passion)." Another malignant phrase, for it was Venus who did this.

94. **tum:** "then," i.e., before Paris brought destruction upon them. **decuit:** is impersonal and governs the infinitive *metuisse*, "it was proper." **tuis:** the dative after *metuisse* indicates the person for whom one fears (see AG §367c). **sera:** "too late." The adjective refers to Venus and implies that her complaints come too late and that she should have been more careful in the past.

95. **et inrita iurgia iactas:** the language borrows from military terminology. *Inrita tela* is said of javelins missing the mark, while *iactare* is a military term often used of the throwing of weapons. The coincidence of ictus and accent in feet 3, 4, 5, and 6 gives the line an unusual rhythm, possibly underscoring Juno's excitement. See appendix on meter.

96-117. *A confused murmur of assent and disagreement follows Juno's words; then, as Jupiter begins to speak, a universal stillness falls on heaven and earth, sky, and sea. Jupiter declares that, since the deities refuse to cease their strife, he will support neither side; then, to confirm his words, he swears by the Styx, and quits the council-chamber.*

Like Jupiter's first speech at the opening of the assembly, this one also has a lofty and quasi-oracular tone and is a masterpiece of ambiguity. Jupiter neither concedes nor promises anything. He declares impartiality (108) and claims both ignorance about the outcome of the war (which he will allow to continue despite his earlier statement to the contrary) and subordination to the will of fate (113). But his claims seem to contradict statements he has made earlier in the poem (see 8 n.). His claim of impartiality rings particularly false since in the new day of battle about to begin he will prevent Pallas and Lausus from meeting in combat (10.436-7), and Mezentius enters the battle "by the warnings of Jupiter" (*Iouis monitis* 10.689). See Horsfall (1995) 143, Thomas (2004-5) 145, O'Hara (2007) 103, Hejduk (2009) 297, and notes on 107-8, 111-12, 436-7, and 689.

96. **orabat:** here "was speaking." **fremebant:** describes low murmurings and anticipates *fremunt* (98) of the following simile*.

caelicolae adsensu vario, ceu flamina prima
cum deprensa fremunt silvis et caeca volutant
murmura venturos nautis prodentia ventos.
tum pater omnipotens, rerum cui prima potestas, 100
infit (eo dicente deum domus alta silescit
et tremefacta solo tellus, silet arduus aether,
tum Zephyri posuere, premit placida aequora pontus):

---

97. **caelicolae**: agrees with *cuncti*, see 6 n. **adsensu vario**: abl. of manner. *Vario*, "divided," i.e., some agreed with Juno and some with Venus. **ceu**: "just as," a poetic archaism* often introducing a simile* in Vergil (cf. Austin *ad* 2.355). **prima**: emphatic at line-end. In epic councils, the reaction of the audience is often described via a simile. Cf. *Aen.* 11.296-9; Hom., *Il.* 2.144-9; Ovid, *Met.* 1.200-5. The imagery of the simile owes something to *Geo.* 1.356-9. For Vergil's similes drawing from the narrative of the *Georgics*, see Briggs (1980).

98-9. **deprensa**: the perfect passive participle "caught" (from *deprehendo*) agrees with *flamina*. Since *deprensa* is often used of trapped animals and *fremunt* of animal noises, the wording suggests an analogy between the trapped winds and trapped animals (Harrison *ad loc.*). **silvis**: locative ablative. **caeca...| murmura**: object of *volutant*, "unseen rumblings"; cf. 12.591 *murmure caeco* (of the buzzing of bees). **volutant**: "send rolling about," cf. 1.725; 5.149.

99. **venturos**: "about to come," future active participle (from *venio*) agreeing with *ventos* (direct object of *prodentia*). **nautis**: dat. after *prodentia*. **prodentia**: "revealing," present participle of *prodo* (3), agreeing with *flamina*. Note the elegant line with alliteration* (*venturos | ventos*) and the interlocked* arrangement in a AbaB pattern (i.e., noun A, adjective b, adjective a, noun B).

100. **omnipotens**: see n. 1. **rerum**: objective genitive after *potestas*. **cui**: dative of possession. **potestas**: sc. *est*. On the relationship between Jupiter's *potestas* and fate/fortune, see 15 n.

101. **infit**: originally meaning "to begin," the term is used by Vergil as a synonym of *inquit*. Here in emphatic position. **eo dicente**: abl. abs. **deum**: see 228-9 n. **silescit**: is juxtaposed to *dicente*. See also *silet* at 102. When Jupiter speaks, not only the gods but also the elements of the universe (here represented by land, air, winds, and water) fall silent. Cf. Neptune calming the sea at 1.147-56 (with a similar blend of simile* and reality).

102. **tremefacta**: sc. *est*. **solo**: is usually explained as a locative "in its foundations," but (like *fundo* at 88) it probably means "from its foundations." **arduus**: see 3 n.

103. **Zephyri**: Zephyrus is the West Wind, but here possibly the term stands for winds in general. **posuere**: i.e., *se posuerunt*. The perfect tense expresses the instantaneous action. The trochaic caesura* after *posuere* underscores the sudden halt of the winds. **placida**: the adjective anticipates the result of the action of the sea (the waters become calm *after* the sea smoothes (*premit*) them) and is therefore proleptic*. Note the alliteration* of *p* (*posuere, premit, placida, pontus*).

'accipite ergo animis atque haec mea figite dicta.
quandoquidem Ausonios coniungi foedere Teucris   105
haud licitum, nec vestra capit discordia finem,
quae cuique est fortuna hodie, quam quisque secat spem,
Tros Rutulusne fuat, nullo discrimine habebo,
seu fatis Italum castra obsidione tenentur
sive errore malo Troiae monitisque sinistris.   110

---

104. **animis:** may be taken as an instrumental ablative, locative ablative, or dative as in *invitant moenibus* (9.676). *Accipite animis* and *haec mea figite dicta* is another example of *dicolon abundans**, see 9-10 n. This line is repeated from 3.250, with the first part modeled on a Homeric formula* (cf. *Il.* 1.297).

105. **quandoquidem:** the *o* is short just as in 7.547. **Ausonios coniungi:** the accusative subject and the present infinitive passive *coniungi* are governed by *haud licitum* (*est*) of the following line. **Teucris:** dative after the compound verb *coniungo*.

106. **haud licitum:** sc. *est*. **discordia:** Jupiter had used the same term in his first speech at the opening of the council. For its meaning, see 9-10 n.

107-8. **quae...spem:** in both relative clauses, the antecedent of the relative pronoun has been attracted into the relative clause (see also 327-8, 642, 903). Construe as *fortuna quae est cuique, spem quam quisque secat.* **fortuna:** here used in its neutral meaning. **hodie:** see 1 n. **quam... spem:** lit. "the hope which each one carves out." The metaphorical* language suggests "carving out" one's way of hope in the carnage of battle (cf. 12.368 *viam secat* of cutting a way through the ranks). See Harrison *ad loc*. The monosyllabic ending and the alliterations* impart solemnity to the utterance. The indefinite pronouns *cuique* and *quisque* add to the vagueness of Jupiter's language. **Tros Rutulusne fuat:** is a disjunctive indirect question after *nullo discrimine habebo*. For the interrogative particle omitted in the first member of a disjunctive indirect question, see AG §335a. **fuat:** archaic* form of the present subjunctive of *sum* (from the root *fu-*). This archaism* lends authority to the speech. **nullo discrimine habebo:** lit. "I will hold with no distinction"; *nullo discrimine* is ablative of manner. As for Zeus' pledge to remain neutral, see 96-117 n.

109-10. **seu fatis...| sive errore...:** "either because of the (good) fortune...or because of the error..." **Italum:** genitive plural (dependent on *fatis*) for *Italorum*, see 2 n. **castra:** i.e., the Trojan camp; subject of *tenentur*. **errore malo Troiae:** "because of the sinful error of Troy," is possibly a reference to Paris' sin (the point made by Juno, 89-93), but, since *error* can also mean "wandering," *errore malo* is also suggestive of the painful wanderings of the Trojans (the point made by Venus, 57-8). **monitisque sinistris:** the expression could be a reference to Juno's claim that the Trojans have come to Italy following unreliable prophecies (67-8), but Jupiter may also hint at the very same claim made ironically* by Venus (31-2), or possibly at Tiberinus' bidding Aeneas to go up river to seek Evander's alliance (8.51-8), thus forcing him to leave the Trojan camp to the care of his men (or of Ascanius, as Juno has it, cf. 68-70). Jupiter remains vague as to the reasons of the Trojans' present misfortunes.

nec Rutulos solvo. sua cuique exorsa laborem
fortunamque ferent. rex Iuppiter omnibus idem.
fata viam invenient.' Stygii per flumina fratris,
per pice torrentis atraque voragine ripas
adnuit et totum nutu tremefecit Olympum.   115
hic finis fandi. solio tum Iuppiter aureo
surgit, caelicolae medium quem ad limina ducunt.

111-12. **nec Rutulos solvo:** parenthetical. Since his last words have referred specially to the Trojans, Jupiter now adds, "nor do I absolve the Rutulians," i.e., I do not necessarily espouse their cause and exempt them from blame. **sua…exorsa:** subject of *ferent*. *Exorsa* is the past participle neuter plural from *exordior*, but here is used as a substantive. Translate as "their own attempts." **laborem:** "suffering," cf. 12.727. **fortunamque:** here "(good) fortune," the opposite of *laborem*. By espousing the view that fate is dependent on human actors, Jupiter shrewdly frees himself of any responsibility for the outcome of the war but contradicts his earlier statement (1.283) in which he had identified himself with fate. For fate and Jupiter, see 15 n. **rex…idem:** sc. *est*. **omnibus:** dative of reference.

113-15. **fata viam invenient:** i.e., without any attempt of mine to modify it (but see 107-8 n.). The expression is repeated from 3.395 (Helenus' prophecy about Aeneas' journey to Italy). For fate and Jupiter, see 15 n. **Stygii per flumina fratris:** for *per* + acc. in oaths and prayers, see 45-6 n. The *frater* is Pluto (Hades) who was king of the Underworld and brother of Jupiter. The adjective *Stygius* ("Stygian") refers to the Styx, the river of the Underworld. It agrees with *fratris* where we would have expected it to agree with *flumina* (*Stygia per flumina*) and is an example of enallage* (transferred epithet; see 230-1 n.). The plural *flumina* is poetic. **per… ripas:** read *per ripas torrentis pice atraque voragine*. *Pice* and (*atra*) *voragine* are descriptive ablatives after *torrentis*. The rivers of the Underworld were proverbially black. **adnuit…:** see 8 n. **tremefecit Olympum:** *tremefecit* picks up *tremefacta* at 102. The expression is Homeric. Cf. 1.530 (similarly at line end). *Stygii…Olympum* is a verbatim repetition of Jupiter's oath to Cybele that he will transform Aeneas' ships into nymphs at 9.104-6. Such repetition is a narratological device meant to reproduce Homeric formulaic* technique (i.e., a technique characteristic of Homeric and oral poetry whereby the same expression (formula*) is regularly used, under the same metrical conditions, to express a particular essential idea). On Vergil's use of formulaic language, see Moskalew (1982) 106-7. Jupiter swearing by the Styx, the most binding among the gods, is somewhat hollow since *de facto* he has committed to nothing other than a vague "the fates will find their way."

116. **fandi:** genitive of the gerund dependent on *finis*. Sc. *fuit*. **aureo:** disyllable by synizesis*.

117. **caelicolae…:** construe as *quem* (i.e., Jupiter) *caelicolae ducunt medium ad limina*. For *caelicolae*, see 6 n. **medium:** the adjective is used adverbially "in the middle," see 54-6 n. Jupiter holds the position of honor in the middle. Servius rightly compares the scene with the *deductio*, the escorting home of newly elected consuls by the senate.

118-307: The return of Aeneas

The narrative switches from heaven to earth where the Trojans are still trapped in their camp, attempting in vain to ward off the Rutulians and their renewed attacks (118-45). At night Aeneas sails down the Tiber back to his camp and, after an unexpected encounter with the ships of his fleet now turned nymphs (see 215-59 n.), he and his Etruscan allies (see 163-214 n.) finally make it to Latium (260-75) and land on its shores (276-307).

The return of Aeneas, placed at the beginning of the third day of battle, that is in the middle of the war (there are five days of battle in the *Aeneid*), marks a sudden and unexpected reversal of fortune. From this moment on, the Trojans go from being besieged to being besiegers, from defenders to attackers, from losers to winners. Most importantly, they go from playing the role of the "ill-fated" Trojans once again besieged in the newborn Troy (see 26-7 n.), to taking on the role of the invading and "victorious" Greeks who eventually, in Book 11, will besiege King Latinus' city which, from this perspective, plays the role of yet another city of Troy.

For detailed analysis of this reversal and its significance in the structure of the last four books of the *Aeneid*, see Rossi (2004) 54-69. For the Trojans playing the role of the Greeks of the *Iliad*, see Quint (1993) 68-83.

> Interea Rutuli portis circum omnibus instant
> sternere caede viros et moenia cingere flammis.
> at legio Aeneadum vallis obsessa tenetur   120
> nec spes ulla fugae miseri: stant turribus altis

118-45. The Rutulians renew the assault and the thin line of Trojan heroes, among whom Ascanius is conspicuous in his youthful beauty, seeks to repulse them with missiles.

118-19. **Interea:** i.e., while the assembly of the gods is taking place. For the chronology of events see 1 n. **portis...omnibus:** "at every gate (locative abl.), all round (*circum*, adverb)." **instant | sternere...cingere:** "press on to lay low (i.e., "to kill")...and to encircle"; for the complementary infinitive after *insto*, see also 130, 354-5. The present tenses add vividness to the entire scene. **caede:** instrumental ablative.

120. **at:** the adversative in initial position underscores the Trojans' opposite state of affairs. **Aeneadum:** genitive plural (from *Aeneades, -ae*), see 4 n. Translate "of the companions of Aeneas." **vallis:** lit. "within the stakes," i.e., within the palisades. *Vallus* was the name of the "stake" used by Roman soldiers to build palisades. Note how the presence of anachronisms in the *Aeneid* pointedly creates temporal dissonances and blurs the boundaries between narrated time and narrating time, mythological past and historical present. See Sandbach (1965-66) and Rossi (2004) 178-88; see also General Introduction to the book.

121. **nec spes ulla fugae:** sc. *est*. The phrase confirms Turnus' threat at 9.131. See also 263 n. **miseri:** the affective vocabulary highlights the Trojans' emotional state. Cf. 9.470-1 *turribus altis | stant maesti*.

> nequiquam et rara muros cinxere corona
> Asius Imbrasides Hicetaoniusque Thymoetes
> Assaracique duo et senior cum Castore Thymbris,
> prima acies; hos germani Sarpedonis ambo 125
> et Clarus et Thaemon Lycia comitantur ab alta.
> fert ingens toto conixus corpore saxum,
> haud partem exiguam montis, Lyrnesius Acmon,

---

122. **nequiquam:** the term, poetic and emphatically isolated in enjambment*, picks up *nec spes* above. **rara:** "thin"; the "ring (*corona*)" of defenders with which they man the wall had many gaps in it (and is thus described as *rara*). **cinxere:** = *cinxerunt*.
123. **Asius…:** many of the names which follow are taken from Homer, but Vergil often assigns the same Homeric name to warriors fighting on opposite sides (e.g. 170-1 n.), blurring the distinction between their identity and, perhaps, calling attention to their common humanity. In general, for the names of Trojans and Latins in the *Aeneid*, see C. F. Saunders (1940) and Reed (2007) especially 1-15. **Asius:** Homer has two Trojans named Asios. The name is possibly intended to suggest his Asian origin. **Imbrasides:** is a patronymic* "son of Imbrasus," from *Imbrasides, -ae*. **Hicetaoniusque:** is a patronymic* in *–ius*, "son of Hicetaon." Cf. also 749 *Lycaonium*. **Thymoetes:** Greek nominative. He will be killed by Turnus at 12.364. The Thymoetes who urges the Trojans to accept the Horse at 2.32-4 is probably an older man.
124. **Assaracique duo:** warrior brothers are common in the *Iliad* and often their relationship is used in Vergil for pathetic effect, cf. 390-3, 575-601. Assaracus is a quintessentially Trojan name, as Assaracus was the grandfather of Anchises, Aeneas' father. **senior:** the comparative adjective is used here as a substantive "an old(er) man." **Thymbris:** the name is possibly derived from that of the river Tembris, a tributary of the Sangaris (or Sagaris) in Phrygia, or else from Thymbra, a town in the Troad.
125. **prima acies:** is in apposition to the list of names given above. **hos:** i.e., the men mentioned above; object of *comitantur* (126). **Sarpedonis:** possessive genitive after *germani ambo*. Sarpedon was a famous Lycian chief and an ally of Troy, slain by Patroclus at *Il*. 16.477-507. For Sarpedon as an important model for several characters in the book, see General Introduction to the book; cf. also 470 n. **ambo:** "two."
126. **Clarus:** the name of this Lycian warrior possibly derives from Clarus, a town in Lycia, famous for a temple of Apollo. **Thaemon:** Greek nominative of the third declension. **alta:** agrees with the ablative (*ab*) *Lycia*. Probably "mountainous," for Lycia was a mountainous region, though the meaning "noble" is also possible; cf. 374.
127. **fert:** the subject is *Lyrnesius Acmon* in the following line. **toto conixus corpore:** "straining with all his force" (lit. "body"). The heavy spondees suggest effort, while the position of *ingens saxum* straddling *toto corpore* reinforces the impression of the rock's overwhelming size. The throwing of large rocks is common in the battles of the *Aeneid* as in those of the *Iliad*.
128. **haud partem exiguam:** is in apposition to *ingens saxum*. **Lyrnesius:** "of Lyrnesus," a town in Mysia. **Acmon:** seems a name appropriate for a warrior carrying weights, since his name means "anvil" in Greek (Harrison *ad loc.*).

nec Clytio genitore minor nec fratre Menestheo.
hi iaculis, illi certant defendere saxis 130
molirique ignem nervoque aptare sagittas.
ipse inter medios, Veneris iustissima cura,
Dardanius caput, ecce, puer detectus honestum,
qualis gemma micat fulvum quae dividit aurum,

---

129. **Clytio genitore:** ablative of comparison after the comparative *minor* (just as *fratre Menestheo*). **Menestheo:** *-eo* scans as one syllable by synizesis*. The topos* of "son rivaling father" is Homeric. For its use in Vergil, cf. also 280-2, 371.

130. **hi...illi:** the subdivision of the scene into smaller narrative units ("these...those") is intended to show the diverse but simultaneous actions of different groups of people. As noted by ancient grammarians such a device adds vividness to the scene. **defendere:** is a complementary infinitive after *certant* (see also *moliri* and *aptare* in the following line.) For the construction, see 118-19 n.

131. **molirique ignem:** "to hurl fire"; the Trojans are to be imagined as throwing flaming torches against the besiegers. **nervo:** "to the sinew," the original material of the bowstring.

132-3. **ipse:** anticipates *Dardanius puer* (i.e., Ascanius). Kyriakidis (2007) 122 notes that Ascanius' position in the middle of the catalogue* mirrors his central position in the scene described. **iustissima cura:** "the very rightful concern," (1) as Venus' grandson, (2) on account of his beauty, and (3) (for Servius) on account of his destiny. Cf. also 1.678 (Venus of Ascanius) *mea maxima cura*. **Dardanius...puer:** for the adjective *Dardanius*, see 92 n. **caput...detectus honestum:** lit. "uncovered in respect to his handsome head." *Caput* is accusative of specification. The construction is influenced by two Greek constructions: (1) a middle verb governing a direct object, (2) the acc. of specification common in Greek with parts of the body. For *honestum = pulchrum*, cf. *Geo*. 2.392 *et quocumque deus circum caput egit honestum* (said of Bacchus). Ascanius is without helmet because Apollo had forbidden him to take part in the fighting (9.646-56). **ecce:** suggests dramatic surprise. Note the intricate word order of the line with nouns and adjectives distributed around *ecce*.

134-7. **qualis...ebur:** in this simile*, Ascanius is compared first to a precious stone (*gemma*) and then to ivory (*ebur*). The point of the two comparisons is the way in which the beauty of Ascanius stands out as he is surrounded by the other warriors who form a frame to it. The bright stone in its gold setting also reflects the contrast between Ascanius' bare head and the gold torque he wears around his neck (see 137-8 n.), while the pale color of the ivory picks up Ascanius' milk-white neck (137). In general, for Vergilian similes, see West (1969) who convincingly shows that many Vergilian similes in the *Aeneid* contain not just one but multiple points of contact with the surrounding narrative. The simile recalls that at 1.592-4, where the divine grace shed round Aeneas by his mother is compared to gold in which silver or marble is set, or to the adornment put upon ivory by the hand of an artist. Feeney (1999) 181-2 views it as an important self-referential moment, suggesting that the beautiful object of jewelry set in the middle of its surrounding reflects the narrative where Ascanius, a beautiful object of contemplation, is set in the middle of the battle narrative (note *per artem* at 135 referring at once to Vergil's and the jeweler's art). Feeney further submits that the reference to artifacts

aut collo decus aut capiti, vel quale per artem 135
inclusum buxo aut Oricia terebintho
lucet ebur; fusos cervix cui lactea crinis
accipit et molli subnectens circulus auro.
te quoque magnanimae viderunt, Ismare, gentes
vulnera derigere et calamos armare veneno, 140
Maeonia generose domo, ubi pinguia culta

---

which circulated in the Augustan imperial court allows the simile to open up a perspective forward in time illustrating the cultural and historical results of the narrated action: the horrors of the narrative, one day, will result in a social order that will produce supremely beautiful work of art to commemorate them.

134. **fulvum...aurum:** read *quae dividit fulvum aurum*. The antecedent of *quae* is *gemma*.

135. **collo...capiti:** datives of reference. **decus:** "an ornament," is in apposition to *gemma*. **quale:** refers to the nominative neuter *ebur* at 137.

136. **inclusum buxo:** "inlaid in box-wood." **Oricia terebintho:** locative ablative. Just like all names of trees in Latin, the terebinth is feminine in gender. *Oricum* or *Oricus* (adj. *Oricius*) is the name of a port/town on the coast of Illyria. Pliny 13.12 describes its wood as *nigri splendoris*; its color would, therefore, stand in stark contrast with that of the ivory. The sense of Oriental finery is enhanced by the Graecizing features of the hiatus* at the caesura* after *buxo*. Note also the quadrisyllabic line ending which Vergil seems to limit mainly to Greek words.

137-8. **fusos...:** construe as *cui* (i.e., to Ascanius, dat. of reference) *cervix lactea et circulus* ("torque-necklace") *molli auro* (abl. of material) *subnectens* (sc. *cervicem*) *accipit fusos crinis*. Note the chiastic* word arrangement around the central *cui*. For Ascanius' erotic beauty, see Harrison *ad loc*. The reading *subnectit* instead of *subnectens* is reported in some manuscripts. In this case construe *cui cervix lactea accipit fulvos crinis et circulus molli auro subnectit* (*fusos crinis*). Ascanius would wear the torque not around his neck, but around his head to confine the hair which at the back escapes from it and flows over the shoulders. If this reading were to be accepted Ascanius would resemble Apollo at 4.147-8 (*mollique fluentem | fronde premit crinem fingens, atque implicat auro*), where the eternally youthful god clearly wears the gold circlet round the head (as a sort of diadem) to confine his hair.

139. **te quoque:** cf. 324, 6.30, and 7.1. With this apostrophe* the narrator expresses sympathy for one of the characters. For more on apostrophe in the *Aeneid*, see Behr (2005). **magnanimae... gentes:** "(your) great-hearted people," i.e., the tribes who followed Ismarus from his "Maeonian (i.e., Lydian) home" (141 n.).

140. **vulnera derigere et...armare:** the accusative subject of the infinitives is *te* at 139. *Vulnera derigere* is a striking expression first found in Vergil. Instead of "throwing weapons" (cf. 401 *validam derexerat hastam*), the Trojans "throw wounds." **calamos:** "reeds"; here used synecdochically* for "arrows," for arrows were made of reeds.

141. **Maeonia...domo:** abl. of origin. Maeonia is the eastern part of Lydia. For the hiatus* *domo ubi*, see 136. **generose:** "high-born." Vocative in agreement with *Ismare*. **pinguia:** Lydia was

exercentque viri Pactolusque inrigat auro.
adfuit et Mnestheus, quem pulsi pristina Turni
aggere murorum sublimem gloria tollit,
et Capys: hinc nomen Campanae ducitur urbi. 145
    Illi inter sese duri certamina belli
contulerant: media Aeneas freta nocte secabat.
namque ut ab Euandro castris ingressus Etruscis
regem adit et regi memorat nomenque genusque

---

famed for its fertility. **culta:** the (neuter accusative plural) perfect passive participle of *colo* is used as a substantive "lands."

142. **Pactolusque...auro:** the Pactolus was a Lydian river famed for carrying gold dust and Servius *auctus* tells the story of King Midas washing away his golden touch in it. For Oriental rivers carrying gold, cf. *Geo.* 2.137-9 with Thomas (1988) *ad loc.*

143-4. **quem...sublimem:** object of *tollit*; the antecedent of *quem* is Mnestheus. **pulsi...Turni:** objective genitive after *pristina gloria*. **pristina...gloria:** subject of *tollit*. Mnestheus had won glory the previous day of battle for he had rallied the beleaguered Trojans to drive Turnus back when he was causing havoc inside the Trojan camp (9.778-98). **aggere:** ablative of place from which after *pulsi*. For the expression *aggere murorum*, see 23-4 n.

145. **hinc:** = *ab hoc* (i.e., *Capys*). Servius *auctus* reports that there was a tradition that made Capys (the founder of Capua) a cousin of Aeneas. **Campanae...urbi:** dative of possession.

146-62. *At night Aeneas sails back to the camp after visiting Tarchon and securing his aid.*

146. **Illi:** i.e., the Latins and the Trojans. **duri certamina belli:** "the contests of hard war"; *duri* is better taken as a genitive singular with *belli* rather than a nominative plural with *illi*.

147. **contulerant...secabat:** the sudden switch of subject (*illi...Aeneas*) and the abrupt introduction of Aeneas mark an almost cinematic change of scene, while the shift of tenses (*contulerant...secabat*) makes clear that "Aeneas was ploughing the straits at midnight" *after* the combat just described had ended. **media...nocte:** ablative of time. **freta...secabat:** the metaphor* ("to cleave the sea") is taken from ploughing and is common in Homer.

148-53. **namque...haud fit mora:** the sentence probably reads "for when (*ut*) having entered the Etruscan camp...he approaches the king...relates...informs him...reminds him...there is no delay" (i.e., straightaway Tarchon unites his forces), with *haud fit mora* functioning as the main clause. Otherwise supply *est* after *ingressus* and make *adit*, *memorat*, etc., the main verbs, beginning a fresh sentence at *haud fit mora*. The narrative is resumed from 8.603, when Aeneas, after leaving Evander (*ab Evandro*), proceeds to the Etruscan camp to ask for Tarchon's aid.

148. **castris...Etruscis:** dative of motion toward, common in poetry (AG §428.h).

149. **regem...regi:** the emphatic polyptoton* and the present tenses (*adit* and *memorat*) stress Aeneas' sense of urgency. **nomenque genusque:** "both (his) name and (his) race."

quidve petat quidve ipse ferat, Mezentius arma 150
quae sibi conciliet, violentaque pectora Turni
edocet, humanis quae sit fiducia rebus
admonet immiscetque preces: haud fit mora, Tarchon
lungit opes foedusque ferit; tum libera fati
classem conscendit iussis gens Lydia divum 155
externo commissa duci. Aeneia puppis

150. **quidve petat quidve...ferat:** two indirect questions introduced by *memorat*. The disjunctive particle *-ve* is often used in Vergil with a sort of vigorous abruptness in direct questions where *-que* would be expected and is retained in indirect questions (cf. also 2.74-5 *hortamur fari, quo sanguine cretus, | quidve ferat*). **petat...ferat:** subjunctives in indirect question. Aeneas asks a favor (alliance) and offers a benefit (help against Mezentius).

150-1. **Mezentius...conciliet:** construe as *quae arma Mezentius sibi conciliet*. *Quae* is an interrogative adjective neuter agreeing with *arma*. *Conciliet* is a subjunctive in the indirect question dependent on *edocet* (here in a first-foot dactyl enjambment*). Mezentius, the abhorred former king of the Etruscans (8.489-95), is mentioned first to the Etruscan Tarchon by Aeneas so as to win his audience's sympathy and attention. **violentaque pectora:** accusative after *edocet*. *Violentus* and *violentia* are solely used of Turnus in the *Aeneid* and are suggestive of his impetuosity. Note how Aeneas' language contrasts dramatically with the embassy sent to Diomedes by the Latins (8.6-17) in which Aeneas is depicted as a foreign aggressor striking alliances with Italian cities with the sole intent of becoming the new king of Latium. This Rutulian perspective had also been contradicted by Aeneas' embassy to Evander, which stressed that Aeneas was the victim of an unfair aggression by the Latins (8.117-51).

152-3. **humanis...rebus:** construe as *quae sit fiducia humanis rebus*. Another indirect question introduced by *quae* (interrogative adjective agreeing with *fiducia*) and governed by *admonet*. The idea that human affairs are unstable is a topos* used to support pleas for help/mercy, but Aeneas is also suggesting that Tarchon may soon need help himself (especially since Mezentius has gathered an army for himself). **rebus:** possessive dative after *sit*. **Tarchon:** though Vergil never states the connection openly, the name of Aeneas' ally evokes the Tarquins, the (in)famous Etruscan kings of Rome, who imposed an Etruscan monarchy in Rome. On Tarchon, see also 287-307 n.

154. **foedusque ferit:** lit. "he strikes a treaty." The expression is explained by Livy (1.24.4) who reports that an agreement of treaty (*foedus*) was ratified by a mortal blow (*ferire*) to a sacrificial animal, symbolizing the punishment for perjury on either side. **libera fati:** "free from fate," i.e., from the opposition of fate, which foretold that the Etruscans could only succeed against Mezentius if they "trusted themselves to a foreign leader" (8.503). The genitive *fati* is a Graecism used in poetry (instead of the ablative) with all words denoting separation or want (AG §356 n.).

155. **iussis...divum:** see 154 n. For the genitive *divum*, see 2 n. **gens Lydia:** subject of *conscendit*. The wording draws attention to the Eastern ethnicity of the Etruscans who were believed to have come to Etruria from Lydia. Just like Aeneas, his allies, too, are linked to the East. See also 157-8 n.

156. **externo...duci:** i.e., Aeneas; dative with compound verb. See 26-7 n. **Aeneia:** is a feminine adjective (nominative) agreeing with *puppis*. For the hiatus* after *duci*, see 136 n.

prima tenet rostro Phrygios subiuncta leones,
imminet Ida super, profugis gratissima Teucris.
hic magnus sedet Aeneas secumque volutat
eventus belli varios, Pallasque sinistro   160
adfixus lateri iam quaerit sidera, opacae
noctis iter, iam quae passus terraque marique.

157-8. **prima:** the neuter plural accusative is the direct object of *tenet*; here translate "first place." **rostro…:** "yoked with Phrygian lions at the beak." For the construction of the perfect passive participle (*subiuncta*) with the accusative of specification (*Phrygios leones*), see 132-3 n. *Rostro* is dative after the compound verb *subiungo* (AG §413a.n). The *rostrum* ("the naval ram," see 166 n.) was a weapon used by the Greeks and Romans, but unknown to Homer. For anachronisms, see 120 n. **Ida:** here a figurehead representing Mount Ida, the mountain near Troy. **super:** adv.; i.e., the figurehead of Mount Ida towers above the Phygian lions. The ship could be Aeneas'. In this case, its decorations, the Phrygian lions (dear to Cybele) and the representation of Mount Ida as its figurehead, are signs of gratitude (158 *gratissima*) to the goddess Cybele, who had granted Aeneas the privilege of building his fleet from a sacred grove of hers on Mount Ida (cf. 9.80-1) when he was escaping from Troy (cf. 158 *profugis* and 3.4-5). However, Aeneas left his ship at Pallanteum and reached Caere on horseback (8.551-3, 585-7) from where he embarks with his Etruscan allies. The ship, therefore, could belong to the Etruscans. In this event, the Eastern motifs on the ships of the Etruscans, which are most dear (*gratissima*) to the Trojans as well, strengthen the Eastern ethnicity of the Etruscans. See 155 n.

159. **Aeneas secumque volutat:** pensiveness is a trait of a good general and Aeneas is similarly represented at 6.157-8.

160-2. **Pallasque…:** this is the first mention of the young man who plays an important role in the book. He had been sent by his father Evander to help the Trojans in their fight against the Latins and had been entrusted to Aeneas (8.513-19). **sinistro…lateri:** dative after the compound verb *adfixus*. He stands on Aeneas' left side either out of modesty (to be on the left side is a sign of respect and subordination) or because Aeneas' right hand holds the tiller (cf. 218). **quaerit sidera:** sc. *ex Aenea*; "he asks (the name of) the stars." The stars were the normal means of navigation in antiquity. Note the contrast between the war-worn and pensive hero and the eager inquisitive boy. Petrini (1997) 62 suggests that by teaching Pallas the art of navigation, Aeneas introduces him to the realities of the iron age, the last of the five mythological ages of man when all manner of evils come into being and which is characterized by the introduction of navigation (cf. *Geo.* 1.136-8 and *Ecl.* 4.31-5). **opacae | noctis iter:** *iter* is in apposition to *sidera*. The stars are called the "path of the dark night" because the sailors follow them as they would follow a road. The expression *opacae noctis* recurs two other times in the *Aeneid*, both times in scenes of treachery and death (4.123; 8.658); here, it, too, may be suggestive that the world Pallas is about to enter is one filled with deception (Petrini (1997) 62). **iam:** repeated from 161, is suggestive of the boy's eagerness. Cf. Austin *ad* 1.120-2. **passus:** sc. *sit*, indirect question introduced by *quaerit* (161). Cf. 1.752-6 where Dido asks of Aeneas similar questions. Because of this similarity (among others) between Dido and Pallas, Putnam (1995) 27-49 suggests that there is an erotically charged relation between Pallas and Aeneas.

163-214: The catalogue of Aeneas' Etruscan allies

After a new invocation to the Muses, Vergil gives a list of the Etruscan allies of Aeneas as they sail with him to join the war against the Latins and Mezentius.

Catalogues* of troops are a feature of epic poetry going back to Homer. The *Aeneid* has two, a longer one of the Italian forces at the end of Book 7, and this shorter one, describing the ships of Aeneas' Etruscan allies. With all the warriors lined up and itemized, catalogues offer an emblem of order that contrasts with the chaos of actual warfare that follows, a tension that, in the case of Vergil, nicely reflects epic and imperial obsession over the relationship between order and violence.

The original purpose of epic catalogues was probably to identify the major participants in the forthcoming action. This seems to be the case in Homer. Vergil's Etruscan catalogue, however, is generally composed of people who have little or no role in the *Aeneid* and disappear quickly from the following narrative. Although this may seem quite puzzling, the quick "disappearance" of these Etruscan warriors from the text may be the very point of the catalogue. The fact that these Etruscan forces are "swallowed up" in the poem (with the notable exception of Asilas, see notes below) without leaving a trace is suggestive of the way the Etruscans, along with other Italians, have disappeared and have been "swallowed up" in history as part of the process of amalgamation of diverse groups into an ever-evolving Roman *civitas* (Feeney (1999) 192-4).

Malamud (1998) has connected Messapus, a warrior in the catalogue of *Aeneid* 7, with Cycnus and Ocnus in the present one, suggesting that these warriors should be read as representatives of epic poets. In particular, she highlights Messapus' and Cycnus' connections to the "swan-poet" image and notes how the "swan-poet" Messapus of *Aeneid* 7, representative of the martial epics of Ennius and of Homer, undergoes a metamorphosis in *Aeneid* 10 by turning into the neoteric* "swan-poet" Cycnus (*cycnus* = swan), representative of the new (Vergilian) epic singer. For details, see notes below. On Messapus as a double of Cycnus, see also O'Hara (1989).

The key model for this catalogue is the Greek Catalogue of Ships of *Iliad* 2. However, the position of this shorter catalogue which follows the longer Catalogue of the Italian Troops of *Aeneid* 7 parallels the position of the Catalogue of the Trojans in *Iliad* 2 which, too, follows the longer one of the Greeks in the same book. On the structure and sources of the catalogue, see Saylor (1974), Basson (1975) 157-92, Courtney (1988), Harrison *ad loc*.

Knauer (1964a) 297 points also to important parallels between this catalogue and the short catalogue of *Iliad* 16 describing the Myrmidons coming to support the ultimately victorious side (168-97). On the structure, arrangement, and sources of the catalogue, see also Saylor (1974), Basson (1975) 157-92, Courtney (1988), Harrison *ad loc*.

For the catalogue of Book 7 and the catalogue of Book 10, both arranged alphabetically with the notable exception of Messapus (in Book 7) and Ocnus (in Book 10), see Malamud (1998).

On epic catalogues, see Kyriakidis (2007). For the catalogue of Book 7, see Ganiban (2021) 106-8.

> Pandite nunc Helicona, deae, cantusque movete,
> quae manus interea Tuscis comitetur ab oris
> Aenean armetque rates pelagoque vehatur.   165
> Massicus aerata princeps secat aequora Tigri,
> sub quo mille manus iuvenum, qui moenia Clusi

163-5. Vergil invokes the Muses

The appeal to the Muses at the outset of a catalogue* is an epic convention that started with Homer who, in the Catalogue of Ships in *Iliad* 2, claims to be unfit to the task of memory without their help (the Muses were the daughters of Mnemosyne = Memory), contrasting the omniscience of the Muses to the ignorance of the mortals who must rely on tradition rather than knowledge (2.484-6. Cf. also *Aen*. 7.745-6).

163. **pandite:** see 1 n. **Helicona:** Greek acc. Mt. Helicon in Boeotia was the home of the Muses (*deae*). **cantusque movete:** supply *in me*. For *moveo* of poetic enterprise, cf. 7.45 *maius opus moveo*. The line is the same as that used to introduce the Catalogue of the Italian Troops in Book 7, suggesting that the two catalogues* are complementary (cf. 7.641).

164. **quae:** the feminine interrogative adjective agrees with *manus* ("band") and introduces the three indirect questions (note the subjective mood of *comitetur, armet, vehatur*). It depends on the idea of "saying" in *cantus movete*.

165. **Aenean:** see 65 n. **armetque rates:** "and mans the ships." **pelagoque:** the locative ablative without a preposition is commonly found to express the idea of motion through or over with verbs of motion.

166-84. Massicus leads a contingent of men from Clusium and Cosa. Along with him come Abas with a contingent from Populonia and Ilva, Asilas from Pisa, and Astur from Caere.

166. **Massicus:** the name is taken from Mt. Massicus in Campania. The region was famous for its wine. **aerata...Tigri:** instrumental ablative. *Aerata* ("bronze-sheathed") is a reference to the bronze-sheathed *rostrum* (i.e., a bronze ram attached to the bow of a warship, used to punch holes into the hull of enemy ships to sink them) of the warship, while Tiger (here, third declension abl.of a Greek noun) is the name of the ship. Roman ships were often named after the devices they bore as figureheads—in this instance a tiger. **princeps:** "(leading as) first." **secat aequora:** for the metaphor*, see 147 n.

167. **sub quo:** sc. *est*; the antecedent of *quo* is Massicus. **mille:** in the singular is an indeclinable adjective. Here it agrees with the genitive *iuvenum*. **Clusi:** "of Clusium" (modern Chiusi), the royal city of Lars Porsena, near Lake Trasimene.

    quique urbem liquere Cosas, quis tela sagittae
    gorytique leves umeris et letifer arcus.
    una torvus Abas: huic totum insignibus armis   170
    agmen et aurato fulgebat Apolline puppis.
    sescentos illi dederat Populonia mater
    expertos belli iuvenes, ast Ilva trecentos
    insula inexhaustis Chalybum generosa metallis.
    tertius ille hominum divumque interpres Asilas,   175

---

168. **urbem...Cosas:** *urbem* is in apposition to *Cosas*. Vergil is the only Latin writer to use the plural form (*Cosae*, -ārum) of the name of this town on the coast of Etruria. **liquere:** = *liquerunt*. **quis:** = *quibus*. The form is archaic* and poetic. The dative is possessive with *sunt* understood.

169. **gorytique:** "quivers"; the noun stands in apposition (together with *sagittae* and *arcus*) to *tela*. The identification of contingents by their arms belongs to catalogue-technique. **umeris:** locative ablative.

170-1. **torvus Abas:** the adjective *torvus* ("grim") seems to agree with his character described at 428 where he is called *pugnae nodumque moramque*. The name Abas is found in Homer of a Trojan victim of Diomedes (*Il.* 5.148). In Vergil, the name is given first to a living Trojan (1.121), then to an Argive warrior killed by Aeneas and whose shield Aeneas fixed on the doors of a temple at Actium (3.286-8), and now to an Etruscan who leads warriors from Populonia and Ilva. He will reappear in the *Aeneid* only to be killed by Lausus at 427-8. On Vergil's use of names, see 123 n. **huic...puppis:** construe as *huic* (i.e., Abas) *totum agmen fulgebat insignibus armis et puppis* (*fulgebat*) *aurato Apolline*. **huic:** dative of reference. **Apolline:** abl.; Apollo is the tutelar deity of the ship. His gilded (*aurato*) image would be set up on the stern; cf. Ov., *Her.* 16.114 *accipit et pictos puppis adunca deos*.

172. **Populonia:** modern Piombino in Tuscany. **mater:** note the affective personification* of the city.

173. **expertos belli:** "skilled in war"; adjectives denoting desire, knowledge, memory, etc. and its opposite often take the genitive, see AG §349a. **ast:** = *at*. See 743-4 n. **Ilva:** modern Elba. **trecentos:** sc. *dederat*.

174. **insula:** is in apposition to Ilva. **inexhaustis...metallis:** "with inexhaustible mines"; abl. of specification after *generosa* ("productive"). **Chalybum:** gen. plural. The Chalybes lived on the south shore of the Black Sea and were famed as great workers of iron; the term stands here, by an easy metonymy*, for iron itself.

175. **ille:** suggests a reputation "that (well-known)." **hominum divumque interpres:** the fundamental notion of *interpres* is one who intervenes *between* (*inter*) two sides. Usually, the genitive which follows only refers to one of these, the other being understood (cf. *interpres divum* = "the interpreter of (the will of) the gods (to men)" *Aen.* 4.356), but here the double relation of the word is expressed "interpreter between (lit. "of") gods and men." Feeney (1999) 192 suggests that the seer Asilas with his Etruscan divinatory arts (extispicy, astrology, ornithomancy, and divination by lightning) represents one of the few elements of Etruscan

cui pecudum fibrae, caeli cui sidera parent
et linguae volucrum et praesagi fulminis ignes,
mille rapit densos acie atque horrentibus hastis.
hos parere iubent Alpheae ab origine Pisae,
urbs Etrusca solo. sequitur pulcherrimus Astur,   180
Astur equo fidens et versicoloribus armis.
ter centum adiciunt (mens omnibus una sequendi)
qui Caerete domo, qui sunt Minionis in arvis,

---

culture to survive and play a role in the Roman world. Asilas is, therefore, one of the few men of the catalogue* allowed to play a role in the narrative and to survive the war (cf. 11.620; 12.127, 12.550; see Tarrant *ad* 12.127). **Asilas:** the name is also given to a Rutulian warrior at 9.571.

176. **cui:** i.e., to Asilas; dative after *pareo*. **fibrae:** "filaments"; they were thread-like markings on the liver from which the *haruspices* deduced the will of the gods. **parent:** the markings, the stars (*sidera*), the cries of the birds (*linguae volucrum*), and the fires of the lightning (*fulminis ignes*) "obey" Asilas for they yield up their meaning to him. For Servius (less convincingly) *parent* = *adparent* ("are clear"), i.e., they have no mystery for him.

177. **linguae volucrum:** "cries of birds." For ornithomancy, see 175 n. **praesagi:** either genitive with *fulminis* or nominative plural with *ignes*.

178. **mille:** sc. *viros* vel sim. **rapit:** "hastens along (with him)," cf. 7.725 *mille rapit populos*. **horrentibus hastis:** is not governed by *densos* like *acie*, but is an ablative of quality with *mille* (*viros*).

179-80. **Alpheae...solo:** construe as *Pisae Alpheae ab origine* ("in origin," i.e., born beside the Alpheus), *urbs Etrusca solo* ("in location," i.e., the town was on Etruscan soil) *iubent hos* (i.e., *mille*, above) *parere* (sc. *ei*, i.e., Asilas). *Pisae* (from *Pisae, - ārum*) is the subject of *iubent*. Vergil has *Pisae* (modern *Pisa*) as a colony of Pisa in Elis near the famous Alpheus River, but there seems no foundation to the story.

180-1. **Astur | Astur:** epanalepsis* is standard in epic catalogues* and here is probably used to further emphasize the hero's beauty (*pulcherrimus*), for Astur's name recalls Greek *astēr* ("star"), and stars were paradigms of beauty (Harrison *ad loc.*). The reading *Astur* (instead of *Astyr*) should be preferred since it is closer to Astura, a river in southern Latium.

181. **equo...armis:** are either ablatives (locative) or datives. *Fido* admits both constructions (AG §431). A connection can be made between the name Astur and the Asturians in Spain who, too, were famous for their horses.

182. **adiciunt:** the subjects are the two *qui* (= *ei qui*) clauses of the following line and *Pyrgi* and *Graviscae* at 184. **mens...una:** sc. *est*. **omnibus:** dative of possession. **sequendi:** genitive gerund.

183. **Caerete domo:** *Caerete* is an adjective from *Caeres, -itis*, or *-etis*. For the abl., see 141 n. **Minionis:** genitive. The Minio River was north of Caere (modern Cerveteri).

et Pyrgi veteres intempestaeque Graviscae.
Non ego te, Ligurum ductor fortissime bello, 185
transierim, †Cuneret†, et paucis comitate Cupavo,
cuius olorinae surgunt de vertice pennae

---

184. **Pyrgi veteres:** "ancient Pyrgi," i.e., the inhabitants of ancient Pyrgi, a town on the coast north of Rome (modern Santa Severa). **intempestaeque:** "unseasonable," "unhealthy"; the epithet* plays on the etymology* of the name: Servius quotes Cato in the *Origines* as explaining *Graviscae, quod gravem aerem sustinent*.

185-97. Next come Cunerus and Cupavo with a crest of swan's feathers. They are leaders of the Ligurian contingent. Vergil tells the legend of Cycnus, Cupavo's father.

The mention of Cupavo's swan-feather crest introduces a digression about a little-known aspect (possibly based on a Hellenistic model) of the well-known myth of Cycnus' love for Phaethon. According to the story, after Phaethon plunged disastrously into the Po River struck by Jupiter's lightning, the grieving Cycnus filled the banks of the river with his laments and was transformed into a swan (Ov., *Met.* 2.333-80). The mythological digression has a parallel in the catalogue* of Book 7 in the story of Hippolytus (761-82), where, again, a myth about a father is narrated on the appearance of his son.

Malamud (1998) 109 observes that the language of the song of Cycnus in the present passage is self-reflexive of Vergilian poetry, for the song of Cycnus points back to the song of Silenus in *Ecl.* 6 and the song of Orpheus in *Geo.* 4, the two Vergilian singers who represent, in many ways, the poetic voice of Vergil himself. See also 163-214 n.

185-6. **Ligurum:** gen. plural after *ductor*. **fortissime:** agrees with the vocative *ductor*. The leader of the Ligurians embodies the quality of its people known in antiquity for their toughness. **bello:** abl. of specification. **transierim:** potential subjunctive. The perfect tense is often used in polite assertion. **Cunere:** vocative. We are finally given the name of the *ductor* above. The manuscripts exhibit many spellings of the first name, but *Cunere*, from *Mons Cunerus* (in Picenum), should be preferred. For the apostrophe*, see 139 n. The combination of litotes* and apostrophe* strikes a panegyrical note (Cf. *Geo* 2.101-2 *non ego te...| transierim, Rhodia, et tumidis, Bumaste, racemis*). Cf. also *Aen.* 10.793 *non...te...silebo*. **comitate:** vocative modifying Cupavo. *Comitor* is one of the many deponent verbs whose past participle may have a passive sense. *Paucis* (sc. *viris*) is here regarded as an ablative of instrument or means (simple abl.) rather than as an ablative of agent (*ab* + abl.). Cf. 1.312 *comitatus Achate*. **Cupavo:** the son of Cycnus (see below) in Vergil. As noted by Ahl and Fantham (2008) *ad loc.* his odd name, not attested elsewhere, has multiple resonanaces: Cupid + *avis* (= "bird-lover"), *pavo* (= "peacock," Juno's special bird). His story, in turn, leads into the story of another bird, Cycnus = "swan." On swans and "swan-poets," see also 163-214 n.

187. **cuius...de vertice:** "from whose top"; for *vertex* understand the helmet as the helmet covers the top of a person's head. Cupavo has swan feathers (*olorinae pennae*) on his helmet.

LIBER DECIMUS 51

(crimen, Amor, vestrum) formaeque insigne paternae.
namque ferunt luctu Cycnum Phaethontis amati,
populeas inter frondes umbramque sororum   190
dum canit et maestum musa solatur amorem,
canentem molli pluma duxisse senectam
linquentem terras et sidera voce sequentem.
filius aequalis comitatus classe catervas

---

188. **crimen:** is in apposition to *pennae*. Translate as "reproach." **vestrum:** "your," agrees with *crimen*. *Vestrum* has been variously interpreted. Page, followed by Harrison, understands *vestrum* = of you, Love (= Cupid), and your mother: the feathers are a reproach to Love and his mother Venus because they have caused a man to lose his human shape and be turned into a swan (for the myth, see 185-97 n.). Alternatively, but less convincingly, *vestrum* has been understood as referring to Cycnus and Phaethon (Kappe) or to Cunerus and Cupavo, whom Conington and Nettleship believed to be two brothers, sons of Cycnus, between whom there existed "a criminal passion." **formaeque insigne paternae:** "the badge of his father's shape"; *insigne* refers again to *pennae*.

189. **ferunt:** "they say" introduces the accusative subject and infinitive *Cycnum* (189) *duxisse* (192). This "reporting" device introducing a story taken from an unnamed source is known as "the Alexandrian footnote" and is often used to signal a scholarly allusion. Cf. 7.765 *namque ferunt fama Hippolytum*. **Phaethontis amati:** objective genitive after *luctu*. For the manner of his death, see 185-97 n.

190. **umbramque sororum:** "the shade of the sisters (of Phaethon)." Phaethon's sisters were turned into poplars as they lamented the death of their brother. The story of their metamorphosis is retold by Vergil in the song of Silenus (*Ecl.* 6.62-3 *tum Phaethontiadas musco circumdat amarae | corticis atque solo proceras erigit alnos*).

191. **canit:** subject is Cycnus. **musa:** instrumental ablative. Here *musa* = "music/song" by metonymy*. **solatur amorem:** the language seems to be self-reflexive as it points back to Vergil's description of the song of Silenus who retells Pasiphae's fateful love for a bull (*Ecl.* 6.45-6 *et fortunatam, si numquam armenta fuissent | Pasiphaen nivei <u>solatur amore</u> iuvenci*) and of the song of Orpheus lamenting the death of Eurydice (*Geo.* 4.464 *cava <u>solans</u> aegrum testudine <u>amorem</u>*). For Silenus and Orpheus as representing the voice of the poet, see 185-97 n.

192. **canentem...duxisse senectam:** "drew over the whiteness of old age (lit. 'the old age whitening') with soft plumage." The artificial expression describes that Cycnus became white, not with the white hairs of age, but with swan's feathers. **duxisse:** probably for *induxisse*, a verb commonly used for the putting on of clothes.

193. **linquentem...sequentem:** refer to Cycnus. **sidera...:** lit. "following the stars with (his) lament." As Cycnus, now a swan, soars upward, he still laments.

194. **filius:** i.e., Cupavo, Cycnus' son. The mention of the son brusquely ends the digression, just as at 7.781. **aequalis:** "of the same age" (as Cupavo). The adjective refers to *catervas*. **comitatus:** is here active in meaning. **classe:** instrumental abl. Note the alliterations* *comitatus classe catervas*.

> ingentem remis Centaurum promovet: ille 195
> instat aquae saxumque undis immane minatur
> arduus, et longa sulcat maria alta carina.
>   Ille etiam patriis agmen ciet Ocnus ab oris,
> fatidicae Mantus et Tusci filius amnis,
> qui muros matrisque dedit tibi, Mantua, nomen, 200
> Mantua, dives avis, sed non genus omnibus unum:

195-6. **Centaurum:** i.e., the name of Cupavo's ship. Cupavo's ship has the same name as the vessel of Sergestus in the boat race (5.122). **ille | instat…minatur:** refer to the actual figure of a Centaur at the prow, while the subject of *et longa sulcat…* (197) is, again, the ship: "and furrows the high seas with its long keel (*longa carina*, instrumental abl.)." **aquae:** dative after the compound verb *insto*. **minatur:** is constructed with a dative of the thing threatened (*undis*) and the accusative of the threat (*saxumque…immane*). The figurehead is that of a rock-throwing centaur. Cf. Prop. 4.6.49 *quodque vehunt prorae Centauros saxa minantis*.

198-212. *Ocnus, founder of Mantua, comes next with a contingent from the city. Last is Aulestes sailing on a ship named Triton after its figurehead.*

Ocnus is the only name out of alphabetical order in the catalogue*. However, as noted by Malamud (1998) 116, the noun could hide the concealed signature of Vergil for the Greek *oknos* means *mora* ("delay") in Latin, which, in turn, is an anagram for *Maro*, Vergil's *cognomen*. With Maro alphabetical order would be restored. For the name Ocnus connected also to the Greek word for "heron," an oracular bird with prophetic powers, see Malamud (1998) 113.

198. **ille…ciet Ocnus:** *ille* is deictic*, "see, (too), that over there Ocnus summons…" **Ocnus:** this is the first time this name is associated with the foundation of Mantua.

199. **Mantus:** "of Manto," Greek genitive (from *Manto, -us,* f.) depending on *filius*. According to Servius, Manto was the daughter of the Theban seer Teiresias. Here she is described as a prophetess and bride of the "Tuscan river" (= the Tiber, cf. 8.473). Note how *fatidicae* ("prophetic") brings out the etymology* of the name since *mantis* means prophet in Greek. Feeney (1999) 194 also notes that another (unmentioned) fate-speaking person of Etruscan ancestry is connected with this place of significant name: Vergil himself. **filius:** in apposition with *Ocnus*.

200. **qui:** i.e., Ocnus. **muros…nomen:** direct objects of *dedit*. Ocnus gave Mantua both walls and name (of his mother). **Mantua:** the emphatic apostrophe* followed by epanalepsis* signals Mantua's special standing in the catalogue* as the poet's birthplace. Mantua receives special mention also at *Geo*. 3.12 *primus Idumaeas referam tibi, Mantua, palmas*.

201. **Mantua dives:** another pun on the etymology* of Mantua (cf. 199). Servius tells us that the name Mantua is derived from *Mantus*, the Etruscan name for the Roman god Dis (another name for Pluto, who was, among other things, the god of wealth). Mantua is *dives* ("rich") because it is named after Dis. **avis:** ablative of specification from *avus* ("ancestor") after *dives*, but note that *avis* is also Latin for "bird." **genus…unum:** sc. *est*. **omnibus:** dative of possession.

gens illi triplex, populi sub gente quaterni,
ipsa caput populis, Tusco de sanguine vires.
hinc quoque quingentos in se Mezentius armat,
quos patre Benaco velatus harundine glauca   205
Mincius infesta ducebat in aequora pinu.
it gravis Aulestes centenaque arbore fluctum
verberat adsurgens, spumant vada marmore verso.
hunc vehit immanis Triton et caerula concha

---

202. **gens...**: sc. *est*; "threefold (is) her race (lit. "threefold is the race to her"), four peoples under (each) race." **illi**: i.e., to Mantua; dative of possession. The three races are probably Etruscans, Gauls, and Veneti. Holland (1935) suggests that Vergil emphasizes the fact that Mantua, Vergil's birthplace, is triracial to compare himself to his epic Roman predecessor Ennius, who claimed to have "three hearts," Oscan, Greek, and Latin (Aulus Gellius, *Noct. Att.* 17.17.1). The twelve *populi* (= "townships") possibly suggest a reference to the confederacy of the *duodecim populi* of Transappennine Etruria.

203. **ipsa caput**: sc. *est*. *Ipsa* refers to Mantua. **populis**: dative of reference. **Tusco**: i.e., Etruscan. **vires**: from *vis* ("strength"). Supply an understood *sunt*. The omission of the verb "to be" in both clauses and the asyndeton* are features of catalogues*.

204. **quingentos**: sc. *viros* vel sim. **in se...**: "against himself." The somewhat paradoxical mode of expression underscores the great hatred the Etruscans feel for Mezentius.

205-6. **quos**: the antecedent is *quingentos*. **patre Benaco**: abl. of origin. The father of the river-god Mincius is Benacus since the river Mincius originates from Lake Benacus (modern Lake Garda). **velatus...| Mincius**: Mincius is the figurehead of the river-god Mincius (modern Mincio), who gives his name to the vessel (cf. 166 n.). Fittingly, it is "veiled (*velatus*) with grey reeds (*harundine glauca*)." **infesta...pinu**: instrumental ablative. *Pinu* ("pine") is used synecdochically* for ship, since ships were made of pine wood. For the gender of *pinu*, see 136 n.

207. **gravis Aulestes**: the name of the Etruscan leader stands here by metonymy* for Aulestes' ship, which is *gravis*. As we learn at 209, the ship itself is actually called Triton from its figurehead. Cf. *Centaurus* and 195-6 n. **centenaque arbore**: instrumental ablative. *Centena* is a distributive form and is used here instead of the cardinal (*centum*), as often in poetry; cf. 213, 329, 565-6. *Arbore* = by metonymy* "oars" because oars were made out of trees. The collective singular combined with *centena* gives an impression of immense size.

208. **marmore verso**: either an ablative absolute or an ablative of cause. *Marmore* = "marble," but here by metonymy* the sea because it is as smooth and gleaming as marble.

209. **hunc**: either Aulestes, the Etruscan leader (see 207 n.) or, less likely, the ship. **immanis Triton**: the reference is again ambiguous. *Triton* most likely refers to the figurehead of the ship, but the ship could be meant. **concha**: instrumental ablative. The conch-shell trumpet was Triton's characteristic instrument, cf. 6.171.

> exterrens freta, cui laterum tenus hispida nanti 210
> frons hominem praefert, in pristim desinit alvus,
> spumea semifero sub pectore murmurat unda.
>   Tot lecti proceres ter denis navibus ibant
> subsidio Troiae et campos salis aere secabant.

215-307: Aeneas' encounter with the Nymphs and return to battle.

As the action resumes, the nymphs, who were once Aeneas' ships, intercept the Trojan hero out at sea (for the transformation of the ships into nymphs, see 9.77-122). Cymodocea tells Aeneas what has befallen his men and then, with her hand, she speeds his ship upon its way. At dawn, Aeneas comes in sight of the Trojan camp.

Aeneas' nocturnal and somewhat fantastic encounter with the nymphs, narrated with a certain lightness, follows an epic tradition of help given to heroes by sea-nymphs (cf. *Od.* 4.364-424) and is reminiscent of Hellenistic poetry. Among its most important models are Apollonius' description of the Argonauts' encounter with Triton (*Argonautica* 4.1537-637) and Catullus 64 where the nymphs, among them Thetis, rise breast-high above the waves to watch the new sea creature that was the ship Argo (12-16).

210-11. **cui...nanti**: dative of reference. The antecedent is Triton (either the figurehead or the ship, see 209 n.). **laterum tenus hispida...| frons hominem praefert**: "the hairy front portrays a man as far as its flanks." **tenus**: the preposition ("as far as") usually follows the genitive or ablative it governs (here the genitive *laterum*). See AG §359b. **in pristim**: *pristim* is an accusative singular of a parisyllabic (i.e., having the same number of syllables in the nominative and genitive) noun in -*is* of the third declension (AG §67). The *pristis* was a large fish or sea mammal often identified as the sawfish. The description here clearly refers to Triton, the figurehead, which is described as a man down to his waist and a sea-monster from its waist down.

212. **semifero sub pectore**: the foaming wave (*spumea unda*) roars *semifero sub pectore* ("under the half-wild breast") since the figurehead is curved to the line of the ship and directly over the water. The alliteration* of *s* and the assonance* of *u* evokes the foam and roar of the waves.

213. **Tot**: "so many," indicates a large number. **ter denis**: = *triginta*. See 207 n.

214. **subsidio**: dative of purpose after *ibant*, "were going to the aid." The construction is common in historians. **Troiae**: for the dative, see 148 n.; for the term, see 26-7 n. **campos salis... secabant**: "were cleaving the fields of sea," suggests the image of ploughing the sea. For the metaphor*, cf. 147 n. **aere**: instrumental ablative. The prows were covered with brass. The catalogue* draws to a close. The formal closing of the catalogue is modeled on the Catalogue of Ships at *Il* 2.760. Cf. also Ap. Rhod., *Arg.* 1.228. By contrast, the Italian catalogue of Book 7 has no formal conclusion.

Vergil, however, introduces an original element to the scene by making Cymodocea and her speech quintessentially Italian (228-9 n.). The episode, therefore, does not simply offer a relief from the reality of war but, more importantly, prepares Aeneas (and Vergil's readers) for the new Italian world from which Rome will emerge. On the topic, see Fantham (1990).

For Cymodocea's deceptive prophecy, see 245 n. and O'Hara (1990) 40-3.

On the episode, see Hardie (1987), Fletcher (2014) 236-43. For the nymphs appropriating elements of dithyrambic choreography (a particularly fitting dance for nymphs who are closely associated with Cybele), see Curtis (2017) 184-95.

> Iamque dies caelo concesserat almaque curru 215
> noctivago Phoebe medium pulsabat Olympum:
> Aeneas (neque enim membris dat cura quietem)
> ipse sedens clavumque regit velisque ministrat.
> atque illi medio in spatio chorus, ecce, suarum

215-59. *Cymodocea bids Aeneas to hasten to the Trojan camp to rescue his companions and assures him of victory. Aeneas prays for Cybele's favor in the battle to come.*

215-16. **caelo:** ablative indicating motion away from. **almaque...Phoebe:** the name of the Titaness Phoebe is used often by Roman poets for Diana in her aspect as moon-goddess as a counterpart to Phoebus Apollo's title as sun-god. See Harrison *ad loc.* **noctivago:** lit. "night-wandering"; the adjective is used only here in Vergil. **medium...Olympum:** "mid-Olympus," (i.e., "mid-sky") indicates a position half-way across the sky, i.e., midnight.

217. **neque...dat cura:** anxiety (*cura*) prevents Aeneas from falling asleep (cf. Dido at 4.5 *nec placidam membris **dat cura** quietem*), 8.29-30 (Aeneas) *Aeneas, tristi turbatus pectora bello, | procubuit seramque dedit per membra quietem*).

218. **velisque:** most likely is a dative after *ministrat* "attends to the sails." If *velis* be taken as an instrumental abl., we would need to supply the direct object *navem*, "attends (the ship) with sails." **ministrat:** historical present.

219. **atque:** a sentence or clause introduced by *atque* (or *ac*) marks a sudden event often closely connected with the preceding sentence. Translate "and suddenly." For other instances, cf. 572; 6.162; 9.754. **illi...:** i.e., to Aeneas. Dative after the compound verb *occurrit*. **chorus:** "band." **ecce:** see 132-3 n.

219-21. **suarum |...comitum:** "of his comrades"; *suarum* is here used (instead of *eius*) because *illi*, to which it refers, is so emphasized as to be felt as the subject of the sentence (AG §301b). The nymphs who come to meet Aeneas were once the ships who had accompanied Aeneas from Troy to Latium before being transformed into nymphs (for their metamorphosis, cf. 9.77-122). Hence, they are called "his comrades." **quas:** the antecedent is *Nymphae*. The relative pronoun is the accusative subject of the infinitives *habere* and *esse* (221) and is dependent on *alma Cybebe* (220) *iusserat* (222). **alma:** the epithet*, etymologically* connected with *alo* ("to nourish"), suits the nurturing Great Mother of the gods (Harrison *ad loc.*). **Cybebe:** another

occurrit comitum: nymphae, quas alma Cybebe 220
numen habere maris nymphasque e navibus esse
iusserat, innabant pariter fluctusque secabant,
quot prius aeratae steterant ad litora prorae.
agnoscunt longe regem lustrantque choreis.
quarum quae fandi doctissima Cymodocea 225
pone sequens dextra puppim tenet ipsaque dorso
eminet ac laeva tacitis subremigat undis.
tum sic ignarum adloquitur: 'vigilasne, deum gens,
Aenea? vigila et velis immitte rudentis.

---

name for *Cybele*. The name, derived from the Greek adjective *kubēbos*, "frantic," is a reference to the ecstatic rites of her priests and is already attested in Catullus (63.9). **numen habere maris**: "to have (divine) power over (lit. "of") the sea." **nymphasque e navibus**: the preposition *e* (or *ex*) is often used to express a change from an earlier condition.

222. **pariter**: "side by side." **fluctusque secabant**: humorously, the language describing the swimming of the nymphs is borrowed from that of sailing ships. See 147 n.

223. **quot**: "as many"; the adjective refers back to *nymphae* (220). **prius**: adv. "previously." **ad litora**: where their metamorphosis took place (cf. 9.118). **prorae**: "prow" is used synecdochically* for "ship."

224. **lustrantque choreis**: "and circle (him) in dance." *Choreis* picks up the description of the nymphs as *chorus* at 219.

225. **quarum...**: construe as *quarum* ("of whom," i.e., the nymphs) *Cymodocea quae* (sc. *est*) *doctissima fandi*. For *quarum* (where we would have expected *earum*), see 384 n. **fandi**: genitive gerund after *doctissima*, cf. 173 n. Vergil is possibly playing with the etymological* connection of the verb *fari* with *fata* ("fate"): Cymodocea is "best at speaking prophetically" (O'Hara (1990) 40). **Cymodocea**: in Greek "the Wave-receiver"; probably here there is also a pun on the element -*doce*, as if it were from the Latin *doce-* ("teach"), since she is the one who "teaches" Aeneas. A Nereid Cymodoce served in the marine escort of Aeneas from Sicily (5.826), but it is unlikely that she was the present Cymodocea.

226-7. **dextra**: sc. *manu*. So *laeva* below. Instrumental ablative. **dorso**: "with her back," abl. of degree of difference (AG §414) for the ablative here indicates the degree by which Cymodocea stands out (*eminet*) from the waves (sc. *ab undis*). Cymodocea lifts her whole torso out of the water, showing her upper, more human and less disturbing half. **ac**: "while," cf. 219 n. The image is indebted to Catullus 64 (14-18) where, similarly, the Nereids lift their whole torso out of the sea as they marvel at the ship of the Argonauts, the Argo. **subremigat**: the metaphor* of rowing is humorously chosen to suggest Cymodocea's previous shape as a ship. Her movement is so gentle as to not make any noise (*tacitis undis*).

228-9. **ignarum**: "unaware"; i.e., Aeneas had not noticed her until she speaks. **vigilasne...vigila**: Cymodocea uses Roman religious language as her words echo the archaic* formula* *vigilasque, rex? Vigila* with which the Vestal Virgins greeted the priest of Janus (Servius). **deum**: archaic* for *deorum*. **gens**: generally "race," but here "offspring." The term, used of a single descendant,

nos sumus, Idaeae sacro de vertice pinus,   230
nunc pelagi nymphae, classis tua. perfidus ut nos
praecipitis ferro Rutulus flammaque premebat,
rupimus invitae tua vincula teque per aequor
quaerimus. hanc genetrix faciem miserata refecit
et dedit esse deas aevumque agitare sub undis.   235
at puer Ascanius muro fossisque tenetur
tela inter media atque horrentis Marte Latinos.
iam loca iussa tenet forti permixtus Etrusco

---

is first found in Vergil. **velis...**: dative after the compound verb *immitto*; lit. "let loose the ropes (*rudentis*) to the sails"; by letting loose the ropes attached at the bottom of the sails, Aeneas would expose more sail to the wind and, therefore, sail faster.

230-1. **nos sumus...**: the main clause is probably *nos sumus...classis tua*, while the words from *Idaeae* to *Nymphae* are explanatory of *nos*. However, the sentence could also read "it is we, pines of Ida from its sacred summit, now nymphs of the sea, your fleet." **Idaeae sacro de vertice pinus:** "pines of Ida from its sacred summit." *Sacro* agrees with *vertice* where we would have expected it to agree with *pinus* (for the gender of *pinus*, see 136 n.) and is an example of enallage* (transferred epithet). For Vergil's use of this device, see Conte (1993) 208 and Conte (2007) 111.

231-2. **perfidus...Rutulus:** subject of *premebat*. The adjective is commonly applied to opponents, cf. *perfidus Hannibal* (Hor., *Carm.* 4.4.49). For the pro-Trojan nymph, Turnus is a treaty breaker (a position shared by Aeneas, cf. 8.540). **praecipitis:** the adjective anticipates the result of Turnus' action (the nymphs become *praecipitis* after Turnus presses them) and is therefore proleptic*. **ferro...flammaque:** instrumental ablative. The pairing is found often in historiography. *Ferro* is a metonymy*, for swords were made of iron. Note the set of alliterations* (*perfidus, praecipitis, premebat, ferro, flammaque*) and the emphatic position of *perfidus* preceding the conjunction *ut*.

233. **vincula:** are the cables by which Aeneas had moored them to the bank (9.118), but the term is also suggestive of the affectional "bond" of the ships/nymphs toward Aeneas.

234. **hanc...faciem...refecit:** "refashioned this (new) shape"; *hanc* is deictic* ("this one that you see"). **genetrix:** i.e., Cybele, cf. 83 n. **miserata:** from *miseror* (1) "having felt pity."

235. **dedit esse:** "granted us to be"; for the construction, see 61-2 n.

236. **Ascanius...tenetur:** the situation was described at 118-45 with *tenetur* recalling *tenetur* of 120. **muro fossisque:** locative ablative ("within the wall and ditches"). The *fossa* was the trench dug around the walls of a Roman military camp.

237. **horrentis Marte:** "bristling with war," describes the *Latinos*. *Marte* is a daring metonymy* that extends the common epic expression "bristling with weapons."

238. **loca...tenet:** "holds (its) station." *Loca tenere* is a military expression. The singular collective *Arcas eques* ("the Arcadian cavalry") is the subject. **Etrusco:** another collective singular. Collective singulars for names of peoples and military units are especially common in

Arcas eques; medias illis opponere turmas,
ne castris iungant, certa est sententia Turno.   240
surge age et Aurora socios veniente vocari
primus in arma iube, et clipeum cape quem dedit ipse
invictum ignipotens atque oras ambiit auro.
crastina lux, mea si non inrita dicta putaris,
ingentis Rutulae spectabit caedis acervos.'   245
dixerat et dextra discedens impulit altam

---

historiography. This is a quite puzzling piece of information for it is the first time we hear that the Arcadian Evander or the Etruscans have dispatched any cavalry to a fixed rendezvous. Further, this squadron never appears in battle, unless we identify them with the cavalry commanded by Pallas. For other inconsistencies of troop-movements in the poem, see, for example, 157-8 n.

239-40. **medias...turmas:** lit. "squadrons (intervening) between." **opponere:** is dependent on *certa est sententia* and governs the dative *illis* (i.e., the Arcadian cavalry) and the direct object *medias turmas*. **ne...iungant:** purpose clause. An accusative should be understood after *iungant*, owing to the common military use of *iungere vires, exercitum, copias*, etc. Otherwise, the verb is used in its middle sense (*iungere se*) and followed by a dative (*castris*), a construction not found before Vergil. **Turno:** possessive dat.

241. **surge age:** the usage of the double imperative is colloquial, cf. 8.59 *surge age, nate dea*. **Aurora...veniente:** ablative absolute. **socios...vocari:** the accusative subject and infinitive are governed by *iube* (242).

242-3. **primus:** is used adverbially "first of all else." **clipeum...auro:** construe as *cape clipeum invictum quem ipse ignipotens dedit* (sc. *tibi*) *atque ambiit* (from *ambio*) *oras auro*. **invictum:** "invincible." Note its emphatic position stressing the invincibility of the shield. **ignipotens:** "the one who has power over fire"; the compound adjective is first found in Vergil and is used for Vulcan. For Vulcan making new armor for Aeneas, see 8.608-731. **oras:** i.e., the rims of the shield.

244. **crastina lux:** subject of *spectabit* (245). **putaris:** = *putaveris* (fut. perfect) in the protasis of a future more vivid conditional clause. Vergil is fond of syncopated* verb forms in speeches for their colloquial tone.

245. **ingentis...:** is a Silver Line (see Golden Line*). Note also the coincidence of word accent and rhythmical ictus in the last three feet, a device often used by Vergil for sonorously rounding off a paragraph. The prophecy seems to be fulfilled almost verbatim at 509 (*cum tamen ingentis Rutulorum linquis acervos!*), but, somewhat ironically*, its fulfillment also brings about Pallas' death (about which Cymodocea remains pointedly silent). See O'Hara (1990) 43.

246. **dextra:** sc. *manu*, instrumental ablative after *impulit*. See 226-7 n. **discedens:** the nominative present participle refers to Cymodocea. Note the alliteration* (*dixerat, dextra, discedens*).

haud ignara modi puppim: fugit illa per undas
ocior et iaculo et ventos aequante sagitta.
inde aliae celerant cursus. stupet inscius ipse
Tros Anchisiades, animos tamen omine tollit.   250
tum breviter supera aspectans convexa precatur:
'alma parens Idaea deum, cui Dindyma cordi
turrigeraeque urbes biiugique ad frena leones,
tu mihi nunc pugnae princeps, tu rite propinques
augurium Phrygibusque adsis pede, diva, secundo.'   255

---

247. **haud ignara:** litotes* for emphasis. **modi:** is genitive after *haud ignara*, see 173 n. The line is humorous: Cymodocea is "not unaware of the way," since she herself was once a ship. **illa:** i.e., Aeneas' ship.

248. **iaculo…sagitta:** are both ablatives of comparison after *ocior*. For the simile*, cf. 5.242-3 (used for Cloanthus' ship after an analogous divine push): *illa Noto citius volucrique sagitta | ad terram fugit.*

249. **aliae:** contrasted with *illa* (247), must mean "the other ships." **cursus:** accusative plural, direct object of *celerant*. **ipse:** i.e., Aeneas. Ignorant (*inscius*) of Cymodocea's action, Aeneas is amazed (*stupet*) at the increased speed of the vessels.

250. **Tros Anchisiades:** "the Trojan son of Anchises." For Aeneas' double naming (and use of the patronymic*) in a similarly solemn context, cf. 6.126. **tollit:** subject is *Tros Anchisiades*. Aeneas "raises his spirits (*animos*) because of the omen (*omine*)" (i.e., because of the increased speed of the ship which he regards as a good omen).

251. **breviter:** qualifies *precatur*. **supera…convexa:** "the vaults above." *Convexa* reflects the ancient view that the heavens were spherical.

252. **alma parens Idaea deum:** lit. "Oh nourishing Idaean mother of gods," i.e., Cybele. For the genitive form *deum*, see 228-9 n. The wording recalls her official title in Rome (*Mater Deum Magna Idaea*) and foreshadows the historical process of Romanization and amalgamation of the Phrygian goddess into the Roman pantheon. See also 215-307 n. For Cybele's relation to Mount Ida, cf. also 157-8 n. and 9.618-21. **cui Dindyma cordi:** sc. *est*. Lit. "to whom Dindyma is dear"; *cordi* is a dative of purpose, *cui* dative of the person affected (i.e., Cybele). For the double dative construction, see AG §382. The construction continues in the following line with additional subjects (i.e., *urbes* and *leones*). Dindyma is a mountain in the Troad sacred to Cybele.

253. **turrigeraeque urbes:** Cybele was traditionally the protectress of cities. The compound epithet* *turrigera* ("tower-bearing") is first found in Vergil and plays on the fact that Cybele is often depicted in art and literature as wearing a "tower-crown." Cf. 6.785 *inuehitur curru Phrygias turrita per urbes*. **biiugique ad frena leones:** "and the lions yoked together in harness." *Biiugus* ("twin-yoked") is a first/second declension adjective. For Cybele's lions, a symbol of her civilizing power, cf. 157-8 n. Cybele' lions are also mentioned at 3.113.

254-5. **tu mihi…:** *sis* (jussive subjunctive) is to be supplied from the jussive subjunctives that follow. **pugnae:** genitive depending on *princeps*. **princeps:** "leader." **propinques | augurium:** *propinquo* is used transitively "may you hasten the (fulfillment of your) prophecy."

tantum effatus. et interea revoluta ruebat
matura iam luce dies noctemque fugarat:
principio sociis edicit signa sequantur
atque animos aptent armis pugnaeque parent se.
    Iamque in conspectu Teucros habet et sua castra   260
stans celsa in puppi, clipeum cum deinde sinistra

Phrygibusque: the term underscores Trojans' Asiatic origins and their close ties with Cybele, a goddess generally associated with Phrygia. For Phrygians' reputation for luxury and effeminacy, see 9.617 (speech of Numanus Remulus) and Turnus' prayer at 12.99 that he overcome "the Phrygian half-man." **pede...secundo:** the expression "lucky foot" refers to the Roman superstition of starting off with the lucky right foot (Harrison *ad loc.*). Cf. 8.302 (prayer to Hercules) *et tua dexter adi pede sacra secundo*.

256-7. **tantum effatus:** see 877 n. **revoluta:** agrees with *dies* (here feminine, see also 467) and is reflexive in sense "having brought (itself) round again". The heaven is regarded as consisting of two hemispheres, one bright and the other dark, which revolve bringing day and night respectively on earth; cf. 2.250 *vertitur interea caelum et ruit oceano nox*. **fugarat:** = *fugaverat*

258-9. **principio:** adv. "first of all." **signa sequantur:** "to follow the standards," is possibly an anachronistic reference to the advancing in formation of the Roman army behind legionary standards. For anachronisms in the *Aeneid*, see 120 n. **sequantur...aptent...parent:** are subjunctives in an indirect command clause after *edicit* with *ut* omitted, see 54-6 n. **animos... se:** *pugnae parent se* repeats with different words the concept expressed in *animos aptent armis* in another instance of *dicolon abundans**, see 9-10 n. The monosyllabic ending and the alliterations* (*animos...armis, pugnae...parent*) give martial vigor to Aeneas' speech. Note also the clash of ictus and word accent at the end of the line.

260-75. *When Aeneas comes in sight of the Trojan camp, he lifts up his shield as a signal to the besieged. The Trojans rise a joyous cry, but the Rutulians, turning round, mark with terror the approaching fleet.*

For the reversal upon Aeneas' return and the historiographical models of the episode, see 118-307 n.

    For Aeneas as a proto-Augustus in this scene, see notes on 261 and 271 and Boyle (1999) 148. For Aeneas as Achilles, see 272-3 n.

260. **habet:** is a historical present.

261. **stans celsa in puppi:** *celsa* (ablative, agreeing with *puppi*) is archaic* and poetic for *altus*. *Puppis* is the stern of a boat and is the natural place for a commander. This image of Aeneas sailing to Latium before his decisive battle with the Latins parallels (with identical language and metrical position) that of his father Anchises arriving in Italy (3.527) and of his descendent Augustus sailing to Actium (8.680) before the final battle against Antony and Cleopatra, a scene engraved on the very center of the shield that Aeneas raises to signal his men. The Trojans (and the readers) see a picture of Aeneas that is just like the picture of Augustus that Aeneas is carrying on his shield. See Boyle (1999) 148. See also 270 n. **cum deinde:** "when (immediately) after"; *deinde* marks that the action described follows immediately on Aeneas sighting the camp. **sinistra:** sc. *manu*.

extulit ardentem. clamorem ad sidera tollunt
Dardanidae e muris, spes addita suscitat iras,
tela manu iaciunt, quales sub nubibus atris
Strymoniae dant signa grues atque aethera tranant   265
cum sonitu, fugiuntque Notos clamore secundo.
at Rutulo regi ducibusque ea mira videri
Ausoniis, donec versas ad litora puppis
respiciunt totumque adlabi classibus aequor.

---

262. **ardentem:** "glowing" (because made of precious metals, 8.445-6), but the language of fire may also underscore its supernatural quality and, possibly, the destructive powers of its owner.

263. **Dardanidae:** nominative plural. It is a masculine noun of the first declension (from *Dardanides, -ae*), as are many words borrowed from the Greek. The patronymic* is a common synonym for *Troiani*, see 92 n. **spes addita:** the unexpected arrival of Aeneas marks a dramatic change of heart in the besieged Trojans. Contrast 121 *nec spes ulla fugae*.

264-6. **quales:** introduces the simile* (cf. 134) and agrees with *Strymoniae grues* (265). **atris:** is an adjective conventional for clouds, but here may also be suggestive of the dangers escaped by cranes and Trojans alike. **Strymoniae...grues:** the "cranes" are called "Strymonian" because the river Strymon in Thrace was a typical habitat for cranes (Harrison *ad loc.*). **dant signa:** "send out their signal (with their cries)," but the phrase is also a military expression meaning "to give the battle-signal" and is therefore perfectly suited here as the cranes are being compared to the Trojan army. **atque:** 219 n. **aethera:** Greek acc. **tranant:** a metaphor* of swimming used for flying. **Notos:** the "South Wind," but here means more generically "stormy weather." The model of the simile is *Il.* 3.3-6 where the shouting of the Trojans entering battle is compared to that of cranes attacking the Pygmies. Vergil adapts the simile to compare the joyous cries of the Trojans at the sight of Aeneas to the exultant cry of the birds.

267-8. **Rutulo regi ducibusque...| Ausoniis:** are datives after *videri*. The Italian leaders are called "Ausonians" because Ausonia was the ancient Greek name for Italy. Note the chiastic* arrangement. **ea:** nominative plural neuter and subject of *videri*, "those things (i.e., the shouts of the Trojans) seem strange (*mira*). **videri:** the historical infinitive conveys suddenness.

268. **donec:** the temporal conjunction ("until") usually takes the subjunctive but is used with the present indicative (*respiciunt*) to state a future fact when there is no idea of expectancy. **versas ad litora puppis:** *puppis* is the object of *respiciunt*. The sterns of the ships are set to face the beach so that the prows can face seaward for ease of relaunching.

269. **totumque...aequor:** the accusative subject (*totum aequor*) and the (deponent) present infinitive (*adlabi*) are governed by *respiciunt*. To the startled Rutulians, the sea rolls in not, as usual, with waves, but with ships.

ardet apex capiti tristisque a vertice flamma 270
funditur et vastos umbo vomit aureus ignis:
non secus ac liquida si quando nocte cometae
sanguinei lugubre rubent, aut Sirius ardor
ille sitim morbosque ferens mortalibus aegris

270-1. **apex:** strictly used of the point in which the cap of a *flamen* (a type of priest) ended, the term here refers to the "tongue of flame," possibly because it resembles the shape of the priest's hat. See also 2.682-3. **capiti:** either an ablative (of place) or a dative of reference. For this form of the ablative (instead of *capite*), cf. Catullus 68.124 *a cano...capiti.* **tristisque...| funditur:** "and a grim flame pours (itself) from its top"; the passive has here a reflexive meaning. Cf. AG §156a. The transmitted text has *cristisque*, but the sentence reads a bit awkwardly "and from his crests from its top stream flames," and the emendation *tristisque* for *cristisque* by Faernus should be accepted. In Vergil and Homer such supernatural flames seem to indicate divine support. Cf. 2.682-4 (head of Ascanius); 7.73-6 (head of Lavinia). Twin flames and the star of his father Julius, the *sidus Iulium*, appear also on the head of Augustus at Actium (8.680-1 *geminas cui tempora flammas | laeta vomunt patriumque aperitur vertice sidus*), furthering the parallel between Aeneas and Augustus. See also 261 n.

271. **umbo:** "the boss of the shield" is used synecdochichally* for "shield." **vomit...ignis:** the golden shield glows in the sun and looks like it "vomits forth huge fires." However, the language also recalls the description of two monsters of the *Aeneid*. The Chimaera's head on Turnus' helmet (7.786) is similarly described as "blasting all the fires of Aetna from its throat" (*Aetnaeos efflantem faucibus ignis*), as is the monster Cacus who is seen as "vomiting black flames from his mouth" (*atros | ore vomens ignis* 8.198-9). The very moment Aeneas comes closest to being connected with Augustus, he is also connected to these violent monsters, leaving a reader to wonder about the real nature of Aeneas (and Augustus).

272-3. **non secus ac...:** "not otherwise than." The simile* is introduced via litotes*, a feature not found in high poetry before Vergil. **liquida...nocte:** ablative of time. **cometae:** nominative masculine; it agrees with *sanguinei*. For its gender, cf. 263 n. **lugubre:** neuter singular of the adjective; it is used adverbially. Vergil's only other mention of comets is at *Geo.* 1.488 (*diri arsere cometae*), where their appearance prefigures the disaster of the Roman Civil Wars when Emathia twice grew rich "with our blood" (*sanguine nostro* 491, repeated at 501). The intertext, again, gives cause for reflection for it suggests that Aeneas' arrival in Latium, in some way, will set in motion a set of bloody civil wars. For the war in Latium as a civil war, see General Introduction to the book. **Sirius:** is used here as an adjective qualifying the noun *ardor* ("the Sirian heat"). Sirius was the so-called Dog Star, rising in July and August. The model for the simile is *Il.* 22.29-31 where Achilles' armor is said "to gleam like the dog-star of Orion, a sign of evil bringing much fever on wretched mortals." In this way, Aeneas-Augustus upon his arrival in Latium begins his metamorphosis into the ruthless Achilles of *Iliad* 22, who had slaughtered Hector and had mercilessly defiled his body.

274. **ille:** "the one which," resumptive and picking up *Sirius ardor.* **mortalibus aegris:** is a rendering of the Homeric *deiloisi brotoisi* and, before Vergil, occurs in Lucretius (6.1).

nascitur et laevo contristat lumine caelum. 275
    Haud tamen audaci Turno fiducia cessit
litora praecipere et venientis pellere terra.
[ultro animos tollit dictis atque increpat ultro:]
'quod votis optastis adest, perfringere dextra.
in manibus Mars ipse, viri. nunc coniugis esto 280
quisque suae tectique memor, nunc magna referto
facta, patrum laudes. ultro occurramus ad undam
dum trepidi egressisque labant vestigia prima.
audentis Fortuna iuvat.'

---

275. **laevo...lumine:** suggests inauspicious light. For the left as unlucky, cf. 254-5 n.

276-86. *Turnus is undismayed and urges his men to attack Aeneas while Aeneas and his allies are engaged in landing.*

276-8. Lines 276 and 278 are repeated almost verbatim from 9.126-7, where, again, Turnus had encouraged his men after a favorable omen for the Trojans. Line 278 is omitted from a number of manuscripts and is somewhat out of context here. It should probably be excluded from the text as a later insertion. **audaci Turno:** dative of separation after *cessit*. The epithet*, usually applied to Turnus and other young warriors in the *Aeneid* (see Pallas below), defines heroic impetuosity. **praecipere...pellere:** the infinitives are dependent on *fiducia*. See also 90-1 n. Turnus' plan is to get to the shore (*litora*) before the enemy ships arrive (*praecipere* = "to seize first") and to drive the invaders from the land (*terra*).

279. **quod:** = *id quod.* **optastis:** shortened form of *optavistis.* **perfringere dextra:** "to crash (them) with (your) right (hand)" explains the relative pronoun *quod* at the beginning of the line.

280. **in manibus Mars:** i.e., the combat is in (your) hands. **in manibus:** = (1) "is before you," or (2) "is to be decided by your valor." **viri:** the vocative, preceded by a comma, found in *codex Romanus* (instead of *viris*, possessive dative) should be accepted for it better suits this short exhortation to the soldiers.

280-2. **nunc...nunc:** note the rhetorical anaphora*. **coniugis...suae tectique:** are genitives after *memor.* **esto...referto:** are (third person singular) future imperatives. Some manuscripts have *referte*, but *referto* ("recall") should be preferred, for *quisque* is to be understood as the subject of both imperatives. **magna...| facta:** "great deeds," explains the following *patrum laudes.* **patrum:** objective genitive; i.e., the deeds that brought praise to your fathers. For the theme of the "son rivaling the father," see also 129 n. **ultro:** "of (our) own accord," i.e., without waiting for them to attack. The mention of home and family and the appeal to the deeds of the ancestors are topoi* of military exhortations, both in epic and historiography. **occurramus:** jussive subjunctive.

283. **trepidi:** sc. *sunt.* **egressisque:** dative of reference, lit. "and (to them) having landed." **vestigia:** "footsteps."

284. **audentis Fortuna iuvat:** a version of the proverbial *fortes fortuna adiuvat* (cf. Ennius fr. 233 Skutch and in *FRL* 1 *fortibus est fortuna viris data*). For the half-line, see 17 n.

haec ait, et secum versat quos ducere contra 285
vel quibus obsessos possit concredere muros.
   Interea Aeneas socios de puppibus altis
pontibus exponit. multi servare recursus
languentis pelagi et brevibus se credere saltu,
per remos alii. speculatus litora Tarchon, 290
qua vada non spirant nec fracta remurmurat unda,

285-6. **quos…quibus:** the interrogative pronouns introduce the two indirect questions (*quos possit ducere contra* and *quibus* (*possit*) *concredere…*) depending on the idea of enquiry in the words *secum versat* (= "ponders"). The subject of both indirect questions is Turnus. **concredere:** "to entrust." Turnus wants to put someone in charge of the besieged Trojan camp (*obsessos muros*) to prevent a sally of the garrison to relieve Aeneas. Unlike the heroes of the *Iliad* and despite his impetuosity, Turnus often shows the good strategic qualities of a Roman general.

287-307. *Aeneas' allies land by gangways or by leaping into the sea; Tarchon, on the other hand, runs his ships ashore, and his vessel is caught on a bank and dashed to pieces by the waves.*

Muse (2007) suggests that the nautical folly of the Etruscan leader is juxtaposed to Aeneas' orderly landing and is an adumbration of traits that will emerge dramatically when his villainous descendants (the Tarquins) will shipwreck the ship of state (see also 290 n.). For parallels between Tarchon and Brasidas, the Spartan general, who in 425 BCE, during the Peloponnesian War, in an attempt to land a force of Peloponnesian allies at Pylos, forced his ship ashore (Thuc. 4.11.4), see Heinze (1993) 193 n. 67.

288. **pontibus:** "by gangplanks," instrumental ablative. **exponit:** "lands." **servare:** "watch for." *Servare* and *credere* are historical infinitives (cf. 267-8 n.) with subject *multi* (288). **recursus:** acc. plural, "ebbing tide." The term, in this meaning, is a Vergilian innovation.

289. **languentis pelagi:** genitive after *recursus*. **brevibus:** "to the shallows"; the (dative) neuter of the adjective is here used as a substantive.

290. **per remos alii:** supply a verb ("came to land," vel sim.). The others came to land either sliding down the oars or using them to support themselves as they struggled, swimming or wading, to the shore. **speculatus:** as made clear in the following lines, Tarchon is looking for a safe path to land his ship ashore. **Tarchon:** for the name, see 152-3 n. and 287-307 n. He was the successor of the exiled Etruscan king Mezentius and had joined forces with Aeneas (*Aen.* 8.506, 603-5). In *Aen.* 11, he is given an *aristeia** in which he rebukes his men for their cowardice (11.725-58).

291. **qua:** adverb, "where." **vada:** subject of *spirant*. **spirant:** "heave"; a metaphorical* usage. The heaving of the sea resembles the act of breathing. Some manuscripts have *sperat*, but *spirant* referring to the heaving of the waters seems to make better sense. Cf. *Geo.* 1.327 *fervetque fretis spirantibus aequor*. **remurmurat:** "roars back"; in this meaning it is first found in Vergil.

sed mare inoffensum crescenti adlabitur aestu,
advertit subito proram sociosque precatur:
'nunc, o lecta manus, validis incumbite remis;
tollite, ferte rates, inimicam findite rostris   295
hanc terram, sulcumque sibi premat ipsa carina.
frangere nec tali puppim statione recuso
arrepta tellure semel.' quae talia postquam
effatus Tarchon, socii consurgere tonsis
spumantisque rates arvis inferre Latinis,   300
donec rostra tenent siccum et sedere carinae
omnes innocuae. sed non puppis tua, Tarchon:

---

292. **sed**: supply *qua* after *sed*. **inoffensum**: has a passive meaning "unobstructed." **crescenti adlabitur aestu**: "glides in with a surging swell."

293. **advertit**: is the main clause of this long sentence. Its subject is Tarchon (290). **proram**: object of *advertit*. The reading *proras* has equal authority. With the singular, *advertit* means that Tarchon turns his own prow to the smooth water and then calls on his followers to do the same; with the plural, that he directs his squadron to turn their prows.

294. **remis**: dative after the compound verb *incumbo* ("lean over"); so as to row faster. The expression *incumbere remis* is first found in Vergil, cf. 5.15.

295-6. **tollite**: Tarchon urges his men to lift (*tollite*) their ships onto the shore with their oar-stroke. **inimicam...terram**: Tarchon bids his men to "plough" (*findite*) the land, ramming it with the *rostrum* (see 166 n.) as if it were an enemy's ship. Note the animated asyndeton* (*tollite, ferte, findite*).

296. **sulcum**: "a furrow"; continues the metaphor* of *findite*. **sibi**: "for itself." **premat**: jussive subjunctive. Subject is *ipsa carina*.

297. **frangere...**: infinitive after *recuso* where in prose we would find *quin/quominus /ne* and the subjunctive. **nec...recuso**: emphatic litotes*. **tali...statione**: Tarchon plays on the double meaning of the word *statio* which can mean both "resting place" and "anchorage." Indeed, the wrecking of the ship will happen at anchorage but be of a permanent nature (Harrison *ad loc.*).

298. **arrepta tellure**: abl. abs.

299. **effatus**: sc. *est*. **consurgere tonsis**: "rise together (or 'vigorously') onto their oars." Cf. 294 n. *Consurgere* (just like the following *inferre*) is a historical infinitive. *Tonsis* is dative after a compound verb.

300. **spumantisque rates**: "the foaming ships." The ships are just like charging war-horses.

301. **siccum**: "dry ground." **sedere**: "have settled." Historical infinitive.

302. **innocuae**: "unharmed." The passive use of *innocuus* is poetical. **sed...**: the vocative and the rare rhythm of the hexameter (with the unusual line ending of three disyllables) mark the dramatic moment. For a similar line ending (more common in the later books of the *Aeneid*), cf. 400, 442, 772.

namque inflicta vadis dorso dum pendet iniquo
anceps sustentata diu fluctusque fatigat,
solvitur atque viros mediis exponit in undis,   305
fragmina remorum quos et fluitantia transtra
impediunt retrahitque pedes simul unda relabens.

308-908: The third day of battle

Highlights of the third day of battle include the double *aristeiai** of Aeneas which neatly frame the duel between the young Pallas and the older and stronger Turnus, and which, so different in mood and nature, dramatically reveal the problematic transformation of Aeneas after the killing of his protégé. In the second half, after Juno's removal of Turnus from the battlefield, Mezentius occupies center stage. Attacked from every side, the Etruscan tyrant, at first, stubbornly holds his own with courage but, eventually, after the death of his beloved son Lausus in the field of battle, rushes all too eagerly to meet his own fate at the hands of Aeneas. (For an analysis of the episodes, see the Introductions to the individual scenes).

Although the return of Aeneas to the battlefield with a new shield seems to pick up the story of the *Iliad* from Book 18 (that is, from Achilles' successful return to battle after the death of Patroclus with a new set of divine armor given by his mother Thetis), the string of duels of *Aeneid* 10—Pallas vs. Turnus, Aeneas vs. Lausus, Aeneas vs. Mezentius—are partly modeled on the chain of Homeric duels that begin in *Iliad* 16 where Sarpedon is killed in a duel by Patroclus, who is himself

---

303. **namque…:** Tarchon's ship strikes a reef or sandbank (*dorsum*) on which it hangs fixed. **inflicta:** "dashed against," the perfect passive participle (feminine nominative singular) refers to the ship. **vadis:** dative after the compound verb *infligo*. **dorso…iniquo:** "on an uneven sandbank (lit. 'ridge')," but the adjective plays also on its meaning "hostile," for it shipwrecks Tarchon's boat. **dum:** introduces both *pendet* and *fatigat*.

304. **anceps:** "in balance," the adjective agrees with *sustentata* ("held up"). **fluctusque fatigat:** for the waves beat and buffet it until they are tired.

305. **solvitur:** "disintegrates." The passive is used in a reflexive sense. Note how the dramatic position of the verb is suggestive of the sudden break-up of the ship. **exponit:** the technical term for disembarking (see 288) is here ironically* used for the dumping of the crew into the sea.

306-7 **fragmina…| impediunt:** construe as *quos fragmina remorum et fluitantia transtra impediunt*. **fragmina…transtra:** are the subjects of *impediunt*. *Transtra* are the "cross-beams" of the ship's structure. **quos:** *viros* at 305 is the antecedent; the relative pronoun is the direct object of *impediunt*.

307. **retrahitque…:** "pulls back"; the subject is *unda relabens*.

dispatched in the same book, with the help of Apollo, by Hector who, in his turn, is killed by Achilles in *Iliad* 22. Somewhat similarly, in *Aeneid* 10, the young Pallas is killed in a duel by Turnus, whose fate is postponed, like Hector's in the *Iliad*, until later in the poem at the end of Book 12. Vergil's adaptation of the Homeric model, however, is not straightforward. No one episode is simply modeled on one Homeric episode. As noted by Quint (2018) 150-79, Vergil's repeated strategy in each of these episodes is to juxtapose the models of two or more different duels from the *Iliad*, making each of Vergil's warriors imitate simultaneously more than one of the figures of the Iliadic chain, Sarpedon-Patroclus-Hector-Achilles. For example, in the duel between Pallas and Turnus, Vergil conflates the two Homeric duels of Sarpedon-Patroclus and Patroclus-Hector. In this way, Pallas is simultaneously cast in the role of the Homeric Sarpedon defeated by Patroclus and in the role of Patroclus, whose death at the hands of Hector, will seal the latter's destiny at the hands of Achilles, just as Pallas' death seals Turnus' death at the hands of Aeneas. Vergil's narrative strategy has thus the effect of blurring the identity of the characters and is suggestive of the leveling effect of war and of "the problem of distinguishing *morally* among characters once they are engaged in battle" (Quint (2018) 175). For Vergil's battle narrative as a reflection of more recent Roman wars, see General Introduction to the book.

In general, Vergil's battle narrative closely follows Homeric narrative conventions. (For Vergil's dynamic appropriation of the Homeric model, see the General Introduction). Just like Homer's *Iliad*, the *Aeneid* alternates between wide-angle views of the movements of the two armies described via quintessentially Homeric-type scenes such as "the advance of the armies," "charges and counter-charges," "the melee," and "the rout" (a catalogue* of continuous killings with each leader of the victorious side killing a named opponent) and close-ups of individual feats. These last ones are represented via duels and *aristeiai**. In the *aristeia**, particular attention is devoted to the victim whose death is often accompanied by an obituary—intensely pathetic at times—in which we are told something special about him, or something of his life before the war. In a number of cases, victims are also distinguished for their special status or some outstanding skills, which, nonetheless, do not prevent them from meeting their destiny.

On Vergil reworking Homeric episodes in the battle scenes of *Aeneid* 10, see Gransden (1984) 126-54, Putnam (2011) 19-65, Barchiesi (2015) 1-52, Quint (2018) 150-90.

On Vergil's war narrative as reflective of the Roman Civil Wars, see Rossi (2004) 150-68, Rijser (2011), Newman (2015). On Vergil's war narrative as resonating with the divisions between Romans and Italians in the Social War, see Barchiesi (2008, in Italian), Marincola (2010), Goldschmidt (2013) 127-31.

On Vergil's battle narrative, see Heinze (1993) 142-94, Krischer (1979), Willcock (1983), Horsfall (1987), S. J. Harrison (1988), S. J. Harrison (1991) xxxi-xxx, Rossi (2004), Barchiesi (2015).

Nec Turnum segnis retinet mora, sed rapit acer
totam aciem in Teucros et contra in litore sistit.
signa canunt. primus turmas invasit agrestis   310
Aeneas, omen pugnae, stravitque Latinos
occiso Therone, virum qui maximus ultro
Aenean petit. huic gladio perque aerea suta,
per tunicam squalentem auro latus haurit apertum.

308-44. *Aeneas' first* aristeia*. *At the sound of the trumpets, the battle begins. Aeneas kills many named warriors (308-24). Cydon is only saved from death by his seven brothers falling on Aeneas. Aeneas then slays Maeon, his spear at the same time cutting across the arm of Alcanor who tries to support his brother.*

The first day of battle had opened detailing the martial feats of Turnus, the leader of the Rutulians. Similarly, the opening of the third day of war details the martial deeds of Aeneas, the leader of the Trojans.

308. **nec...segnis...mora:** "no slow delay"; but Vergil plays with *segnis* since the adjective also means "cowardly" (cf. 592 *fuga segnis*). Tarchon's shipwreck apparently solves Turnus' tactical dilemma (285-6) and firms his resolve. With swiftness and courage Turnus positions his troops to face those of Aeneas. **rapit:** "hurries along"; the verb is similarly used of the deployment of troops at 178.

309. **contra:** here an adverb, i.e., facing the Trojans. **sistit:** the standard term for stationing troops.

310. **signa canunt:** a standard military phrase where *signa* ("the signals for battle") stands for the instruments which give the signal. Absent in Homeric battle scenes, trumpets signaled the beginning of battle in the Greek and Roman world. For anachronisms in the *Aeneid*, see 120 n. **turmas...agrestis:** at 7.681 the Italian army is similarly represented as an "unwarlike" army of farmers: *hunc legio late comitatur agrestis*. Lyne (1987) 8 points out that the term "farmers" applied to the Italians is particularly troubling as it underscores that Aeneas' "imminent destruction of the Italians will destroy those who have the potential to embody essential qualities of peace and morality."

311. **omen pugnae:** is in loose apposition with the preceding clause (*primus...Aeneas*). The "forecast" refers to Aeneas' initial success in battle. For a similar expression, cf. 9.53 *principium pugnae* (of Turnus).

312. **occiso Therone:** abl. abs. His name may mean "wild animal" from Greek *thēr*. **virum:** archaic* genitive for *virorum*. It is a partitive genitive after the superlative *maximus* ("the largest"). **ultro:** "of his own accord." The adverb goes closely in sense with *maximus*; it is his giant size which makes him seek out Aeneas.

313-14. **Aenean:** see 65 n. **huic:** i.e., to Theron; dative of reference. **gladio:** instrumental abl. **perque...| per:** "both through... (and) through..." The repeated preposition marks the sword as passing through two objects: the *aerea suta* ("the bronze coat of mail") and *tunicam squalentem auro* (the "shirt stiff with gold" worn beneath the corselet). **latus haurit apertum:** "(Aeneas) gouges the exposed side"; *haurit* may also mean "drains (the life-blood from) his side (*latus*)" (cf. 11.804), in which case *apertum* = "laid open (by the sword)."

> inde Lichan ferit exsectum iam matre perempta 315
> et tibi, Phoebe, sacrum: casus evadere ferri
> quo licuit parvo? nec longe Cissea durum
> immanemque Gyan sternentis agmina clava
> deiecit leto; nihil illos Herculis arma
> nec validae iuvere manus genitorque Melampus, 320
> Alcidae comes usque gravis dum terra labores
> praebuit. ecce Pharo, voces dum iactat inertis,
> intorquens iaculum clamanti sistit in ore.

---

315. **Lichan:** Greek accusative. See also *Gyan* at 318. **exsectum...:** "cut out (from the womb)." **matre perempta:** ablative of separation. Such infants were dedicated to Apollo (see 316), who cut his own son Asclepius from the womb of the dead Coronis. For pathetic anecdotes on the victim's life, see also 320-2, 391-6, 417-20.

316-17. **Phoebe:** i.e., Apollo, who, as it often happens to the gods in the *Aeneid*, is powerless and cannot save his protégé. Cf. 11.843-4 (Diana and Camilla) and, in this book, 457-65 (Hercules and Pallas) and 537-42 (Apollo and Haemonides). **casus...parvo?:** construe as *quo licuit parvo* (i.e., to the infant) *evadere casus ferri*. **ferri:** genitive dependent on *casus*. The steel here is the surgeon's steel with which the infant was cut out from his mother's womb. Lychas was able to survive the steel of the surgeon but not that of Aeneas' sword. **quo...:** "to what end?" *Evadere* and *parvo* are respectively the infinitive and the dative dependent on *licuit*. **Cissea:** Greek accusative. A Cisseus was also the father of Hecuba. See 703-6.

318. **immanemque Gyan:** a wordplay. Gyas is gigantic (*immanem*) because his name resembles that of the giant Gyēs. **sternentis:** acc. plural referring to both Cisseus and Gyas. **clava:** "with a club" = *Herculis arma* in the next line.

319-20. **leto:** for the dative, see 148 n. **nihil:** "not at all," adverbial accusative. Note the emphatic initial position. **illos:** direct object of *iuvere* (320). **Herculis arma:** is the subject (together with *validae manus* and *genitorque Melampus*) of *iuvere*. **iuvere:** = *iuverunt*. **genitorque Melampus:** i.e., the fact that they are descended from Melampus, a comrade of Hercules (321), did not prevent their death. The name Melampus (meaning "black foot") is that of a famous seer of Greece (cf. *Od.* 11.288-97).

321. **Alcidae:** genitive of Hercules' patronymic* "of Alcides" (= "of the descendant of Alceus"). For the declension, see 263 n. **comes:** refers to Melampus. **usque...dum:** "all the time...so long as." For *dum* with the perfect indicative (*praebuit*), see 43 n. **gravis...labores:** a reference to the well-known Labors of Hercules.

322-3. **ecce:** 132-3 n. **Pharo:** dative of reference with *clamanti* below. The name, phonetically close to the Greek pharynx ("throat"), nicely fits the man and his destiny: the "talkative" Pharus is killed by Aeneas who plants his javelin in his mouth. For a similar wound, see 347. The reading *Pharo* should be preferred to the reading *Pharon* (nominative) of some manuscripts, as it sets up a greater degree of tension and drama. **iactat:** "throws"; instead of throwing weapons, Pharus throws empty words (*voces inertis*). **intorquens iaculum:** "hurling a javelin," i.e., Aeneas. **sistit:** "he planted (it)," i.e., the javelin.

> tu quoque, flaventem prima lanugine malas
> dum sequeris Clytium infelix, nova gaudia, Cydon, 325
> Dardania stratus dextra, securus amorum
> qui iuvenum tibi semper erant, miserande iaceres,
> ni fratrum stipata cohors foret obvia, Phorci
> progenies, septem numero, septenaque tela

324-5. **tu quoque:** is the subject (with *infelix Cydon* of the following line) of *sequeris* (325), *stratus* (326), and *iaceres* (327). For the apostrophe*, cf. 139 n. **flaventem…Clytium:** direct object of *sequeris*. **prima lanugine:** instrumental ablative. **malas:** acc. of specification depending on (*Clytium*) *flaventem*. Cf. also 132-3 n. Vergil describes Cydon's beloved Clytius in words reminiscent of *Ecl.* 2.51 (*cana legam tenera lanugine mala*) and thus pointedly recalls the love affair between Corydon and Alexis. See Boyd (1983). **infelix:** the epithet* denotes sympathy for the victim. **nova gaudia:** is in apposition to Clytius. The term is borrowed from love elegy. The theme of the pair of homosexual warriors is most prominently explored in the *Aeneid* in the story of Euryalus and Nisus (9.176-450 with Hardie *ad loc.*), but see also 160-2 n. (Aeneas and Pallas) and 189-93 (Cycnus and Phaeton). On homosexuality in Vergil, see Lilja (1983) 62-70, Oliensis (2019). On Roman homosexuality, see C. A. Williams (2010). **Cydon:** the name can also mean "Cretan" (cf. also *Aen*. 12.858 where Cydon is an elegant substitute for "Cretan," with Tarrant *ad loc.*) and a link with Crete (famed for pederasty) is suggested by Cydon's character (*amorum | qui iuvenum tibi semper erant* 326-7).

326-7. **Dardania…dextra:** instrumental ablative dependent on *stratus* (perfect passive participle from *sterno*). The Dardanian hand is that of Aeneas. For the adjective referring to the Trojans, see 92 n. **securus…erant:** construe as *securus amorum iuvenum qui tibi semper erant*. **securus amorum:** "untroubled by love," i.e., forgetting his loves in death. For the genitive after *securus*, see 154 n. **iuvenum:** "for young men," objective genitive dependent on *amorum*. The noun is attracted into the relative clause. **tibi:** dative of possession. **miserande:** the same apostrophe* is used for the dead youths Marcellus (6.882), Pallas (11.42), and in this book Lausus (825).
iaceres: imperfect subjunctive in the apodosis of a present contrary-to-fact conditional clause.

328. **fratrum stipata cohors:** "the close-packed formation of the brothers." *Cohors* is the subject of *foret* and is hyperbolic. The seven brothers are hyperbolically called a cohort, a Roman military unit of about five hundred soldiers. **foret:** = *esset*; imperfect subjunctive in the protasis of a present contrary-to-fact conditional clause. The description of an almost fatal situation narrated by means of a contrafactual pattern is Homeric, and commonly used also in historiography. In this instance, however, Cydon's survival comes somewhat as a surprise with *iaceres* postponed, and *Dardania stratus dextra* seeming at first to be factual rather than contrafactual.

329. **progenies:** is in apposition to *cohors*. **septem…septenaque:** the variation of cardinal and distributive numbers is common in Vergil (cf. 565-6) as is Vergil's use of distributives for cardinals (see 207 n). **numero:** ablative of specification.

LIBER DECIMUS 71

    coniciunt; partim galea clipeoque resultant   330
inrita, deflexit partim stringentia corpus
alma Venus. fidum Aeneas adfatur Achaten:
'suggere tela mihi, non ullum dextera frustra
torserit in Rutulos, steterunt quae in corpore Graium
Iliacis campis.' tum magnam corripit hastam   335
et iacit: illa volans clipei transverberat aera
Maeonis et thoraca simul cum pectore rumpit.
huic frater subit Alcanor fratremque ruentem
sustentat dextra: traiecto missa lacerto
protinus hasta fugit servatque cruenta tenorem,   340

330-2. **coniciunt:** although the subject is singular (*cohors*), the verb agrees *ad sensum* in number with the genitive plural *fratrum*. **galea clipeoque:** ablatives indicating motion away from after *resultant* ("rebound"). **inrita:** "in vain"; like *stringentia* below, the adjective qualifies *tela* above. The javelins are repelled because Aeneas' armor is divine. **stringentia corpus:** "grazing the body." **Venus:** divine intervention in battle is common in the *Iliad*, but highly unusual in the *Aeneid*. When Vergilian gods intervene directly in the action of war, they do so only to save their protégés. Cf. 9.638-71 (Apollo stops Ascanius from any daring enterprise), 9.745-6 (Juno deflects a javelin aimed at Turnus), 10.606-88 (Juno forges a phantom image of Aeneas to save Turnus), 12.766-90 (Venus restores the javelin to Aeneas after Juturna hands the sword back to Turnus).

333-4. **non ullum...:** "not any" (sc. *telum*). **dextera:** sc. *manus*. **torserit:** Aeneas presents the action as already completed by using the future perfect. **steterunt quae:** construe as (*eorum telorum*) *quae steterunt* = "(of those javelins) which have been planted (lit. 'stood')." **corpore** is sing. because the idea is collective. **Graium:** genitive plural for *Graiorum*, see 2 n. Aeneas fights with the same weapons with which he fought at Troy (and which he had extracted from his victims, as is usual in the *Iliad*) and is sure that the weapons which did not fail him at Troy will not fail him now against another enemy.

336. **et iacit:** note the emphasis secured by the pause after the first dactyl. **illa:** i.e., *hasta*. **clipei... aerea:** i.e., the bronze layers of the shield.

337. **Maeonis:** gen. The name Maeon is that of a Greek in Homer (*Il.* 5.394). **thoraca:** Greek accusative.

338. **huic:** i.e., Maeon. Dative after the compound verb *subeo*. **frater...fratremque:** i.e., Alcanor and Maeon respectively. The repetition emphasizes the brotherly affection which prompts Alcanor to rush to his falling brother (*fratrem ruentem*); cf. 600. **Alcanor:** "man of strength," the name is connected to the Greek *alkē* ("strength") and *anēr* ("man"). The same name is given to a Trojan at 9.672.

339-41. **dextra:** instrumental ablative; i.e., Alcanor holds up his brother with his right arm. **traiecto...lacerto:** "the arm (of Alcanor) having been sliced through," abl. abs. **missa:** perfect passive participle nominative feminine agreeing with *hasta*. **protinus:** with *fugit* "flies

dexteraque ex umero nervis moribunda pependit.
tum Numitor iaculo fratris de corpore rapto
Aenean petiit: sed non et figere contra
est licitum, magnique femur perstrinxit Achatae.
    Hic Curibus fidens primaevo corpore Clausus   345
advenit et rigida Dryopem ferit eminus hasta
sub mentum graviter pressa, pariterque loquentis
vocem animamque rapit traiecto gutture; at ille

---

onward." **hasta:** subject of *fugit*. **servatque…tenorem:** "keeps its course." **cruenta:** the adjective qualifies *hasta*. **dexteraque:** "the right (arm)," subject of *pependit*. **nervis:** "by the sinews," instrumental ablative. **moribunda:** i.e., the right arm is already half lifeless. Aeneas' spear of 335-6 passes first through Maeon and then, maintaining its forceful course, into the top of Alcanor's arm (as he attempts to support his brother from behind), which it severs. For fantastic wounds as part of the epic repertoire, see Fenik (1968) 195-6, K. B. Saunders (1999).

342. **Numitor:** the name is also that of Romulus' and Remus' grandfather. **iaculo…rapto:** ablative absolute. **fratris de corpore:** "from the body of the brother," a pathetic inversion of the extraction of the spear by the killer (Harrison *ad loc.*). Cf. 383-4.

343-4. **Aenean:** see 65 n. **non et…| est licitum:** "it is not allowed (sc. *ei*, to him, i.e., Numitor), too (*et*)." **figere:** infinitive after *est licitum*. Numitor aims at Aeneas, but he, too, cannot hit him. **contra:** "in return" for his brother's death but also "opposite," as Aeneas stands in front of him. **magnique femur…Achatae:** the motif of the *alienum vulnus* (i.e., "warrior aims at one enemy but ends up striking another one") is Homeric (Fenik (1968) 126-8). For other examples in Vergil, see 402, 781.

345-61. Clausus kills Dryopes, three Thracian brothers, and Halaesus. On both sides the combat is waged desperately.

After Aeneas' *aristeia**, the narrative turns to Italian successes and eventually wraps up with a wide-angle view of the two armies fighting evenly against each other.

345. **Hic:** adverb. **Curibus:** "from Cures." Ablative of origin. Cures (a Sabine town) is also mentioned in the context of the war between Rome and the Sabines depicted in the shield of Aeneas (*Aen.* 8.638). **primaevo corpore:** ablative after *fidens*, see 181 n. *Primaevus* translates the Homeric *prōthēbēs*. **Clausus:** the name is linked to the *gens Claudia*, an ancient Sabine family, whose leader was Attus Clausus, Latinized as Appius Claudius. Livia, the wife of Augustus, belonged to the *gens Claudia*. See 7.706-9.

346. **rigida…hasta:** instrumental ablative. **Dryopem:** a Trojan Dryops is killed in Homer (*Il.* 20.455). **ferit:** observe the balanced symmetry between Clausus' act of violence and its result. Just as Clausus strikes (*ferit*) Dryops, so the dying Dryops strikes the ground (*ferit terram* 349). **eminus:** "at a distance."

347-8. **pressa:** refers to *rigida hasta* above. The heavy spondaic movement of the first half of the hexameter mimics the weighty pressure applied to the spear. **loquentis | vocem…rapit:** for a similar wound where a "talkative" enemy is killed by a wound to the throat, cf. 322-3 n. **traiecto gutture:** abl. abs. **ille:** i.e., Dryops.

fronte ferit terram et crassum vomit ore cruorem.
tres quoque Threicios Boreae de gente suprema   350
et tris quos Idas pater et patria Ismara mittit,
per varios sternit casus. accurrit Halaesus
Auruncaeque manus, subit et Neptunia proles,
insignis Messapus equis. expellere tendunt
nunc hi, nunc illi: certatur limine in ipso   355

---

349. **fronte:** instrumental ablative. **ore:** ablative of motion from. A graphic description with graphic alliterations* (*fronte ferit* and *crassum cruore*). Note how the word *ore* ("mouth") is subsumed in the word *cruorem* ("gore") and thus mimics the hideous fact that Dryops' mouth is now indeed nothing but gore (Feeney (1999) 181). For grotesquely vivid details in Vergilian battle scenes, see S. J. Harrison (1988).

350-1. **tres...tris:** is an elegant variation and this reading should be preferred to *tris...tris* found in some manuscripts. **Threicios:** the Thracians were Troy's allies also in the *Iliad*. **Boreae:** "of Boreas." Genitive of a masculine noun of the first declension. Cf. 263 n. In Greek mythology Boreas (the North Wind) is regularly personified as a deity dwelling on Mt. Haemus in Thrace. **de gente suprema:** *de* + abl. indicates place of origin. *Suprema* means here "most exalted." The term is used of Jupiter with a similar meaning. **Ismara:** is either a neuter plural noun (from *Ismara, -orum*), in apposition to *patria*, or a (nominative) feminine singular adjective (from *Ismarus, a, um*), agreeing with *patria*. Ismara was the Homeric town of the Cicones in Thrace situated on a mountain of the same name, famous for its wine and Dionysiac connections. **mittit:** both *Idas pater* and *patria Ismara* are its subject. The verb is singular because the two subjects are considered as a single whole (AG §317 b).

352. **sternit:** the subject is still Clausus (345). **casus:** lit. "fall"; a poetic euphemism* for "death." **Halaesus:** Halaesus and his contingent (the *Aurunci*) come from Campania and appear in the Italian catalogue* at 7.723-4. His ensuing death comes as he tries to shield Imaon with his own body during Pallas' *aristeia** (10.424-5).

353. **Auruncae manus:** *manus* (nom. feminine plural of the 4th declension) here means "bands." **Neptunia proles:** is in apposition to Messapus (354). Messapus is so called for he was the son of Neptune.

354-5. **Messapus:** he was introduced in the Italian catalogue* as the leader of a contingent from Etruria (7.691-4). **equis:** abl. of specification after *insignis*. Messapus' association with horses, here and elsewhere, reflects the equine connections of his father Neptune who was worshipped also as a god of horses by the Romans. **expellere:** "to expel," i.e., each other. The infinitive is complementary after *tendunt*, see 118-19 n. **nunc:** the temporal deictic* *nunc*, the deictic pronouns *hi* and *illi*, and the grammatical present (*tendunt*) add vividness to the scene allowing the reader to become a virtual spectator, witnessing the event as it unfolds. **hi...illi:** i.e., the Trojans and the Latins. **certatur:** the impersonal passive, commonly used by historians, places the emphasis on the action, rather than on the subject of the action.

    Ausoniae. magno discordes aethere venti
    proelia ceu tollunt animis et viribus aequis;
    non ipsi inter se, non nubila, non mare cedit;
    anceps pugna diu, stant obnixa omnia contra:
    haud aliter Troianae acies aciesque Latinae   360
    concurrunt, haeret pede pes densusque viro vir.

362-438: The *aristeiai** of Pallas and Lausus

After rallying his men, Pallas overthrows hero after hero in a major *aristeia** (362-425). On the other side, the young Lausus strikes back and, at last, the two young warriors seek each other, but in vain (426-38). The description of the two young heroes' *aristeiai** is narratologically important. It establishes their martial valor and builds up expectations for the important role each of them will play later in the book.

From their very first appearance in battle, Pallas and Lausus are modeled on the Homeric pair Sarpedon-Patroclus with Pallas and Lausus playing, in turn, both Sarpedon and Patroclus. Pallas first enters the fray rallying his men who are yielding to the Latins. His actions and speech are structurally parallel to (and are fashioned on) those of Sarpedon in *Iliad* 16 (419-25), who rallies his Lycians fleeing before Patroclus. His subsequent *aristeia**, which lists Pallas' victims in order of

---

356-7. **Ausoniae:** see 267-8 n. **magno...aethere:** locative ablative. **discordes...venti:** the adjective applied to the winds is notably reminiscent of *discordia*, the term often used by Roman authors to define the Roman Civil Wars. See 9-10 n. **ceu:** is used to introduce similes* (see 97) and is often postponed in Vergil. **animis et viribus aequis:** "with matched courage and strength," ablatives of manner. The winds are personified to match the warriors they describe.

358-9. **non...non...non:** a triple anaphora*. **ipsi:** i.e., the winds. Supply *cedunt*. **nubila:** sc. *cedunt*. **obnixa:** "steadfast." **contra:** "against each other," is used adverbially. The simile* describes the stalemate produced by equal forces in conflict: the Trojans and the Italian cannot move each other just as conflicting winds cause the clouds and the sea to remain motionless under the impact of contrary forces. Similes comparing human battles to conflicting winds are in the epic tradition. Cf. *Il.* 9.4-7; 16.765-9; *Aen.* 2.416-19.

360. **Troianae acies aciesque Latinae:** note how the chiastic* word order juxtaposes the two opposing sides and how the proximity of the two opposing armies in the hexameter reflects their close-quarters combat.

361. **haeret pede pes...:** *haeret* usually requires a dative but *haeret* here is not so much "sticks to" as "is held tight by," so that *pede* is to be taken as a sort of instrumental ablative. The double polyptoton* (cf. *viro vir*) describing a close military encounter is first found in Homer (*Il.* 13.131) and, in Latin, in Ennius (fr. 584 Skutsch and in *FRL* 1 *premitur pede pes atque armis arma teruntur*).

their deaths (cf. *primum* 380, *tum* 399), recalls, however, Homer's description of the warriors who fall to Patroclus (*Iliad* 16.692-7 and 399-418). Pallas, thus, shifts role and is cast as a new Patroclus, while Lausus, holding his ground and rallying the Latins against Pallas (426-32), now plays the role of Sarpedon holding the line against Patroclus.

Both young heroes are, however, also quintessentially Vergilian. From his first appearance on the battlefield, Pallas shares with other young Vergilian warriors an excessive desire for fame and a youthful daring, which eventually seals his fate and untimely death. Lausus, closely abiding to a Homeric code of behavior in his *aristeia**, later in the book gives up his life to save his father in a striking manifestation of filial love. He thus becomes an exemplum of self-sacrifice and of *pietas*, two themes that are central to the Vergilian poem.

On Pallas and his relation with Aeneas, see 160-2 n., Putnam (1995) 27-9 and Carstairs-McCarthy (2018). On Pallas and the attractions of the world of heroism which threatens and finally destroys childhood, see Petrini (1997) 48-86.

> At parte ex alia, qua saxa rotantia late
> impulerat torrens arbustaque diruta ripis,
> Arcadas insuetos acies inferre pedestris
> ut vidit Pallas Latio dare terga sequaci   365

362-79. When Pallas sees his men in difficulty, he rallies them urging that, with the sea in front and flight impossible, they must cut their way through to the Trojan camp.

Pallas' address to his men bears the typical elements of a general's exhortation as we find them in the *Iliad* and in ancient historiography: pleas, appeal to shame, analysis of the situation, and call to action. Its main model is, however, Sarpedon's speech to his men fleeing in front of Patroclus (*Il.* 16.419-26). For clear linguistic echoes of the speech, cf. 365 *ut vidit Pallas* (= *Il.* 16.419 as Sarpedon saw) and 369 *quo fugitis, socii* (= *Il.* 16.422 O Lykians, where are you fleeing?).

362. **At:** 120 n. **qua:** 291 n. **saxa rotantia:** "stones rolling," is the object of *impulerat*. *Roto* is transitive, but the participle is used intransitively. **late:** "far and wide."

363. **torrens:** subject of *impulerat*. **arbustaque:** another object of *impulerat*. **ripis:** abl. of separation after *diruta*. The Arcadians are walking down the dry bed of a river, among the boulders and the trees which the river (*torrens*) had brought down when in flood.

364-5. **Arcadas insuetos acies inferre pedestris:** lit. "the Arcadians unaccustomed to advance the infantry formations" (i.e., to attack in infantry formations). *Arcadas* is subject accusative of *dare terga* (365) and is governed by *vidit* in the temporal clause *ut vidit Pallas* (365). The infinitive *inferre* is directly dependent on the adjective *insuetos*. The construction follows a Greek idiom (AG §461). The verb is used transitively as often with similar expressions, cf. *signa inferre, pedem inferre*. The Arcadians were cavalry (239) and were unaccustomed to fighting as infantry. **Latio...sequaci:** note the bold personification*. The name of the country standing for the name of its people is a device common in Roman historiography.

(aspera aquis natura loci dimittere quando
suasit equos), unum quod rebus restat egenis,
nunc prece, nunc dictis virtutem accendit amaris:
'quo fugitis, socii? per vos et fortia facta,
per ducis Euandri nomen devictaque bella   370
spemque meam, patriae quae nunc subit aemula laudi,
fidite ne pedibus. ferro rumpenda per hostis
est via. qua globus ille virum densissimus urget,
hac vos et Pallanta ducem patria alta reposcit.

366-7. **aspera...loci:** the sentence is a real textual crux. Mynors, Geymonat, and Harrison emend *aspera quis* to *aspera aquis*. I adopt *aquis*, taking *aquis* as an ablative of means explaining *aspera*. The phrase would read "the nature of the place rough because of the water." The emendation, however, results in an odd word-order, leaving the conjunction *quando* ("since") postponed almost to the end of its clause. For other emendations, see Trappes-Lomax (2005). **dimittere:** supply the accusative subject *eos* (i.e., the Arcadians). For the construction accusative and infinitive after *suasit*, see 9-10 n. **suasit:** subject is *natura* (366). **equos:** object of *dimittere* ("to let go" or "dismount their horses"). **unum quod...restat:** is in apposition to the following line. **rebus...egenis:** either abl. abs. or dative of reference after *restat*.

368. **dictis...amaris:** i.e., reproaches. A mix of praises and reproaches is common in a general's exhortation to his soldiers, cf. *Il.* 12.267; 17.431; Livy 21.30.1 *varie militum versat animos castigando adhortandoque*.

369. **per vos et fortia facta:** the verb of entreaty (*precor* vel sim.) is omitted (cf. also 597) to underscore the urgency of the plea. For similar appeals in which the general recalls his soldiers' past (glorious) deeds, cf. Livy 26.41.23 *traducite in terras cum multis fortibus factis saepe a vobis peragratas* and Sall., *Cat.* 59.6 *plerosque ipsos factaque eorum fortia noverat: ea commemorando militum animos accendebat*.

370. **devictaque bella:** i.e., by Evander. The accusative *bella* (like *spemque meam* below) is still governed by the preposion *per*.

371. **patriae:** is feminine dative singular (from the adjective *patrius*) with *laudi*. **quae:** the antecedent is *spemque meam*. **subit:** "rises," i.e., in my mind. Pallas hopes to equal the deeds of his father. For the heroic theme of the son rivaling the father, cf. 129 n. **laudi:** dative after *aemula* ("striving to equal").

372-3. **fidite ne:** the conjunction is postponed. *Ne* + present imperative expresses prohibition, cf. 11 n. **pedibus:** dat. after *fidite*. **ferro:** instrumental ablative; chiastically* juxtaposed to *pedibus*. For a similar expression, cf. Sall., *Cat.* 58.7 *ferro iter aperiendum est*. **rumpenda...| est via:** passive periphrastic.

373-4. **qua...| hac:** "where..., there..." **globus ille virum densissimus urget:** "that mass of men presses (being) the thickest." *Ille* is deictic*. For the genitive *virum*, see 312 n. **Pallanta:** Greek acc. *Pallanta ducem* picks up *ducis Evandri* (370), signaling Pallas' wish to parallel his father's deeds. **alta:** "noble"; the adjective is a common epithet* of places. Cf. 126 *Lycia ab alta*. **reposcit:** "claims (you and the leader Pallas) as its due."

numina nulla premunt, mortali urgemur ab hoste   375
mortales; totidem nobis animaeque manusque.
ecce maris magna claudit nos obice pontus,
deest iam terra fugae: pelagus Troiamne petamus?
haec ait, et medius densos prorumpit in hostis.
     Obvius huic primum fatis adductus iniquis   380
fit Lagus. hunc, magno vellit dum pondere saxum,
intorto figit telo, discrimina costis
per medium qua spina dabat, hastamque receptat

375-6. **mortali...| mortales:** an emphatic polyptoton*. **totidem...manusque:** sc. *sunt*; the meaning is "we have one life and two hands apiece just as they do." Cf. Hom., *Il.* 21.568-9, said of Achilles. *Nobis* is dative of possession.

377. **ecce:** see 132-3 n. **maris...:** construe as *pontus claudit nos magna obice maris* and take the genitive *maris* as associated with *magna obice* rather than with *pontus*. It is a Vergilian feature to have the subject of the sentence (*pontus*) resumed by means of an equivalent noun (*maris*), see Conte (1993) 209 and cf. 1.246 *it mare proruptum et pelago premit arva sonanti*. **magna... obice:** "with the great barrier"; *obice* (from *obex*) scans as a dactyl since the word originally read obiice with the first *i* consonantal, making the first syllable long by position.

378. **deest...:** the dative (*fugae*) is usual after compounds of *sum*. For the language, cf. Livy 22.6.6 *locus fugae deest* and *Il.* 15.735-7. *Deest* scans as a monosyllable by synizesis*. **pelagus Troiamne:** objects of *petamus*. *Troiam* is possibly the Trojan camp (see 26-7 n.) rather than the city of Troy, for the city of Troy means nothing to the Arcadian soldiers. **petamus:** deliberative subjunctive. This variant is to be preferred to *petemus* (future) as more appropriate to the end of Pallas' arousing speech (Harrison *ad loc.*).

379. **medius:** "in the middle," is proleptic* (it anticipates the result of *prorumpit*) and is used adverbially (cf. 54-6 n.). **densos:** picks up *densissimus* at 373. Pallas acts as he preaches. The fast-paced sequence of Pallas' slaying in the following lines reflects his ardor.

380-98. Pallas' aristeia*. After his speech, Pallas charges the enemy and overthrows hero after hero. He kills Lagus, Hisbo, Sthenius, Anchemolus, and the twin brothers Larides and Thymber.

380. **huic:** i.e., to Pallas. Dative after *obvius*. **primum:** the stress on the sequence of slaying is modeled on Patroclus' *aristeia** (*Il.* 16.692-7). For Pallas playing the role of Patroclus, see 362-438 n. **iniquis:** the adjective (ablative with *fatis*) casts a sympathetic light on the victim.

381. **Lagus:** his name is connected with Greek *lagos* ("hare"). **hunc:** i.e., Lagus, object of *figit* (382). **magno...:** *dum* is here postponed. Construe as *dum* (*Lagus*) *vellit saxum magno pondere*. **magno...pondere:** ablative of quality. Rocks wielded in epic fightings are usually large.

382-3. **intorto...telo:** instrumental ablative. **figit:** Pallas is the subject. **discrimina...dabat:** construe as *qua* ("where") *spina dabat discrimina* ("made a parting") *costis* (lit. "to the ribs," i.e., separated the ribs; dative after *discrimina dare*) *per medium* ("(running) between them"). **dabat:** the final syllable is lengthened before the caesura*. The lengthening can be explained by the fact that the "silence" created by the caesura was seen as equivalent to the so-called

ossibus haerentem. quem non superoccupat Hisbo,
ille quidem hoc sperans; nam Pallas ante ruentem, 385
dum furit, incautum crudeli morte sodalis
excipit atque ensem tumido in pulmone recondit.
hinc Sthenium petit et Rhoeti de gente vetusta
Anchemolum thalamos ausum incestare novercae.
vos etiam, gemini, Rutulis cecidistis in agris, 390
Daucia, Laride Thymberque, simillima proles,

"lengthening by position." **receptat:** i.e., Pallas. The verb is a frequentative form of *recipio* "he tugs repeatedly at." After having killed Lagus, Pallas recovers the javelin that was lodged in Lagus' bone.

384. **quem:** refers to Pallas; Latin often uses a relative pronoun where English would use a demonstrative. **non superoccupat:** "does not forestall from above," i.e., as Pallas is stooping to pull out the spear. The verb commonly contains the idea of doing something before another can prevent it. **Hisbo:** his name shows a close resemblance to the Roman cognomen *Hispo*.

385. **ille quidem hoc sperans:** "(although) he indeed hoped it (lit. 'hoping this')," concessive participial clause, see also AG §496. **Pallas:** the final *a* is long. Distinguish Pallăs from Pallăs *Athena* (Minerva) where the final *a* is short. **ante:** is adverbial with *excipit* (387). **ruentem:** i.e., Hisbo, object of *excipit*.

386. **dum furit:** i.e., Hisbo. **incautum:** qualifies *ruentem*. **crudeli morte:** ablative of cause. The adjective casts a sympathetic light on the victim (and may possibly express Hisbo's perspective), see 380 n. **sodalis:** suggests a close companionship, explaining Hisbo's frenzy and heedless behavior.

387. **tumido:** "swelling," i.e., with rage; cf. 6.407 *tumida ex ira tum corda residunt*.

388. **hinc:** is here used of time rather than place, "after this." **Sthenium:** "the mighty one" (from Greek *sthenos*). **Rhoeti de gente vetusta:** "from the ancient family of Rhoetus," ablative of origin. For a similar expression, cf. 9.284 *Priami de gente vetusta*. Here Rhoetus is the king of the Marsi and father of Anchemolus (389). Rhoetus is also the name of a Rutulian killed by Euryalus during the night raid (9.344).

389. **thalamos:** poetic plural. **incestare:** is dependent on *ausum* and means "to pollute" (in a sexual sense). According to Servius, Anchemolus seduced his stepmother and afterward fled to the court of Daunus, Turnus' father. Harrison *ad loc.* sees in his name the Greek *anchimolos* "coming near" and reads it as a reference to the fact that Anchemolus "approached" his stepmother Casperia sexually.

390. **vos:** for the apostrophe*, see 139 n.

391. **Daucia...proles:** the string of nouns and adjectives are vocatives and are in apposition to *gemini* at 390. **Daucia:** i.e., of Daucus, father of the twins. **Laride:** is a Greek vocative (AG §82). The names *Daucus, Larides*, and *Thymber* occur only here. **simillima proles:** the superlative highlights the similarity between the twins.

indiscreta suis gratusque parentibus error;
at nunc dura dedit vobis discrimina Pallas.
nam tibi, Thymbre, caput Euandrius abstulit ensis;
te decisa suum, Laride, dextera quaerit   395
semianimesque micant digiti ferrumque retractant.
Arcadas accensos monitu et praeclara tuentis
facta viri mixtus dolor et pudor armat in hostis.
   Tum Pallas biiugis fugientem Rhoetea praeter

---

392. **indiscreta:** "indistinguishable," with *proles*. In this sense, the adjective is first found in Vergil. **suis:** "to their own," and not *vestris*, generalizes the picture as the poet returns to the descriptive mode. **gratusque...error:** "a welcome mistake." **parentibus:** dative of reference. The pathetic detail of twins indistinguishable even to their parents, who are, however, made different in death, is Homeric. This line and the next are imitated by later poets, who often expand with gory variations. Cf. Lucan 3.603-8 and Statius, *Theb.* 9.292-5.

393. A highly pathetic line starting with the strong adversative *at*, underscoring the dramatic change. Note the harsh alliteration* *dura dedit discrimina* (for the sympathetic *dura*, see 380) and the shift back to the second person (*vobis*).

394. **Thymbre:** as if from *Thymbrus*, not *Thymber*, for which the vocative is *Thymber* (as at 391); for the two forms of the nominative, cf. *Teucer, Teucrus*. The vocative resumes the pathetic apostrophe*. **caput:** *-put* is lengthened before the caesura* (cf. 382-3). **Evandrius:** adjective with *ensis*. In epic fashion Pallas carries the sword of his father Evander.

395. **te...suum...quaerit:** "seeks you (*te*) as its (master)." **decisa...dextera:** subject of *quaerit*. *Dextera* is the right hand; *decisa* is a metaphor* for pruning. The line is highly pathetic. Note the personification* of the severed limb and the different cases of the second personal pronoun *te* and *tibi* (394), underscoring the different fate of the twin brothers.

396. **semianimesque:** "dying." *Semianimes* is scanned as a tetrasyllable by synizesis* of the semivowel *i* (= *y*). **micant:** can be used of anything twitching. The main model for the description is Ennius fr. 484 Skutsch and in *FRL* 1 *semianimesque micant oculi lucemque requirunt*. The twitching of the fingers recalls Lucretius' similar description of a severed leg (3.653 *digitos agitat propter moribundus humi pes*). For the personification* of the limb, cf. also Ov., *Met.* 6.560 *et moriens (lingua) dominae vestigia quaerit*.

397-8. **monitu:** ablative of cause, i.e., Pallas' speech. **praeclara...| facta:** direct object of (*Arcadas*) *tuentis*. **mixtus dolor et pudor:** subjects of *armat*. For the use of the verb in the singular, see 350-1 n. They feel *dolor* at being chastised by their leader for their cowardice (*accensos monitu*) and *pudor* ("shame") for they have witnessed Pallas' glorious deeds (*praeclara...facta viri*) and are ashamed of their inaction.

399-425. *Pallas' glorious exploit kindles the fire of battle in his followers until it bursts into a general blaze. Halaesus, however, makes havoc in their ranks until he, too, is slain by Pallas.*

399. **biiugis:** instrumental ablative, "with (his horses) yoked in pairs" (from the adjective *biiugus*). The term is here used by synecdoche* to mean chariot (*bigae*). **Rhoetea:** Greek acc. Both Rhoeteus and Ilus (400) evoke the toponymy of the Trojan War, since Rhoeteus

traicit. hoc spatium tantumque morae fuit Ilo; 400
Ilo namque procul validam derexerat hastam,
quam medius Rhoeteus intercipit, optime Teuthra,
te fugiens fratremque Tyren, curruque volutus
caedit semianimis Rutulorum calcibus arva.
ac velut optato ventis aestate coortis 405
dispersa immittit silvis incendia pastor,

---

correlates to Rhoeteum (small town near Troy and the site of a cenotaph erected by Aeneas for Priam's son Deiphobus at *Aen.* 6.505-6) as *Ilus* does to Ilium. **praeter:** adverbial with *fugientem* ("speeding by").

400-1. **spatium:** indicates here an interval of time, "respite." **morae:** partitive genitive after *tantum*. **Ilo | Ilo:** the first *Ilo* is dative of advantage, while the second is an indirect object. Note the emotional epanalepsis* of the name. For the line ending with three disyllables at 400, see 302 n. **namque:** *namque* is postponed from its normal initial position, cf. 614, 815 and 585 (*nam*). Such postponement is first found in Latin in neoteric* poets of the first century BCE. **derexerat:** i.e., Pallas.

402. **quam:** the antecedent is *hastam*. **medius:** "(being) in the middle" (i.e., finding himself between Pallas and Ilus). **intercipit:** possibly an ironic* play on *intercipere* which, in its legal use, means "to appropriate another's property" (Servius *auctus*). For the topos* of *alienum vulnus*, see 343-4 n. **optime Teuthra:** vocative.

403. **fugiens:** refers to Rhoeteus. Rhoeteus intercepts the javelin aimed at Ilus while he is fleeing Teuthras and his brother Tyres. **Tyren:** Greek acc. His name has (Eastern) associations with the city of Tyre. **volutus:** is here used with an active meaning, as often in Vergil.

404. **semianimis:** either a third declension nominative singular (from *semianimis, -e*) agreeing with *Rhoeteus* or a second declension ablative plural (from *semianimus,-a,-um*) agreeing with *calcibus* ("with dying heels"). For a similar image, cf. 730-1 *calcibus atram | tundit humum exspirans*. The model is *Od.* 18.99. **Rutulorum:** genitive after *arva*.

405-9. **ac velut:** introduces similes* eleven other times in the *Aeneid*. **optato:** lit. "it having been prayed for," a single-word ablative absolute used here adverbially ("according to his (i.e., the shepherd's) wish") and referring to the ablative absolute *ventis coortis*. The shepherd has waited for the winds to fire a wooded tract. **aestate:** ablative of time. **dispersa...incendia:** i.e., the shepherd (*pastor*) sets (*immittit*) "scattered fires" in the woods. **silvis:** dative after the compound *immittit*. **correptis...mediis:** ablative absolute, "all in between suddenly having been seized (by fire)," i.e., the space between the separate fires (*dispersa incendia*). **extenditur:** the passive has a reflexive meaning "stretches (itself) out," see 270-1. **una:** either adverb with *extenditur*, "in an unbroken stretch," or adjective referring to the subject *acies*, "one terrifying (*horrida*) line (*acies*) of fire (*Volcania*)." **horrida...acies:** *acies* refers here to the long thin line of a blaze, while *horrida* suggests the jagged appearance of the line of the flame. The language, however, also evokes the image of an army with bristling spears and is apt for a simile which compares the line of fire with the army (*acies*) of Pallas' soldiers. **ovantis:** the adjective suggests

> correptis subito mediis extenditur una
> horrida per latos acies Volcania campos,
> ille sedens victor flammas despectat ovantis:
> non aliter socium virtus coit omnis in unum   410
> teque iuvat, Palla. sed bellis acer Halaesus
> tendit in adversos seque in sua colligit arma.
> hic mactat Ladona Pheretaque Demodocumque,
> Strymonio dextram fulgenti deripit ense
> elatam in iugulum, saxo ferit ora Thoantis   415
> ossaque dispersit cerebro permixta cruento.

---

the image of the shepherd as a victorious (*victor*) Roman general welcomed by a cheering crowd during an ovation (a processional entrance into Rome by a victorious commander, of lesser honor than a triumph). West (1969) 48 notes the detailed correspondence between simile and narrative (*Pastor | Pallas, extenditur | coit, una | in unum*) and calls attention to the military terms used metaphorically* in the simile (*coortis, immittit, extenditur, horrida acies, victor, ovantis*).

410. **socium:** = *sociorum*. **virtus...omnis:** abstract for concrete. **in unum:** *unum* is neuter accusative, "to one place." Note the juxtaposition *omnis | unum*, which underscores how all the Arcadians now become almost one single body.

411. **teque iuvat, Palla:** *iuvat* here can either mean "aids" or "gives pleasure." This kind of sympathetic apostrophe* is usually reserved for the fallen, and so here foreshadows Pallas' approaching end. For the vocative Pallā, see 385 n. **bellis:** abl. of specification after *acer*. **Halaesus:** Pallas' last victim is awarded special treatment: he is the only one to have his share of victims before succumbing to his enemy. Ovid will make Halaesus the eponymous hero of the Falisci (an early Italic tribe) and the founder of their capital, Falerii, in Etruria (*Amores* 3.13.31-5).

412. **tendit:** "proceeds"; the verb here is intransitive. **in adversos:** sc. *viros vel sim.* **seque...:** "and gathers himself up within his shield," so as to leave no part exposed as he attacks. In 12.491 (*et se colligit in arma*) the same attitude is adopted for defense.

413. **hic:** i.e., Halaesus. **mactat:** is used of the killing of sacrificial victims (e.g., 8.85). **Ladona...:** the list of names is given a Greek rhythm by the absence of the masculine caesura* in the third or fourth foot and by its polysyllabic ending (Williams *ad loc.*). *Ladona* and *Phereta* are Greek accusatives. The name *Pheres* appears in Homer (*Od.* 11.259).

414. **Strymonio:** either possessive dative after *dextram* or dative of reference. **dextram:** "the right arm," see 339-41 n. **fulgenti...ense:** instrumental ablative.

415. **elatam:** refers back to *dextram*. **in iugulum:** i.e., Halaesus' throat. Halaeus chops off Strymonius' arm while the latter was raising his arm against him to strike the death blow. **saxo:** instrumental ablative. **Thoantis:** genitive of *Thoas*.

416. **ossa:** here the "skull." **cerebro...cruento:** "with bloody brain," cf. *Il.* 11.97-8.

fata canens silvis genitor celarat Halaesum;
ut senior leto canentia lumina solvit,
iniecere manum Parcae telisque sacrarunt
Euandri. quem sic Pallas petit ante precatus: 420
'da nunc, Thybri pater, ferro, quod missile libro,
fortunam atque viam duri per pectus Halaesi.
haec arma exuviasque viri tua quercus habebit.'
audiit illa deus; dum texit Imaona Halaesus,
Arcadio infelix telo dat pectus inermum. 425

---

417. **fata canens:** is a descriptive phrase. The father (*genitor*) "singing fates" is a seer. For *cano* of prophetic utterances, cf. 7.79 *namque fore inlustrem fama fatisque canebant* (prophecy about Lavinia). **celarat:** = *celaverat*. Cf. also 244 n. The pathetic anecdote is modeled on *Il.* 2.831-4 (the seer Merops tries to keep his two sons from going to Troy).

418. **ut:** "when." **senior:** the comparative is used as a substantive and here emphasizes the father's old age. **leto:** should be best taken as a locative ablative "in death." **canentia lumina:** "the eyes becoming white"; it refers to the whitening of the iris of the eye in old age. **solvit:** "loosed," refers to the relaxation of the eyelids in death (cf. 5.856).

419-20. **iniecere manum:** = *iniecerunt manum*, "laid (their) hand." Servius connects the expression to *manus iniectio*, a form of arrest or of claiming property where the creditor would lay his hands on the debtor (cf. Ov., *Am.* 1.4.40 *et dicam "mea sunt" iniciamque manus*). **Parcae:** the three female goddesses who determined human destiny and especially the span of a person's life. **telisque...| Evandri:** "to the arms of Evander." For Pallas wearing the arms of his father, see 394 n. **sacrarunt:** = *sacraverunt*. *Sacro* ("to dedicate") is usually applied to a thing dedicated by a man to a god, but here is used of the act of a god to a mortal. Cf. also 12.141. **quem:** the relative pronoun (where we would expect a demonstrative, see 384 n.) refers to Halaesus. **sic:** goes with *precatus*, "so having prayed first (*ante*)." Cf. 4.364 *sic accensa profatur*.

421-3. **da...habebit:** a plain petition and a plain promise put side by side with the connection between the two left unexpressed because obvious. **Thybri pater:** "father Tiber," *Thybri* is a vocative of a Greek noun of the third declension. Note the scansion Thȳbrĭ. The divinity is highly appropriate, since the battle is taking place at the mouth of the Tiber, while Pallanteum (future Rome), Pallas' city, is on the banks of the Tiber. **ferro:** see 9-10 n. **missile:** is in apposition to *quod* and refers back to *ferro*. **libro:** "poise to throw." **tua quercus:** trees were perpetually dedicated to particular deities. Pallas' promise of dedication of the spoils contrasts with Turnus keeping (and wearing) Pallas' belt later in the book and with Mezentius giving Lausus Palmus' spoils to wear (701 n.). For Aeneas' dedication of the spoils of Mezentius, see 904-5 n. and 11.5-11.

424. **dum texit:** i.e., with his shield. **Imaona:** Greek accusative. The name is found only here.

425. **Arcadio...telo:** "to the Arcadian spear." Pallas' father Evander, according to Book 8 (51-4), had migrated from Arcadia in Greece to Italy. **infelix:** the epithet* denotes sympathy for the victim, see 324-5 n. **inermum:** from *inermus,-a,-um* (and not from the more common *inermis*,

> At non caede viri tanta perterrita Lausus,
> pars ingens belli, sinit agmina: primus Abantem
> oppositum interimit, pugnae nodumque moramque.
> sternitur Arcadiae proles, sternuntur Etrusci
> et vos, o Grais imperdita corpora, Teucri.   430
> agmina concurrunt ducibusque et viribus aequis.
> extremi addensent acies nec turba moveri
> tela manusque sinit. hinc Pallas instat et urget,
> hinc contra Lausus, nec multum discrepat aetas,

-e) Halaesus' breast is undefended because he is covering Imaon with his shield. The expression picks up Pallas' prayer that his weapon go *duri per pectus Halaesi* (422). Note how Halaesus' death, highly anticipated by Pallas' prayer and by the pathetic anecdote, is omitted from the narrative.

426-38. *Lausus'* aristeia*. *On the other side, Lausus rallies his panic-stricken men and charges against the enemy. Thanks to the valor of Pallas and Lausus, both outstanding in beauty and of similar age, the battle evens up. Soon, however, both heroes will meet their fate at the hands of a greater enemy and will be denied the return to their homeland.*

426-7. **At:** the adversative marks a shift in the situation with the battle eventually balancing out (*ducibusque et viribus aequis* 431) thanks to Lausus' valiant efforts. **non...agmina:** construe as *Lausus, pars ingens belli, non sinit agmina perterrita caede tanta viri.* **non:** goes with *sinit* in the following line, "does not allow." **caede...tanta:** is an ablative of cause after *perterrita agmina* (object of *sinit*). **viri:** either (i) *viri* = Halaesus, "by the death of so great a hero," with *tanta* referring to *caede* by hypallage (see enallage*) or (ii) *viri* = Pallas, "the hero's wide death-dealing." *Viri* is objective genitive in (i), subjective genitive in (ii). **pars ingens belli:** is in apposition to *Lausus*. For the expression, cf. 737; 2.6 *et quorum pars magna fui.* **primus:** is quasi-adverbial as at 242, "first of all". **Abantem:** see 170-1 n.

428. **pugnae nodumque moramque:** is in apposition to *Abantem. Nodus* probably refers to a knot in the wood which is hard to cut through. For *mora*, see 485 n.

429. **Arcadiae proles:** "the offspring of Arcadia." The Arcadians are called sons of their country. Note the line pattern with anaphora*, asyndeton* (to underscore the speed of the killing) and variation in verb number.

430. **et vos...Teucri:** is the climax of the rhetorical tricolon*. **Grais imperdita corpora:** "bodies unscathed by the Greeks," is in apposition to *Teucri*; i.e., the Trojans who escaped from the Trojan War. *Grais* is dative of the personal agent (see AG §375).

432-3. **extremi:** "those in the rear." **addensent acies:** "make compact the ranks." **sinit:** governs the acc. subject (*tela manusque*) and the infinitive passive (*moveri*). See AG §563c. The final syllable of *sinit* is lengthened at the caesura* (see 382-3 n.).

433-4. **hinc Pallas...| hinc...Lausus:** the matching structure of the two clauses underscores the two youths' matching behavior. **Pallas:** see 385 n. **contra:** adverb "in return." **multum:** adverb "much."

egregii forma, sed quis Fortuna negarat 435
in patriam reditus. ipsos concurrere passus
haud tamen inter se magni regnator Olympi;
mox illos sua fata manent maiore sub hoste.

439-509: Pallas' duel with Turnus

The young Pallas is sought out in duel by Turnus, a far superior opponent (439-56). Vain are Pallas' prayers to Hercules. The demigod can only weep, mourning the fate of his protégé, as Jupiter reminds him that destiny is inescapable (457-73). Turnus kills Pallas and strips him of his sword-belt. The poet comments that a day will come when Turnus will bitterly regret his deed (474-509).

Placed in the middle of *Aeneid* 10, the duel between Pallas and Turnus is the most consequential episode of the book. The duel has two major Homeric models. The most obvious is the duel between Hector and Patroclus in *Iliad* 16. The points of contact are numerous. Juturna, the immortal sister of Turnus, urges Turnus to fight against Pallas (439-41), just as the god Apollo spurs Hector to battle against Patroclus (16.712-30), the slayer of Sarpedon. Like Patroclus, Pallas is led by a desire for valor into tragic combat against a stronger enemy. And just as it was for Hector, the victory of Turnus is simultaneously the peak of his success and the basis for his defeat: Hector had sealed his fate by killing and stripping Patroclus; so, too, Turnus consigns himself to certain death by killing Pallas and stripping him of his belt. And yet, an important moment of the duel between Sarpedon and Patroclus is also reworked into this episode. Hercules' weeping (465) in response to Pallas' prayers is modeled on Zeus' grief over his son Sarpedon's imminent death at *Iliad* 16.459, a moment that Vergil's Jupiter, in a sort of reflexive allusion, evokes in his speech to

---

435. **egregii:** is in apposition to Pallas and Lausus. **forma:** abl. of specification. Beauty is a heroic quality but its mention in connection with the anticipation of the two young heroes' death is highly pathetic. **quis:** 168 n. **negarat:** = *negaverat*.

436-7. **reditus:** direct object of *negarat*. **ipsos:** is the accusative subject of the infinitive *concurrere* and is governed by *passus* (sc. *est*, from *patior*). **regnator:** i.e., Jupiter, subject of *passus* (*est*). Jupiter's intervention contradicts his promise of neutrality earlier in the assembly of the gods. Cf. 107-8 n. Quint (2018) 161 suggests that the language, which recalls Apollo's warning to Patroclus that he is not fated to win Troy (*Il.* 16.707-9), assimilates both heroes to Patroclus. On the topic, see 362-438 n.

438. **mox:** "soon enough." **sua:** is used here emphatically to underscore their own fate as opposed to that of others, see AG §301c. **manent:** here is transitive ("awaits") and governs *illos*. For a similar foreshadowing in the *Aeneid*, cf. e.g., 471, 503 (Turnus). In general, for the technique of foreshadowing in epic, see Duckworth (1933). **maiore sub hoste:** Pallas is slain by Turnus (see 479-80) and Lausus by Aeneas (see 815-16).

Hercules: *quin occidit una | Sarpedon, mea progenies* (470-1). Thus, again, the intertextual identities of our two contenders become blurred as both Turnus and Pallas, at different moments of the duel, play the role of the Homeric Patroclus, and each one is made to fight, in a way, an image of his own self (on the topic, see also 308-908 n.).

Vergil, however, also establishes another important set of parallels within his own text, between this duel and that of Lausus and Aeneas at the end of the book, where, too, another young man, Lausus, is prematurely taken away from his father's affection and killed at the hands of a stronger hero. The parallelism of the two episodes sets in sharp contrast the difference of behavior between Turnus and Aeneas. Turnus is boastful and arrogant (cf. 443, his wish that Evander were present to watch; 491-5, his boast over the dead body; 500, his excessive delight in his triumph). His tone and treatment of Pallas alienate the readers' sympathy, a result reinforced by the narrator's direct intervention into the narrative (501-2, 507-10). Aeneas, by contrast, in his hour of victory, shows deep restraint, *humanitas*, and *pietas* toward the fallen youth. He offers him a heroic consolation (829-30) and, in a chivalrous act, himself picks up the body of the fallen Lausus (830-2). On this topic, see also General Introduction to Book 10.

The Homeric models for this episode are analyzed by Lyne (1983), Barchiesi (2015) 1-34, Quint (2018) 160-2. For parallels between this duel and that of Aeneas and Lausus, see Barchiesi (2015) 1-34, Stahl (2016) 143-54. For uneven duels in the *Aeneid*, see Krisher (1979). For the topos* of "immature death," see Conte (1986) 185-95, Petrini (1997) 48-86. For a narratological analysis of the duel, see Bonfanti (1985) 31-56 (in Italian), who notes that almost all the verbs in the narrative of the duel relate to the visual experience of Pallas or Hercules, while Turnus, the victor of the contest, is merely the object of such visual experience. On the topic, see also Conte (2007) 23-57.

> Interea soror alma monet succedere Lauso
> Turnum, qui volucri curru medium secat agmen.   440
> ut vidit socios: 'tempus desistere pugnae;

439-56. *Urged by his sister Juturna to come to Lausus' rescue, Turnus seeks Pallas in a duel. Pallas, though amazed at his giant size, accepts the challenge.*

439-40. **soror:** i.e., Juturna. She is an Italian nymph, sister of Turnus. She is formally introduced at 12.138-41 (and named for the first time at 12.146). **alma:** is a common epithet* for goddesses. **succedere...| Turnum:** infinitive and accusative subject after *moneo* (see 9-10 n.). **Lauso:** dative after the compound verb *succedere*. **volucri curru:** instrumental ablative.

441. **ut vidit socios:** the omission of the verb of saying before Turnus' speech conveys excitement. **tempus:** sc. *est*. **desistere:** is an infinitive after *tempus* (*est*) (AG §504 n. 2). **pugnae:** is a genitive of separation, a construction borrowed from the Greek, cf. 9.789 *Turnus paulatim excedere pugnae*.

solus ego in Pallanta feror, soli mihi Pallas
debetur; cuperem ipse parens spectator adesset.'
haec ait, et socili cesserunt aequore iusso.
at Rutulum abscessu iuvenis tum iussa superba 445
miratus stupet in Turno corpusque per ingens
lumina volvit obitque truci procul omnia visu,
talibus et dictis it contra dicta tyranni:

---

442. **Pallanta**: Greek accusative. **feror**: the passive seems to underscore that his action has been dictated by an external force (i.e., Juturna). The triple anaphora* (in different cases) *solus...soli, ego...mihi, in Pallanta...Pallas* highlights Turnus' desire to meet Pallas in single combat. Contrast Aeneas' attempt to dissuade Lausus from fighting him (811-12). For the unusual line ending with three disyllables, see 302 n. The line presents another example of *dicolon abundans**, see 9-10 n.

443. **cuperem**: optative subjunctive. The imperfect expresses an unfulfilled wish in the present "I wish" (but my wish cannot be fulfilled, see AG §441). Turnus' hideous desire to have Evander witness the duel (and the death) of his own son pairs him with Pyrrhus of *Aen.* 2 who forced Priam to witness his own son's death (2.538-9 *qui nati coram me cernere letum | fecisti et patrios foedasti funere vultus*). For Pyrrhus, see also 491 n., 535-6 n., 555 n., 580 n. By contrast, Aeneas, at the sight of Lausus' dead body, is moved by the thought of his paternal loyalty (824). **ipse parens**: i.e., Evander. **spectator**: is in apposition to *ipse parens*. **adesset**: an imperfect subjunctive after *cuperem* with *ut* omitted, see 54-6 n. The tense is determined by the sequence of tenses.

444. **aequore iusso**: ablative of separation. The *aequor* here is the level fighting ground. The manuscript reading *iusso* (instead of the emendation *iussi*) should probably be retained as another example of transferred epithet or hypallage (see enallage* and 230-1 n.).

445. **Rutulum**: archaic* genitive plural used often in the *Aeneid* for *Rutulorum*. **abscessu**: abl. of attendant circumstance. **tum**: picks up *Rutulum abscessu = cum Rutuli abscessissent*; after they had retired, Pallas *then* had a full view of Turnus. **iussa superba**: direct object after *miratus*; the adjective reflects Pallas' point of view.

446. **stupet in Turno**: *stupeo in* + abl. is used of dazed admiration. Cf. Hor., *Serm.* 1.6.17 *qui stupet in titulis et imaginibus*. **corpusque per ingens**: Turnus has a (heroically) formidable physique.

447. **lumina volvit**: "causes the eyes to travel restlessly," see OLD s.v. 8. **obit**: the sense of "to survey with the sight" is first found in Vergil. **truci...visu**: ablative of manner. Although Pallas "marvels" at Turnus' arrogance and is "amazed" at his size, he is not yet daunted.

448. **talibus et dictis**: = *et talibus dictis*. The postponement of *et* is a neoteric* feature. **it contra dicta**: the expression suggests an analogy between this verbal skirmish and the coming physical confrontation (Harrison *ad loc.*). **tyranni**: the derogatory term, like *superba* above, reflects Pallas' point of view.

'aut spoliis ego iam raptis laudabor opimis
aut leto insigni: sorti pater aequus utrique est. 450
tolle minas.' fatus medium procedit in aequor;
frigidus Arcadibus coit in praecordia sanguis.
desiluit Turnus biiugis, pedes apparat ire
comminus; utque leo, specula cum vidit ab alta
stare procul campis meditantem in proelia taurum, 455
advolat: haud alia est Turni venientis imago.

---

449. **spoliis...raptis...opimis:** take it either as an ablative of cause or an ablative absolute. The *spolia opima* were the spoils taken when the general on one side slew the general of the enemy in single combat (cf. Livy 4.20.5 *quae dux duci detraxit*). According to tradition they had been won three times in Roman history, by Romulus (752 BCE), by Cossus (428 BCE), and by Marcellus who had killed the leader of the Insubrian Gauls (222 BCE). M. Licinius Crassus, grandson of the triumvir, had claimed them unsuccessfully in 29 BCE, reviving interest in the institution.

450. **leto insigni:** ablative of cause. Death, too, would be glorious since it would come by the hand of an enemy commander. **sorti...utrique:** dat. after *aequus*. Pallas answers Turnus' taunt at 443. Evander, like a good Roman father, will bear "calmly" whatever befalls Pallas, provided it is not dishonor. Neither Evander (11.152-81) nor Aeneas (10.510-15), however, will show equanimity over his death.

451. **aequor:** see 444 n.

452. **frigidus...sanguis:** the blood freezes in fear; cf. 3.30 *gelidusque coit formidine sanguis*. **Arcadibus:** dat. of reference. **in praecordia:** motion toward because the blood rushes into their breasts. For the emotional response of the internal spectators of the duel channeling the response of the external spectators (i.e., the audience), see Rossi (2004) 154-68.

453. **biiugis:** see 399 n. **pedes:** "on foot," the noun (lit. "person on foot") is a nominative singular in apposition to Turnus, the implied subject of *apparat*.

454-6. **utque:** introduces the simile*. **vidit:** the perfect tense imitates the Greek use of the gnomic aorist in similar contexts and the effect is a timeless description. **stare...taurum:** infinitive and accusative subject after *vidit*. **procul:** is used as a preposition "far from" (with the ablative *campis*). **meditantem in proelia:** the construction *in* + accusative indicates purpose "practicing for (the purpose of) battle," i.e., with some rival bull. The phrase points to Pallas' bellicose spirit. **imago:** possibly a wordplay; *imago* describes "the impression of Turnus on the onlookers" as elaborated in the simile*, but it is also itself the standard word for simile (Harrison *ad loc.*). The simile foreshadows Pallas' upcoming death, since Pallas is compared to a bull who is brave yet doomed against a superior opponent. While the lion simile is positioned in the narrative to parallel Homer's simile comparing both Hector and Patroclus to lions fighting over a deer at *Iliad* 16.756-75, just before Hector kills Patroclus, its content recalls the lion-bull simile used of Patroclus as he stands over the dying Sarpedon (*Iliad* 16.487-9). For the conflation of the two duels, see 439-509 n.

hunc ubi contiguum missae fore credidit hastae,
ire prior Pallas, si qua fors adiuvet ausum
viribus imparibus, magnumque ita ad aethera fatur:
'per patris hospitium et mensas, quas advena adisti,   460
te precor, Alcide, coeptis ingentibus adsis.
cernat semineci sibi me rapere arma cruenta
victoremque ferant morientia lumina Turni.'

457-63. *Pallas casts a spear against Turnus and asks Hercules to grant him victory against his opponent.*

457-8. **hunc...Pallas:** construe as *ubi* ("when") *Pallas credidit hunc* (i.e., Turnus) *contiguum fore* (= *futurum esse*) *missae hastae, prior ire*. **hunc...fore:** the accusative subject and infinitive are governed by *credidit*. **contiguum:** a rare use (and attested here for the first time) of the term in the passive sense of "reachable" (i.e., "within reach"). **missae...hastae:** dative dependent on *contiguum*. **ire:** historical infinitive (267-8 n.). **prior:** comparative, for Turnus is the implied second term of comparison. **si qua:** = *si (ali)qua via* ("if by any way"); abl. of means. **adiuvet:** the present subjunctive is used either to express Pallas' thoughts (subjunctive in indirect discourse) or to indicate doubt about the result (protasis of a future less vivid conditional clause); cf. 1.18 *si qua fata sinant*, of Juno's desire to win universal empire for Carthage. **ausum:** masculine accusative perfect participle of the semideponent *audeo* (referring to Pallas "(him) having dared"). If taken to be the neuter accusative singular of the neuter noun *ausum, -i* ("deed"), a comma should be placed after it and *viribus imparibus* would go with *ire prior*.

459. **viribus imparibus:** either ablative of manner or means. The duel between Turnus and Aeneas at the end of the poem is similarly described. Cf. 12.216 *impar pugna* and 12.218 *non viribus aequos*, with Tarrant *ad loc*. **aethera:** Greek accusative singular. Cf. 11.556 *ita ad aethera fatur*.

460. **per...hospitium et mensas:** hendiadys* (= *hospitium mensae*). **patris:** i.e., Evander. The story of Evander entertaining Hercules is told at 8.362-5. For the importance of the tie of hospitality, cf. 494-5. **advena:** i.e., Hercules; nominative in apposition to an implied *tu*.

461. **Alcide:** i.e., Hercules. Greek vocative. Cf. 391 n. The patronymic* derives from his grandfather Alcaeus. **coeptis ingentibus:** dat. depending on *adsis* (optative subjunctive). For the expression (a standard prayer-formula), cf. 9.296 *tuis ingentibus...coeptis*.

462-3. **cernat...ferant:** optative subjunctives. The subjects are, respectively, Turnus (implied) and *morientia lumina*. The subjunctives reply to Turnus' *cuperem ipse parens spectator adesset* at 443, with *cernat* responding directly to Turnus' *spectator*. **semineci sibi:** dative of separation after *rapere* (see 50 n.). The adjective *seminex* means "dying" rather than "half-dead." *Sibi* is reflexive because it refers to the person who is the subject of *cernat*. **me rapere:** subject accusative and infinitive dependent on *cernat*.

463. **victoremque:** sc. *me*. Direct object of *ferant*.

audiit Alcides iuvenem magnumque sub imo
corde premit gemitum lacrimasque effundit inanis.   465
tum genitor natum dictis adfatur amicis:
'stat sua cuique dies, breve et inreparabile tempus
omnibus est vitae; sed famam extendere factis,

464-78. Hercules hears Pallas' prayer and sheds tears. Jupiter tells his son that Pallas' fatal hour has come. Turnus, too, will meet his fate soon. Pallas' javelin only grazes Turnus' body.

The model for the passage is Zeus' grief for the death of his son Sarpedon at *Il.* 16.431-61 (see 439-509 n.). Vergil, however, reworks the episode thoroughly: he excludes Hera's and Jupiter's divine squabble which opened the Homeric scene, "replaces" Zeus with the demigod Hercules, and changes what was Zeus' rain of bloody drops (a portent with precise honorific function) into Hercules' sympathetic but useless tears for the victim-to-be. Jupiter, still present in the Vergilian scene, is made to play the more dignified role of the *voice of fate* who, in a didactic and somewhat detached tone, presents Hercules, the voice *of compassion*, with the great laws of fate governing human affairs.

For an overall analysis of the passage and Vergil's reworking of the Homeric model, see Feeney (1991) 156-7, Barchiesi (2015) 6-19. For the stark contrast between this helpless and all-too-human Hercules and Evander's "heroic" Hercules, see Petrini (1997) 62-5. Hejduk (2009) rightly notes that, whereas the Homeric Zeus groans that he cannot fight against Moira and save Sarpedon, Vergil's Jupiter does not show any emotional connection with human suffering. For the consolatory commonplaces in Jupiter's speech, see Harrison *ad loc.*

464-5. **Alcides:** for the patronymic*, see 461 n. **magnumque...premit gemitum:** "held back a great groan," as he attempts to control himself. **lacrimasque...inanis:** Hercules hears the prayer but cannot fulfill it. Hence the ineffectual tears. This image of Hercules is all the more effective if we consider that in the ancient tradition he was the exemplar of the long-suffering hero who never wept (Barchiesi (2015) 11). For the expression, cf. 4.449 *lacrimae volvuntur inanes* (where it is unclear whether the tears are Dido's or Aeneas').

466. **genitor:** Jupiter. **natum:** Hercules was son of Jupiter (cf. also 8.301 *uera Iouis proles*) by Alcmene and the two gods were commonly joined in Roman cult. The juxtaposition *genitor | natum* stresses their family ties. **dictis...amicis:** ablative of manner. As noted by Hejduk (2009) 299, the term is somewhat ambiguous. Is Jupiter exhibiting true "kindness," as expected of a father toward his son, or is he simply giving "friendly advice"?

467. **stat:** indicates immovable fixity (see Harrison *ad loc.*). For the expression, cf. Lucret., *DRN* 1.563-4 *et finita simul generatim tempora rebus | stare. **sua...dies:** *dies* is feminine when it means a particular day (cf. 256-7). For the usage of the possessive *sua*, see 219-21 n. **cuique:** dat. (of reference) of the indefinite pronoun. **inreparabile:** Vergil is fond of adjectives with negative prefixes.

468. **omnibus:** dat. of possession. **vitae:** genitive dependent on *tempus* (467). **famam extendere factis:** *factis* is instrumental ablative. Note the opposition between the idea of stretching implied in *extendere* and the *breve tempus* of Pallas' life. For the expression, cf. 6.806 *virtutem*

hoc virtutis opus. Troiae sub moenibus altis
tot gnati cecidere deum, quin occidit una 470
Sarpedon, mea progenies: etiam sua Turnum
fata vocant metasque dati pervenit ad aevi.'
sic ait, atque oculos Rutulorum reicit arvis.
at Pallas magnis emittit viribus hastam
vaginaque cava fulgentem deripit ensem. 475
illa volans umeri surgunt qua tegmina summa
incidit, atque viam clipei molita per oras
tandem etiam magno strinxit de corpore Turni.

---

extendere factis (Anchises' speech to Aeneas in the Underworld). For the rhetorical commonplace, cf. Sall., *Cat.* 1.3. *quoniam vita ipsa, qua fruimur, brevis est, memoriam nostri quam maxume longam efficere.*

469. **hoc...opus:** sc. *est.* The clause is in apposition to *famam extendere factis.*

470. **gnati:** archaic* spelling of *nati.* These sons were Achilles (son of Thetis), Cycnus (son of Neptune), Ascalaphus (son of Ares), Memnon (son of Eos), and Sarpedon (son of Jupiter). **cecidere:** = *ceciderunt* (from *cado*). **deum:** = *deorum*, see 228-9 n. **quin:** "in fact," cf. 23-4 n. **una:** adv., "together" (i.e., with so many other sons of gods). Jupiter uses another common consolatory scheme, the *consolatio per exemplum*, as he reminds the grieving Hercules that others have suffered the same fate before Pallas (Barchiesi (2015) 14).

471. **sua:** see 219-21 n.

472. **metasque...:** construe as *ad metas aevi dati* (i.e., to him) *pervenit* (i.e., Turnus). The image is that of a race nearing its completion since the *meta* was the turning post at a racetrack.

473. **Rutulorum:** genitive after *arvis.* **reicit:** is scanned as a dactyl. **arvis:** ablative of motion away from with preposition *ab* omitted, as often in poetry (AG §428g). Jupiter's gesture has been interpreted in various, often antithetical, ways: as a sign of sorrow (Harrison *ad loc.*, Stahl (2016) 164; cf. also 12.151 where Juno states that she cannot bear to witness the duel between Turnus and Aeneas, *non pugnam aspicere hanc oculis*), as an expression that Jupiter renounces interfering in human affairs (Barchiesi (2015) 14 n. 40), or as a sign of his detachment (Hejduk (2009) 301-2; for similar behavior by the Homeric Zeus, cf. also *Il.* 13.2-3).

474. **magnis...viribus:** instrumental ablative.

476-7. **illa...| incidit:** construe as *illa* (i.e., *hasta*) *volans incidit qua tegmina summa umeri surgunt.* For *qua*, see 291 n. *Tegmina summa* refers to the top of the breastplate and probably to the projecting shoulder-pieces of the Roman *lorica.* **viam...molita:** "forcing (its) way," cf. *molitur iter* (6.477, said of difficult progress). **clipei...per oras:** "through the rim of the shield." The plural *oras* is poetic.

478. **strinxit:** *stringo* is usually transitive and takes the accusative. Here understand a direct object like *aliquid*, "grazed (a portion) of the great body." For *magno de corpore*, used almost like a partitive genitive, cf. also 4.324 *hoc solum nomen quoniam de coniuge restat?* (speech of Dido).

LIBER DECIMUS 91

> Hic Turnus ferro praefixum robur acuto
> in Pallanta diu librans iacit atque ita fatur: 480

479-509. Turnus kills Pallas and strips the gold-decked baldric from his body, little thinking in his pride that the trophy would one day decide his doom. The narrator interrupts the narrative to comment on Turnus' action.

Turnus' stripping of Pallas' sword-belt (and later his wearing it as a spoil of war) marks a decisive moment in the poem. With these actions, Turnus seals his fate: at the end of the poem, it is the sight of Pallas' sword-belt that triggers Aeneas' furious rage and prompts him to kill an already wounded (and suppliant) Turnus.

The death of Pallas conflates, once again, events from two Homeric duels, the one between Patroclus and Sarpedon and the one between Hector and Patroclus, with the effect of further blurring the identities of these Vergilian heroes. Pallas' pulling of Turnus' spear out of his own chest and tearing out his life with it echoes the action of Patroclus, who steps on the chest of Sarpedon and pulls both his spearhead and the life out of the vanquished Sarpedon (*Il.* 16.503-5). Turnus' stepping on the body of Pallas (495) to strip him of his baldric is modeled, instead, on Hector's stepping on the body of Patroclus to remove his spear (*Il.* 16.862-3). However, while Hector's action serves to retrieve the spear from the body of Patroclus, Turnus' gesture is gratuitous and is evidence of his lack of restraint (cf. *servare modum* 502). On Vergil's reworking of the Homeric code model, see General Introduction to the book. The passage, however, also evokes the moment when Hector strips Patroclus of the armor of Achilles at *Iliad* 17.183-97, since the narrator's warning that Turnus will pay a price for spoiling Pallas of his baldric (501-4) recalls the moment in the Iliadic passage when Zeus spells out that Hector is soon destined to be killed by Achilles (*Il.* 17.201-8).

As for Pallas' baldric, the elaborate design engraved on it carries important symbolic meanings that foreshadow the destiny of both Pallas and Turnus. The slaughter of young men on their wedding night in the baldric's design not only reflects Turnus' impious deed but also foreshadows Turnus' fate. By killing Pallas, Turnus has deprived Pallas of the hope of maturity and progeny just as the Danaids have deprived the sons of Aegyptus of their future. Yet by wearing Pallas' baldric with its ominous design, Turnus has also inadvertently consigned himself to the same premature death of Pallas and the sons of Aegyptus. For the myth of the Danaids, see 497 n. On the ecphrasis*, see Conte (1986) 185-95, Fowler (1987), Lyne (1989) 158, Mitchell (1991), Spence (1991), Hardie (1993) 33, Putnam (1994), Stahl (2016) 118-32. On the belt of Pallas and the Colonnade of the Danaids on the Palatine, see Lefèvre (1989). On the story of the Argive Danaids (and the story of the Argive Io on Turnus' shield) as a representation of Turnus' most salient mythological past (Turnus is of Argive origin), see Kirichenko (2013). For the erotic representation of the fallen body of Pallas, see Reed (2007) 34-40. On Pallas' death as a substitute for the death of Aeneas' own son, see Quint (2018) 178. For Turnus stepping on the dead body of Pallas, see Barchiesi (2015) 18.

479. **Hic:** adverb "at this point." **ferro…acuto:** instrumental ablative. **robur:** "wood," but by metonymy* a "wooden spear-shaft."

480. **diu:** qualifies *librans*.

'aspice num mage sit nostrum penetrabile telum.'
dixerat; at clipeum, tot ferri terga, tot aeris,
quem pellis totiens obeat circumdata tauri,
vibranti cuspis medium transverberat ictu
loricaeque moras et pectus perforat ingens.   485
ille rapit calidum frustra de vulnere telum:
una eademque via sanguis animusque sequuntur.
corruit in vulnus (sonitum super arma dedere)
et terram hostilem moriens petit ore cruento.

---

481. **num…sit:** indirect question after *aspice*. **mage:** archaic* for *magis*. **nostrum…telum:** arrogantly, Turnus uses the royal "we." **penetrabile:** active = "piercing."

482-4. **at clipeum…:** construe as *at cuspis vibranti ictu transverberat medium clipeum—tot terga ferri, tot (terga) aeris, quem pellis tauri circumdata totiens obeat—loricaeque moras*. **tot…terga:** is in apposition to *clipeum*. *Terga* literally "a hide," is then used of a "layer of hide" on a shield and so here of a layer of iron; cf. also 784 (*linea terga*). **quem…totiens obeat:** *clipeum* is the antecedent of the relative pronoun. *Obeat* is subjunctive in a concessive relative clause with *quem = quamvis eum* (AG §535e). *Totiens* qualifies *obeat* and picks up *tot* of the previous line: the bull's hide placed around the shield (*pellis circumdata tauri*) goes around it (*obeat*) a number of times equal to the number of layers of iron and bronze. The sentence structure keeps the narrative in suspense. It begins with the object (*clipeum*), followed first by phrases in apposition to it (*tot…, tot…*), and then by the adjective *vibranti* which qualifies *ictu* (at the end of the line) and which precedes both the subject *cuspis* and main verb *tranverberat*. The sentence then ends with the reiteration of the object with *medium*. The tricolon* *tot…tot… totiens* highlights how, despite its elaborate making, the shield fails to protect Pallas.

485. **loricaeque moras:** "his corselet's barrier." Pallas' cuirass is meant to slow down the course of the attacker's weapon, i.e., to be a "delay" (*mora*), cf. 428 and 12.541 *clipei mora*. **ingens:** certainly with *pectus*, as its position demands. Huge size is regularly attributed to gods and heroes (cf. 5.241; 6.413).

486-7. **ille:** i.e., Pallas. **frustra:** take with *rapit*. Similarly, Camilla pulls out the fatal spear in a vain attempt to save herself at 11.816 *illa manu moriens telum trahit*. For the Homeric subtexts, see 479-509 n.

487. **una eademque via:** "at the same time and by the same path." The ablative *eadem* is disyllabic by synizesis* for the first two vowels combine to form one long vowel. **sanguis:** *-is* is long before the caesura*, see 382-3 n.

488. **in vulnus:** "onto the wound," i.e., onto his breast where he was wounded. **super:** either adverb "on top," or preposition with *eum* understood ("over him"). For the image, cf. *Il*. 4.504 and Ennius fr. 4112 Skutsch and *FRL* 1 *sonitum simul insuper arma dederunt*.

489. **hostilem:** because this is where he dies. **ore cruento:** instrumental ablative. Pallas falls on his face, cf. 349.

LIBER DECIMUS 93

    quem Turnus super adsistens: 490
'Arcades, haec' inquit 'memores mea dicta referte
Euandro: qualem meruit, Pallanta remitto.
quisquis honos tumuli, quidquid solamen humandi est,
largior. haud illi stabunt Aeneia parvo
hospitia.' et laevo pressit pede talia fatus   495
exanimem rapiens immania pondera baltei
impressumque nefas: una sub nocte iugali

490. **quem:** = *eum*, see 384 n. **super:** a preposition (*super quem*), not an adverb. For speeches introduced with half-lines, see 17 n. Turnus' boast stands in stark contrast with Aeneas' restrained and sympathetic behavior toward the dead Lausus (see 824-32).

491. **Arcades:** vocative plural. The final syllable is short in this Greek form. **memores...referte:** Turnus' wording echoes Pyrrhus' taunt to Priam, cf. 2.547 *referes* | *referte*, 2.549 *memento* | *memores*. See also 443 n.

492. **Evandro:** scan the first syllable as the diphthong *eu*. **qualem...remitto:** lit. "such as (i.e., dead) he (Evander) has deserved, I send back Pallas." That Pallas should be sent back dead was exactly what Evander had "earned" as a repayment for his conduct. Contrast Aeneas' sympathetic words to the dead Lausus at 827-8. Turnus adopts a number of commercial metaphors*: *meruit, largior, haud stabunt parvo*. Cf. also 532 *belli commercia*. For a similar taunt, cf. *Il.* 14.501-2.

493. **quisquis...tumuli:** sc. *est*. **quidquid:** is a pronoun (like *quisquis*) used adjectivally, cf. Hor., *Carm.* 2.13.9 *quidquid nefas*. See also 9-10 n. For a similar idea, cf. 828 n. **humandi:** genitive of the gerund.

494-5. **illi:** i.e., to Evander. **stabunt:** "will cost." **Aeneia...| hospitia:** subject of *stabunt*. For the contemptuous tone, cf. 1.671-2 *Iunonia* | *hospitia* (said ironically* by Venus). **parvo:** abl. of price (cf. 2.104 *magno mercentur Atridae*). **laevo...pede:** instrumental ablative. The use of the left foot is ominous, see 254-5 n.

496. **exanimem:** is used as a substantive and is the object of *pressit*. **immania pondera:** is suggestive both of the weight of the baldric and of the enormity of Turnus' deed (Harrison *ad loc.*). **baltei:** scanned as a spondee by synizesis*. The *balteus* was a strap worn diagonally across the shoulder and was used to support a sword, shield, or quiver (cf. 12.941-2 *umero cum apparuit alto* | *balteus*). Turnus presses his foot on the body of his defeated enemy and strips him of his sword-belt. His behavior stands in stark contrast with Aeneas', who refrains from taking Lausus' weapons and, in a chivalrous gesture, picks up Lausus' body himself. For Vergil's reworking of the Homeric code model, see 479-509 n.

497. **impressumque nefas:** "and the imprinted crime," i.e., the story of the Danaids. The Danaids were the fifty daughters of Danaus. They fled Argos to avoid a forced marriage to the fifty sons of Danaus' twin brother Aegyptus. Eventually they relented, but, on their wedding night, they all (except for Hypermnestra) slaughtered their cousin-husbands. For the story, see also Aeschylus, *Prometheus Bound* 846-69 and *Suppliants* 5-19. For an analysis of the myth, see Petrini (1997) 81-4, Kirichenko (2013). **una sub nocte iugali:** "under (the cover of) one wedding night." *Una* is in emphatic position. The single night contrasts with the mass murder.

caesa manus iuvenum foede thalamique cruenti,
quae Clonus Eurytides multo caelaverat auro;
quo nunc Turnus ovat spolio gaudetque potitus. 500
nescia mens hominum fati sortisque futurae
et servare modum rebus sublata secundis!
Turno tempus erit magno cum optaverit emptum
intactum Pallanta, et cum spolia ista diemque

---

498. **caesa manus iuvenum:** "the band of young men killed." *Caesa manus* should be in the accusative agreeing with *nefas*, but since the words *una...cruenti* are really a separate clause stating what the representation is, a transition to the nominative is natural. **foede:** either "with shame" and referring to the young boys, "who died ingloriously" because killed "in bed and not in battle" (see Conte (1986) 187), or "barbarously" and characterizing the act of *caedere* (Stahl (2016) 123). **thalamique cruenti:** nominative plural.

499. **quae:** neuter accusative plural; picks up the picture described at 497-8. **Eurytides:** patronymic*, "son of Eurytus." **multo...auro:** abl. of material.

500. **quo...spolio:** i.e., the balteus; *quo = eo*. The ablative is governed by *ovat* which borrows the ablative construction usual after *gaudet*. For Turnus' joy, cf. *Il.* 18.131-2 (of Hector wearing the armor of Achilles taken from Patroclus).

501-5. **nescia...:** contrary to Homeric praxis, Pallas dies without a final speech, which, in this episode, is significantly "replaced" by the narrator's own comments (Bonfanti (1985) 48).

501. **fati sortisque futurae:** objective genitives after *nescia*. The moralizing comment of the poet calls attention to Turnus' premature elation. The model is *Il.*17.201-8, where Zeus predicts Hector's future death. However, the speech of the Iliadic Zeus focuses mainly on the ineluctability of death and lacks Vergil's moralizing overtones (Barchiesi (2015) 32). Lyne (1983) 188-203 points out that Vergil passes adverse judgment not on Turnus' triumph, but on his exultation in that triumph. For the importance of Homeric scholia for lines 501-5, see Barchiesi (2015) 32.

502. **servare:** infinitive after *nescia*; cf. *nescia vinci | pectora* (12.527-8). The infinitive after adjectives, common in poetry, follows Greek idiom (AG §461). As noted by Behr (2005), the problem of preserving the right conduct toward the conquered was a central issue in contemporary Roman political discourse. **rebus...secundis:** instrumental ablative or ablative of cause.

503-4. **Turno:** dat. of reference. **magno:** "at a great price," abl. of price with *emptum*. **cum optaverit:** is a temporal clause. The subject is Turnus. The future perfect is used because when that fatal hour comes, his wish will be "over and done with." The reference is to 12.940-4, when Aeneas, although half-disposed to spare him, eventually slays Turnus after he catches sight of this *balteus*. **emptum | intactum:** "that Pallas had been bought unspoiled," i.e., with the belt not taken. The accusative subject (*Pallanta*) and perfect infinitive passive (*emptum* sc. *esse*) are governed by *optaverit*. The poet adopts the same commercial metaphor* used by Turnus in his taunts.

504. **ista:** agrees with *spolia* but applies also to *diem*. The demonstrative evokes a dialogical dimension between the narrator and his audience (Barchiesi (2015) 28).

oderit. at socii multo gemitu lacrimisque   505
impositum scuto referunt Pallanta frequentes.
o dolor atque decus magnum rediture parenti,
haec te prima dies bello dedit, haec eadem aufert,
cum tamen ingentis Rutulorum linquis acervos!

510-605: Aeneas' second *aristeia**

Roused by the sad tidings of Pallas' death, Aeneas launches an offensive, pitilessly killing his opponents, and taking prisoners with the intent of sacrificing them at his friend's pyre.

Aeneas' brutality in his second *aristeia** (cf. 308-44 n.) is clearly modeled on that of Achilles in his rage after Patroclus' death (*Il.* 21), with the three Italian warriors whom Aeneas kills after denying their pleas for mercy (Magus (521-36), Tarquitus (550-60), and Liger (595-601)) playing the role of the suppliant Lycaon, the son of Priam, whom Achilles dispatches without mercy (*Il.* 21.34-135). Just like Achilles (and just like Turnus), Aeneas cannot restrain himself in his hour of maddening frenzy.

Aeneas' problematic behavior has received a lot of critical attention. A school of critics views Aeneas' anger as justified by his *pietas* toward Pallas and necessary for Aeneas' final victory (e.g., Harrison *ad* 510-605; Stahl (2016) 132-41). Others call attention to how Aeneas' impious and merciless behavior casts a problematic shadow on Aeneas as a proto-Roman (and proto-Augustan) founder of that

---

505. **oderit:** another temporal clause introduced by *cum* at 504. In this case, the future perfect has the meaning of a simple future (AG §205). **gemitu lacrimisque:** ablative of manner. The rhythm, with an unusual quadrisyllabic word at line-end producing clash of ictus and accent in the fifth foot, is intended to suggest discordant sounds.

506. **scuto:** dative after the compound *impositum*. Pallas is carried back laid on his shield, as befits a warrior, cf. 841. **frequentes:** "all thronging together."

507. **dolor...:** is in apposition (together with *decus magnum*) to the vocative *rediture* (i.e., Pallas). The narrator juxtaposes sorrow and public recognition but seems to subordinate grief to the celebration of public virtue, thus imposing on the narrative a "providential" perspective. See Behr (2005) 206. **rediture:** future active participle: "(you) who are about to come back." As noted, again, by Behr (2005) 207, Pallas' return, however, is granted only as a dead body memorialized in the praise of the poet. **parenti:** for the dative of motion to, see 148 n.

508. **haec...prima dies...dedit:** "this first day gave." The personification* of the crucial day of battle belongs to the epic repertoire (Harrison *ad loc.*). For *dies* (feminine), see 467 n.

509. **cum tamen:** "although in spite of all." The rare use of the indicative with concessive *cum* adds dramatic vividness to the poet's apostrophe*. This line repeats three words from the prophecy at 245 (see note).

Roman Empire which claimed to be known for its *pietas, clementia*, and *iustitia* (e.g., Lyne (1987) 111-12; O'Hara (2007) 98-100; Putnam (2011) 19-48). Particularly troubling in this regard is Aeneas' human sacrifice, an act which seems ethically condemned and viewed as "un-Roman" by the Romans of the first century BCE (cf. Livy 22.57.6 who describes the practice as "wholly alien to the Roman spirit"). For readings that interpret Aeneas' act as an allusion to Octavian's alleged sacrifice of three hundred senators and knights at the capture of Perusia, see Farron (1985) and Farrell (2021) 174.

Quint (2018) 163 suggests that Aeneas, in this passage, also plays the role of the out-of-control Patroclus in his *aristeia** at *Iliad* 16 and is therefore cast simultaneously in the role of the vindictive Achilles and of Patroclus whom Achilles is out to avenge.

> Nec iam fama mali tanti, sed certior auctor   510
> advolat Aeneae tenui discrimine leti
> esse suos, tempus versis succurrere Teucris.
> proxima quaeque metit gladio latumque per agmen
> ardens limitem agit ferro, te, Turne, superbum

510-42. Aeneas takes eight prisoners to sacrifice on Pallas' pyre and avenge his death. He kills Magus who had pleaded in vain for his life and Haemonides, priest of Apollo and Diana.

510. **certior auctor:** "a more reliable author," i.e., a messenger.

511-12. **Aeneae:** dative after *advolat*. See 148 n. **tenui discrimine...| esse suos:** construe as *suos (viros) esse tenui discrimine leti*. The accusative subject and infinitive depend upon the action of reporting in *auctor*. *Tenui discrimine* is an ablative of quality (AG §415). Cf. 3.685 *utrimque viam leti discrimine parvo*. **tempus:** sc. *esse*. For the infinitive *succurrere* after *tempus*, see 441 n. **versis...Teucris:** dative after the compound *succurrere.*.

513. **proxima quaeque:** "everything near," is an idiomatic use of *quisque* with a superlative (AG §313b). The expression highlights Aeneas' lack of discrimination in his desire for revenge. **metit:** "mows"; an agricultural metaphor*. The verb, used only here by Vergil, points back to Catullus 64.353-5, where it is used in a simile* to describe the savagery of Achilles: *namque velut densas praecerpens __messor__ aristas | sole sub ardenti flaventia __demetit__ arva, | Troiugenum infesto prosternet corpora ferro* (Putnam (2011) 18-20). **latumque:** goes with *limitem* and is suggestive of cutting a path through a field. Aeneas drives a line where he slaughters, as a reaper does where he reaps.

514. **ardens:** Aeneas is connected more than once to the imagery of fire in this *aristeia**, see 566-8 n. **ferro:** instrumental ablative (like *gladio* at 513). See 231-2 n. for the meaning of the term. **te:** emphatic apostrophe*. **superbum:** is explained by the ablative of cause *caede nova* "recent killing" (515). As in 445, the adjective seems to reflect Aeneas' perspective.

caede nova quaerens. Pallas, Euander, in ipsis 515
omnia sunt oculis, mensae quas advena primas
tunc adit, dextraeque datae. Sulmone creatos
quattuor hic iuvenes, totidem quos educat Vfens,
viventis rapit, inferias quos immolet umbris
captivoque rogi perfundat sanguine flammas. 520
inde Mago procul infensam contenderat hastam.
ille astu subit, at tremibunda supervolat hasta,

515-16. **Pallas, Evander...mensae:** the broken opening of the sentence and the asyndeton* mark Aeneas' excitement. **in ipsis |...oculis:** "before his very eyes"; the expression suggests a vivid mental vision. **advena:** "he (as a) foreigner," i.e., Aeneas. It is the nominative subject of *adiit* (517). **primas:** with *quas*. Evander was the first to offer hospitality to Aeneas. Several words are adapted from Pallas' prayer to Hercules at 460-1: *per patris hospitium et mensas, quas advena adisti, | te precor.*

517. **dextraeque datae:** "the right hands given," i.e., the pledges. **Sulmone:** abl. of origin after *creatos*. *Sulmo* is a man (cf. 9.412), not the town of that name.

518. **hic:** "at this point." **quos educat Ufens:** "whom Ufens rears" = "who are sons of Ufens"; hence the present. Cf. 8.141 (*Maiam*) *idem Atlas generat.* The antecedent of *quos* is *totidem* "just as many" (i.e., four). Ufens is one of Turnus' most important lieutenants (7.744-9). He will be killed by the Trojan Gyas at 12.460. His name has association with the topography of Italy and the fabric of the *res publica* for *Ufens* is the name of a river in Latium (7.802) and *Ufentina* is the name of one of the thirty-five Roman voting tribes.

519. **inferias...:** construe as *quos immolet inferias umbris. Inferias* is in apposition to *quos.* They were the "sacrifices" offered to the souls of the deceased (*umbris*). **immolet:** subjunctive in a relative clause of purpose (cf. also *perfundat* at 520). *Immolo* (used of sacrificial victims) is also used for Aeneas' killing of Turnus at the end of the poem (12.949). Aeneas' sacrifice of eight prisoners to the shade of Pallas matches the worst excesses of the Homeric Achilles when he avenged Patroclus' death (cf. *Il.* 21.26-33). In Homer, the victims remain anonymous. Vergil, by contrast, mentions the name of the fathers of the prisoners, giving poignant emphasis to the family relationship (Putnam (2011) 23-5). For the description of the sacrifice, see 11.81-2 *vinxerat et post terga manus, quos mitteret umbris | inferias, caeso sparsurus sanguine flammas.* For human sacrifice as "un-Roman" and sacrilegious, see 510-605 n.

520. **captivoque...sanguine:** instrumental ablative. **rogi:** genitive after *flammas.*

521. **Mago:** dative. Magus is one of the three Italian warriors who ask, in vain, for mercy, and who are killed by a merciless Aeneas. For the Homeric model, see 510-605 n. His name, not attested elsewhere, derives from the Greek *magus* "magician" or "charlatan" and is perhaps relevant to his cleverness in ducking under Aeneas' spear (Harrison *ad loc.*).

522. **astu:** adverbial ablative, "craftily." **tremibunda:** "quivering."

et genua amplectens effatur talia supplex:
'per patrios manis et spes surgentis Iuli
te precor, hanc animam serves gnatoque patrique.   525
est domus alta, iacent penitus defossa talenta
caelati argenti, sunt auri pondera facti
infectique mihi. non hic victoria Teucrum
vertitur aut anima una dabit discrimina tanta.'
dixerat. Aeneas contra cui talia reddit: 530
'argenti atque auri memoras quae multa talenta

---

523. **genua amplectens:** "embracing (his, i.e., Aeneas') knees"; the expression in the *Aeneid* is used only here and at 3.607 (*dixerat et genua amplexus genibusque volutans*), when the Greek Achaemenides appeals, successfully, to Aeneas for mercy. **supplex:** Aeneas' refusal to spare the "suppliant" Magus stands in stark contrast with Anchises' teaching of sparing the defeated (6.853 *parcere subiectis*).

524. **per…:** *per* + accusative is introduced by *precor* (525) and is the typical language of prayers, see 45-6 n. **patrios manis:** "the spirit of the dead of your father" (i.e., Anchises). The plural is here used rhetorically by Magus. Aeneas had similarly pleaded (successfully) with the Sybil in the name of his son and father at 6.116 -17 (*gnatique patrisque, | alma, precor, miserere*). The plea here is, however, rejected by Aeneas. **surgentis Iuli:** objective genitive, "(the hopes that center) on growing Iulus"; the metaphor* is that for the growth of plants.

525. **hanc animam serves:** construe as *ut serves hanc animam*. For the omission of *ut* (here after *precor*), cf. 54-6 n. **gnatoque patrique:** dative of reference or advantage. For *gnato*, see 470. Magus' reference to his son and father parallels that to Anchises and Iulus in the preceding line. Aeneas' rejection of the appeal to family *pietas* is particularly troubling for a family-minded Roman culture.

526. **domus alta:** suggests a wealthy home. **talenta:** a *talentum* is a large unit of weight. Cf. 5.112. *argenti aurique talenta* (one of the prizes for the races in *Aeneid* 5).

527-8. **pondera:** the *pondus* is a unit of weight equal to twelve ounces. **facti | infecti:** are the normal terms for "wrought" and "unwrought" metal. **mihi:** dative of possession.

528-9. **hic…:** = *in me*. **Teucrum:** = *Teucrorum*. **vertitur:** the verb characterizes Magus' life as a pivot, "does the victory of the Trojans turn"; the passive is used here in a reflexive sense. For a similar expression, cf. Cic., *Verr.* 1.1.20 *omnia in unius potestate…vertentur*. **una:** is in pointed juxtaposition with *tanta*.

530. **Aeneas:** Aeneas' speeches to Magus (531-4), Tarquitus (557-60), and Liger (599-600) echo sections of Achilles' terrible words to suppliant Lycaon (*Iliad* 21.99, 106, 122-5), before and after he kills him. See 521 n. **contra:** adverbial, "in reply." **cui:** = *ei*, see 384 n.

531-2. **argenti…:** construe as *multa talenta argenti atque auri quae memoras*. **gnatis:** "for your sons," dative of advantage. For this archaic spelling of *natus*, see 470 and 525. Note the word order of the sentence: Aeneas raises Magus' hopes by mentioning the money first only to dash them with *natis parce tuis*. **parce:** governs the accusative *talenta* = "be thrifty of the talents."

gnatis parce tuis. belli commercia Turnus
sustulit ista prior iam tum Pallante perempto.
hoc patris Anchisae manes, hoc sentit Iulus.'
sic fatus galeam laeva tenet atque reflexa   535
cervice orantis capulo tenus applicat ensem.
nec procul Haemonides, Phoebi Triviaeque sacerdos,
infula cui sacra redimibat tempora vitta,
totus conlucens veste atque insignibus albis.

532-3. **belli commercia...ista:** "that trafficking of war." For the expression, cf. Tac., *Hist.* 3.81 *dirempta belli commercia*.

533. **sustulit:** perfect of *tollo*. **prior:** goes adverbially with *sustulit*. **tum:** "at that moment when." **Pallante perempto:** abl. abs.

534. **hoc:** i.e., Aeneas' killing of Magus. **manes:** sc. *sentiunt*. **sentit:** used in its legal meaning "approves" or "judges." **Iulus:** Aeneas' speech ends picking up Magus' *per patrios manis et spes surgentis Iuli* (524), at the opening of Magus' plea. Ironically*, Aeneas' claim that this is the verdict of his father Anchises stands in stark contrast to what was Anchises' essential dictum about sparing suppliants at the climax of his speech in *Aeneid* 6. See 523 n.

535-6. **laeva:** sc. *manu*. **reflexa | cervice:** abl. abs. **capulo tenus:** "to the hilt." For *tenus* (always postpositive) with the abl., see AG §221.26. But cf. 210 where it instead takes the genitive. The two lines bear close resemblance to Pyrrhus' merciless killing of Priam (2.552-3 *implicuitque comam laeva, dextraque coruscum | extulit ac lateri capulo tenus abdidit ensem*). Just as Turnus' behavior when killing Pallas recalled that of Pyrrhus (cf. 443 n., 491 n.), so, too, Aeneas, when killing Magus, assumes the posture of a new Pyrrhus, the degenerate descendant of Achilles who, in his treatment of Priam, proved himself unworthy even of his own father Achilles (2.540-1 *at non ille, satum quo mentiris, Achilles | talis in hoste fuit Priamo*).

537. **procul:** sc. *erat*. **Phoebi Triviaeque:** the two deities (Phoebus = Apollo; Trivia = Diana) are often found together and are often joined in cult. **sacerdos:** is in apposition to Haemonides. Priest-warriors are not uncommon in epic. For the *Aeneid*, see also 9.327 and 11.768.

538. **infula:** subject of *redimibat*. The *infula* was a woolen headband worn by priests and sacrificial victims. Haemonides wears it in its double capacity for he is a priest but will also become Aeneas' sacrificial victim (note the verb *immolat* used of sacrificing victims). In general, for the language of sacrifice in the *Aeneid*, see Bandera (1981). **cui:** i.e., to Haemonides, dative of reference. **sacra...vitta:** may be either ablative of quality, a fillet "with a holy band," or instrumental ablative, "to whom a fillet wreathed the temples with its holy band." **redimibat:** from *redimio*, archaic* form of the imperfect indicative of the fourth conjugation (instead of *redimiebat*).

539. **veste...insignibus:** ablatives of cause. **albis:** the manuscripts report *armis* but Probus' reading *albis*, a reference to the white *insigna* ("badges") worn by Roman priests, should be accepted for it better explains *conlucens* ("shining").

quem congressus agit campo, lapsumque superstans 540
immolat ingentique umbra tegit, arma Serestus
lecta refert umeris tibi, rex Gradive, tropaeum.
    Instaurant acies Volcani stirpe creatus

---

540. **quem congressus:** "having met with him" (i.e., having joined him in battle). *Quem = eum*, see 384 n. *Congredior* with the accusative is found only here in Vergil. **agit campo:** "pursues over the plain." *Campo* is locative ablative, see 165 n. **superstans:** "standing over"; a pose akin to that of Turnus at 10.514 (*superbum*).

541. **immolat:** see 538 n. **ingentique umbra:** instrumental ablative. The shade is that of Aeneas' own mighty body which stands in sharp contrast with the brightness of Haemonides' dress, but the expression is also suggestive of the darkness of death. **Serestus:** close comrade and trusted officer of Aeneas (cf. 1.611, 4.288, 9.171-3). Just as in the *Iliad*, the lesser hero carries the weapons for the greater (cf. *Il.* 12.297).

541-2. **arma... | lecta:** is the object of *Serestus refert*. **umeris:** = *in umeris*. **rex Gradive:** i.e., Mars. He is called by his title *Gradivus* (cf. also 3.35). The meaning of the epithet* is obscure and it may mean either "the Rejoicer" or "the Marcher." **tropaeum:** is in apposition to *arma*. Aeneas is not above carrying away the armor of those he kills as trophies to Mars, even if he has it done by the surrogate Serestus. At the opening of Book 11, Aeneas personally constructs a similar *tropaeum* (7) to the God of War out of the arms of Mezentius (5-8). For Aeneas playing the role of the Iliadic Patroclus who gives Sarpedon's armor to carry back to the Greek ships to his companions at *Iliad* 16.664-5, see Quint (2018) 163.

543-74. Aeneas kills the boastful Anxur, Tarquitus, and a host of others, seeming to wield a hundred arms like the fabled giant Aegaeon. Next, Aeneas hurls Niphaeus from his four-horse car.

The simile* comparing Aeneas to the Titan Aegaeon is problematic for a number of reasons. First, Vergil follows an unusual variant of the myth: while Homer and Hesiod have the Hundred-hander help Zeus fight against the Titans (*Il.* 1.401-6, *Th.* 713-35), Vergil, possibly following the Hellenistic poet Callimachus, has him fighting on the side of the Titans against Jupiter (a fact of which the reader is, however, suddenly and unexpectedly made aware only in the second half of the third line). Second, the simile presents *pius* Aeneas, who in the poem is, in many ways, presented as "Jupiter's man," as the impious and barbaric Titan, an emblem of uncontrolled and irrational wildness who once attempted to overthrow Jupiter's orderly kingdom.

O'Hara (2007) 98-100 rightly notes that the Aegaeon simile embodies the ambiguities of the poem's allusions to Gigantomachy. Cf. also Putnam (2011) 40 who suggests that, through the simile, Aeneas becomes the "savage embodiment of seemingly limitless physical bestiality at work and the personification* of inclemency spurred by the need for vengeance carried to an irrational extreme." For a positive reading of the simile (as exalting Aeneas' strength), see Stahl (2016) 135-6. Cf. also G. Williams (1983) 180 who points out that the simile portrays Aeneas in a negative light because it represents the way the Latins see Aeneas.

543. **Instaurant acies:** either "repair the ranks" or "renew the fight." Subjects are *Caeculus* and *Umbro* (544). **stirpe:** abl. of origin after *creatus Caeculus*.

LIBER DECIMUS

Caeculus et veniens Marsorum montibus Vmbro.
Dardanides contra furit. Anxuris ense sinistram   545
et totum clipei terrae deiecerat orbem
(dixerat ille aliquid magnum vimque adfore verbo
crediderat, caeloque animum fortasse ferebat
canitiemque sibi et longos promiserat annos):
Tarquitus exsultans contra fulgentibus armis,   550

---

544. **Caeculus:** founder of Praeneste, he is introduced in the catalogue* of Turnus' allies at 7.678-90. Vergil makes Caeculus the son of Vulcan (*Volcani*), the god of fire, a possible rationalization of an old legend (reported by Servius at *Aen.* 7.678) in which Caeculus' mother was made pregnant by a spark from the fire. **montibus:** see 473 n. **Vmbro:** in the catalogue* of Turnus' allies, he is presented as an Italian warrior and priest from Marruvium, skilled in the Marsian art of snake charming (7.750-60).

545. **Dardanides:** in the moment he is about to kill an Italian opponent, the patronymic* (used here for the first time of Aeneas) reminds the reader of Aeneas' Italian ancestry. Dardanus (see 92 n.) was supposedly born in Corythus, modern Cortona, in Etruria (cf. *Aen.* 3.165-71). The patronymic will be used, once more, of Aeneas at 12.775, in his final duel with Turnus (see Tarrant *ad loc.*). **contra:** adverb "on the other side." **furit:** describes madness and loss of control. Aeneas is similarly described at 802. Cf. also 604 *furens*. On *furor*, see 63 n. **Anxuris... sinistram:** "the left arm of Anxur," not "hand," for it carries the shield with it. Cf. 341. *Sinistram* is the object of *deiecerat* (together with *totum orbem*). The name Anxur seems to be connected to the town of Anxur (modern Terracina). **ense:** instrumental ablative.

546. **totum clipei...orbem:** lit. "all the circle of the shield." **terrae:** "to the ground." For the dative of motion to, see 148 n. Harrison *ad loc.* observes the pointed juxtaposition between *terrae* and *caelo* (548). Anxur's ambitions for heaven fall together with his shield to earth. All manuscripts read *ferro* for *terrae*, but *ense* (545) and *ferro* cannot stand in the same sentence as they mean the same thing. Jasper's emendation *terrae* should be accepted. For a similar expression, see 555.

547-8. **ille:** i.e., Anxur. **aliquid magnum:** "something great" (i.e., boastful). **vimque adfore verbo:** "that there would be force (to help) his talk"; the accusative subject and (future) infinitive (of *adsum*) are governed by *crediderat*. **verbo:** dative after *adsum*. Anxur had wrongly believed that his strength would equal his words.

548. **caeloque...:** lit. "it may well be he was raising his spirit to the sky," i.e., perhaps he was carried away by a soaring ambition. The expression suggests arrogant hope for heroic apotheosis (Harrison *ad loc.*). For the dative *caelo*, cf. 148 n. *Fortasse* seems sarcastic.

549. **canitiemque...:** a poetic metonymy* for "old age"; but only gods can promise a long life.

550-2. **Tarquitus...obtulit:** after the parenthesis at 547-9, these words are introduced as a separate statement, though they should strictly form a clause subordinate to *Anxuris... deiecerat*. The connection of thought is "he had just lopped off Anxur's arm when Tarquitus advanced." The name Tarquitus recalls that of the two Tarquin kings of Rome and his characterization as boastful and arrogant may reflect Roman views on that dynasty (see

silvicolae Fauno Dryope quem nympha crearat,
obvius ardenti sese obtulit. ille reducta
loricam clipeique ingens onus impedit hasta,
tum caput orantis nequiquam et multa parantis
dicere deturbat terrae, truncumque tepentem   555
provolvens super haec inimico pectore fatur:
'istic nunc, metuende, iace. non te optima mater
condet humi patrioque onerabit membra sepulcro:

152-3 n). **contra:** "on the other side," is adverbial and qualifies *exsultans*. **fulgentibus armis:** should possibly be taken as an ablative of quality.

551. **silvicolae…:** construe as *quem nympha Dryope crearat* (= *creaverat*) *silvicolae Fauno. Fauno* is a dative of reference. Faunus is either Faunus himself, father of Latinus (*Aen*. 7.47), or just simply one of the Fauni who lived in Latium (*Aen*. 8.314-15, Evander's speech). Dryope is Greek nominative. She is a wood-nymph.

552-3. **ardenti:** i.e., Aeneas, dative after the compound *obtulit*; picks up *ardens* at 514 (see note). **sese:** = *se*. **ille…:** i.e., Aeneas. **reducta |…hasta:** "with the spear drawn back," abl. abs. Understand that first Aeneas draws back his spear and then throws it. The latter action is not described but is implied. **loricam…impedit:** lit. "entangles the cuirass and the mighty burden of the shield." *Impedio* means "to restrict the movement by entangling" and describes how Aeneas hampers the action of Tarquitus who is thus unable to defend himself and is easily slain.

554. **caput:** object of *deturbat*. **orantis…parantis:** genitives after *caput*. **nequiquam:** cf. Magus who, too, had pleaded in vain for his life (*orantis*, 536). See 523 for Aeneas' behavior toward suppliants in this *aristeia**. **multa:** sc. *verba*, object of *dicere*.

555. **deturbat:** is a vivid word, used at 5.175 of "pitching a man overboard," and at 6.412 of "bustling" the ghosts out of Charon's boat, but here perhaps Vergil connects it mentally not so much with the noun *turba* ("crowd") as with *turbo* ("whirlwind"), meaning either "send spinning" or possibly "with a whirling stroke." **terrae:** see 148 n. Note the heavy alliteration* of *d* and *t* in this gruesome line. **truncumque tepentem:** Putnam (2011) 37-8 suggests that Aeneas' beheading of Tarquitus once more (see 535-6 n.), brings us back to the last night of Troy when Pyrrhus kills (and beheads) the suppliant Priam (2.557-8 *iacet ingens litore truncus | avulsumque umeris caput et sine nomine corpus*). Note also the grim humor of the image: Tarquitus, who was the son of the forest-god Faunus and Dryope ("Oak-face"), has now become a "trunk" himself (Ahl and Fantham *ad loc*.).

556. **super:** adverbial, "over it," i.e., the trunk. Cf. 540 *superstans* (of Aeneas, again, looming over his victim). **inimico pectore:** ablative of manner. This personification* is already found in Greek poetry.

557. **metuende:** vocative gerundive; the apostrophe* is sarcastic. **optima:** the superlative is conventionally used of virtuous women, but here is sarcastic.

558. **humi:** locative. **patrioque…sepulcro:** "with the sepulcher of your fathers," i.e., the bones of the dead will not be weighed down by the ancestral tomb. Another example of *dicolon abundans** as this clause repeats, with different words, *non mater condet humi*, see 9-10 n.

alitibus linquere feris, aut gurgite mersum
unda feret piscesque impasti vulnera lambent.'   560
protinus Antaeum et Lucam, prima agmina Turni,
persequitur, fortemque Numam fulvumque Camertem,
magnanimo Volcente satum, ditissimus agri
qui fuit Ausonidum et tacitis regnavit Amyclis.
Aegaeon qualis, centum cui bracchia dicunt   565
centenasque manus, quinquaginta oribus ignem
pectoribusque arsisse, Iovis cum fulmina contra
tot paribus streperet clipeis, tot stringeret ensis:

---

559. **alitibus...feris**: "for the wild birds." **linquere**: second person of the fut. passive indicative. **gurgite**: locative ablative. **mersum**: i.e., Tarquitus, object of *unda feret*. Aeneas' sarcastic speech reworks that of Achilles to the dead Lycaon (*Il*. 21.122-5). Vergil's addition of prideful scorn (*metuende*) makes it even more vicious, while the reference to Tarquitus' mother and father (*patrio sepulcro*) make it more emotionally charged (Putnam (2011) 37).

560. **impasti**: "hungry."

561. **prima agmina**: "the front rank," is in apposition to *Antaeum* and *Lucam*.

562. **Numam**: another very Italian name. Numa was the name of the second king of Rome.

563-4. **magnanimo Volcente**: ablative of origin, 517 n. **satum**: is in apposition to *Camertem*. **ditissimus agri |...Ausonidum**: construe as *qui fuit Ausonidum* (partitive genitive; for *Ausonius* = Italian, see 267-8 n.) *ditissimus agri* (genitive of respect). Cf. 7.536-7 *iustissimus unus | qui fuit Ausoniisque olim ditissimus arvis*. **tacitis...Amyclis**: locative ablative (from *Amyclae, -ārum*). Amyclae is a town in Latium. Three explanations are given by ancient commentators for *tacitis*: (1) since the citizens had been often falsely alarmed by reports of invasion, a law was passed that no one should report "the arrival of an enemy," and that, as a consequence of this "silence," on the occasion of an actual invasion, the town was captured; (2) because desolate; (3) the inhabitants were followers of Pythagoras, who enjoined silence.

565-6. **Aegaeon**: note the emphatic position before *qualis* which introduces the simile*. Aegaeon is another name of the hundred-armed Briareus. The giant appears also in Vergil's Underworld (6.287) where he is one of the many monsters Vergil places before the entrance court leading to the Underworld. For the simile and its interpretation, see 543-74 n. **centum...manus**: construe as *cui* (dative of possession) *dicunt centum bracchia centenasque manus* (sc. *fuisse*). *Bracchia* and *manus* and the understood *fuisse* are the accusative subjects and infinitive dependent on *dicunt*. **centum...centenasque**: see 329 n. **dicunt**: see 189 n.

566-8. **quinquaginta...ignem |...arsisse**: the accusative subject and (perfect) infinitive are still governed by *dicunt*. **oribus...| pectoribusque**: are locative abl. The breathing forth of fire from lungs is a characteristic of malevolent monsters, but here the verb draws also upon *ardens* (514) and *ardenti* (552), said of Aeneas. In Homer, Aegaeon is portrayed as a figure of such a might as to scare the Olympian gods (*Il*.1.401-6). Hesiod describes him as a monster with one hundred arms and fifty heads (*Th*. 147-53; 713-15). Vergil adds one hundred hands to Hesiod's

sic toto Aeneas desaevit in aequore victor
ut semel intepuit mucro. quin ecce Niphaei   570
quadriiugis in equos adversaque pectora tendit.
atque illi longe gradientem et dira frementem
ut videre, metu versi retroque ruentes
effunduntque ducem rapiuntque ad litora currus.
   Interea biiugis infert se Lucagus albis   575

---

one hundred arms, and the fifty heads gain specificity by flashing fire (Putnam (2011) 39). For Aeneas as Aegaeon, see 543-74 n. **cum...streperet:** "when he made a clashing," i.e., he tried to match the noise of Jupiter's thunderbolt by clashing his shields. **contra:** is the preposition (postponed) and governs *fulmina*. **tot paribus...clipeis:** instrumental ablative, "with so many (i.e., fifty, one for each left arm) shields all alike (*paribus*)." **tot...ensis:** "so many (i.e., fifty, one for each right arm) swords." Aegaeon holds fifty shields and fifty swords in his one hundred arms. **stringeret:** = (*cum*) *stringeret*.

570. **ut semel:** "when once." **intepuit:** "grew warm (with blood)." This is the first use of the verb *intepesco* in Latin. The warmth of Aeneas' sword is reminiscent of Tarquitus' *truncum tepentem* (555), still warm with blood (Putnam (2011) 39). With *desaevit* of the previous line, the expression conveys Aeneas' bloodlust. **mucro:** "sword-point"; a synecdoche* for sword. **quin:** see 23-4 n. **ecce:** see 132-3 n. **Niphaei:** the name *Nyphaeus* means "Snowy."

571. **quadriiugis in equos:** "against the horses (yoked) in a team of four." *Quadriiugis* is a third declension accusative plural (from *quadriiugis, -e*). **pectora:** i.e., of the horses. **tendit:** Aeneas is the subject.

572. **atque illi:** "and they (i.e., the horses)," is the subject of *ut videre* (= viderunt) at 573. For *atque*, see 219 n. **gradientem...frementem:** supply *eum* (i.e., Aeneas). They are the direct objects of *ut videre*. The assonance* is intended to suggest terror. Putnam (2011) 41 suggests a wordplay between *gradientem* and *Mars Gradivus*, who was so called, according to Festus, "for striding (*gradiendo*) to and fro from battle." Aeneas, thus, would be nothing less than the War God whose approach terrifies the horses of Niphaeus. For the etymology* of *Gradivus*, see also 541-2 n. **dira:** the neuter plural accusative is a cognate accusative with *frementem* (AG §390b). Translate as an adverb "dreadfully." Cf. 12.398 *acerba fremens*.

573. **metu:** ablative of cause. **versi:** the perfect passive participle is reflexive in meaning. **retroque:** adv. "backward."

574. **rapiuntque:** the verb emphasizes the speed of the fleeing horses.

575-605. *Aeneas slays Lucagus and Liger, who attack him in a chariot drawn by white steeds, and eventually forces his way to the camp, from which Ascanius comes to meet him.*

575. **biiugis...albis:** instrumental ablative. For *biiugus* = "chariot," see 399 n. **Lucagus:** the name appears only here and may mean "White Chief" in Greek, and it is possibly a pun on *albis* (Harrison *ad loc.*).

in medios fraterque Liger; sed frater habenis
flectit equos, strictum rotat acer Lucagus ensem.
haud tulit Aeneas tanto fervore furentis:
inruit adversaque ingens apparuit hasta.
cui Liger: 580
'non Diomedis equos nec currum cernis Achillis
aut Phrygiae campos: nunc belli finis et aevi
his dabitur terris.' vesano talia late
dicta volant Ligeri. sed non et Troius heros
dicta parat contra, iaculum nam torquet in hostis. 585

---

576. **in medios:** sc. *viros*, vel sim. **fraterque...sed frater:** of the two brothers, one drives the chariot (Liger), while the other (Lucagus) does the fighting. For other sets of brothers, see 124 n. Note the repetition of the word *frater* picked up at the end of the episode (600 *fratrem ne desere frater*) and, hence, the emphasis on the relationship between Liger and Lucagus. The name Liger is Latin for the river Loire. **habenis:** instrumental ablative.

577. **rotat:** "whirls," showing off his dexterity with the sword.

578. **tanto fervore:** abl. of manner, qualifies the accusative *furentis* (i.e., Liger and Lucagus).

579. **adversaque...hasta:** is an ablative loosely connected with *ingens apparuit* "(Aeneas) appeared mighty (i.e., to them) with (his) hostile spear."

580. **cui Liger:** supply *dixit* vel sim., cf. 2.547 *cui Pyrrhus*. See also 17 n.

581. **Diomedis equos...:** in the *Iliad*, Aeneas was rescued from Diomedes by Aphrodite (5.311-17) and from Achilles by Poseidon (20.290-339). Liger, who seems to have been a keen "reader" of the *Iliad*, tells Aeneas that he will find no such means of escape now. For a similar taunt, cf. Turnus at 9.154-5 and Numanus Remulus at 9.602. **Achillis:** this form of the genitive (instead of the more regular *Achilli*) appears to be a Vergilian innovation (Austin *ad* 2.275).

582. **Phrygiae campos:** i.e., the plains of Troy. Phrygia was actually a region east of the Troad (where Troy was), but in Vergil Phrygia and the Phrygians are often one and the same with Troy and the Trojans, cf. 1.468; 2.68, etc. **aevi:** i.e., (the end) of your life. *Aevum* meaning "life" is poetic.

583-4. **vesano:** is in emphatic initial position. The adjective agrees with *Ligeri* (the dative is that of reference and is almost equal to a genitive). For the expression *talia dicta volant*, cf. 11.381 (*verba*) *quae tuto tibi magna volant*.

584-5. **sed non...contra:** lit. "but not also (*et*) the Trojan hero prepares words in reply." The striking repetition of *dicta* underscores that Aeneas will not reply with words to Liger's taunts, but rather will resort to action as befits a hero. **Troius heros:** a fitting label, since Aeneas has just been reminded of events of his Trojan past. However, throughout his *aristeia**, Aeneas has played the role of a Greek in this new Trojan War, having taken on the part of Achilles (see 510-605 n.). In this new role, he proves to be more than a match for Liger. **nam:** see 400-1 n.

Lucagus ut pronus pendens in verbera telo
admonuit biiugos, proiecto dum pede laevo
aptat se pugnae, subit oras hasta per imas
fulgentis clipei, tum laevum perforat inguen:
excussus curru moribundus volvitur arvis.   590
quem pius Aeneas dictis adfatur amaris:
'Lucage, nulla tuos currus fuga segnis equorum
prodidit aut vanae vertere ex hostibus umbrae:
ipse rotis saliens iuga deseris.' haec ita fatus
arripuit biiugos; frater tendebat inertis   595
infelix palmas curru delapsus eodem:

586-8. **Lucagus...pronus:** construe as *ut* ("just as") *Lucagus pronus*. **pendens in verbera:** "bending forward for the lash" i.e., to apply the lash. Lucagus is leaning forward to whip his horses. *In* expresses purpose, see 454-6 n. **telo:** instrumental abl. Here, the flat of Lucagus' sword. **biiugos:** see 399 n. **proiecto...pede laevo:** ablative absolute, "with his left foot thrust forward." **pugnae:** dative of purpose "for the battle." **subit:** "rose"; the subject is *hasta*. The compound (*sub + eo*) emphasizes that the javelin is struck from a lower position as Aeneas is on foot. Lucagus, though the combatant (577), in his eagerness leans forward to goad on the horses himself, and then, advancing his left foot to get a firm stand, puts himself in position for the moment when he will attack Aeneas, but meantime the spear of Aeneas suddenly (note the position of *subit*) strikes him from below. **oras...per imas:** a poetic plural. **laevum... inguen:** the spear hits the inside of Lucagus' leg, which was thrust forward.

590. **moribundus:** "dying." **volvitur:** see 403 n. **arvis:** see 165 n. Note the alliteration* of *u* and *r* in the line.

591. **quem:** = *eum*, see 384 n. **pius:** although the epithet* seems somewhat ironic* applied here to a merciless Aeneas, its presence calls attention to the conflicting and irreconcilable meanings of *pietas*. Aeneas may indeed show *pietas* to Pallas by ruthlessly avenging his death, but, by so doing, he rejects the all-important appeal to family *pietas* of his victims. **dictis...amaris:** "with bitter words." Aeneas' grim battlefield humor brings us back once more to *Iliad* 16 (745-50) and to Patroclus who, after launching a stone that kills Kebriones, Hector's charioteer, compares him to an acrobat and a diver.

592-3. **nulla...:** construe as *nulla fuga segnis equorum prodidit tuos currus*. The accusative plural *tuos currus* is poetic. The scornful allusion is to the events at 574 where instead Niphaeus had been abandoned by his horses. **vanae...umbrae:** "empty shadows," again a sarcastic reference to the events narrated at 572-3 where the horses of Niphaeus had been scared by the sight of Aeneas advancing against them. **vertere:** = *verterunt*. Supply *eos* (i.e., the horses).

594. **rotis...:** "from the chariot." Both *rotis* and *iuga* are used synecdochically* for chariot.

595-6. **arripuit:** "he laid hold of." **biiugos:** see 399 n. **frater:** i.e., Liger. **tendebat inertis |... palmas:** the gesture of a suppliant. **infelix:** see 324-5 n. **curru...eodem:** "from the same car" from which his brother Lucagus had just been "hurled" (590 *excussus*).

'per te, per qui te talem genuere parentes,
vir Troiane, sine hanc animam et miserere precantis.'
pluribus oranti Aeneas: 'haud talia dudum
dicta dabas. morere et fratrem ne desere frater.' 600
tum latebras animae pectus mucrone recludit.
talia per campos edebat funera ductor
Dardanius torrentis aquae vel turbinis atri
more furens. tandem erumpunt et castra relinquunt
Ascanius puer et nequiquam obsessa iuventus. 605

606-88: The phantom of Aeneas

Meanwhile in heaven, Juno obtains permission from Jupiter to save Turnus from immediate death (606-32). She fashions a phantom figure of Aeneas and, when Turnus follows it on a ship, cuts the cable and sets the vessel loose, bringing ship and protégé safely to Ardea (633-64). While carried back to his hometown, Turnus, humiliated and once again deceived by the gods, delivers a speech bitterly complaining about his enforced absence from the battlefield (665-88).

---

597. **per...parentes:** construe as *per parentes qui te talem genuere* (= *genuerunt*). For a similar appeal, see 524 n. Liger is the third suppliant who pleads his case in vain during Aeneas' *aristeia**. See 521 n.

598. **sine hanc animam:** "spare this life"; a rare construction of *sino* with the accusative (cf. 9.620). **miserere:** second person present imperative of *misereor*. **precantis:** genitive after *misereor* (AG §354a).

599. **pluribus:** sc. *verbis*, "with more words"; instrumental ablative. **Aeneas:** sc. *dixit*, vel sim. The double ellipsis* underscores excitement. **dudum:** "just now." The expression is colloquial.

600. **morere:** 598 n. The imperative "die" clearly echoes Achilles' similar injunction to Lycaon (*Il.* 21.106 *thane*). See also 743-4 n. (Mezentius to Orodes). **fratrem...frater:** the cruel reply shows Aeneas' twisted sense of family *pietas*: the brother needs to die so as not to leave his dead brother alone. **ne desere:** see 11 n. **frater:** is in apposition to an understood *tu*.

601. **latebras animae:** "the hiding place of the soul"; is in apposition to *pectus*. **mucrone:** instrumental ablative; for the term, see 570 n.

603. **Dardanius:** see 545 n. **torrentis...atri:** the genitives are dependent on the ablative *more* ("in the manner of"). **atri:** *ater* means "dark and destructive"; see 77. For the expression, cf. *volat atri turbinis instar* (12.923), said of Aeneas' spear, about to wound Turnus at the end of the book. Putnam (2011) 162 n. 151 suggests that this verbal parallel forms one of several links between the moment in Book 10 where Aeneas goes wild and the poem's conclusion.

604. **furens:** this key word for madness and loss of control marks the end of Aeneas' *aristeia**. Cf. 545 n. **erumpunt:** see 890-1 n.

The structural parallel for the episode is Apollo's rescue of Hector from Achilles at *Il.* 20.443-54 which had, likewise, allowed for the postponement of the final encounter between the two major heroes of the poem, Achilles and Hector. Juno's fashioning of a phantom of Aeneas and her removal of Turnus from the battlefield, however, clearly recall the episode of *Iliad* 5 when Apollo similarly saves Aeneas from Diomedes by whisking him off the field and leaving a replica of Aeneas' body on the field to distract Diomedes (444-53). Thus, in this scene, Aeneas, once again, intertextually reenacts the Trojan past and successfully overcomes it by playing the role of a victorious Greek (Achilles) rather than that of the defeated Trojan (Hector). Turnus, by contrast, is not only cast in the role of Hector but also plays the role of the Homeric Aeneas, who needs to be saved by a protecting god.

For analysis of the episode in relation to its Homeric models, see Gransden (1984) 145-51, Quint (1993) 72-4, (2018) 165-6. Feeney (1999) 184-5 gives a metapoetic reading of the passage, suggesting that Juno's fashioning of a "copy" that imitates Aeneas parallels the poet's fashioning of a "copy" that imitates Homer, for it is from Homer that Vergil has taken the model of the phantom of Aeneas. Feeney further notes that, in this way, Vergil calls attention to the fundamentally illusory nature of poetry's mimetic art (something insubstantial that deludes us into thinking it real) and to the terrible risks of artistic failure.

> Iunonem interea compellat Iuppiter ultro:
> 'o germana mihi atque eadem gratissima coniunx
> ut rebare, Venus (nec te sententia fallit)
> Troianas sustentat opes, non vivida bello

606-32. Jupiter mockingly calls Juno's attention to the success of the Trojans. As she humbly laments that she now lacks power over his heart to win some pity for Turnus, he allows her to save Turnus from immediate death.

606. **interea**: see 1 n. **ultro**: "on his own accord," i.e., unaddressed.

607. **o germana…**: Juno and Jupiter were both children of Saturn, cf. 1.46-7 *ast ego, quae divum incedo regina, Iovisque | et soror et coniunx*, where Juno is speaking. **mihi**: dative after *gratissima* (AG §384). **eadem**: "at the same time" (OLD s.v. *idem, eadem, idem* 8). **gratissima coniunx**: Jupiter's tone here and in the entire speech is mockingly ironic*, while Juno's reply is highly devious.

608. **ut rebare**: = ut *rebaris* (imperfect indicative from *reor*), "as you thought."

609-10. **vivida bello**: *vivida* agrees with *dextra* in the following line. *Bello* is an abl. of specification after *vivida*. For a similar expression, cf. 5.754 *bello vivida virtus*. **viris**: see 583-4 n. Jupiter is being sarcastic for the opposite is true (i.e., the Trojans owe their success to their own prowess, not to Venus' help). **pericli**: a syncopated* form (for *periculi*) and an objective genitive. Hejduk (2009) 302-4 notes that Jupiter's approval—his only openly stated approval of any human action—comes after Aeneas' most cruel rampage.

dextra viris animusque ferox patiensque pericli.' 610
cui Iuno summissa: 'quid, o pulcherrime coniunx,
sollicitas aegram et tua tristia dicta timentem?
si mihi, quae quondam fuerat quamque esse decebat,
vis in amore foret, non hoc mihi namque negares,
omnipotens, quin et pugnae subducere Turnum 615
et Dauno possem incolumem servare parenti.
nunc pereat Teucrisque pio det sanguine poenas.
ille tamen nostra deducit origine nomen

---

611. **cui:** = *ei*, see 384 n. **summissa:** "submissive"; sc. *dixit*, vel sim. **quid:** is used adverbially "why?" **pulcherrime coniunx:** balances the half-mocking *gratissima coniunx* above.

612. **sollicitas:** sc. *me* "taunt" or "torment." The latter better fits Juno's self-portrayal as helpless victim (cf. *aegram* and *timentem*). **tua tristia dicta:** object of *timentem*.

613. **mihi:** dative of possession after *vis in amore foret* (614). **quae:** anticipates *vis* (*in amore*) of the following line. **fuerat:** the pluperfect expresses the state of affairs before things changed. **quamque esse:** acc. subject and infinitive after *decebat*. The antecedent of *quamque* is still *vis* (*in amore*).

614. **foret:** = *esset*; imperfect subjunctive in the protasis of a contrary-to-fact condition. **namque:** is emphatic, "indeed." For *namque* postponed, cf. 400-1 n.

615-16. **omnipotens:** the epithet* is pointed as it implies that Jupiter can fulfill her request. **quin...possem:** "that I could..."; the *quin* clause is explanatory of *hoc*, the object of *negares*. *Quin* is common after verbs of "hindering" (here *negares*), see AG §558. **pugnae:** see 50 n. During the assembly of the gods (81-2), Juno had accused Venus of interfering in human affairs and rescuing her son from Diomedes, as described in *Iliad* 5 (312-18). Now, Juno turns around and does the same for Turnus. Her attitude is especially hypocritical, if we also recall her conversation with Zeus at *Iliad* 16, when she convinced him not to rescue Sarpedon (440-9) and her speech to Poseidon, when she argued against the saving of Aeneas (*Il.* 20.310-17).

616. **Dauno...parenti:** dative of advantage. The mention of Turnus' father adds pathos to Juno's plea. Turnus' father was from Ardea and was a hero for whom Vulcan had once fashioned a sword dipped in the Styx (12.90-1). **incolumem:** read *eum incolumem*, i.e., Turnus.

617. **nunc:** "as it is"; i.e., since I no longer possess your love and, hence, everything is indifferent to me. Juno hides her real intentions (i.e., to save Turnus) by proposing its opposite. **pereat...det:** jussive subjunctives. The understood subject is Turnus. **pio...sanguine:** instrumental ablative. In Juno's words Turnus is as *pius* as *Aeneas* and thus deserves as much regard as he does.

618. **ille:** i.e., Turnus. **nostra...origine:** ablative of origin, "from our (i.e., divine) stock." **nomen:** "lineage."

Pilumnusque illi quartus pater, et tua larga
saepe manu multisque oneravit limina donis.'   620
cui rex aetherii breviter sic fatur Olympi:
'si mora praesentis leti tempusque caduco
oratur iuveni meque hoc ita ponere sentis,
tolle fuga Turnum atque instantibus eripe fatis:
hactenus indulsisse vacat. sin altior istis   625
sub precibus venia ulla latet totumque moveri
mutarive putas bellum, spes pascis inanis.'
et Iuno adlacrimans: 'quid si, quae voce gravaris,
mente dares atque haec Turno rata vita maneret?

619-20. **Pilumnusque:** sc. *est*; for Pilumnus, see 76 n. **illi:** i.e., Turnus, dative of possession. Note how the polyptoton* *ille* (618) and *illi* (619) puts the focus on Turnus. **tua…limina:** "your thresholds" (i.e., of Jupiter's temples). **larga |…manu:** "with generous hand," instrumental ablative (together with *multisque donis*). Cf. also *saepe*, and *oneravit*, all stressing Turnus' generosity and *pietas* toward the gods. **oneravit:** subject is Turnus.

621. **cui:** see 384. **breviter:** see 16-17 n.

622-3. **praesentis leti:** "from (lit. "of") imminent death." **tempusque:** "respite." **caduco…iuveni:** dative of advantage, "for the doomed (lit. "about to fall") youth." For the *dicolon abundans**, see 9-10 n.

623. **meque hoc ita ponere:** the subject accusative (*me*) and infinitive (*ponere*) are governed by *sentis* ("and you realize"). **hoc:** i.e., a respite. **ita:** "on these terms," i.e., under the strict condition that it is only a respite. Jupiter's language is formal and legalistic: *ponere* ("to lay down rules and conditions," *OLD* s.v. 17), *ita* (a limiting formula of the law, "on these terms"), *hactenus* at 625 (common of legal limitation).

624. **instantibus…fatis:** ablative of separation. **eripe:** sc. *eum* (i.e., Turnus).

625-6. **indulsisse:** see 14 n. **vacat** is used impersonally, "there is room"; i.e., fate "admits of" being delayed but not reversed. **altior…venia ulla:** "any other far-reaching favor."

626-7. **moveri | mutarive:** "to be thrown into confusion or to be changed." The (passive) infinitives and the accusative subject (*totum bellum*) are governed by *putas*. **spes pascis inanis:** the image modifies the traditional "feeding on empty hope" to that of "feeding empty hopes" (Harrison *ad loc.*).

628-9. **Iuno:** sc. *dixit*. **quid si…dares:** "what if you were to grant." Juno puts what is really a fresh appeal in the shape of a supposition which presents itself to Juno's mind only to be dismissed as impossible (note the imperfect subjunctive). **quae:** the antecedent is an understood nominative neuter plural *ea*. **gravaris:** "refuse." This meaning of the verb is colloquial and found only here in Vergil. **Turno:** dative of reference. **rata:** "fixed," i.e., if Turnus could remain alive. These lines are difficult to interpret. Juno presents the common contrasts between speech and thought and is perhaps pointing to the fact that the fate here spoken (by Jupiter) does not necessarily express the nature of his thoughts.

nunc manet insontem gravis exitus, aut ego veri 630
vana feror. quod ut o potius formidine falsa
ludar, et in melius tua, qui potes, orsa reflectas!'
 Haec ubi dicta dedit, caelo se protinus alto
misit agens hiemem nimbo succincta per auras,
Iliacamque aciem et Laurentia castra petivit. 635
tum dea nube cava tenuem sine viribus umbram
in faciem Aeneae (visu mirabile monstrum)
Dardaniis ornat telis, clipeumque iubasque

630. **manet:** with the acc. = "awaits." The indicative picks up and answers the vain hope of *maneret* (629). **insontem:** "an innocent," i.e., Turnus. The term is rhetorically powerful as it describes Turnus as an innocent victim of the war but is somewhat exaggerated as it comes after Turnus' treatment of Pallas. **veri:** for the genitive after *vana* ("empty of"), cf. 154 n.

631-2. **feror:** is used of a vague, drifting movement; cf. 4.110 *sed fatis incerta feror*. **quod ut o potius...| ludar:** "but how I would rather be deluded." *Quod* is an accusative of respect "with regard to which" (= "but") and is often used as a loose connective to continue an argument (AG §397a). **ut:** the usage of *ut* to introduce an optative subjunctive (*ludar* and *reflectas*), here intensified by *o*, is archaic* and poetic (AG §442a). **in melius...reflectas:** "you would turn back to the better"; the phrase seems to be pointedly reminiscent of Jupiter's prophecy about Juno at 1.281 *consilia in melius referet*. For Jupiter's power to change the end of the story as mirroring that of the poet, see Feeney (1999) 188. **qui potes:** is an expression of prayer-language. **orsa:** "counsels," lit. a line of action just begun.

633-52. Juno descends to earth and fashions a phantom figure of Aeneas, decking it out with Trojan weapons, a wonder marvelous to behold. The phantom flies before Turnus and challenges him, eventually taking refuge on one of the Etruscan ships.

633-4. **caelo...alto:** see 143-4 n. **se...| misit:** Juno shows her real concern for Turnus by acting in person and not through an agent. **agens hiemem:** "driving a storm." Juno's stormy descent suggests her power over the weather (Harrison *ad loc.*). **nimbo succincta:** "girded in cloud." The gods in Homer and Vergil are typically shrouded in clouds when they come among men.

635. **Iliacam:** i.e., Trojan, see 61-2 n. **Laurentia castra:** see 87 n. Note the symmetrical placing of the opposing proper names.

636. **nube cava:** abl. of material after *tenuem umbram*. Cf. 6.293 *volitare cava sub imagine formae*, of the ghosts of the dead.

637. **in faciem Aeneae:** *in* + accusative ordinarily represents motion. Here it gives the picture of the transformation as it happens. **visu mirabile:** "remarkable to behold." This kind of phrase (with the supine *visu*) often marks a supernatural event in Vergil. Cf. 7.78 *id vero horrendum ac visu mirabile ferri*.

638. **Dardaniis...telis:** for Dardanus, see 92 n. **iubasque:** are helmet-crests of horsehair.

> divini adsimulat capitis, dat inania verba,
> dat sine mente sonum gressusque effingit euntis: 640
> morte obita qualis fama est volitare figuras
> aut quae sopitos deludunt somnia sensus.
> at primas laeta ante acies exsultat imago
> inritatque virum telis et voce lacessit.
> instat cui Turnus stridentemque eminus hastam   645
> conicit, illa dato vertit vestigia tergo.
> tum vero Aenean aversum ut cedere Turnus
> credidit atque animo spem turbidus hausit inanem:

---

639. **divini...capitis:** i. e. Aeneas. *Caput* is used by synecdoche* for the whole body, which is divine since Aeneas has divine parentage. **adsimulat:** "counterfeits." **inania verba:** the "words" are "empty" because they are mindless utterances. For the expression, cf. Lucret., *DRN* 4.995 *inania cervorum simulacra*. See also *sine mente sonum* below.

640. **euntis:** present participle of *eo*; gen. singular dependent on *gressus*.

641. **morte obita:** the ablative absolute should be read as part of the clause beginning with *qualis*. **qualis fama est...figuras:** "just as it is rumored the shades." *Qualis* is acc. plural agreeing with *figuras*; its antecedent (i.e., *talis*) is suppressed as often in the case of correlatives. *Fama est* governs the accusative subject (*figuras*) and the infinitive (*volitare*). For the expression, see 189 n.

642. **somnia:** has been attracted to the relative clause. The correlatives are understood from the *qualis* above. The full construction would be *talis figura est* (i.e., of Aeneas) *qualia sunt somnia quae...* The wording of the simile* borrows from Lucretius (*morte obita* 1.135; *volitare figura* 2.380) and so does its content, conjoining two elements found often paired in Lucretius, the apparent but untrue perception of ghosts and the deceptive nature of dreams. See Harrison *ad loc*.

644. **inritatque...telis:** "provokes the man with darts," i.e., by brandishing, not by throwing, darts. **virum:** i.e., Turnus. **lacessit:** "harasses."

645. **cui:** i.e., Aeneas' phantom. Dative after the compound verb *insto*. **Turnus:** note the balanced alternation of the names of the two heroes, *Turnus* (645), *Aenean* (647), *Turnus* (647), *Aenea* (649) (Harrison *ad loc.*).

646. **illa:** i.e., the phantom. **dato...tergo:** abl. abs. **vestigia:** "feet."

647. **Aenean aversum...cedere:** the accusative subject and infinitive are governed by *ut Turnus credidit*. Note how there is a grammatical transformation here, whereby the *imago* (f.) in 643-6 finally becomes *Aenean aversum* in 647 (from Turnus' perspective).

648. **atque...hausit:** understand *ut* as also introducing this second subordinate clause, the main clause being "he said" supplied from 649-50. For *hausit* lit. "drank in" (but translate "conceived"), cf. also 12.26 *simul hoc animo hauri*. **animo:** locative ablative. **spem...inanem:** picks up Juno's *spes...inanis* at 627. Turnus' hope of victory is as vain as Juno's hope of changing

'quo fugis, Aenea? thalamos ne desere pactos;
hac dabitur dextra tellus quaesita per undas.' 650
talia vociferans sequitur strictumque coruscat
mucronem, nec ferre videt sua gaudia ventos.
   Forte ratis celsi coniuncta crepidine saxi
expositis stabat scalis et ponte parato,

---

the course of the war. **turbidus:** "storming," is applied literally to wind and rain and figuratively to human beings. Cf. 763 (applied to Mezentius) and 9.57; 12.10, 671 (applied, again, to Turnus).

649. **ne desere:** 11 n. **pactos:** "promised," is sarcastic. Cf. 79 n.

650. **hac...dextra:** sc. *manu*, instrumental ablative. **tellus quaesita:** Turnus plays on the thought that Aeneas is seeking land: he will give it to him, but in a form of a grave. For a similar taunt, cf. 12.359-60 *en agros, et quam bello, Troiane, petisti | Hesperiam metire iacens* (Turnus' words as he kills Eumedes).

651-2. **coruscat:** this transitive sense ("cause to flash") is first found in Vergil. **mucronem:** see 570 n. For Vergil's transitive use of intransitives, see e.g., *stupet...donum* (2.31); *tela...exit* (5.438). **nec ferre...ventos:** the infinitive and the subject accusative is dependent on *videt*. Servius states that *venti ferunt gaudia* was a proverb (cf. also 9.312-13). Yet here the expression is more pointed, since winds will also be responsible for carrying Turnus away from the battle.

653-88. *Turnus follows Aeneas' phantom onto the ship. Juno cuts the cable, and, when the vessel is well at sea, the phantom vanishes, leaving Turnus to reproach the gods for having lured him to abandon his comrades. Juno, with difficulty, prevents him from killing himself, and the vessel reaches Ardea.*

While the fashioning of a phantom is clearly modeled on *Iliad* 5.449-53 (see 606-88 n.), the tactic by which Juno lures Turnus into the boat recalls still another Iliadic passage and affords the Rutulian hero, if only for a brief moment, another heroic role, that of Achilles. At the end of *Iliad* 21, Apollo encloses the Trojan Agenor in a cloud of mist and takes his place. In his likeness, the god runs away from Achilles, who chases him up and down the battlefield, allowing the routed Trojans to safely withdraw into the city (21.600-12).

   For echoes of the speech of Turnus in the speech of Juturna in *Aeneid* 12, see Newman (2015) 365.

653. **Forte:** "by chance"; the adverb is commonly used to introduce an ecphrasis*. Cf. *Aen*. 3.22 (Polydorus' mound), 12.766 (description of a wild olive tree). **coniuncta:** *coniungo* usually takes a dative or the ablative with *cum*, only occasionally the simple ablative as here (*crepidine*). **crepidine:** *crepido* is usually a raised platform supporting a building or a statue; in this instance understand the projection of a (lofty) rock (*celsi saxi*).

654. **expositis...scalis:** abl. of manner (like *ponte parato*). *Scalae* are the landing ladders. **ponte:** "bridge," but here "gangway" (see also 658). Cf. English "pontoon."

>   qua rex Clusinis advectus Osinius oris.   655
>   huc sese trepida Aeneae fugientis imago
>   conicit in latebras, nec Turnus segnior instat
>   exsuperatque moras et pontis transilit altos.
>   vix proram attigerat, rumpit Saturnia funem
>   avulsamque rapit revoluta per aequora navem.   660
>   tum levis haud ultra latebras iam quaerit imago,   [663]
>   sed sublime volans nubi se immiscuit atrae.   [664]
>   illum autem Aeneas absentem in proelia poscit,   [661]

---

655. **qua:** the relative pronoun (in the ablative) refers to *ratis*, "by which." **rex...Osinius:** in the Etruscan catalogue* (166-7), Massicus was presented as the leader of the contingent from Clusium. This Osinius must be, therefore, a subordinate chief/king under Massicus. **Clusinis...oris:** see 143-4 n. **advectus:** sc. *erat*.

656. **huc:** "hither," picks up the narrative after the ecphrasis* of *forte...stabat*.

657. **in latebras:** see 601. **nec...segnior:** the litotes* emphasizes Turnus' eager pursuit. Cf. 4.149 *haud illo segnior ibat*.

658. **moras:** "obstacles," cf. 485 n. **pontis...altos:** see 654 n.

659. **vix...attigerat, rumpit Saturnia:** "scarce had he touched... (when) Juno snaps," an example of parataxis*, wherein two independent clauses are placed side by side without a subordinating conjunction. This is especially common in Vergil after *vix* and the pluperfect in the first clause; cf. 5.857-8; 8.520; 12.650-1. **Saturnia:** patronymic* of Juno, the daughter of Saturn. Here, however, the patronymic is also suggestive of her siding with the Latins (and Italians) for Saturn was also the great-grandfather of Latinus (*Aen*. 7.45-9), and *Latium* (and Italy), being the place where Saturn hid out from his son Jupiter, was also called "the land of Saturn"; see 8.329 (*Saturnia tellus*).

660. **revoluta per aequora:** lit. "over back-churned waters." Juno possibly created an ebb tide to increase the speed of the boat.

661-4. The text is possibly corrupted, for *tum* of 663 makes little sense after 662, nor does *interea* of 665 after 664. One attractive solution is to assume that lines 661-2 were transposed by mistake before 663-4. With the proper order restored, we should understand 661-2 as added parenthetically to show (1) Turnus' personal disgrace and (2) the general disaster caused by his absence.

663. **levis:** the adjective *lĕvis* (not *lēvis*) here modifies *imago* and is commonly used for ghosts and phantoms. **haud ultra...quaerit:** for the phantom has achieved its scope of luring Turnus into the ship.

664. **sublime:** the neuter singular is used adverbially, "up high," i.e., into the sky. **nubi...atrae:** dative after the compound verb *immisceo*. The phantom returns to its element.

661. **illum:** i.e., Turnus. **Aeneas:** i.e., Aeneas himself, not the phantom. **in proelia:** "for battle," note the accusative. For the construction, 454-6 n.

obvia multa virum demittit corpora morti, [662]
cum Turnum medio interea fert aequore turbo. 665
respicit ignarus rerum ingratusque salutis
et duplicis cum voce manus ad sidera tendit:
'omnipotens genitor, tanton me crimine dignum
duxisti et talis voluisti expendere poenas?
quo feror? unde abii? quae me fuga quemve reducit? 670
Laurentisne iterum muros aut castra videbo?
quid manus illa virum, qui me meaque arma secuti?

---

662. **obvia multa virum...corpora:** a striking image of lifeless bodies. *Obvia* is another example of transferred epithet (see enallage*), for we would expect *obvia* to agree with *virum*, "bodies of men in his way" (i.e., *obviorum*). **virum:** = *virorum*, see 312 n. **morti:** dative after *demittit*. See 148 n.

665. **cum...interea:** "while all the time," suggests a link between two simultaneous actions (Aeneas' killing and Turnus' drifting) and supports the placement of lines 661-2 after 663-4 (cf. 661-4 n.). **medio...aequore:** 165 n.

666. **respicit:** i.e., Turnus. **rerum:** for the genitive, see 173 n. The expression echoes *rerumque ignarus imagine gaudet* (8.730), said of Aeneas when receiving the shield from his mother Venus, but, while the latter rejoices in the image of the shield, the *imago* of Aeneas brings misery to the former (Hejduk (2009) 317). **ingratusque:** is exceptionally used with the genitive (*salutis*) to balance *ignarus rerum*.

667. **duplicis...manus:** "both hands." **tendit:** "stretches" is in zeugma*, for the verb is appropriate to *manus* but not to *vox*.

668. **omnipotens genitor:** Turnus erroneously believes Jupiter to be responsible for his deception. **tanton...crimine:** abl. after (*me*) *dignum*. *Tanton* (= *tantone*, from *tanto* + enclitic *ne*), is a colloquial shortening. See also 12.503 *tanton placuit concurrere motu*.

669. **expendere:** the subject is *me* understood from the previous line. **poenas:** "penalty." In heroic fashion, Turnus views his abandoning the field as a crime and the dishonor following such action as the punishment.

670. **feror:** see 442 n. **quae me fuga quemve reducit?:** lit. "what flight (withdraws) me (i.e., from battle)? whom does (flight) withdraw?" Turnus apparently is not even sure of his identity as he finds himself running away from the enemy.

671. **Laurentis:** adjective agreeing with *muros*, "of Laurentum," i.e., the city of King Latinus. For the name of the city, see 87 n. and 7.59-63. **castra:** i.e., the Trojan camp in front of it (see 635).

672. **quid:** "what of," with ellipsis* of a verb (= "what is to be said of"). Such ellipses are very common and colloquial. **virum:** see 312 n. **secuti:** sc. *sunt*. Note the anaphora* and alliteration* (*quid, qui, quosne, quid, quae* at 675), characteristic of the language of prayers.

quosne (nefas) omnis infanda in morte reliqui
et nunc palantis video, gemitumque cadentum
accipio? quid ago? aut quae iam satis ima dehiscat   675
terra mihi? vos o potius miserescite, venti;
in rupes, in saxa (volens vos Turnus adoro)
ferte ratem saevisque vadis immittite syrtis,
quo neque me Rutuli nec conscia fama sequatur.'
haec memorans animo nunc huc, nunc fluctuat illuc,   680
an sese mucroni ob tantum dedecus amens
induat et crudum per costas exigat ensem,
fluctibus an iaciat mediis et litora nando

673. **quosne:** the antecedent is *virum* above. The interrogative particle *ne* (repeated from 671) joined to the relative pronoun is rare, and it converts the relative clause into a fresh question (What of the men whom...?) The irregularity indicates the speaker's excitement. **nefas:** an exclamation, "what a crime."

674. **palantis:** present participle accusative plural (from *pālor*). **cadentum:** = *cadentium*, is genitive after *gemitumque*. As a good general, Turnus is concerned for the men he has left behind.

675. **quid ago:** the indicative, instead of the deliberative subjunctive, lends directness and urgency; cf. 12.637 *nam quid ago* (12.637 Turnus; 4.534 *en, quid ago*? Dido). **quae:** interrogative adjective agreeing with *terra*. **dehiscat:** potential subjunctive, "would gape open." A similar wish of despair is expressed by Turnus' own sister Juturna (12.883-4 *o quae satis ima dehiscat | terra mihi*) and by Dido (4.24 *sed mihi vel tellus optem prius ima dehiscat*).

676. **mihi:** dative of reference. **vos:** vocative (with *venti*), but *vos* at 677 is accusative after *adoro*. **miserescite:** sc. *mei*.

677. **in...:** anaphora*, asyndeton*, and alliteration* (cf. *volens vos*) mark Turnus' excitement. **volens:** used adverbially ("willingly"). The term is a formula* of Roman prayer language. **adoro:** = *oro* ("I beseech"); this meaning of the verb is a poetic archaism*.

678. **saevisque vadis:** dative after the compound *immittite*. **syrtis:** gen. sing. "of some Syrtis" or "sandbank." The *Syrtes* are two noted sandbanks off the coast of North Africa (1.111), but the word here is used for sandbank in general.

679. **quo...:** purpose clause introduced by the relative adverb *quo* ("where, to what place"). **Rutuli:** i.e., the rebukes of his comrades. **conscia:** i.e., aware of my guilt.

680. **memorans:** here "saying" as it defines Turnus' soliloquy. **animo:** locative ablative with *fluctuat*. **fluctuat:** "wavers," the water metaphor* befits Turnus' physical surroundings.

681-3. **an...| induat...an iaciat:** *an...an* (instead of *utrum...an*) to introduce an indirect disjunctive interrogative question is an archaic* and poetic construction. **sese mucroni...| induat:** *induo* is usually used of "putting on" clothes but here Turnus would "put himself on the sword," i.e., he would impale himself. **dedecus:** in heroic fashion, Turnus is concerned about the "shame" resulting from his action. **crudum...ensem:** Servius understands *crudus* as "cruel." The expression is found again at 12.507-8. Cf. also *crudo...caesto* at 5.69. As noted by

curva petat Teucrumque iterum se reddat in arma.
ter conatus utramque viam, ter maxima Iuno   685
continuit iuvenemque animi miserata repressit.
labitur alta secans fluctuque aestuque secundo
et patris antiquam Dauni defertur ad urbem.

689-754: Mezentius' *aristeia**

With Turnus removed from the battlefield, Mezentius, an older and mightier fighter, takes his place at the forefront of the Latins, warding off Trojans' attacks from all sides in a valiant *aristeia**.

When mentioned earlier in the poem, Mezentius was introduced as a *contemptor divum* (7.648, 8.7) by the narrator and, later, in Evander's account (8.481-90), he is presented as an impious and cruel tyrant given to sadistic methods of torture, hated by his own people and eventually driven into exile by them. In Books 9 and 10, however, Mezentius grows progressively sympathetic and seems to undergo a deep transformation. The present *aristeia**, made particularly Homeric by the frequency of similes* (three extended similes in just about sixty lines, all of them

---

Tarrant (*ad* 507-8), the hyperbaton* enacts verbally the progress of the sword blade through the body. **fluctibus...mediis:** 148 n. **iaciat:** supply *sese* from 681. **nando:** ablative of the gerund.

684. **petat:** present subjunctive for the clause is still part of the indirect (disjunctive) question (see also *reddat*) introduced at 681. **Teucrum...in arma:** lit. "against the weapons of the Trojans," i.e., to the battle with the Trojans. *Teucrum* is genitive plural (see 528-9 n.).

685. **ter...ter:** see 885 n. **conatus:** sc. *est*. **utramque viam:** "each course of action," i.e., suicide or a return to battle. **maxima Iuno:** the epithet* *maxima* is also used of Juno at 4.371 and 8.84.

686. **animi miserata:** "pitying in her heart"; *animi* is a locative after verbs and adjectives indicating feeling (AG §358). Juno had similarly felt pity for Dido about to die (4.693 *tum Iuno omnipotens longum miserata dolorem*). Juno, unlike Jupiter, seems to be able to show compassion and pity for humans.

687-8. **labitur...defertur:** the passive *defertur* underscores Turnus' impotence. **alta:** neuter accusative plural. Translate "the deep," i.e., the sea. **secans:** "cleaving," for the verb, see 147 n. Turnus, the passenger, is described as if he were the ship itself (Harrison *ad loc.*). **fluctuque aestuque secundo:** instrumental ablatives. The winds and current that carry Turnus swiftly away are certainly created by Juno.

688. Note the interlocking* word order. **ad urbem:** i.e., Ardea. The town was located in Latium on the coast of the Mediterranean sea, close to Antium. The boat that carries Turnus out of battle takes him back to his homeland and the city of his father Daunus. Similarly, in Book 11.593-4, Diana promises to carry the corpse and armor of Camilla back to her homeland. Both episodes recall *Iliad* 16 (450-7, 666-83), when the dead body of Sarpedon is brought back to his homeland in Lycia by the divine transport of Death and Sleep (Quint (2018) 166).

based on Homeric originals), establishes him as a strong and noble warrior (*ardens* 689; *impavidus* 717; *alacer* 729; *haud furto melior sed fortibus armis* 735; *imperterritus* 770) who does not deign to hit an enemy from behind (732-3).

Continuing his practice of alternating and juxtaposing Homeric models, Vergil has Mezentius play multiple Homeric characters in this episode. During his *aristeia**, Mezentius is cast in the role of Iliadic warriors in their moment of victory: Achilles, Hector, Patroclus. However, in his defeat at the hands of Aeneas, he, too, finds himself in the role of the defeated Sarpedon, who, in many ways, is "the emblematic Homeric victim." See Quint (2018) 169.

The bibliography on Mezentius is long. Among the most comprehensive studies are Glenn (1971), Leach (1971), and Gotoff (1984). Kronenberg (2005) reads Mezentius as an allegorical Epicurean in a way that allows for an Epicurean reading of the *Aeneid*, which problematizes the very concept of *pietas* and redefines *impietas* as true piety.

> At Iovis interea monitis Mezentius ardens
> succedit pugnae Teucrosque invadit ovantis.   690
> concurrunt Tyrrhenae acies atque omnibus uni,
> uni odiisque viro telisque frequentibus instant.
> ille (velut rupes vastum quae prodit in aequor,

689-718. *Spurred on by Jupiter, Mezentius joins the fray and, though assailed by all the Trojans, maintains his ground unmoved, like a rock assailed by winds and waves, slaying warrior after warrior, until at last none dare approach him as he rages like a wild boar at bay.*

689. **Iovis...monitis:** "because of the instructions of Jupiter." Somewhat ironically*, the actions of Mezentius, "the despiser of gods" (7.648), seem to be partly controlled by the will of the gods. Note how Jupiter's direct intervention in human affairs contradicts his assertions of neutrality (cf. 107-8 n.).

690. **pugnae:** see 439-40 n. **Teucrosque...ovantis:** the Trojans are triumphant because of their successes. For *ovantis*, see 405-9 n.

691-2. **Tyrrhenae acies:** "the Etruscan lines"; they are singled out because of their hatred for Mezentius, their ex-king. For Mezentius' story, see 689-754 n. **omnibus...odiisque...telisque frequentibus:** instrumental ablatives. For the unusual combination of abstract and concrete (*odiis...telis*), cf. Hor., *Carm.* 1.15.12 *currusque et rabiem parat*. The combination of abstract and concrete is a favorite one with Tacitus. Note the elision of the long syllable *-ae* of *Tyrrhenae* and -ī of ūnī (692) before a short vowel. **uni...viro:** dative after *instant*. See 26-7 n. The repetition of *uni* at line break (epanalepsis*) has an intensely emphatic effect (cf. also 180 -1 n.). Note also the meaningful juxtaposition of *uni* and *omnibus*, with *unus* underscoring the "isolation" of Mezentius, the tyrant, hated by all, whose only bond is, with tragic consequences, the one with his devoted son Lausus.

693-6. **vastum:** qualifies *aequor*. **quae:** the antecedent is *rupes*. **furiis:** dative after *obvia*. In the simile* it refers to the wrath of the sky and the sea, but the term is also suggestive of the more literal wrath of the angry Etruscans. See also *minas*, below. **expostaque:** syncope* for

obvia ventorum furiis expostaque ponto,
vim cunctam atque minas perfert caelique marisque   695
ipsa immota manens) prolem Dolichaonis Hebrum
sternit humi, cum quo Latagum Palmumque fugacem,
sed Latagum saxo atque ingenti fragmine montis
occupat os faciemque adversam, poplite Palmum
succiso volvi segnem sinit, armaque Lauso   700
donat habere umeris et vertice figere cristas.

---

expostaque. **caelique marisque**: are both genitives after *vim* and *minas*. The cliff is able to resist both the fury of the winds (*caeli*) and of the sea (*maris*). The model for the simile comparing a warrior unperturbed by the assaults of the enemy to a rock resisting the stormy weather is *Il.* 15.618-21, already used by Vergil at 7.586-90 to describe Latinus' resistance to the war-party. In this instance, however, unlike Latinus, Mezentius remains completely unmoved.

696-7. **prolem...humi**: resumes the narrative proper. The point of comparison between the cliff and Mezentius seems to be the following: just as Mezentius resists his attackers by killing them, so, too, the cliff resists the high waves by breaking their power and "laying them low." **prolem**: is in apposition to *Hebrum*, direct object of *sternit*. **Hebrum**: like many other warriors in the poem, Hebrus shares his name with a river. The river Hebrus (modern Maritza), in Western Thrace, is mentioned by Vergil in *Ecl.* 10.65, *Geo.* 4.463, and *Aen.* 1.317. **sternit**: subject is *ille* at 693. **humi**: locative. **cum quo**: i.e., together with Hebrus. Supply *sternit*.

698. **saxo atque ingenti fragmine montis**: "with a rock and a mighty fragment of a mountain," an example of hendiadys* (the expression of a single idea by two words connected with "and"). The expression is repeated from 9.569.

699. **occupat**: 384 n. **os faciemque**: "mouth and face," are accusatives of specification. Cf. 132-3 n. For a similar construction (with direct object (*Latagum*) and accusative of specification), cf. *Aen.* 12.275-6 *egregium forma iuvenem | transadigit costas*.

699-700. **poplite...| succiso**: abl. abs., "with his hamstrings having been cut." **Palmum |... segnem**: the accusative and infinitive (*volvi*) are governed by *sinit* ("allows"). *Segnem* here means "slow = crippled," because his hamstring has been cut. **volvi**: the infinitive passive is used as a deponent (i.e., with active meaning), see 403 n. As a contrast to Latagus, who meets his enemy face to face (cf. *adversam*), Palmus was described as *fugax* (697, not merely "fleeing," but "prone to flee"). Mezentius now spoils his capacity to run away by hamstringing him from behind, and then contemptuously leaving him to writhe with his useless limbs. **armaque**: direct object of *habere*, just as *cristas* is the object of *figere*.

701. **donat habere**: "gives to wear"; for the infinitives *habere* and *figere* after *dono*, cf. also 61-2 n. **umeris**: locative abl. (cf. also *vertice*). Instead of dedicating the spoils to a divinity, Mezentius offers them to his son, who is in his thoughts even before appearing on the scene. At 774-6 Mezentius similarly vows to deck his son with the spoils of Aeneas. Yet to wear the spoils of the dead brings bad luck in the *Aeneid*, and Lausus, too, will soon meet his fate. Cf. 421-3 n.

nec non Euanthen Phrygium Paridisque Mimanta
aequalem comitemque, una quem nocte Theano
in lucem genitore Amyco dedit et face praegnas
Cisseis regina Parim; Paris urbe paterna 705
occubat, ignarum Laurens habet ora Mimanta.
ac velut ille canum morsu de montibus altis
actus aper, multos Vesulus quem pinifer annos
defendit multosque palus Laurentia, silva
pascit harundinea, postquam inter retia ventum est, 710

---

702. **Evanthen…Mimanta:** Greek accusatives from *Evanthes* and *Mimas*. *Evanthes* is Greek for "fair-flowering." In the *Argonautica* of Apollonius, Mimas is the name of a Bebrycian warrior killed by Polydeuces (2.105). **Paridisque:** gen. after *aequalem comitemque*.

703-6. **una…nocte…et:** "on the same night as." When meaning "the same," *unus* may be followed by *et, ac, or atque*, meaning "as." **quem:** refers to *Mimas* and is the object of *dedit in lucem* ("gave birth to"). **Theano:** nominative singular subject of *dedit in lucem*. In Homer we have a Theano, daughter of Cisseus, as the wife of Antenor (*Il.* 5.70). **genitore Amyco:** abl. of origin. Bentley's emendation *genitore* (instead of *genitori*) should be accepted, since, otherwise, both *genitori* and *in lucem* would be complements of *dedit*. **Cisseis regina:** sc. *dedit in lucem* (object is *Parim*). Hecuba, daughter of Cisseus (*Cisseis* is the patronymic*, nom. singular), wife of Priam, dreamed that she was about to give birth to a firebrand (*face praegnas* "pregnant with a torch"). The child born was Paris. **regina…| occubat:** the manuscript tradition reads *regina Parim creat: urbe paterna occubat*, a reading that does not have a subject for *occubat*. Bentley's emendation *regina Parim: Paris urbe paterna occubat* is adopted by many editors and beyond question improves the text. **ignarum:** is active in sense, "a stranger to it" (i.e., the coast). The accusative adjective qualifies *Mimanta*. **Laurens…ora:** "the Laurentian shore," subject of *habet*. Note the stark juxtaposition: Paris lies in the land of his fathers, while Mimas is buried in a country in which he is a stranger. For the epic theme of dying in a foreign country, see Griffin (1980) 106.

707. **ille:** with *aper* at 708 "that boar"; is deictic* and draws attention to the boar. Cf. 11.809-11 *ac velut ille…|…lupus*. The main verb is *substitit* at 711. **canum:** genitive after *morsu*. Note that this i-stem noun has the genitive plutral in *-um* (rather than the expected *-ium*). **morsu:** abl. of means after *actus*. For the image, cf. *venator cursu canis et latratibus instat* (12.751, said of Aeneas pursuing Turnus).

708. **multos…:** construe as *quem* (antecedent is *aper*) *Vesulus pinifer defendit multos annos* (acc. of duration). **Vesulus:** *Mount Viso* in which the Po rises. Servius notes that the simile* provides an appropriate location for the Etruscan Mezentius.

709-10. **multosque…:** sc. *annos*, understood from the previous clause; *-que* is disjunctive for there are two boars envisioned here (one mountain-defended, the other reed-fed); in English we should use "or." **palus Laurentia:** subject of *pascit*; modern Pantano di Lauro. **silva |…harundinea:** "with reedy thick growth," abl. of means. **ventum est:** impersonal passive. Cf. 354-5 n.

substitit infremuitque ferox et inhorruit armos,
nec cuiquam irasci propiusque accedere virtus,
sed iaculis tutisque procul clamoribus instant;
haud aliter, iustae quibus est Mezentius irae,
non ulli est animus stricto concurrere ferro, 715
missilibus longe et vasto clamore lacessunt.
ille autem impavidus partis cunctatur in omnis
dentibus infrendens et tergo decutit hastas.
 Venerat antiquis Corythi de finibus Acron,
Graius homo, infectos linquens profugus hymenaeos; 720

---

711. **infremuit**: the compound of *fremo* is first found here. **inhorruit armos**: lit. "bristles as to his shoulders." For the accusative, see 132-3 n. The perfects seem gnomic, "has been known to halt, roar, and bristle."

712. **cuiquam**: possessive dative. **irasci...accedere**: the infinitives depend on *virtus* (sc. *est*); cf. 90-1 n. *Irasci* is picked up by *irae* of the narrative at 714.

713. **iaculis...clamoribus**: instrumental ablatives. **procul**: contrasts *propiusve* of the previous line.

714-15. **iustae...animus**: construe as *animus non est ulli (eorum), quibus Mezentius est iustae irae*. **irae**: dative of purpose or, less likely, gen. of quality. For *iusta ira*, cf. *merita ira* (8.501), said by Evander (reporting the speech of a soothsayer) of the rage of his citizens toward Mezentius. **concurrere**: depends on *animus non est*. See 90-1 n. **ferro**: see 231-2 n.

716. **missilibus...vasto clamore**: instrumental ablatives; the behavior of Mezentius' enemies picks up the behavior of the hunters at 713.

717-18. **partis cunctatur in omnis**: Mezentius holds his ground (*cunctatur*) by moving in every "direction" (hence the *in* + acc. of motion toward). **tergo**: ablative of motion away from. Some editors have transposed these two lines to follow 713 on the ground that *dentibus infrendens* ("gnashing (lit. 'with,' instrumental ablative) his teeth") can hardly refer to a human (but cf. 3.664 of Polyphemus and 8.230 of Hercules) and that *tergum* meaning "shield" is exceptional. Objections to this transposition are stronger: (1) the want of textual authority; (2) the awkwardness of *ille autem* after *sed iaculis...*; (3) the fact that Mezentius' actions, in Vergilian fashion, nicely pick up those of the boar (*cunctatur | substitit, dentibus infrendens | infremuitque ferox, et tergo decutit hastas | inhorruit armos*); and 4) in Vergil the language of the simile* often trespasses into that of the narrative. For fuller discussion on trespassing, see O'Hara (1991).

719-46. Mezentius is likened to a ravening lion, urged on by maddening hunger, and slays Acron. He then kills Orodes, who warns him of his own impending doom.

719. **venerat...**: the formula* is often used to introduce a new character (cf. 544 *veniens Marsorum montibus Vmbro*). **Corythi**: possibly Cortona, a city near Lake Trasimene.

720. **infectos...hymenaeos**: lit. "the uncompleted marriage." The pathetic theme "warrior dies before consummating marriage" is both Homeric (e.g., *Il.* 11.242-3) and reminiscent of Pallas' baldric (497-9). **profugus**: note the lengthening of *-us* in *profugus* in arsis*.

hunc ubi miscentem longe media agmina vidit,
purpureum pennis et pactae coniugis ostro,
impastus stabula alta leo ceu saepe peragrans
(suadet enim vesana fames), si forte fugacem
conspexit capream aut surgentem in cornua cervum,   725
gaudet hians immane comasque arrexit et haeret
visceribus super incumbens—lavit improba taeter
ora cruor—
sic ruit in densos alacer Mezentius hostis.
sternitur infelix Acron et calcibus atram   730

---

721. **hunc:** i.e., Acron. **ubi…vidit:** the subject is Mezentius. **longe:** "from afar." Construe with *vidit*. Acron can be seen from afar because of his rich clothes. **media agmina:** object of *miscentem*; Acron is spreading confusion in the midst of the ranks.

722. **purpureum:** the color of love (cf. Ov., *Am.* 2.1.38 *purpureus Amor*) is highly appropriate in this context of marital affection. **pennis…ostro:** ablatives of specification. They are, respectively, the feathers of the crest and the cloak "of his promised wife" (*pactae coniugis*), i.e., given to him by his promised wife.

723-8. This simile*, written in Homeric fashion, closely follows the previous one (707-18) and is modeled on *Il.* 3.23-6. The first line and a half is partly repeated from 9.339-40, where Euryalus is compared to an unfed lion among full sheepfolds: *impastus ceu plena leo per ovilia turbans | (suadet enim vesana fames) manditque trahitque*.

723. **impastus:** "unfed," qualifies *leo* ("lion") and is placed in emphatic initial position to underscore the lion's maddening hunger (*vesana fames* 724) and, therefore, Mezentius' maddening thirst for blood. **stabula alta:** "deep lairs," cf. 6.179 *itur in antiquam silvam, stabula alta ferarum*. **ceu saepe:** "as often," = "as, which often happens." For *seu* introducing a simile* and often postponed in Vergil, see 356-7 n.

725. **surgentem in cornua:** lit. "rising to its horns," i.e., "with lofty antlers"; the phrase artistically contrasts the proud stag with the "timid (*fugacem*) roe-deer."

726. **immane:** adverbial, governed by *hians*. **comasque arrexit:** "and bristled up his mane." **haeret:** the change of tense marks the first action (*arrexit*) as preceding the second.

727. **visceribus:** dative after *haeret*. **super incumbens:** "coming down from above." The reading *incumbens* should be preferred to *accumbens* "reclining (to eat)" since it better describes the action of the lion attacking its prey and because lions do not recline to eat. **lavit:** "washes." Both Vergil and Horace prefer to use forms from the older (third conjugation) *lavĕre* rather than from the first conjugation *lavāre* in the indicative present. **improba:** "ruthless," is often applied to predators. Cf. 9.62 (a wolf), 12.250 (an eagle).

730. **sternitur…Acron:** the lofty Acron (*akros* = "topmost" in Greek) is "laid low" (*sternitur*), see Harrison *ad loc*. **infelix:** see 324-5 n.

tundit humum exspirans infractaque tela cruentat.
atque idem fugientem haud est dignatus Oroden
sternere nec iacta caecum dare cuspide vulnus;
obvius adversoque occurrit seque viro vir
contulit, haud furto melior sed fortibus armis.   735
tum super abiectum posito pede nixus et hasta:
'pars belli haud temnenda, viri, iacet altus Orodes.'
conclamant socii laetum paeana secuti.

---

731. **infractaque tela:** i.e., for the javelin breaks off in the wound as he falls. The plural is poetic.

732. **idem:** i.e., Mezentius. **haud est dignatus:** "did not deem worthy." Mezentius strictly abides to the ideals of epic heroism and refuses to kill a man who is fleeing. **Oroden:** Greek acc. For the etymology*, see 737 n. Orodes is also the name of the Parthian king who destroyed the army of Marcus Licinius Crassus at the battle of Carrhae in 53 BCE.

733. **sternere:** complementary inf. after *est dignatus* (like *dare*). **iacta...cuspide:** abl. abs. *Cuspis* ("spear-point,") is used by synecdoche* for the entire spear. **caecum...vulnus:** "an unseen wound," i.e., given from behind.

734-5. **obvius adversoque occurrit:** lit. "he runs to meet (*occurrit*) (him) face to face (*obvius*) and (he runs to meet him) as he (i.e., Orodes) stands facing him (*adverso*)." The *-que* is logically correct. Orodes is "seeking to escape," and Mezentius runs (1) to cross his path and (2) to make Orodes stand and face him. **seque...| contulit:** "and rushed himself (to meet him) man to man." *Viro* is dative after *se conferre*. For the phrase *viro vir* and the monosyllabic ending, cf. 361. **furto...armis:** abl. of specification. Note the rhetorical assonance* between *furto* and *fortibus*. For Mezentius' heroic ethic, see 732 n.

736. **super abiectum:** "over the one cast down," i.e., Orodes. **posito...:** lit. "having made an effort with planted foot and with (his) spear," i.e., pressing with his foot so as to pull out the spear. Both the planted foot (which gives leverage) and the spear are *instrumental* ablatives dependent on *nixus*. The spear is only actually withdrawn at 744. For a similar, but, in that case, gratuitous gesture, see Turnus' planting of his foot on the dead Pallas (494-5 n.).

737. **pars...temnenda:** cf. 426-7 n. The litotes* *haud temnenda* is emphatic. **altus Orodes:** *altus*, often used of gods and demigods (cf. 9.697), is here used derisively. Note the etymological* wordplay in *altus Orodes* (Orodes = "mountainous" in Greek) and the clear antithesis* between *altus* and *iacet*; once so lofty, now so low (Harrison *ad loc.*).

738. **paeana:** Greek accusative. It can be taken either as the direct object of *conclamant* (the comrades (*socii*) of Mezentius shout together a paean (a cry of triumph) while they follow their leader) or of *secuti* (the comrades of Mezentius shout together following Mezentius' cry of triumph). If the former interpretation is accepted, compare *Il.* 22.391 where Achilles bids his comrades to "sing a paean" after his slaying of Hector (Hom. *Il.* 22.391).

ille autem exspirans: 'non me, quicumque es, inulto,
victor, nec longum laetabere; te quoque fata   740
prospectant paria atque eadem mox arva tenebis.'
ad quem subridens mixta Mezentius ira:
'nunc morere. ast de me divum pater atque hominum rex
viderit.' hoc dicens eduxit corpore telum.
olli dura quies oculos et ferreus urget   745
somnus, in aeternam clauduntur lumina noctem.
   Caedicus Alcathoum obtruncat, Sacrator Hydaspen

---

739. **exspirans:** sc. *dixit*. The models for this prophecy are the words of the dying Patroclus foretelling to Hector his death at the hands of Achilles (*Il*. 16.843-54) and of the dying Hector foretelling to Achilles his imminent death (*Il*. 22.355-60). In general, the dying are thought to have prophetic powers. **me...inulto:** the ablative absolute goes adverbially with *laetabere* (= *laetaberis*). **quicumque es:** Orodes must be a Trojan for he does not know who Mezentius is.

740-1 **nec:** "nor," links *longum* (an adverbial accusative "for long," cf. 272-3) with *me inulto*. Mezentius will not rejoice at Orodes' death without a penalty nor for long. **te...fata |...paria:** "a similar fate looks on you too." Orodes uses a rather bold personification*; he has Mezentius' own end (fate) watching Mezentius.

742. **ad quem:** sc. *respondit*. **subridens:** *sub-* may suggest here a sneer rather than a smile; cf. 9.740 *olli subridens sedato pectore Turnus*. Mezentius' response, commanding Orodes to die and placing himself in the hands of the king and father of the gods, brings us back to that moment in the *Iliad* when Achilles tells Hector to die and leaves Zeus to determine his own death (22.365-6). **mixta...ira:** ablative of manner.

743-4. **morere:** present imperative; cf. 600 (Aeneas to Liger). **ast:** archaic* form of *at*. **de me...:** responds to Orodes' *te quoque*. **divum...rex:** for Servius this dignified description of Jupiter (cf. 2 n.) is distinctly scornful as befits Mezentius, a *contemptor divum*. **viderit:** the future perfect postpones consideration of the question, suggesting indifference.

745-6. **olli:** dative of reference, is archaic* and poetic for *illi*. **ferreus...| somnus:** is an adaptation of the Homeric "sleep of bronze." The expression *dura quies* and *ferreus somnus* are parallel expressions, "each coupling a harsh adjective with a noun of opposite connotation" (Tarrant *ad* 12.309-10). **lumina noctem:** for the effective juxtaposition, cf. Cat. 51.11-2 *teguntur | lumina nocte*. The lines are repeated at 12.309-10, but with *conduntur* for *clauduntur*. In both cases the lines mark the end of a battle narrative. For line repetition in the *Aeneid*, see 113-15 n.

747-54. Mezentius' companions counterattack, stirred up by their leader: Caedicus kills Alcathous, Sacrator Hydaspes, Rapo Parthenius and Orses, Messapus Clonius and Erichaetes, Valerus Agis, but then the Italian Salius kills the Trojan (or Arcadian) Thronius and is immediately killed by the Trojan Nealces.

747. **Caedicus:** a Latin, as shown by his name, just like Sacrator, Rapo, Messapus, Valerus, and Salius. **obtruncat:** literally "decapitates." **Hydaspen:** Greek accusative, just like *Orsen* at 748 and *Erichaeten* at 749.

Partheniumque Rapo et praedurum viribus Orsen,
Messapus Cloniumque Lycaoniumque Erichaeten,
illum infrenis equi lapsu tellure iacentem,   750
hunc peditem. pedes et Lycius processerat Agis,
quem tamen haud expers Valerus virtutis avitae
deicit; at Thronium Salius Saliumque Nealces
insignis iaculo et longe fallente sagitta.

748. **Partheniumque Rapo:** supply *obtruncat*, vel sim. here and at 749. Rapo's (evoking the verb *rapere* "rape," "ravish") killing of Parthenius ("Maiden" in Greek) may allude to sexual violation. Cucchiarelli (2001) 53 suggests that the context of the line in Book 10 is significant as Turnus has just killed another youth, Pallas, and Aeneas will soon kill Lausus, burying his sword in a youthful body and therefore furthering the thread whereby a life prematurely cut down is imagined as an act of sexual violation. Cucchiarelli (2001) further notes that Rapo comes in immediate succession after Caedicus and Sacrator with the result that a kind of synonymity of murder is rounded off: *caedere, sacrare, rapere.* **viribus:** abl. of specification.

749. **Lycaoniumque:** "son of Lycaon," cf. 123 n. **Erichaeten:** Greek accusative.

750. **illum...iacentem:** i.e., Clonius. **infrenis equi:** genitive after *lapsu*, see 154 n. The adjective *infrenis* ("unbridled") may indicate that Erichaetes rides without a bridle like the *Numidae infreni* (4.41), or that he has lost the bridle. **lapsu:** ablative of cause after *iacentem*. **tellure:** locative ablative.

751. **hunc peditem:** i.e., Erichaetes. **pedes:** nom. sing, "on foot" (describing Agis). **Lycius...Agis:** "the Lycian Agis."

752. **Valerus:** his name suggests a connection with the *gens Valera*. Vergil's positive comments on Valerus as showing "ancestral courage" may be a tribute to Marcus Valerius Messalla, patron of poets during the age of Augustus (Harrison *ad loc.*). **virtutis avitae:** gen. after *expers* ("devoid of"); see 154 n.

753. **at:** the adversative signals the end of the rout with the battle turning into an even fight when the Italian Salius kills the Trojan Thronius and the Trojan Nealces kills, in turn, Salius. Salius is possibly connected to Latin *salio* "to leap," while Nealces has a Greek root which means "fresh strength." Thronius is probably derived from the city of Thronium in Locri.

754. **insignis:** nominative singular qualifying Nealces. This reading should be preferred to the variant *insidiis*. It is unlikely for Nealces to have killed Salius with both javelin and arrow. Further, archery and javelin-throwing are paired elsewhere as elements of heroic prowess (Williams, *ad loc.*). **iaculo...sagitta:** ablatives of specification after *insignis*. **longe fallente:** referring to *sagitta* "deceiving from afar."

755-832: The duel between Mezentius and Aeneas and the death of Lausus

The battle hangs in even balance, moving the pity of the gods until, at last, Mezentius meets Aeneas in combat. Aeneas wounds Mezentius and is about to dispatch him when young Lausus rushes in to intercept the blow (755-802). After vainly warning Lausus, Aeneas kills him. However, moved by a deep sympathy and compassion for this young hero who has sacrificed his life for that of his father, Aeneas lifts up his body and restores it to his comrades (802-32).

Mezentius, who, so far, has played the roles of Iliadic victors (see 689-754 n.), is now cast as yet another new Sarpedon (for Vergilian warriors taking on the role of the Iliadic Sarpedon, see General Introduction to the book). In *Iliad* 5, Sarpedon had been wounded in the groin and carried out of the fray by his followers (660-7). Somewhat similarly, Mezentius is struck by Aeneas' spear and helped out of the fighting by his companions (after being saved, in Mezentius' case, by the intervention of his beloved son Lausus). Subsequently Mezentius recovers beneath a tree, surrounded by his companions (833-8); Sarpedon, likewise, lies beneath an oak tree to have the spear removed from his thigh and to recover (*Iliad* 5.692-8). These two episodes frame the death of Lausus, who now takes his father's place in combat against Aeneas. A young warrior, Lausus is no more a match for Aeneas than Pallas was for Turnus, and Aeneas warns Lausus not to get carried away by filial piety (810-11); then, his wrath kindled (812-13), Aeneas kills the young man. The moment of Lausus' death contains a double Iliadic echo, for it imitates the formula* Homer used to describe both the death of Patroclus (16.855-7) and that of Hector (22.361-3). Here, too, Vergil "exploits links already made by the *Iliad* to suggest how heroic deaths have become identical and to blur together the models he evokes: Lausus plays both Patroclus and Hector, Aeneas both Hector and Achilles" (Quint (2018) 169).

Although the duel between Mezentius and Aeneas closely follows the Homeric narrative code, it differs in one important detail. Contrary to Homeric praxis it is the victim Mezentius and not the victor Aeneas who occupies center stage in the narrative. This important shift in narrative focus further problematizes the audience's response to the character of Mezentius who, in the previous books, had been described solely as a ruthless tyrant. On the topic, see Gotoff (1984) and Bonfanti (1985) 68-84. On Mezentius, see also 689-754 n.

For parallels between the duel between Aeneas and Lausus and that between Turnus and Pallas, see 439-509 n., with relevant bibliography. On Lausus' death, see also Pogorzelski (2009) and Stover (2011) who argue that in killing Lausus, Aeneas has, in fact, killed his own double. See further Putnam (1995) 134-51 who describes Lausus as an emblem of piety, irreconcilable with the maddened and irrational weapons of war and, therefore, with the teleology of Roman destiny personified in Aeneas. Important Lucretian intertexts and imagery used in the episode of Lausus' death are analyzed by Coppolino (2005).

> Iam gravis aequabat luctus et mutua Mavors 755
> funera; caedebant pariter pariterque ruebant
> victores victique, neque his fuga nota neque illis.
> di Iovis in tectis iram miserantur inanem
> amborum et tantos mortalibus esse labores;
> hinc Venus, hinc contra spectat Saturnia Iuno: 760
> pallida Tisiphone media inter milia saevit.

755-68. In the palace of Jupiter, the gods watch the battle and pity the futile anger of the mortals. Mezentius is compared to the giant Orion.

Feeney (1999) 189 reads the response of the gods as a metaphor* for the response of the audience: the gods who take pity on the humans but remain ultimately detached by virtue of their immortality/invulnerability mirror the audience of the text passionately involved in the action but ultimately detached by virtue of the fact of its awareness that the story is pure fiction.

For parallels between Polyphemus and Orion (both giants, blinded, wading through the sea, and wielding tree-trunks as clubs), and, therefore, implicitly between Mezentius and Polyphemus see 763-8 below, Glenn (1971) 148-9, Leach (1971), Hardie (1986) 266-9. For the duel between Aeneas and Mezentius as a sort of Gigantomachy with Aeneas having been compared previously to the giant Aegaeon and Mezentius now to the giant Orion, see Conte (2007) 165.

755. **gravis:** "grim," adjective modifying *Mavors*. **Mavors:** the archaic* name of Mars. For Mars understand the semiabstract form of the spirit of war, not the god himself (who in the *Aeneid* never intervenes directly in the fight).

756. **caedebant...ruebant:** the two verbs aptly describe the alternate killing (*caedebant*) and falling (*ruebant*) of the two armies and are nicely picked up by *victores* and *victi* of the following line. Note the chiastic* arrangement of *caedebant...ruebant* and how the balance of words imitates the even balance of the strife.

757. **fuga nota:** sc. *erat*.

758. **di:** = *dei*. **tectis:** see 5 n. **miserantur:** governs both the accusative *iram inanem* and the accusative and infinitive (*tantos...esse labores*). **inanem:** "futile," indicating the pointlessness of human quarrels in the eyes of superior beings.

759. **amborum:** i.e., Trojans and Latins. **mortalibus:** dative of possession. The term is here pointed as it highlights what distinguishes them from the gods ("the immortals").

760. **contra:** is used adverbially. **Saturnia:** see 659 n.

761. **pallida Tisiphone:** she was the daughter of Pluto and the sister of Allecto and Megaera, the other two Furies. She is first mentioned at 6.555, where she is described as the sleepless sentinel of Tartarus who tortures with her whips and snakes those souls judged guilty by Rhadamanthus. Her name means the "avenger" from Greek *tisis*. **media:** can be either a nominative singular with *Tisiphone* or accusative plural with *milia*. While the gods look at the human strife "from the halls of Jove" (758), Tisiphone, moving "in the midst of the thousands," shares and sharpens their rage. A colon, instead of a full stop, after *Iuno* makes the contrast clearer.

at vero ingentem quatiens Mezentius hastam
turbidus ingreditur campo. quam magnus Orion,
cum pedes incedit medii per maxima Nerei
stagna viam scindens, umero supereminet undas, 765
aut summis referens annosam montibus ornum
ingrediturque solo et caput inter nubila condit:
talis se vastis infert Mezentius armis.
   Hunc contra Aeneas speculatus in agmine longe
obvius ire parat. manet imperterritus ille 770

---

763. **turbidus:** "storming"; cf. 648 n. **campo:** "over the plain," see 165 n. **quam magnus Orion...:** the order is inverted and should read (*tam*) *magnus quam Orion* (*est*). This is similar to the attraction into the relative clause at 327. The fourth full-scale simile* of Mezentius in sixty lines compares him to the giant Orion. For the simile*, see 755-68 n.

764-5. **pedes:** "on foot," nominative singular. **medii...Nerei:** "of mid-sea." Nereus is used metonymically* to indicate the sea. It scans as a spondee by synizesis*. **per maxima...| stagna:** "through the greatest depths"; *stagna* is often used as a synonym for sea. **viam scindens:** recalls the ploughing metaphor* traditional for sailing. Orion is described as a large ship (Harrison *ad loc.*).

765. **umero:** abl. of degree of difference. **supereminet:** is used transitively.

766. **summis...montibus:** ablative indicating motion away from. **referens annosam...ornum:** "carrying an old ash tree." Servius believes Orion to be carrying a tree, apparently as a staff or club, uprooted by himself on the mountains. This would agree sufficiently with *Od.* 11.573-5 where Homer describes Orion as a carrier of a brazen club, but the substitution of a tree for a club of brass would remind the reader also of Vergil's Polyphemus who wields a pine-tree (*trunca pinus*) as a stick at 3.659.

767. **ingrediturque solo:** "strides over the ground," parallels Mezentius' *ingreditur campo* at 763; for *solo*, see 165 n. **caput inter nubila condit:** cf. *Aen.* 3.678 *Aetnaeos fratres caelo capita alta ferentes* (said of the Cyclops).

768. **vastis...armis:** either "with his vast weapons," echoing *ingentem hastam* at 762 and corresponding to the tree-trunk staff of the simile* (766) or *armis* = "with shoulders" (from *armus*). In the latter case, the line would emphasize Mezentius' huge body and would correspond to the description of Orion's huge size with his head rising up to sky. *Vastus* is used twice by Vergil of Polyphemus (3.617, 656). Note the heavy spondaic rhythm of the line.

769-90. At last Mezentius meets Aeneas and hurls a spear which misses him but kills Antores. Aeneas wounds Mezentius with his spear. The young Lausus groans at the sight of his wounded father.

769. **hunc:** i.e., Mezentius. This reading is preferable to *huic* as it provides the object to *speculatus*. **contra:** is adverbial and defines Aeneas' position: "on the other side, Aeneas." **longe:** goes with *speculatus* and is preferable to the variant *longo*, the point being that Aeneas spots Mezentius from a distance.

LIBER DECIMUS 129

hostem magnanimum opperiens, et mole sua stat
atque oculis spatium emensus quantum satis hastae:
'dextra mihi deus et telum, quod missile libro,
nunc adsint! voveo praedonis corpore raptis
indutum spoliis ipsum te, Lause, tropaeum   775
Aeneae.' dixit, stridentemque eminus hastam
iecit. at illa volans clipeo est excussa proculque
egregium Antoren latus inter et ilia figit,
Herculis Antoren comitem, qui missus ab Argis
haeserat Euandro atque Itala consederat urbe.   780

---

771. **et mole sua stat:** "and stands (immovable) by his own sheer bulk"; cf. 7.588-9 *sese... | mole tenet*, of a crag; Lucan 1.139 *pondere fixa suo est*, of an old oak. The rhythm with its monosyllabic ending suggests rugged strength. Again, *moles* is used also of Polyphemus at 3.656 *vasta se mole mouentem*. For parallels between Mezentius and Polyphemus, see notes above.

772. **oculis:** instrumental ablative. **quantum:** agrees with *spatium*. **satis:** sc. *sit* (subjunctive in indirect question). **hastae:** dative after *satis*, see AG §368.2. Cf. 457. For the line ending, see 302 n.

773. **deus:** is in apposition to *dextra*. Mezentius, the *contemptor divum*, acknowledges his strength as his only deity. **missile:** is in apposition to *quod*.

774-6. **adsint:** optative subjunctive. A similar prayer is uttered by the blasphemous Capaneus in Statius' *Thebaid* (9.548-50) *ades o mihi, dextera, tantum | tu praesens bellis et inevitabile numen, | te voco, te solam superum contemptor adoro*. **voveo...:** construe as *voveo ipsum te, Lause, indutum spoliis raptis corpore praedonis, tropaeum Aeneae*. **praedonis:** genitive; the term is derogatory meaning "robber" or "pirate." Aeneas is similarly called *perfidus praedo* by Amata (7.362) and *Phrygii praedonis* by the Latin women (11.484). **corpore:** abl. of separation. **raptis |...spoliis:** abl. after *indutum*. **tropaeum:** is in apposition to *te*. The arms of a defeated foe were frequently set up on a tree trunk (11.4-11) as a trophy dedicated to some god (e.g., Mars, 11.8). Mezentius mocks this practice by vowing that his living son, decked in the arms of the vanquished, will be the trophy of his victory over Aeneas. Mezentius had already given Lausus the spoils of Palmus at 701 n.

777. **clipeo:** see 330-2 n. **proculque:** "some way away." *Procul* does not necessarily imply that the distance between two things is great, but merely that they are separated.

778-9. **Antoren...Antoren:** see 180-1 n. **latus...:** construe as *inter latus et ilia*, "between the flank and the groin."

780. **haeserat:** for the meaning "attaching oneself to a person (with the dative)," see OLD s.v. *haereo* 4. **Itala...urbe:** locative ablative, i.e., Pallanteum, Evander's city.

sternitur infelix alieno vulnere, caelumque
aspicit et dulcis moriens reminiscitur Argos.
tum pius Aeneas hastam iacit; illa per orbem
aere cavum triplici, per linea terga tribusque
transiit intextum tauris opus, imaque sedit   785
inguine, sed viris haud pertulit. ocius ensem
Aeneas viso Tyrrheni sanguine laetus
eripit a femine et trepidanti fervidus instat.
ingemuit cari graviter genitoris amore,

781-2. **infelix:** see 324-5 n. **alieno vulnere:** instrumental ablative, see 343-4 n. **caelumque | aspicit:** he gazes up at the sky that he is about to lose; cf. 898-9 n. The model for the line is possibly Ennius (fr. 484 Skutsch and in *FRL* 1 *semianimesque micant oculi lucemque requirunt*. Cf. also *Aen.* 4.691-2 *oculisque errantibus alto | quaesivit caelo lucem* (of Dido). Note the hypermetric line* at 781. **dulcis...Argos:** the adjective reflects Antores' feeling (internal focalization*). The memory of his homeland Argos is particularly sweet to Antores who is about to die in a foreign land. **reminiscitur:** the accusative after verbs of remembering is used of things which one has experienced (as here), while the genitive is used when the verbs of remembering means to be mindful of or to think of somebody and something (AG §350).

783-4. **pius:** the epithet* draws attention to the contrast between "pious" Aeneas and "impious" Mezentius but is somewhat ironic*, for Aeneas is just about to kill Lausus, a paradigm of *pietas*. **per orbem | aere cavum triplici:** "through the hollow shield of triple brass" or "shield (shaped) hollow with triple brass"; the abl. (*aere...triplici*) is of material. For a similar portentous shield, see 482-3. **linea:** "of linen." **terga:** = "layers"; see also 482-4 n.

784-5. **tribusque |...tauris:** "with (the hides of) three bulls," abl. of material after *intextum*. *Taurus* = "ox-hide"; by whole-for-part synecdoche*. **intextum...opus:** the accusative is still governed by the preposition *per*.

785-6. **imaque sedit | inguine:** *ima* = *ima hasta* "the bottom part of the spear." Alternatively, *ima* (adv.) = "low down (in the groin)," denoting position. The first alternative should be preferred as this seems to be a case where the adjective is transferred from the adverbial phrase to the subject (*hasta*). See 230-1 n. **sed...pertulit:** "but it did not carry force (with it)," for Aeneas' spear lost most of its force as it broke through Mezentius' shield. **ocius:** modifies *eripit* at 788. The comparative is used instead of the positive (*ociter*); the positive does not seem to be attested in Latin before Apuleius.

787. **viso...sanguine:** abl. of cause after *laetus*. **Tyrrheni:** "of the Etruscan," i.e., of Mezentius.

788. **a femine:** = "from his thigh," ablative singular of *femor*. *Femine* (rather than the more common *femore*) is attested here by all manuscripts and Servius. **trepidanti:** supply *Mezentio*. Dative after *instat*, see 26-7 n.

789. **ingemuit...graviter:** note the dramatic placing of the verb in initial position. The phrase recurs at 823, but there describes Aeneas at the moment of Lausus' death. For the way in which Vergil fuses the character of Aeneas and Lausus in this episode, see Putnam (1995) 138. **cari**

ut vidit, Lausus, lacrimaeque per ora volutae. 790
Hic mortis durae casum tuaque optima facta,
si qua fidem tanto est operi latura vetustas,
non equidem nec te, iuvenis memorande, silebo.
Ille pedem referens et inutilis inque ligatus

---

genitoris: objective genitive governed by *amore*. Hated by all, Mezentius is a "dear father" to Lausus.

790. **volutae**: sc. *sunt*. For the active meaning of the verb, see 403 n.

791-3. The narrator praises Lausus' valor.

As he had done for Euryalus and Nisus (9.446-9) and Pallas (see 507-9), the narrator interrupts the narrative to apostrophize in his own person the youth, praising his valor and promising immortal glory through his song. Note how, in this case, the emphasis of the apostrophe* is increased by the word order, with accusatives at 791, and a subordinate clause at 792 before the subject and verb at 793.

791. **Hic**: "here." **mortis durae casum**: the plain, unfigured, form would have been *mortis durum casum*. For enallage*, see 230-1 n.

792. **si qua...vetustas**: = *si aliqua vetustas*. **fidem**: "credibility." The line is of difficult interpretation but seems to mean that Lausus' deed, which if reported of modern times would be justly disbelieved, should be thought credible because it is sufficiently ancient and possibly because "antiquity" is the age of heroes. **est...latura**: "is about to bring." *Latura* is the future active participle of *fero*, nominative feminine singular agreeing with *vetustas*.

793. **non equidem**: with *silebo*. **nec te**: *nec* links *te* with *casum* and *fata*. **memorande**: voc. of the gerundive; it is in artistic juxtaposition with *silebo*: "worthy of song and so not unsung." For the poet memorializing the deeds of the fallen from a future perspective, cf. 507 n. **silebo**: in its transitive sense (its objects are *casum, facta*, and *te*) means "be silent about," "leave unsung."

794-832. Aeneas would have killed Mezentius with his sword had not young Lausus rushed in to intercept the blow. Meanwhile his followers carry off Mezentius and rain their darts upon Aeneas, who maintains his place until the storm is over and then, after vainly warning Lausus, kills him. Aeneas, struck with pity at the sight of the youth's pale dead face, returns both his body and his weapons to the boy's companions.

Reed (2007) 36-43 compares Vergil's sensual description of Lausus' beautiful body to that of Adonis, the strikingly handsome and sexually ambiguous youth loved by Aphrodite who died after being wounded by a boar, and he further suggests an equation between the slaying of an umarried youth (here Lausus) and defloration. For Lausus as a primeval version of the young Scipio Africanus who, in the battle of Ticinus, saved the life of his father, see Goldschmidt (2013) 180. For Aeneas' behavior toward Lausus juxtaposed with that of Turnus toward Pallas, see 439-509 n. For the death of Lausus replaying the death of Antilochus in the *Aithiopis*, where the youth has similarly saved his father Nestor from Memnon, see Quint (2018) 185-9.

794. **Ille**: i.e., Mezentius. **pedem referens**: lit. "carrying back his foot," i.e., "moving back." **inutilis**: "unfit for fight." **inque ligatus**: = *inligatusque*, "hampered"; rather common in other poets (Ennius and Lucretius), tmesis* is rare in Vergil.

cedebat clipeoque inimicum hastile trahebat.   795
proripuit iuvenis seseque immiscuit armis,
iamque adsurgentis dextra plagamque ferentis
Aeneae subiit mucronem ipsumque morando
sustinuit; socii magno clamore sequuntur,
dum genitor nati parma protectus abiret,   800
telaque coniciunt perturbantque eminus hostem
missilibus. furit Aeneas tectusque tenet se.
ac velut effusa si quando grandine nimbi

---

795. **cedebat...trahebat:** the imperfects underscore the slow and painful withdrawal from the field. **clipeoque:** "with his shield." **inimicum hastile:** i.e., the enemy's javelin (stuck on his shield), but the javelin is also hostile for it wounded him.

796. **proripuit:** "dashed forward." The emphatic initial position of the verb reflects the youth's (*iuvenis*) eagerness to come to his father's aid. **armis:** dative after *immiscuit*; see 26-7 n.

797-8. **adsurgentis...mucronem:** construe as *subiit mucronem* (see 570 n.) *Aeneae adsurgentis dextra (et) ferentis plagam.* **adsurgentis...ferentis:** gens. referring to *Aeneae* of the following line. **dextra:** "with his right (arm)," instrumental abl. **subiit mucronem:** "slipped under the sword" (of Aeneas). For the transitive use of *subeo*, see AG §370b. **morando:** ablative of the gerund.

799. **sustinuit:** the object is *ipsum* at 798 (i.e., Aeneas). **sequuntur:** here the meaning is not that his companions (*socii*) "follow" Lausus with a loud shout (*magno clamore*), but that they "back up" his action with a shout.

800. **dum...abiret:** subjunctive because *dum* marks their purpose (AG §553). For the use of a secondary tense after an historical present (*sequuntur*), see AG §485e. **genitor nati:** are pathetically set one next to the other to emphasize Lausus' filial devotion. **parma:** instrumental abl.; the light shield of Lausus (*nati*) emphasizes the boy's youth. The *parma* was carried by light-armed soldiers (*velites*), usually the youngest soldiers of the army.

802. **tectusque:** "and protected (by the shield)." **tenet se:** lit. "holds himself," i.e., holds his ground. Note the short sentence, the alliteration* of *t* and the monosyllabic ending, expressing Aeneas' angry frustration (*furit*).

803-8. The comparison of showers of missiles to rain, hail, or snow belongs to the epic tradition (cf. e.g., *Il.* 12.156; Ennius, fr. 266 Skutsch and in *FRL* 1; *Aen.* 12.284), while the *agricola* appears in other Vergilian similes* (cf. 2.628; 12.453). Note the number of correspondences between simile and context (*tectus | tuta latet arce, dum pluit | dum detonet*) and how the language of the narrative, in Vergilian fashion, uses weather imagery (e.g., *obrutus, nubem belli, detonet*). For these Vergilian features, see also 134-7 n. and 405-9 n.

803. **effusa...grandine:** abl. abs.

praecipitant, omnis campis diffugit arator
omnis et agricola, et tuta latet arce viator 805
aut amnis ripis aut alti fornice saxi,
dum pluit in terris, ut possint sole reducto
exercere diem: sic obrutus undique telis
Aeneas nubem belli, dum detonet omnis,
sustinet et Lausum increpitat Lausoque minatur: 810
'quo moriture ruis maioraque viribus audes?
fallit te incautum pietas tua.' nec minus ille
exsultat demens, saevae iamque altius irae
Dardanio surgunt ductori, extremaque Lauso

804-5. **praecipitant**: is here used intransitively, "plunge down." **omnis...arator | omnis... agricola**: emphatic anaphora*. **campis**: see 473 n. **diffugit**: for the tense, see 103 n. **tuta...arce**: locative ablative, "in safe shelter."

806. **ripis**: locative ablative (plural); it refers to the overhanging banks of some mountain stream (*amnis*). **fornice**: "in the vault," locative ablative; the term is used also at 6.631.

807-8. **dum pluit in terris**: for *dum* and the present ind., see 43 n. For the expression, cf. *cum pluit in terris* (Lucret., *DRN* 6.630). **ut possint**: purpose clause. The subjects are the *arator*, the *agricola*, and the *viator* mentioned above. **sole reducto**: abl. abs.

808-9. **exercere diem**: lit. "keep the day busy," i.e., spend the rest of the day at their work, once the sun returns. **obrutus**: "overwhelmed," but the term can also mean "flooded" and is an instance of the weather imagery of the simile* leaking or trespassing into the language of the narrative, just like *nubem* and *detonet* at 809. **nubem**: object of *sustinet* at 810. **detonet**: "cease to thunder." For the subjunctive, see 800 n. The suffix *de* implies completion of action. The verb is first found in Vergil. **omnis**: sc. *nubes*, nominative singular, subject of *detonet*.

810. **Lausum...Lausoque**: cf. Turnus at 10.442-3 *solus ego in Pallanta feror, soli mihi Pallas | debetur*. **minatur**: takes the dative (*Lauso*); see AG §367.

811. **quo**: "to what end?" **moriture**: for the future active participle used of people destined to certain death, cf. 881 and *periture* (11.856). **viribus**: abl. of comparison after *maiora*.

812. **pietas tua**: Aeneas touches on an important point: up to what point can/should *pietas* justify excessive or impulsive behavior? Cf. 591 n. Putnam (1995) 135 suggests that here Aeneas questions the meaning of *pietas*, the virtue that, in many ways, is his own defining characteristic, and the reader is, therefore, left to wonder about the overall value of the virtue. **ille**: i.e., Lausus.

813-14. **exsultat**: describes Lausus' defiant behavior; cf. 550 and 643. **demens**: suggests doomed folly. **altius**: the comparative adverb qualifies *surgunt* at 814. **Dardanio...ductori**: dative of reference. Aeneas was already "enraged" (*furit* 802) at being robbed of his prey and attacked by the followers of Mezentius, but "now in (lit. 'to') the Dardanian leader fierce anger rises higher." Aeneas' anger similarly builds up in his final duel with Turnus (12.494 *tum vero adsurgunt irae*). The metaphor* seems to be taken from the movement of water (Harrison *ad loc.*). **Lauso**: dative of reference.

Parcae fila legunt: validum namque exigit ensem 815
per medium Aeneas iuvenem totumque recondit.
transiit et parmam mucro, levia arma minaci,
et tunicam molli mater quam neverat auro,
implevitque sinum sanguis; tum vita per auras
concessit maesta ad manis corpusque reliquit. 820
at vero ut vultum vidit morientis et ora,
ora modis Anchisiades pallentia miris,

---

815. **Parcae:** the Fates, and especially Clotho, spin the thread of each human life, and, when it draws near its end, "gather up the last threads (*extrema fila*)," i.e., the last portions of the thread, which they finally cut. **namque:** see 400-1 n.

816. **iuvenem:** underscores Lausus' young age. Cf. also 793, 796. **totumque:** refers to the sword. Aeneas buries his sword in Pallas' body "in all its length."

817-18. **et…| et:** "both…and." **parmam:** see 800 n., object of *transiit* together with *tunicam*. **mucro:** see 570 n. Subject of *transiit*. **levia arma:** is in apposition to *parmam*. **minaci:** a dative after *levis* and is preferable to the variant *minacis*, "weapons (too) slight for one (so) threatening." **molli…auro:** = *quam mater neverat molli auro*. **molli…auro:** lit. "from pliant gold." abl. of material. The touching detail is suggestive of her love. Wiltshire (1989) 54 links Lausus' cloak to that woven for Euryalus by his mother (9.488), another doomed boy fated to die before reaching manhood.

819-20. **tum vita…:** the formula* recalls the one Homer used for the deaths of Patroclus and Hector which Vergil reworks also for the deaths of Camilla and Turnus (11.831 = 12.952 *vitaque cum gemitu fugit indignata sub umbras*). See 755-832 n. Cf. also *in ventos vita recessit* (4.705, death of Dido). **corpusque reliquit:** repeats with different wording *vita per auras | concessit…ad manis* and is another example of *dicolon abundans**, see 9-10 n.

821-2. **at vero ut vultum vidit:** Aeneas' transition from anger to pity is presented in slow spondees with strong alliteration* of *v*'s. **ora | ora:** the same epanalepsis* over line break is found at 6.495-6; for other similarly pathetic epanalepsis, cf. also 2.405-6 (*lumina frustra | lumina*) and 10.180-1. **ora modis…pallentia miris:** "the face (growing) pale in a surprising way." *Miris modis* is adapted from *Geo.*1.477 to describe the apparitions at Caesar's death (*simulacra modis pallentia miris*), a line that, in turn, was taken verbatim from Lucretius' description of the dead (*DRN* 1.123). Vergil uses the same expression at 1.354 (*ora modis atollens pallida miris*, the apparition of Dido' unburied husband during her sleep), at 6.738 (*modis inolescere miris*, of the many long-accumulated contagions that are deeply engrained in the soul), and 7.89 (*multa modis simulacra videt volitantia miris*, apparitions to Latinus during his sleep). **Anchisiades:** the patronymic* (used here for the last time in the poem), reminds the reader of Aeneas' own filial responsibilities toward his father at the very moment another son loses his life saving his own father. The indirect mention of Anchises, however, also brings to mind the other father who will now have to endure the loss of his son killed by the "son of Anchises": Mezentius.

ingemuit miserans graviter dextramque tetendit,
et mentem patriae subiit pietatis imago.
'quid tibi nunc, miserande puer, pro laudibus istis,   825
quid pius Aeneas tanta dabit indole dignum?
arma, quibus laetatus, habe tua; teque parentum
manibus et cineri, si qua est ea cura, remitto.
hoc tamen infelix miseram solabere mortem:

---

823. **miserans**: used absolutely. **dextramque tetendit**: Aeneas stretches his hand as a sign of compassion. This gesture is described only here in the poem. Contrast *dextram tendit* (11.672), where the hand is held out to give actual support.

824. **patriae...pietatis**: the adjective *patriae* (from *patrius, a, um*) is objective in sense, "of the *pietas* (shown) toward his own father." **imago**: has the double meaning of "image" and "replica" (i.e., Lausus' *pietas* toward his father is also a replica of Aeneas' *pietas* toward his own). Both meanings are surely present for, as Hardie (1994) *ad* 9.294 rightly suggests, the power of the line lies in its open-endedness as emotions and relationships in Vergil tend to merge into one another. For *imago* in Lucretius (used to denote corporeal and transitory images) and a possible Lucretian subtext in this passage, see Coppolino (2005). For Turnus' different reaction at his killing of Pallas, see 443.

825-6. **quid tibi**: sc. *est*. **miserande puer**: see 326-7 n. **pro laudibus istis**: "in return for these praiseworthy deeds of yours," is possibly a pun on the boy's name (*Lausus/laudibus*) signaled by Aeneas' immediate reference to Lausus' *indoles* (nature) in the following line (826). See Stover (2011) 353. **pius**: the use of the epithet* is particularly relevant here since Aeneas is paying tribute to Lausus' *pietas* but also somewhat ironic* since he has just taken issue with Lausus' *pietas*. See 812 n. **Aeneas**: cf. 73. For the lines, compare "*quae vobis, quae digna, viri, pro laudibus istis | praemia posse rear solvi?*" (9.252-3 Auletes praising Euryalus' and Nisus' act of courage). **tanta...indole**: abl. after *dignum*.

827. **laetatus**: sc. *es; es* is rarely omitted (cf. 1.237; 5.687), but here the extreme clearness of the phrase makes it allowable. For Aeneas' gesture, see also 496 n. **habe**: "keep." **parentum**: "of the ancestors," genitive after *manibus* and *cineri*.

828. **manibus**: dative plural from *manes*, "to the shades"; the *manes* were the spirits of dead ancestors. Their cult was celebrated at the Roman festivals of the *Feralia, Lemuria*, and *Parentalia*. **si qua est ea cura**: sc. *tibi*, "if that be any (*qua = aliqua*) care to you." Honors paid to the dead are ever accompanied by a natural doubt whether such things concern them at all. Cf. also 493. **remitto**: see 492 n. Aeneas speaks as if the spirits of the dead are still lingering around their place of burial. He gives back the body so that Lausus may rejoin them.

829. **hoc**: ablative of cause, anticipates the explanation of the following line. **solabere**: = *solaberis* ("you will bring solace for").

Aeneae magni dextra cadis.' increpat ultro 830
cunctantis socios et terra sublevat ipsum
sanguine turpantem comptos de more capillos.

833-908: Mezentius' death

The wounded Mezentius inquires about Lausus' fate, showing a deep and sincere concern for his son. Upon hearing of his son's death, he rides forth with his horse and challenges Aeneas to a duel only to meet his death at the hands of the Trojan hero. The depth of Mezentius' sorrow for his son's death and the nobility with which he meets his own fate add an altogether new dimension to his character: in his final hour, Mezentius, the impious, becomes the epitome of paternal *pietas*. His behavior calls to mind that of the old father Priam of the *Aeneid*, who too, although old and no longer fit to fight, after the death of his son Polites, seeks his own death at the hands of the ruthless Pyrrhus.

Quint (2018) 172 suggests that in the duel with Aeneas, Mezentius is cast, initially, in the role of Achilles out to avenge the death of Patroclus and, later, in that of Hector pleading with Achilles for burial. He therefore concludes that "the book thus closes where one would expect, with the normative epic model of Achilles and Hector—and it looks forward to Book 12, where the final duel of Aeneas and Turnus will elaborately imitate the duel of Achilles and Hector in *Iliad* 22."

For bibliography on Mezentius, see notes on 689-754, 755-832, 755-68. More specifically, on Mezentius' death as reenacting the torture inflicted on his enemies whereby the body of a living person was tied to a cadaver (*Aen.* 8.478-88), see Rosati (2017).

---

830. **Aeneae magni...**: for this heroic consolation, cf. *Il*. 7.89-91; *Aen*. 11.688-9 *nomen tamen haud leve patrum | manibus hoc referes, telo cecidisse Camillae*. Note the bucolic diaeresis* at the end of the speech. By referring to himself grandiloquently in the third person, Aeneas effectively plays up his status as a warrior. **ultro**: "of his own initiative"; qualifies *increpat* "reproaches."

831. **cunctantis socios**: object of *increpat*. They are Lausus' companions. Lausus' companions were cowed at seeing their young leader fall, and Aeneas chides them for not coming to fetch the body. **ipsum**: i.e., Lausus.

832. **comptos...capillos**: object of *turpantem*. **de more**: "in the traditional way." The "hair arranged stylishly" is the mark of an attractive young man. The passage is modeled on *Iliad* 24.589 where Achilles personally places Hector's body onto the bier to be delivered to the Trojans. See Barchiesi (2015) 50 n.19. For a comparison with Turnus' behavior, see 496 n. For Lausus as an Adonis-figure and the eroticism of his death scene, see Reed (2007) 36-7 and 794-832 n. Coppolino (2005) 13 notes that Vergil in this line adopts the language used by Lucretius in his description of the sacrifice of Iphigenia (*DRN* 1.85-87).

LIBER DECIMUS

Interea genitor Tiberini ad fluminis undam
vulnera siccabat lymphis corpusque levabat
arboris acclinis trunco. procul aerea ramis 835
dependet galea et prato gravia arma quiescunt.
stant lecti circum iuvenes; ipse aeger anhelans
colla fovet fusus propexam in pectore barbam;
multa super Lauso rogitat, multumque remittit
qui revocent maestique ferant mandata parentis. 840
at Lausum socii exanimem super arma ferebant

833-57. Mezentius sends messenger after messenger to call back Lausus from the battle and, when he sees Lausus' companions bring back his corpse, he bitterly reproaches himself for having now caused his son's death as before he had sullied his life.

833. **genitor:** Mezentius is sympathetically reintroduced as Lausus' father.

834. **lymphis:** "with water"; the term is poetic. Mezentius "was stanching" (*siccabat*) the blood with water. **levabat:** "eased." All major manuscripts have *lavabat* "to wash" which adds very little to *siccabat lymphis*. Servius is surely right to read *levabat*.

835. **acclinis:** "leaning against." **trunco:** dative after *acclinis*. **procul:** Cf. 777 n.

836. **prato:** locative abl. **gravia arma quiescunt:** the running water of a stream (*ad fluminis undam*), the green meadow (*prato*), and the tree (*trunco*) and its shade (*ramis*) are traditional elements of the topos* of the *locus amoenus* (an idealized place of safety or comfort), which here provides a pointed contrast with the reality of war (Harrison *ad loc.*). In this place, weapons "lie silent." For this landscape of serenity as evoking an Epicurean ideal of tranquility and self-sufficiency, see also Kronenberg (2005) 411.

837. **lecti...iuvenes:** i.e., his most trusted warriors. **circum:** adverb qualifying *stant*. **aeger anhelans:** i.e., Mezentius. Note the juxtaposition of alliterative words of increasing semantic force.

838. **fovet:** the verb is common of medicinal bathing, but here it could simply mean that Mezentius tries "to make his neck (*colla*) comfortable," by leaning against the tree. **propexam...barbam:** retained accusative after *fusus* (lit. "spread out with regards to his beard combed forward on his chest"), see 132-3 n.

839. **multa...multumque:** the rhetorical polyptoton* (the second *multum* (= *saepe*) is adverbial) and the frequentative *rogitat* emphasize Mezentius' concern. **super:** see 42 n.

840. **qui:** the antecedent of the relative pronoun is an understood *viros* vel sim. **revocent... ferant:** subjunctives in a relative clause of purpose. **parentis:** see 833 n.

841. **at Lausum:** the strong adversative *at* and the repetition of Lausus' name in emphatic position (*Lauso...at Lausum*) dramatically juxtapose Mezentius' expectations and the harsh reality of Lausus' death. **super arma:** i.e., on top of his shield. So too the young Pallas, cf. 506 n.

flentes, ingentem atque ingenti vulnere victum.
agnovit longe gemitum praesaga mali mens.
canitiem multo deformat pulvere et ambas
ad caelum tendit palmas et corpore inhaeret.   845
'tantane me tenuit vivendi, nate, voluptas,
ut pro me hostili paterer succedere dextrae,
quem genui? tuane haec genitor per vulnera servor
morte tua vivens? heu, nunc misero mihi demum
exitium infelix, nunc alte vulnus adactum!   850

842. **flentes:** i.e., the *socii* (841). The spondee followed by a pause marks melancholy (cf. *Ecl.* 5.20-1 *exstinctum Nymphae crudeli funere Daphnim | flebant*), and the heavy movement of the next words *ingentem atque ingenti*, followed by strong alliteration* *vulnere victum*, heightens the effect. **ingentem:** "a mighty (warrior)." **ingenti vulnere:** instrumental ablative after *victum*.

843. **agnovit longe gemitum:** cf. *Il.* 22.447 (Hector's wife, Andromache, discovers that her husband has been killed by Achilles as she hears noises of mourning coming from the walls of the city), 4.672 *audiit* (Anna, of Dido's death). **mali:** objective genitive dependent on *praesaga* ("foretelling"). **mens:** for the monosyllabic ending, see 2 n.

844. **canitiem...:** described up to this point as mighty and fearless, Mezentius seems to age suddenly after his son's death. See Gotoff (1984) 209. For *canities* as symbolic of old age, cf. 549. For a similar act of mourning, cf. *canitiem immundo perfusam puluere turpans* (12.611, Latinus). Cf. also Achilles who befouled himself at the news of Patroclus' death (*Il.* 18.22-4).

845. **corpore:** i.e., of Lausus. The simple abl. (locative) after *inhaereo* (instead of the more common dative) is poetic, cf. Ov., *Met.* 11.403 *inhaerentem...cervice*. For Mezentius' cleaving to his son's dead body, see Rosati (2017).

846. **vivendi:** genitive of the gerund after *voluptas*. For *vivendi voluptas* as a marked Epicurean expression which defines the inescapable drive to seek pleasure that shapes the ethical world of Epicureans and constitutes their *summum bonum*, see Kronenberg (2005) 413. Observe the emotional alliterations* (*tanta tenuit; vivendi voluptas*).

847. **ut...paterer:** result clause. Supply *te* as antecedent to *quem genui* and as object of *paterer*. **hostili...dextrae:** dative after the compound *succedere*.

848. **quem genui:** "whom I begat," repeats the idea expressed with *nate* at 846 and is again picked up by *genitor* ("I, your father") and *nate* at 851. **tuane haec...per vulnera:** construe as *per tua haec vulnera*. Note also the emphatic repetition of *tuane...tua* and the juxtaposition *morte tua vivens* (848-9). In this speech of bitter self-reproach, Mezentius reveals a deep love for his son and a great contempt of death.

849. **morte tua:** instrumental ablative. **misero mihi:** dative of reference.

850. **exitium infelix:** sc. *est*. *Exitium* is the reading of the manuscripts and should be preferred to the reading *exilium* attested in Servius and defended by Dewar (1988). After Lausus' death, Mezentius can say: "now at last...my end is truly wretched," since his son has died before him. **alte vulnus adactum:** sc. *est*, "the wound has been thrust deep." The verb *adigo* is often used of a sword being thrust into an enemy (cf. 9.431 *ensis adactus*), but here Vergil adapts the more

idem ego, nate, tuum maculavi crimine nomen,
pulsus ob invidiam solio sceptrisque paternis.
debueram patriae poenas odiisque meorum:
omnis per mortis animam sontem ipse dedissem!
nunc vivo neque adhuc homines lucemque relinquo.   855
sed linquam.' simul hoc dicens attollit in aegrum
se femur et, quamquam vis alto vulnere tardat,
haud deiectus equum duci iubet. hoc decus illi,

---

common phrase and has the wound itself being thrust into the enemy. The meaning of the sentence is that, though Aeneas has wounded him, it is Lausus' death that has made the wound yet deeper. The *dicolon abundans** (9-10 n.) gives force to the idea.

851. **crimine:** "with (this) crime" (instrumental ablative), i.e., the charge of being the son of a villainous father. **nomen:** i.e., good name, reputation.

852. **pulsus ob invidiam:** "driven because of hatred." In 8.483-95 Evander describes to Aeneas Mezentius' horrible crimes toward his own people and how he has been expelled by his own citizens. The expression is repeated at 11.539 of Metabus (Camilla's father).

853-4. **debueram...poenas:** the pluperfect indicates that the debt had been incurred long before the present events, "I already owed (my) punishment." **patriae...odiisque:** indirect objects of *debueram*. **meorum:** subjective genitive, i.e., the hatred my fellow citizens felt for me. **omnis per mortis:** *per* is instrumental. The expression seems to mean "through every kind of death" rather than "through death from every quarter." **dedissem:** either jussive subjunctive "I ought to have yielded (= *debueram dare*)" or optative (= *utinam dedissem*).

855. For the *dicolon abundans**, see 9-10 n.

856-7. **sed linquam:** "but I will leave (sc. *homines* and *lucem* from 855)." Note the strong brevity of this final sentence. **attollit in aegrum | se femur:** "he raised himself on his weak thigh," where he had been wounded.

857. **tardat:** "fails," because of the deep wound (*alto vulnere*). Alternatively, *tardat* may be taken to mean "makes (sc. him) slow." In this case, "vis" = "(his diminished) strength."

858-72. Bereft of his son, Mezentius turns to his beloved horse Rhaebus. In a highly moving speech, he pledges to either live or die with him to avenge the "pains of Lausus."

Mezentius' speech has two important models. The first is Achilles' conversation with his horse Xanthus (*Il*. 19.397-423). Both take place before the two heroes' return to battle and both anticipate their death. However, in Mezentius' case the horse remains dramatically silent after his master's speech, unable to utter words of comfort. Rhaebus, unlike Xanthus, mourns in silence. For Mezentius as Achilles, see Quint (2018) 172. The second is the speech that Polyphemus, just blinded by Odysseus, addresses to his ram (*Od*. 9.447-60). This second subtext further strengthens the parallel Mezentius-Polyphemus (cf. 768 n. and 771 n). On the topic, see Glenn (1971) 140-9.

858. **deiectus:** sc. *animo*. **equum duci:** accusative subject and infinitive (passive) introduced by *iubet*.

> hoc solamen erat, bellis hoc victor abibat
> omnibus. adloquitur maerentem et talibus infit: 860
> 'Rhaebe, diu, res si qua diu mortalibus ulla est,
> viximus. aut hodie victor spolia illa cruenta
> et caput Aeneae referes Lausique dolorum
> ultor eris mecum, aut aperit si nulla viam vis,
> occumbes pariter; neque enim, fortissime, credo, 865
> iussa aliena pati et dominos dignabere Teucros.'
> dixit, et exceptus tergo consueta locavit

858-9. **hoc:** refers to the horse. We might have expected *hic* (masc.) as referring to *equus*, but *hic* is attracted to the gender of its predicate *decus*. **decus:** "pride." **illi:** dative of reference. **solamen:** "consolation," cf. 3.660-1, where the sheep of the Cyclops are *sola voluptas | solamenque mali*. Cf. 858-72 n.

859. **hoc:** this third *hoc* is an ablative of means ("with this").

860. **maerentem:** i.e., the horse, cf. 11.89-90 *post bellator equus positis insignibus Aethon, | it lacrimans, guttisque humectat grandibus ora* (Pallas' charger sheds tears at his master's funeral). **infit:** see 101 n.

861-2. **Rhaebe:** "bandy-legs," in Greek. **diu...:** the anaphora* of *diu* is emphatic, while the perfect *viximus* (862) suggests the additional thought, "and now our life is over"; Dido meets her death with a similar philosophic pronouncement (*vixi et quem dederat cursum fortuna peregi* 4.653). **res si...est:** *qua* is feminine sing. adjective (nominative) of the indefinite (ali)*qui, -a, -quod*, "if any thing at all is for a long time for mortals." **mortalibus:** dat. of reference.

862. **cruenta:** "bloody," for they will be stained with Aeneas' blood. *Illa* is deictic*. The reading *cruenta* should be preferred over *cruenti*, for *cruentus* in Vergil is always used of people (or objects) covered in blood and never to mean "bloodthirsty," a necessary meaning if we read *cruenti* (agreeing with the genitive *Aeneae*) instead of *cruenta*.

863. **caput Aeneae referes:** "you will carry back the head of Aeneas," i.e., Mezentius threatens to decapitate Aeneas. **Lausique dolorum:** can either mean "of the pains felt by Lausus" (subjective genitive) or "of the pains (I feel) for the death of Lausus" (objective genitive). Possibly both ideas are present.

864. **ultor eris mecum:** Polyphemus similarly wishes his ram to help him take revenge on Odysseus who has blinded him (*Od.* 9.456-60). Cf. 858-72 n. **viam vis:** the alliteration* and monosyllabic ending suggest force.

865. **pariter:** "together," i.e., you will die along with me, cf. 9.182 *pariterque in bella ruebant* (of Euryalus and Nisus). **fortissime:** the epithet*, better suited for humans than for animals, reflects Mezentius' humanization of his horse.

866. **iussa...dominos:** both objects are governed by the infinitive *pati* (from *patior*). **dignabere:** = *dignaberis* from *dignor* ("you will not deign").

867. **exceptus tergo:** "received on his (horse's) back." *Exceptus* suggests the horse's willingness to accept his well-known rider and stands in contrast with *neque... iussa aliena pati et dominos dignabere* (cf. also *consueta membra*). **locavit:** "he placed."

membra manusque ambas iaculis oneravit acutis,
aere caput fulgens cristaque hirsutus equina.
sic cursum in medios rapidus dedit. aestuat ingens   870
uno in corde pudor mixtoque insania luctu.
[et furiis agitatus amor et conscia virtus.]
   Atque hic Aenean magna ter voce vocavit.
Aeneas agnovit enim laetusque precatur:
'sic pater ille deum faciat, sic altus Apollo!   875
incipias conferre manum.'

---

869. **aere:** instrumental ablative, a reference to Mezentius' helmet which was made of bronze. **caput:** acc. of specification. Cf. 132-3 n. **cristaque...equina:** "(shaggy) with his horse-hair crest."

870-1. **in medios:** sc. *hostes* vel sim. **aestuat:** "seethes," the metaphor* is taken from the movement of water. **ingens |...pudor:** the shame for having caused Lausus' death and for still being alive, while his son is dead. **uno in corde:** calls attention to the variety of conflicting emotions experienced, at once, by Mezentius. **insania:** the maddening anger he feels against Aeneas. **luctu:** the sorrow he feels for Lausus' death. Line 871 is used of Turnus at 12.667 after Turnus receives the news of the siege of the city of King Latinus and of the death of Amata. For the relation between the two passages (possibly underscoring points of similarity between Mezentius and Turnus), see Tarrant *ad loc*. Line 872 is absent in the best manuscripts and should be omitted.

873-908. *Mezentius rides forth to challenge Aeneas. Mortally wounded by Aeneas, he meets his death with dignity. He asks for no pity and only begs to be buried with his son. He then accepts the death blow.*

Although the duel between Aeneas and Mezentius closely follows Homeric conventions, it departs from them in one important detail: in the typical staging of the epic duel, the rule holds good that whoever emerges victorious in the encounter is either the only one to speak or the last one to speak. In a significant violation of this epic code, Vergil grants Mezentius this privilege, leaving Aeneas, the alleged protagonist, in the background. For the death of Mezentius as marked by a submerged cultural model traceable to gladiatorial games, see Conte (2007) 195. For Homeric models as important subtexts to the duel, see 833-908 n.

873. **Aenean:** Greek accusative. **ter:** is a conventional number, see also 885 n. **voce vocavit:** is a favorite Vergilian assonance*, solemn in tone; cf. 4.680-1; 6.247, 506; 12.483, 638.

874. **agnovit enim:** "indeed did Aeneas recognize him"; *enim* = "indeed" is an archaic use of the word. After *agnovit* is emphatic and stresses the verb.

875. **ille...altus:** if *ille* here merely means "mighty," we may take the following *altus* as "lordly." However, since this is a prayer addressed to heaven, it seems more forcible to give both *ille* and *altus* a local meaning (respectively "up there" and "on high"). **deum:** see 228-9 n. **faciat:** jussive subjunctive.

876. **incipias:** many take *incipias* as dependent on *faciat*, "so may Jove grant that you should begin," with *sic* meaning somewhat awkwardly, "even as I desire." Both *faciat* and *incipias* are,

tantum effatus et infesta subit obvius hasta.
ille autem: 'quid me erepto, saevissime, nato
terres? haec via sola fuit qua perdere posses:
nec mortem horremus nec divum parcimus ulli.   880
desine, nam venio moriturus et haec tibi porto
dona prius.' dixit, telumque intorsit in hostem;
inde aliud super atque aliud figitque volatque
ingenti gyro, sed sustinet aureus umbo.
ter circum astantem laevos equitavit in orbis   885
tela manu iaciens, ter secum Troius heros

---

however, better taken as independent jussive subjunctives, with the second clause explaining *sic* in the first.

877. **tantum effatus:** lit. "having spoken so much (and no more)," a speech-formula already used at 256.

878. **ille autem:** sc. *dixit vel sim.* The omission of the verb of speaking before Mezentius' reply conveys excitement. **quid:** see 611 n. **erepto...nato:** abl. abs. **saevissime:** the superlative adjective (vocative) is pointedly placed between *erepto nato* which explains it. Aeneas is "most cruel" because he has taken Mezentius' son away from his father.

879. **terres:** i.e., with your threatening words and movements. **via:** "way," i.e., by robbing me of my son. **qua...posses:** relative clause of purpose with *qua* meaning "such that by it." **perdere:** "destroy (me)."

880. **divum...ulli:** *ulli* is dative after *parcimus*. For *divum*, see 2 n. **parcimus:** "we have regard for," see OLD s.v. 4. *Pius* Aeneas had just appealed to the gods, and now Mezentius, the scorner of the gods, states that he will not refrain from his attack out of regard for any of them. Kronenberg (2005) has noted that Mezentius' statement that he has no fear of death (*nec mortem horremus*) or regard for the gods reads as the manifesto of Epicurean philosophy for, according to Epicureanism, both fear of death and fear of the gods threaten human happiness and should be dismissed. For Mezentius as an Epicurean philosopher, see also 689-754 n.

881. **desine:** imperative, "cease," is used absolutely. **moriturus:** see 811 n., but this time, Mezentius uses it about himself for he knows (and welcomes) the destiny awaiting him.

882. **dona:** i.e., the spears he carries. The term is used ironically*. **prius:** adv. "before," i.e., he will not go down before fighting against Aeneas.

883-4. **super:** adv. ("in addition"). **figitque volatque |...gyro:** "he (Mezentius) implants (sc. them, i.e., the javelins) as he speeds round (Aeneas) in a great circle." **sustinet:** "withstands," i.e., the javelins. **aureus:** but *aerato* at 887; both brass and gold had been used by Vulcan in the making of Aeneas' shield, cf. 8.445 (*fluit aes rivis aurique metallum*). **umbo:** see 271 n.

885. **ter:** "three times," is the number for unsuccessful attacks in epic. The fourth attempt, when made, is usually successful. **circum astantem:** "around (Aeneas) standing." **laevos...in orbis:** "in leftward circuits"; in this way Mezentius has his left side, which is protected by his shield, facing Aeneas.

immanem aerato circumfert tegmine silvam.
inde ubi tot traxisse moras, tot spicula taedet
vellere, et urgetur pugna congressus iniqua,
multa movens animo iam tandem erumpit et inter   890
bellatoris equi cava tempora conicit hastam.
tollit se arrectum quadripes et calcibus auras
verberat, effusumque equitem super ipse secutus
implicat eiectoque incumbit cernuus armo.
clamore incendunt caelum Troesque Latinique.   895
advolat Aeneas vaginaque eripit ensem

---

887. **immanem...silvam:** object of *circumfert*. The expression offers a visual image of darts stuck in the shield. **circumfert:** "moves around in a circle." As Mezentius is riding in circles around Aeneas, Aeneas rotates the shield (and the darts stuck in it) to defend himself from Mezentius' attacks. **tegmine:** locative ablative. *Tegmen* means "covering," but here (as at 9.577) is used metaphorically* for "shield."

888. **inde:** "then." **tot...moras:** "so many delays," object of *traxisse*. As noted by Conington and Nettleship *ad loc.*, the more regular wording should be *"tantum morae,"* but Vergil probably wished to balance *"tot spicula."* **traxisse:** like *vellere* depends on the impersonal *taedet*. **taedet:** supply *eum* (i.e., Aeneas) as this impersonal verb takes the accusative of the person affected,"when it wearies him."

889. **urgetur...:** "and is hard-pressed." **pugna...iniqua:** because he is on foot; ablative of cause. **congressus:** the perfect (deponent) participle refers to Aeneas.

890-1. **multa movens animo:** lit. "moving many things in his soul," i.e., Aeneas is possibly thinking about possible tactics to adopt. **erumpit:** "(Aeneas) bursts out," is the military term for making a sortie. **inter |...cava tempora:** the temples are a vital spot.

892. **arrectum:** i.e., on its hind legs. **quadripes:** "four-footer," is poetic for "horse." Subject of *tollit*. **calcibus:** "with its hooves," i.e., the horse "paws" the air with its forefeet.

893-4. **effusumque...| implicat:** construe as *ipse secutus super implicat equitem effusum*. *Ipse secutus* refers to the horse while *equitem effusum* is Mezentius, who has fallen from the horse when the horse "struck" the air with its feet. **super:** is used adverbially "on top." **implicat:** "holds fast." **eiectoque...armo:** abl. abs. *Eicere* = "to dislocate" is technical, while *armus* for the forequarter of an animal is standard. **cernuus:** the adjective, used before Vergil by the archaic poet Lucilius of a tumbler, seems to mean "headlong." The horse after rearing "pitched on to its head" putting its shoulder out.

895. **clamore incendunt caelum:** "set the sky alight with a shout," in a daring image, the sound is described in terms of heat. Cf. 11.147 *incendunt clamoribus urbem*; 9.500 *incendentem luctus*. In general, for the role of spectators in a duel reflecting the role of the readers of the text, see also 452 n. and Rossi (2004) 150-68. **Troesque Latinique:** doubled *-que*, "both...and." For the hypermetric line*, see also 781.

et super haec: 'ubi nunc Mezentius acer et illa
effera vis animi?' contra Tyrrhenus, ut auras
suspiciens hausit caelum mentemque recepit:
'hostis amare, quid increpitas mortemque minaris?   900
nullum in caede nefas, nec sic ad proelia veni,
nec tecum meus haec pepigit mihi foedera Lausus.
unum hoc per si qua est victis venia hostibus oro:
corpus humo patiare tegi. scio acerba meorum
circumstare odia: hunc, oro, defende furorem   905

897. **super**: see 556 n. **haec**: sc. *verba dixit*. **ubi nunc…**: sc. *est*. The taunt, although typical of a Homeric hero, reads particularly cruel in light of Mezentius' reply.

898-9. **contra Tyrrhenus**: sc. *dixit*. *Tyrrhenus* underscores Mezentius' Italian lineage. **auras | suspiciens**: "gazing at the air," see 781-2 n. Cf. also Dido (about to die) 4.691-2 *ter revoluta toro est oculisque errantibus alto | quaesivit caelo lucem ingemuitque reperta*. **hausit caelum**: either "drank the sky (by the eye)" or "drew in breath" with *caelum* = air. Conte (2007) 208 notes that "to gaze at the air and to breathe in the sky" is an example of double enallage* which stretches the connections between the words. **mentemque recepit**: his fall had stunned him, but now he recovers his senses.

900. **hostis amare**: vocative. *Amarus* is echoed by assonance* by *minaris*. *Hostis amare* transfers the bitterness of the words metonymically* to their speaker. **quid**: "why," see 611 n.

901. **nullum…nefas**: sc. *est*. **in caede**: locative ablative. Mezentius is referring to his own death. **sic**: "on such terms," i.e., to be spared by Aeneas.

902. **nec…Lausus**: either "Lausus, when he attacked you (and lost his life), did not suppose that you would spare me," or "Lausus by his death sealed the covenant that neither of us was to spare the other." But it is quite possible that both meanings may be included. **meus**: is movingly affectionate. **pepigit**: from *pango*, with *haec foedera* "made this bargain." **mihi**: dative of reference.

903. **unum hoc…oro**: "this one thing I beg"; *hoc* is explained by the next line. **per si qua est… venia**: understand *per veniam si (ali)qua est*, "by mercy, if there is any." **victis…hostibus**: dative of reference.

904-5. **corpus…tegi**: supply *meum*. Subject acc. and present inf. passive dependent on *patiare*. Mezentius' plea that Aeneas guarantee his burial recalls Hector's plea to Achilles to return his body for burial (*Il.* 22.338-43). *Aen.*11.5-11 suggests that Aeneas will not honor Mezentius' dignified request. See Anderson (1999) 198 and Thomas (2001) 138, who argue that as Aeneas sets up the trophy of Mezentius' arms, the breastplate with its twelve perforations suggests (as already noted by Servius) a ritual desecration of the corpse by each of the twelve Etruscan cities from which Mezentius had asked Aeneas' protection. **patiare**: = *patiaris*, a subjunctive depending on *oro* (with omission of *ut*, see 54-6 n.). **acerba…odia**: sc. *me* (as direct object of *circumdare*), while *meorum* is a subjective genitive, the bitter hatred of my people (toward me.) The personification* is particularly fitting because the Etruscans are watching the duel (895). **hunc…defende furorem**: "ward off this rage."

et me consortem nati concede sepulcro.'
haec loquitur, iuguloque haud inscius accipit ensem
undantique animam diffundit in arma cruore.

906. **consortem:** is in apposition to *me*. **nati:** gen. depending on *consortem*: "me as partner of my son." **sepulcro:** locative ablative.
907. **haud inscius:** "not unknowing," the litotes* marks Mezentius' resolute firmness. **accipit ensem:** the phrase is borrowed from the gladiatorial games in which the vanquished was said *ferrum recipere*, and it was a point of honor to receive, unmoved, the fatal stroke. For hints of a philosopher's suicide in Mezentius' complete willingness to die, see Kronenberg (2005) 424 n. 79.
908. **animam diffundit:** "and pours out his life." **in arma:** "onto his armor."

Appendix 1: Vergil's Meter[1]

The **dactylic hexameter** was the meter of Greek epic, and beginning with Ennius' *Annales* [2] (early second century BCE), it became the meter of Roman epic as well. Its basic rhythm can be felt in the following line from the opening of Longfellow's Evangeline:

This is the | forest pri | meval. The | murmuring | pines and the | hemlocks

Here five dactyls (búm-ba-ba) are followed by a final disyllabic foot. These metrical units (as with English verse more generally) are created through the use of natural word stress to create patterns of stressed and unstressed syllables. Thus, a dactyl in English poetry is a stressed syllable followed by two unstressed syllables (e.g., "Thís is the" and "múrmuring). Classical Latin meter, however, differs in an important way. Metrical feet are based not on word stress but on the quantity of individual syllables (i.e., whether they are long or short). Thus, in Latin a dactyl contains one long syllable followed by two shorts (–⌣⌣).

As the name indicates, "dactylic hexameter" literally consists of a line made from six (Gr. *hexa*) feet, each foot containing either a long syllable followed by two short syllables (a dactyl: –⌣⌣)[3] or two long syllables (a spondee: – –). The first four feet may be either dactyls or spondees.[4] The fifth foot is normally (but not always) a dactyl. The sixth foot is an anceps, that is, either

---

1 For more on Vergil's meter, see Jackson Knight (1944) 232-42, Duckworth (1969) 46-62, Nussbaum (1986), and Ross (2007) 143-52.
2 The early Latin epics by Livius Andronicus and Naevius were composed in Saturnian verse, a meter that is not fully understood.
3 The word "dactyl" comes from the Greek word *dactylos*, "finger." A metrical dactyl with its long and two shorts syllables resembles the structure of a finger: the bone from the knuckle to the first joint is longer than the two bones leading to the fingertip.
4 More technically the two short syllables of a dactyl are "contracted" into one long; together with the first long syllable, they form a spondee.

a long-long (– –) or long-short (– ⏑). A line of dactylic hexameter will follow this pattern:

$$-\smile\smile \mid -\smile\smile \mid -\smile\smile \mid -\smile\smile \mid -\smile\smile \mid -\underline{X}$$

(Here "|" separates metrical feet; "-" = a long syllable; "⏑"= a short syllable; and "x"= an *anceps* ("undecided") syllable, one that is either long or short.)

Very rarely a spondee is used in the fifth foot, in which case the line is called spondaic.

To scan a line (i.e., to identify a line's rhythm and meter), long and short syllables must be identified. A syllable can be *long* in two ways; by nature, if it contains a vowel that is inherently long or a diphthong;[5] or by position, if it contains a naturally short vowel followed either by a double consonant (*x* or *z*) or, in most cases, by two consonants.[6] In general, all other syllables are short. If, however, a word ending in a vowel, diphthong, or *-m* is followed by a word that begins with a vowel, a diphthong, or *h*, the first vowel or diphthong is elided (cf. *laeti* in 1.35 below; elided syllables are enclosed in parentheses in the examples below). As a result, the two syllables merge and are scanned as one—a phenomenon called *elision*. *Elision* occurs frequently in Vergil.

By applying these rules, we may scan hexameter lines as follows:

Mūltă sŭ/pēr Prĭă/mō rŏgĭ/tāns, sŭpĕr/ Hēctŏrĕ/ mūltă   (*Aen.* 1.750)

prōtrăhĭt / īn mĕdĭ/ōs; quaē/ sīnt ĕă/ nūmĭnă/ dīvŭm   (*Aen.* 2.123)

vēlă dă/bānt laē/t(i) ēt spū/mās sălĭs/aērĕ rŭ/ēbānt   (*Aen.* 1.35)

---

5   One can determine if a vowel is long by nature by looking the word up in a dictionary to see if it has a macron over it or by checking inflected endings in a grammar (for example, some endings like the first and second declension ablative singular (*-a*, *-o*), are always long; others, like the second declension nominative neuter plural (*-a*), are always short.

6   An exception to this general rule: if a short vowel is followed by a mute consonant (*b, c, d, g, p, t*) and a liquid (*l, r*), the resulting syllable can be either short or long. Cf. 2.663 where *patris* and *patrem* are short and long respectively: *natum ante ora pătris, pātrem qui obtruncat ad aras*. It should also be noted that *h* is a breathing, not a consonant; it therefore does not help make a vowel long by position.

A long syllable generally takes twice as long to pronounce as a short, and the first syllable of each foot receives a special metrical emphasis known as the *ictus*.

The flow of the line is affected not only by its rhythm but also by the placement of word breaks. A word break between metrical feet is called *diaeresis*:[7]

ēt iăcĭt. / ārrēc/ tāē mēnt / tēs stŭpĕ /fāctăquĕ / cōrdă   (*Aen.* 5.643)

Here, diaereses occur after *iacit* and after *stupefactaque*;[8] the former helps reinforce the syntactic pause after *iacit*. A word break within a metrical foot is called *caesura*. When a caesura falls after the first syllable of the foot, it is called "strong" (as after the first *super* in 1.750); if it falls after the second syllable in a dactylic foot, it is called "weak" (as after *multa* in 1.750). The most important caesura in any given line often coincides with a sense break and is called the main or principal caesura.[9] It most frequently falls in the third foot, but also occurs not uncommonly in the second or fourth (or sometimes both). The slight pause implied in the main caesura helps shape the movement of each verse by breaking it into two (or more) parts. Here are the first seven lines of the *Aeneid*, scanned and with the principal caesurae marked ("‖"):

ārmă vĭ/rūmquĕ că/nō, ‖ Trō/iāē quī /prīmŭs ăb /ōrīs

Ītălĭ/ām fā/tō prŏfŭ/gŭs‖ Lā/vīniăquĕ/ vēnĭt

lītŏră,/ mūlt(um) īll(e) / ēt tēr/rīs ‖ iāc/tātŭs ēt/ āltō

vī sŭpĕ/rūm, ‖ saē/vāē mĕmŏ/rēm Iū/nōnĭs ŏb / īrăm,

mūltă quŏ/qu(e) ēt bēl/lō pās/sūs, ‖ dūm/ cōndĕrĕt/ ūrbĕm

---

7   When a *diaeresis* occurs just before the fifth foot, it is often called a *bucolic diaeresis* because this type of *diaeresis* was used frequently in pastoral poetry: e.g., *nos patriam fugimus: tu, Tityre,* ‖ *lentus in umbra* (*Ecl.* 1.4).

8   In the combinations *qu, gu, su* (e.g., *-que, sanguis, suesco*), note that the *u* is consonantal but that the combinations themselves count as a single consonant for the purpose of scansion.

9   Readers may differ on where (or even if) there is a main caesura in a given line.

īnfĕr/rētquĕ dĕ/ōs Lătĭ/ō; ‖gĕnŭs / ūndĕ Lă/tīnŭm
Âlbā/nīquĕ pă/trēs ‖ ātqu (e) āltā͞e / mō͞enĭă/ Rōmā͞e.

(note that in line 2, *Laviniaque* is pronounced as four (not five) syllables, as if the second "I" were a consonant.)

In addition to metrical length, words also have a natural accent,[10] which may coincide or clash with the metrical stress (ictus), which falls on the first long syllable of each foot. Coincidence of word accent and metrical stress produces fluidity in the verse; clashing of word accent and metrical stress creates tension. For example:

<pre>
x   x   /   x   /   /
īnfān/dūm, rē/gīnă, iŭ/bēs rĕnŏ/vārĕ dŏ/lōrĕm   (Aen. 2.3)
</pre>

(Naturally accented syllables are in boldface; "/" = ictus that coincides with word accent; "x"= ictus that clashes with word accent.)

In this line, there are several clashes in the first four feet (wherein the word accent generally does not coincide with the verse accent), followed by coincidence in the final two feet.[11] In creating such clashes, the placement of caesurae can be particularly important. For example, "if a word of two or more syllables ends after the first long of a foot (that is, producing a strong caesura), there will be a clash between accent and ictus in the foot," because the final syllable of such words is not accented.[12] The strong caesura in 2.3 (above) and in 2.108, 199 (below) display the principle well.

One of Vergil's artistic feats was to manage the sequence of clash and coincidence of ictus and word accent in such a way as to achieve a rhythmically varied and pleasing line. In general we find that Vergilian hexameters

---

10   Disyllabic words have their accent on their initial syllable: *caris, dabant, molis*. If, however, words are three syllables or longer, the word accent falls: on the penultima (second to last), if it is long (*ruébant, iactátos*) but on the antepenultima (the syllable preceding the penultima), if the penultima is short (*géntibus, mária, pópulum*).

11   Classical Latin speakers would presumably have pronounced the word accents in reading lines, while still maintaining the basic rhythm of the hexameter. Otherwise, the ictus would have transformed the basic sound of the word.

12   Ross (2007) 146. For word accentuation, see n. 10 (above).

are characterized by the clash of ictus and word accent in the first four feet and by the coincidence of ictus and word accent in the last two feet,[13] which results in a pleasing resolution of stress at line end.

    /   x   x   x   /   /
saepĕ **fŭ**gām **Dă**nāī **Trō**iā cŭpĭĕrĕ rĕlīctā (*Aen.* 2.108)

    /   x   x   x   /   /
hīc ălĭūd **mā**iūs **mĭ**sĕrīs **mūl**tōquĕ **trĕ**mḗdŭm (*Aen.* 2.199)

This rhythmical innovation constitutes an advance over Vergil's predecessors, who could write such lines as, for example, Ennius' *spársis / hástis / lóngis/ cámpus/ spléndet et/ hórret*, which exhibits a monotonous coincidence of ictus and word accent throughout the entire line.

---

13   Vergil sometimes avoids such resolution for special effect, though he does so rarely. For example, in the following line, a clash between ictus and word accent occurs in the final foot: *sternitur/ exani/misque tre/mens pro/cumbit hu/mi bos* (5.481).

Appendix 2: Stylistic Terms

Vergil's skillful use of language is a defining element of his artistry. He often employs rhetorical figures and stylistic devices to reinforce the content of his poetry. Careful attention should therefore be paid both to what Vergil says and to how he says it. The following list defines many of the terms (primarily rhetorical, stylistic, and metrical) that are encountered in studying Vergil and that are used in the commentary. For more information on the terms, see Lanham (1991), Brogan (1994), and Lausberg (1998). Fuller information on Vergilian style can be found in Jackson Knight (1944) 225-341, Camps (1969) 60-74, O'Hara (2019), Conte (2007) 58-122, and Dainotti (2015). Stylistic analyses of Vergilian passages are presented in Horsfall (1995) 237-48 and Hardie (1998) 102-14.

NB: all line references are to Aeneid 10 unless otherwise noted.

Alliteration: the repetition of an initial letter or sound in neighboring words. Alliteration is frequent in Vergil and employed for a variety of purposes; for example, to emphasize words, to suggest connections between words, to create special effects such as onomatopoeia or simply to please the ear. Some examples: *venturos...ventos* (99), ***p**osuere,* ***p**remit **p**lacida aequora **p**ontus* (103). Cf. also 212 where the alliteration of *s* and the assonance of *u* evokes the foam and roar of the waves, *spumea semifero sub pectore murmurat unda.*

Anaphora (Gr. "bringing back"): the repetition of a word at the beginning of consecutive sentences or clauses. It is commonly used to convey emphasis, emotion, or stylistic elevation: for example, *quid repetam exustas Erycino in litore classis, / quid tempestatum regem ventosque furentis* (36-37). In this instance, the anaphora of *quid*, conveys Venus' indignation.

Antithesis (Gr. "opposition"): the juxtaposition of contrasting ideas usually within a balanced or parallel construction: for example, 737 *iacet altus Orodes*. Here there is a clear antithesis between *iacet* and *altus*: once so lofty, now so low.

Apostrophe (Gr. "turning away"): a sudden shift of address to figure (or idea) absent or present. In Vergil, a characteristic effect is of pathos since the apostrophe heightens the emotional register of the passage. Cf. *te, Turne, ...quaerens* (514-15), said of Aeneas seeking out Turnus after the death of Pallas.

Archaism: a word or expression no longer used in the spoken language or prose. In the *Aeneid*, archaisms are usually used to underscore remoteness and solemnity. In *Aeneid* 10, the speech of Jupiter in the assembly of the gods presents many archaisms to underscore its formal nature.

Aristeia (pl. aristeiai): a type-scene in the dramatic conventions of epic poetry where a hero in battle has his finest moments (*aristos* = "best") and kills a number of named opponents.

Arsis, lengthening in: the lengthening of a final short syllable of a word when it occurs in *arsis* (i.e., the first long syllable of a hexameter foot, which receives the *ictus*, the metrical stress). It is (usually) followed by a strong caesura for the "silence" created by the caesura was seen as equivalent to the so-called "lengthening by position." (cf. 720... *Graius homo, infectos linquens profugūs hymenaeos*).

Assonance (Lat. "answer with the same sound"): the repetition of vowel sounds in neighboring words or phrases. Latin is rich in vowel sounds, making assonance a natural and frequent poetic feature: for example, 572 *gradientem...frementem*. Here the assonance is intended to suggest terror.

Asyndeton (Gr. "unconnected"): the omission of connectives between words, phrases, or sentences. Asyndeton can convey effects such as emphasis, suddenness, and vehemence: for example, *liceat dimittere ab armis / incolumen Ascanium, liceat superesse nepotem* (46-7); or cf. *sternitur Arcadiae proles, sternuntur Etrusci* (429). Here the asyndeton combined with anaphora underscores the speed of the killing.

Bucolic Diaeresis: in dactylic hexameter, the bucolic diaeresis (so called for its frequency in Theocritus) is the fourth foot diaeresis, a not infrequent feature of Homeric verse. See also **Diaeresis**.

Caesura (Lat. "cutting down"): a word break within a metrical foot. Caesurae (plural) are often described as strong or weak: a *strong caesura* is one that falls after the first syllable of a foot; a *weak caesura* is one that falls after the second syllable of the dactylic foot. The most important *caesura* in any given line often coincides with a sense break and is called the main or principal caesura. It most frequently falls on the third foot, but it also occurs not uncommonly in the second or fourth (or sometimes in both). For examples, see Appendix 1 on Vergil's meter.

For lengthening before the caesura, see **Arsis, lengthening in**.

Catalogue (Gr. "list, register"): a poetic list, as of place names, military forces, crew members. Catalogues are a feature of epic poetry. The *Aeneid* counts two; one in Book 7 (the Catalogue of Italian Forces) and one in Book 10 (the Catalogue of Etruscan Forces).

Chiasmus (Gr. "crossing"): an arrangement of words whereby parallel constructions are expressed in reverse word order. Cf. 137.

a	B
fusos	cervix
b	A
lactea	crinis

Deixis (Gr. "pointing"): a word or a phrase (such as "this," "that," "now," "then") that points to time, place, or situation in which the speaker is speaking.

Diaeresis (Gr. "division"): a word break between metrical feet. For examples, see Appendix 1 on Vergil's meter. See also **Bucolic Diaeresis**.

Dicolon Abundans: the restatement of an initial phrase in different language: for example, 9-10 *quis metus aut hos / aut hos <u>arma sequi ferrumque lacessere suasit</u>?* In this case, *lacessere ferrum* ("to provoke the sword") is simply a variation of *arma sequi* ("to follow the course of war") but with a different language. Cf. also 31, 46-7, 104, 259, 295-6, 442-3, 557-8, 622-3, 677-8, 819-20, 855.

Ecphrasis: a vivid description of an object, person, or event. However, in a more restricted sense, the term is applied to a detailed description of a work of art.

Ellipsis (Gr. "leaving out"): the omission of a syntactically necessary word or words that must be supplied. Cf. *quid manus illa virum* "what of that maniple of men" (672). In this instance, after *quid* we must infer "is to be said." Ellipses are particularly common with forms of *esse* and are colloquial.

Enallage (Gr. "interchange"): the distortion of the "syntactic relations among words," whereby one element of the phrase, often the adjective, is referred not to the element to which it belongs by a logical or grammatical connection but to another one more or less nearby. Cf. *Idaeae sacro de vertice pinus* (230). Here we have a double enallage since *Idaeus* should go more naturally with *vertex*, linking Aeneas' ships with their protector the *Mater Idaea*, while *sacer* should go with *pinus* in the context of the story. The term **hypallage** is often used interchangeably with enallage.

Enjambment (Fr. "crossing over"): the continuation of the sense or syntactic unit from one line to the next. The feature is frequent in Vergil and plays with our expectations that clauses will be contained within an individual hexameter: for example, *atque iterum in Teucros Aetolis surgit ab Arpis / Tydides* (28-9).

Epanalepsis (Gr. "taking up again"): the syntactically unnecessary repetition of a word or phrase for emphasis: for example, *Astur…Astur* (180-1); *Mantua…Mantua* (200-1); *Ilo…Ilo* (400-1).

Epithet (Gr. "added"): an adjective or descriptive phrase that accompanies or substitutes the name. The use of epithets is Homeric where they are important compositional elements for oral poetry. In Vergil, they become literary devices that help create epic tone: for example, *alma Cybebe* (220); *Venus aurea* (16).

Etymology (Gr. "true word"): the study of the derivation of a word. Etymologies were particularly characteristic of Hellenistic writers. Vergil often engages in etymological wordplay. Note, for example, *altus Orodes* at 737. Here *altus* "explains" *Orodes* which in Greek means "mountainous."

Euphemism (Gr. "use of an auspicious word"): the substitution of an agreeable, less offensive, or indirect expression for one that may seem harsh, offensive, or unnecessarily blunt. For example, 352 *casus* (lit. "fall") is a poetic euphemism for "death."

Focalization: The perspective through which a narrative is presented. For example, a narrative where all information presented reflects the subjective perception of that information by a certain character is said to be internally

APPENDIX 2: STYLISTIC TERMS   155

focalized. Focalization, therefore, enables the Vergilian text to encompass a range of possible interpretations through the multiplication of different perspectives. Cf. 782 *dulcis moriens reminiscitur Argos*. The memory of his homeland Argos is sweet (*dulcis*) to Antores who is about to die in a foreign land.

Formula: an expression that is regularly used, under the same metrical conditions, to express a particular essential idea. In Homeric verse, for example, a phrase like "rosy-fingered dawn" occupies a certain metrical pattern that fits into the hexameter and aids the bard in *extempore* composition.

Golden Line and Variations: in dactylic hexameter, the golden line is an artful arrangement of two adjective/substantive phrases with a verb in between. It usually takes the form abVAB where V is the verb/participle, while aA and bB are both adjective-noun phrases and interlocked. Virgil uses a golden line when he describes how Dido is dressed for the hunt (*Aen.* 4.139):

      a   b   V   A   B

auream purpuream subnectit fibulam vestem

The variation abVBA is often called a Silver Line, in which the two adjective-noun phrases are not interlocked; rather one phrase frames the other (245):

      a   b   V   B   A

ingentis Rutulae spectabit caedis acervos

Hendiadys (Gr. "one through two"): the expression of one idea through two terms joined by a conjunction: for example, *per patris hospitium et mensas* (460). Here *per hospitium et mensas* really means "for the hospitality of the tables."

Hiatus (Gr. "gaping"): the gap created when two syllables which would normally be elided are not. This usually happens when the preceding syllable receives special emphasis: for example, *o hominum* (18). Here there is no elision between *o* and *hominum*.

Hypallage: see **Enallage**

Hyperbaton (Gr. "transposed"): a distortion of normal word order: for example, *securus amorum / qui iuvenum* for *securus amorum iuvenum* (326-7).

Hypermetric Line (Gr. "beyond measure"): an extra syllable at the end of the line, often *-que* which elides with the first letter of the following line, emphasizing its connection to the next line: for example, 781-2:

> *sternitur infelix alieno vulnere, caelumque*
> *aspicit.*

Interlocking Word Order (or Synchysis): an arrangement of two phrases that interweave their members in an abAB pattern (e.g., adjective a, adjective b, noun A, noun B) or AbaB (e.g., noun A, adjective b, adjective a, noun B) with the result that the two phrases are interlocked. Cf. 99 *murmura*(A) *venturos*(b) *nautis prodentia*(a) *ventos*(B).

Irony (Gr. "dissembling"): saying one thing but with its opposite somehow implied or understood. At 89-90 Juno asks whether it was she who pitted the wretched Trojans against the Greeks (*an miseros qui Troas Achivis / obiecit?*). Here Juno's question is ironic for what she implies is that the Trojan War was Venus' doing.

Litotes (Gr. "simplicity"): the affirmation of a thing by denial of its contrary. Litotes provides emphasis through understatement. Its opposite is hyperbole. Litotes are not unusual in Vergil. Cf. *haud ignara modi* (247) = "not unaware of the way" said of Cymodocea pushing Aeneas' ship, that is, skilled (since she was a ship before). Cf. also *nec...segnior* (657) where the litotes emphasizes Turnus' eager pursuit.

Metaphor (Gr. "transference"): the application of a word or phrase from one field of meaning to another, thereby suggesting new meaning. For example, *freta secabat* (147), said of sailing, suggests the image of ploughing the sea.

Metonymy (Gr. "change of name"): the substitution of one word for another somehow closely related. In Vergil metonymy often involves names. Cf. *horrentis Marte* (237). Here *Marte* stands in for "war." Cf. also *Nerei* at 764 where the sea god stands for "sea." But metonymy can involve other types of relationships, for example, qualities. *Marmore* ("marble") at 208 is said of the sea to indicate that the sea is smooth and gleaming as marble. *Robur* (oak, timber) at 479 defines the "spear-shaft" made of oak or timber. See also **Synecdoche**.

Neoteric (Neoteric Poets): circle of poets, also known as *poetae novi*, writing in the first century BCE, who rejected traditional social and literary norms.

Their poetry is characterized by tight construction, playful use of genre, punning, and complex allusions. The most significant surviving Latin Neoteric is Catullus.

Parataxis (Gr. "placing side by side"): the juxtaposition of sequential main clauses without a subordinating conjunction. Parataxis is a feature of archaic and epic style. An example from Book 10 is *vix proram attigerat, rumpit Saturnia funem* (659). Though the two sentences are independent, in sense one is subordinate to the other: "Scarcely had he reached the stern, when Juno cut the cable." Its opposite is *hypotaxis* in which there is a subordination that explicitly clarifies the hierarchical relationship between clauses.

Patronymic (Gr. "father's name"): a name formed by attaching a suffix to the name of a father or ancestor: for example, 499 *Eurytides*, "son of Eurytus"; 822 *Anchisiades*, "son of Anchises."

Personification: the representation of inanimate things as if they were human, endowing them with human characteristics or feelings. Cf. 740-1 *fata / prospectant*. Here the fates are said to "see."

Polyptoton (Gr. "in many cases"): the repetition of a word in its inflected cases: for example, *regem...regi* (149). Here the emphatic repetition of *rex* stresses Aeneas' sense of urgency in his speech to Tarchon. Cf. also *haeret pede pes densusque viro vir* (361). Here we see a double polyptoton to describe the close military encounter between the two armies.

Praeteritio (Lat. "passing over"): the mentioning of a subject in order to state that it should not be mentioned: for example, <u>quid</u> *repetam exustas Erycino in litore classis, /* <u>quid</u> *tempestatum regem ventosque furentis* (36-7).

Prolepsis (Gr. "anticipation"): the use of a word or phrase that anticipates a later event or outcome. Consider *premit placida aequora pontus* (103). Here *placida* anticipates the result of the action of the sea ("the sea smoothed its waters <u>to calm</u>").

Silver Line: see Golden Line and Variations.

Simile (Lat. "similar"): a figurative comparison between two different things. It is an important component of epic style: for example, *qualis gemma micat fulvum quae dividit aurum, / aut collo decus aut capiti, vel quale per artem / inclusum buxo aut Oricia terebintho / lucet ebur; fusos cervix cui lactea crinis / accipit et molli subnectens circulus auro* (134-8). In this simile, the point of the two comparisons is the way in which the beauty of Ascanius stands out as he is surrounded by the other warriors who form a frame to it. The bright jewel in its gold setting also reflects the contrast between Ascanius' bare head and its gold torque (138), while the pale color of the ivory picks up Ascanius' milk-white neck (137).

Syncope (Gr. "a cutting"): the omission of a letter or short syllable from within a word. Cf. *expostaque* for *expositaque* (694).

Synecdoche (Gr. "understanding one thing with another"): a type of **metonymy** that uses the part for the whole (or the reverse). For example, at 399 *biiugis* "horses" is used to mean car (*bigae*); again at 594 *rotis* "wheels" is used for chariot.

Synizesis (Gr. "collapse"): the collapsing of two vowels into one: for example, *aureo* (116) which scans as a disyllable.

Tmesis (Gr. "cutting"): the separation of the two parts of a compound verb. Common in Ennius, tmesis involving compound verbs often has an archaic flavor: for example, *inque ligatus* = *inligatusque* (794).

Topos (Gr. "place"): a standardized method of constructing or treating an argument in the context of classical Greek rhetoric.

Tricolon (Gr. "having three limbs"): the grouping together of three parallel clauses (cola) or phrases: for example, *num linquere castra / hortati sumus aut vitam committere ventis? / num puero summam belli, num credere muros* (68-70). When the third element is the longest, the tricolon is said *tricolon abundans*. Alternatively, when the last clause is the shortest (as in the case above), it is called *tricolon decrescens*.

Type-scene: may be regarded as a recurrent block of narrative with an identifiable structure, such as a sacrifice, the donning of armor, a duel, a death scene. In the *Iliad*, almost all battle narrative consists of an extensive store of "typical" or repeated details which undergo numerous and repeated combinations.

Zeugma (Gr. "yoking"): the governing of two or more words by one verb or adjective, which is strictly appropriate for just one of them: for example, 13 *exitium magnum atque Alpis immittet apertas*. The verb *immittet* is easily comprehensible with *exitium*, but less with *Alpis apertas*. With rhetorical boldness the "opened Alps" themselves are said to be "let loose" on Rome because they let loose the invaders through their passes.

Bibliography

Adler, E. (2003) *Vergil's Empire: Political Thought in the* Aeneid. Lanham, MD.

Ahl, F., and E. Fantham (2008) *Vergil*, Aeneid. Oxford World's Classics. Oxford.

Allen, G. (2000) *Intertextuality*. London.

Anderson, W. S. (1957) "Vergil's Second *Iliad*." *Transactions and Proceedings of the American Philological Association* 88: 17-30. Reprinted in S. J. Harrison (ed.) (1990), 239-52.

———. (1969 1st ed.; 2005 2nd ed.) *The Art of the* Aeneid. Wauconda, IL.

———. (1999) "*Aeneid* 11: The Saddest Book." In *Reading Vergil's* Aeneid: *An Interpretative Guide*, ed. C. Perkell, 195-209. Norman, OK.

Armstrong, D., J. Fish, P. A. Johnston, and M. Skinner (eds.) (2004) *Vergil, Philodemus, and the Augustans*. Austin, TX.

Austin, R. G. (1964) *P. Vergili Maronis* Aeneidos *Liber Secundus*. Oxford.

———. (1971) *P. Vergili Maronis* Aeneidos *Liber Primus*. Oxford.

Bandera, C. (1981) "Sacrificial Levels in Virgil's *Aeneid*." *Arethusa* 14: 217-39.

Barchiesi, A. (2008) "*Bellum Italicum*: L'unificazione dell'Italia nell'*Eneide*." In *Patria diuersis gentibus una*, ed. G. Urso, 243-60. Pisa.

———. (2015) *Homeric Effects in Vergil's Narrative*. Princeton; trans. and adapted from *La traccia del modello* (1984). Pisa.

Basson, W. P. (1975) *Pivotal Catalogues in the* Aeneid. Amsterdam.

Behr, F. (2005) "The Narrator's Voice: A Narratological Reappraisal of Apostrophe in Virgil's *Aeneid*." *Arethusa* 38: 186-221.

Benario, H. W. (1967) "The Tenth Book of the *Aeneid*." *Transactions and Proceedings of the American Philological Association* 98: 23-36.

Bonfanti, M. (1985) *Punto di vista e modi della narrazione nell'Eneide*. Pisa.

Boyd, B. W. (1983) "*Cydonea mala*: Virgilian Wordplay and Allusion." *Harvard Studies in Classical Philology* 87: 169-74.

Boyle, A. J. (1999) "*Aeneid* 8: Images of Rome." In *Reading Vergil's* Aeneid: *An Interpretative Guide*, ed. C. Perkell, 148-61. Norman, OK.

Breed, B., C. Damon, and A. Rossi (eds.) (2010) *Citizens of Discord: Rome and Its Civil Wars*. Oxford.

Bretzigheimer, G. (1993) *Jupiter Tonans in Ovids Metamorphosen*. Munich.

Briggs, W. Ward. (1980) *Narrative and Simile from the* Georgics *in the* Aeneid. Leiden.

———. (1981) "Virgil and the Hellenistic Epic." In *Aufstieg und Niedergang der römischen Welt* 2.31.2: 948-84.

Brogan, T. V. F. (ed.) (1994) *The New Princeton Handbook of Poetic Terms.* Princeton.

Cairns, F. (1989) *Virgil's Augustan Epic.* Cambridge.

Camps, W. A. (1969) *An Introduction to Virgil's* Aeneid. Oxford.

Carstairs-McCarthy, A. (2018) "Dido, Pallas, Nisus and the Nameless Mothers in *Aeneid* 8-10." *Classical Quarterly* 68: 199-219.

Clausen, W. (1987) *Virgil's* Aeneid *and the Tradition of Hellenistic Poetry.* Berkeley, CA.

———. (1994) *A Commentary on Virgil*, Eclogues. Oxford.

———. (2002) *Virgil's* Aeneid: *Decorum, Allusion, and Ideology.* Munich. A revised and expanded version of Clausen (1987).

Coleman, R. (ed.) (1977) *Virgil*: Eclogues. Cambridge.

Conington, J., and H. Nettleship (1858-83) *The Works of Virgil.* 3 vols. London.

Conte, G. B. (1986) *The Rhetoric of Imitation: Genre and Poetic Memory in Virgil and Other Latin Poets.* Ithaca, NY.

———. (1993) Review of *Virgil*, Aeneid *10*, by S. J. Harrison. *Journal of Roman Studies* 83: 208-12.

———. (1999) "The Virgilian Paradox: An Epic of Drama and Sentiment." *Proceedings of the Cambridge Philological Society* 45: 17-42. A revised version is included in Conte (2007), 23-57.

———. (2007) *The Poetry of Pathos: Studies in Virgilian Epic.* Oxford.

Coppolino, N. (2005) "The Death of Lausus: Lucretian Intertext as Propaganda Foil in *Aeneid* 10.801-32." *New England Classical Journal* 32:5-18.

Courtney, E. (1988) "Vergil's Military Catalogues and Their Antecedents." *Vergilius* 34: 3-8.

Crook, J. (1996) "Political History: 30 B.C. to A.D. 14." In *The Augustan Empire: 43 B.C.- A.D. 69.* 2nd ed., ed. A. Bowman, E. Champlin, and A. Lintott, 70-112. Vol. 10 of *The Cambridge Ancient History.* Cambridge.

Cucchiarelli, A. (2001) "Vergil on Killing Parthenius (*Aen.* 10.748)." *Classical Journal* 97: 51-4.

Curtis, L. (2017) *Imagining the Chorus in Augustan Poetry.* Cambridge.

Dainotti, P. (2015) *Word Order and Expressiveness in the* Aeneid. Berlin.

Dekel, E. (2012) *Virgil's Homeric Lens.* New York.

Dewar, M. (1988) "Mezentius' Remorse." *Classical Quarterly* 38: 261-2.

Duckworth, G. E. (1933) *Foreshadowing and Suspense in the Epics of Homer, Apollonius, and Vergil.* Princeton.

———. (1969) *Vergil and Classical Hexameter Poetry: A Study in Metrical Variety.* Ann Arbor, MI.

Edmunds, L. (2001) *Intertextuality and the Reading of Roman Poetry*. Baltimore.

Fantham, E. (1990) "*Nymphas...e navibus esse*: Decorum and Poetic Fiction in *Aeneid* 9.77-122 and 10.215-59." *Classical Philology* 85: 102-19.

Farrell, J. (1991) *Vergil's* Georgics *and the Traditions of Ancient Epic: The Art of Allusion in Literary History*. Oxford.

———. (2005) "The Augustan Period: 40 BC-AD 14." In *A Companion to Latin Literature*, ed. S. J. Harrison, 44-57. Oxford.

———. (2019) "Virgil's Intertextual Personae." Reprinted with revisions in F. Mac Góráin and C. Martindale (eds.), 299-325.

———. (2021) *Juno's* Aeneid: *A Battle for Heroic Identity*. Princeton.

Farron, S. (1985) "Aeneas' Human Sacrifice." *Acta Classica* 28: 21-33.

Feeney, D. (1984) "The Reconciliations of Juno." *Classical Quarterly* 34: 179-94.

———. (1991) *The Gods in Epic: Poets and Critics of the Classical Tradition*. Oxford.

———. (1999) "Epic Violence, Epic Order: Killings, Catalogues, and the Role of the Reader in *Aeneid* 10." In *Reading Vergil's* Aeneid: *An Interpretative Guide*, ed. C. Perkell, 178-94. Norman, OK.

Fenik, B. (1968) *Typical Battle Scenes in the* Iliad: *Studies in the Narrative Techniques of Homeric Battle Description*. Wiesbaden.

Fletcher, K. F. B. (2014) *Finding Italy: Travel, Nation, and Colonization in Vergil's* Aeneid. Ann Arbor, MI.

Fowler, D. (1987) "Vergil on Killing Virgins." In *Homo Viator: Classical Essays for John Bramble*, ed. M. Whitby, P. Hardie, and M. Whitby, 185-98. Bristol.

———. (1990) "Deviant Focalisation in Vergil's *Aeneid*." *Proceedings of the Cambridge Philological Society* 36: 42-63.

———. (1997) "On the Shoulders of Giants: Intertextuality and Classical Studies." *Materiali e discussioni per l'analisi dei testi classici* 39: 13-34.

Fratantuono, L. (2007) *Madness Unchained: A Reading of Virgil's* Aeneid. Lanham, MD.

Gale, M. R. (2000) *Virgil on the Nature of Things: The* Georgics, *Lucretius and the Didactic Tradition*. Cambridge.

Galinsky, G. K. (1988) "The Anger of Aeneas." *American Journal of Philology* 109: 321-48.

———. (1996) *Augustan Culture: An Interpretive Introduction*. Princeton.

———. (2003) "Greek and Roman Drama and the *Aeneid*." In *Myth, History, and Culture in Republican Rome: Studies in Honour of T. P. Wiseman*, ed. S. Braund and C. Gill, 275-94. Exeter.

———. (ed.) (2005) *The Cambridge Companion to the Age of Augustus*. Cambridge.

Ganiban, R. T. (2021) Aeneid: *Book 7*. Indianapolis, IN.

George, E. V. (1974) Aeneid *VIII and the* Aitia *of Callimachus*. *Mnemosyne*, Supplement 27. Leiden.

Glenn, J. (1971) "Mezentius and Polyphemus." *American Journal of Philology* 92: 129-55.

Goldberg, S., and G. Manuwald (eds.) (2018) *Fragmentary Republican Latin*. 2 vols. Cambridge, MA.

Goldschmidt, N. (2013) *Shaggy Crowns: Ennius'* Annales *and Virgil's* Aeneid. Oxford.

Gotoff, H. C. (1984) "The Transformation of Mezentius." *Transactions of the American Philological Association* 114: 191-218.

Gransden, K. W. (1984) *Virgil's* Iliad: *An Essay on Epic Narrative*. Cambridge.

Griffin, J. (1980) *Homer on Life and Death*. Oxford.

Gurval, R. A. (1995) *Actium and Augustus*. Ann Arbor, MI.

Hardie, P. (1986) *Cosmos and Imperium*. Oxford.

———. (1987) "Ships and Ship Names in the *Aeneid*." In *Homo Viator: Classical Essays for John Bramble*, ed. M. Whitby, P. Hardie, and M. Whitby, 163-72. Bristol.

———. (1991) "The *Aeneid* and the *Oresteia*." *Proceedings of the Virgil Society* 20: 29-45.

———. (1993) *The Epic Successors of Vergil*. Cambridge.

———. (1994) *Virgil,* Aeneid *IX*. Cambridge.

———. (1998) *Virgil*. Greece and Rome: New Surveys in the Classics, no. 28. Oxford.

———. (2012) *Rumour and Renown: Representations of Fama in Western Literature*. Cambridge.

———. (2019) "Virgil and Tragedy." Reprinted with revisions in F. Mac Góráin and C. Martindale (eds.), 326-44.

Harrison, E. L. (1984) "The *Aeneid* and Carthage." In *Poetry and Politics in the Age of Augustus*, ed. T. Woodsman and D. West, 95-115. Cambridge.

Harrison, S. J. (1986) Review of *La traccia del modello*, by A. Barchiesi (1984). *Journal of Roman Studies* 76: 318-21.

———. (1987) Review of *Punto di vista e modi della narrazione nell'Eneide*, by M. Bonfanti (1985). *Classical Review* 37: 173-5.

———. (1988) "Vergil as a Poet of War." *Proceedings of the Virgil Society* 19: 48-68.

———. (ed.) (1990) *Oxford Readings in Vergil's* Aeneid. Oxford.

———. (1991) *Vergil,* Aeneid *10*. Oxford.

Heinze, R. (1993) *Virgil's Epic Technique*, trans. H. Harvey, D. Harvey, and F. Robertson. Bristol. Published in German as *Virgils epische Technik* (1915). 3rd ed. Leipzig.

Hejduk, J. (2009) "Jupiter's *Aeneid: Fama* and *imperium*." *Classical Antiquity* 28: 279-327.

———. (2013) "The Bough and the Lock: Fighting Fate in the *Aeneid*." *Illinois Classical Studies* 38: 149-57.

Hershkowitz, D. (1998) *The Madness of Epic: Reading Insanity from Homer to Statius*. Oxford.

Heyworth, S. (2005) "Pastoral." In *A Companion to Latin Literature*, ed. S. J. Harrison, 148-58. Oxford.

Hinds, S. (1998) *Allusion and Intertext: Dynamics of Appropriation in Roman Poetry*. Cambridge.

———. (2000) "Essential Epic: Genre and Gender from Macer to Statius." In *Matrices of Genre*, ed. M. Depew and D. Obbink, 221-44. Cambridge, MA.

Holland, L. A. (1935) "Place Names and Heroes in the *Aeneid*." *American Journal of Philology* 56: 202-15.

Horsfall, N. (1987) "*Non viribus aequis*—Some Problems in Virgil's Battle-Scenes." *Greece & Rome* 34: 48-55.

———. (1995) *A Companion to the Study of Virgil*. Leiden.

———. (2000) *Virgil: Aeneid 7*. Leiden.

———. (2003) *Virgil: Aeneid 11*. Leiden.

———. (2006) *Virgil: Aeneid 6*. Leiden.

Hunter, R. L. (2006) *The Shadow of Callimachus: Studies in the Reception of Hellenistic Poetry at Rome*. Cambridge.

Jackson Knight, W. F. (1944) *Roman Vergil*. London.

Johnson, W. R. (1976) *Darkness Visible: A Study of Vergil's Aeneid*. Berkeley, CA.

———. (2005) Introduction to *Virgil: Aeneid*, trans. S. Lombardo, xv-lxxi. Indianapolis, IN.

Johnston, P. (1980) *Vergil's Agricultural Golden Age: A Study of the Georgics*. Mnemosyne Supplementum 60. Leiden.

Jones, A. H. M. (1970) *Augustus*. London.

Kennedy, D. (1992) "'Augustan' and 'Anti-Augustan': Reflections on Terms of Reference." In *Roman Poetry and Propaganda in the Age of Augustus*, ed. A. Powell, 26-58. Bristol.

Kirichenko, A. (2013) "Virgil's Augustan Temples: Image and Intertext in the *Aeneid*." *Journal of Roman Studies* 103: 65-85.

Knauer, G. N. (1964a) *Die Aeneis und Homer*. Göttingen.

———. (1964b) "Vergil's *Aeneid* and Homer." *Greek, Roman and Byzantine Studies* 5: 61-84. Reprinted in S. J. Harrison (ed.) (1990), 390-412.

———. (1981) "Vergil and Homer." *Aufstieg und Niedergang der römischen Welt* ii 31.1: 870-918.

Krisher, T. (1979) "Unhomeric Scene Patterns in Vergil." *Papers of the Liverpool Latin Seminar* 2: 143-54.

Kronenberg, L. (2005) "Mezentius the Epicurean." *Transactions of the American Philological Association* 135: 403-31.

Kyriakidis, S. (2007) *Catalogues of Proper Names in Latin Epic Poetry: Lucretius - Virgil - Ovid*. Newcastle.

Lanham, R. A. (1991) *A Handlist of Rhetorical Terms.* 2nd ed. Berkeley, CA.

Lausberg, H. (1998) *Handbook of Literary Rhetoric: A Foundation for Literary Study.* Leiden.

Leach, E. W. (1971) "The Blindness of Mezentius (*Aeneid* 10.762-768)." *Arethusa* 4: 83-90.

Lefèvre, E. (1989) *Das Bildprogramm des Apollo-Tempels auf dem Palatin.* Konstanz.

Lilja, S. (1983) *Homosexuality in Republican and Augustan Rome.* Helsinki.

Lowrie, M. (2010) "Vergil and Founding Violence." In *A Companion to Vergil's* Aeneid *and Its Tradition*, ed. J. Farrell and M. C. J. Putnam, 391-403. Malden, MA.

Lyne, R. O. A. M. (1983) "Vergil and the Politics of War." *Classical Quarterly* 33: 188-203.

———. (1987) *Further Voices in Vergil's* Aeneid. Oxford.

———. (1989) *Words and the Poet.* Oxford.

Mac Góráin, F., and C. Martindale (eds.) (2019) *The Cambridge Companion to Virgil.* 2nd ed. Cambridge.

Mahoney, A. (2001) *Allen and Greenough's New Latin Grammar.* Newburyport, MA. Reprint (with additional material) of the 1903 edition.

Malamud, M. (1998) "Gnawing at the End of the Rope: Poets on the Field in Two Virgilian Catalogues." *Ramus* 27: 95-126.

Marincola, J. (2010) "*Eros* and Empire: Virgil and the Historians on Civil War." In *Ancient Historiography and Its Contexts*, ed. C. Kraus, J. Marincola, and C. Pelling, 183-204. Oxford.

Martindale, C. (1993) "Descent into Hell: Reading Ambiguity, or Virgil and the Critics." *Proceedings of the Virgil Society* 21: 111-50.

Mitchell, R. N. (1991) "The Violence of Virginity in the *Aeneid.*" *Arethusa* 24: 219-37.

Morgan, G. (2019) "'To Heaven on a Hook' (Dio Cass. 60.35.4): Ennius, Lucilius and an Ineffectual Council of the Gods in *Aeneid* 10." *Classical Quarterly* 69.2: 636-53.

Moskalew, W. (1982) *Formular Language and Poetic Design in the* Aeneid. Leiden.

Muse, K. (2007) "Sergestus and Tarchon in the *Aeneid.*" *Classical Quarterly* 57: 586-605.

Mynors, R. A. B. (ed.) (1969) *P. Vergili Maronis* Opera. Oxford.

———. (ed.) (1990) *Virgil,* Georgics. Oxford.

Nappa, C. (2005) *Reading after Actium: Vergil's* Georgics, *Octavian, and Rome.* Ann Arbor, MI.

Nelis, D. (2001) *Vergil's* Aeneid *and the* Argonautica *of Apollonius Rhodius.* Leeds.

Newman, J. K. (2015) "Virgil's *Iliad:* Reflections on a Secondary Epic." In *Virgilian Studies: A Miscellany Dedicated to the Memory of Mario Geymonat*, ed. H. C. Günther, 343-403. Studia Classica et Mediaevalia 10. Nordhausen.

Nussbaum, G. B. (1986) *Vergil's Metre: A Practical Guide for Reading Latin Hexameter Poetry*. London.

O'Hara, J. J. (1989) "Messapus, Cycnus and the Alphabetical Order of Vergil's Catalogue of Italian Heroes." *Phoenix* 43: 35-8.

———. (1990) *Death and the Optimistic Prophecy in Vergil's* Aeneid. Princeton.

———. (1991) "Vergilian Similes, Trespass, and the Order of *Aeneid* 10.707-18." *Classical Journal* 87: 1-8.

———. (2007) *Inconsistency in Roman Epic: Studies in Catullus, Lucretius, Vergil, Ovid and Lucan*. Cambridge.

———. (2010) "The Unfinished *Aeneid*?" In *Companion to Vergil's* Aeneid *and Its Tradition*, ed. J. Farrell and M. C. Putnam, 96-106. Oxford.

———. (2017) *True Names: Vergil and the Alexandrian Tradition of Etymological Wordplay*. Expanded from O'Hara (1996) *True Names: Vergil and the Alexandrian Tradition of Etymological Wordplay*. Ann Arbor, MI.

———. (2019) "Virgil's Style." Reprinted with revisions in F. Mac Góráin and C. Martindale (eds.), 368-86.

Oliensis, E. (2019) "Sons and Lovers: Sexuality and Gender in Virgil's Poetry." In *The Cambridge Companion to Virgil*. 2nd ed., ed. F. Mac Góráin and C. Martindale, 425-44. Cambridge.

Osgood, J. (2006) *Caesar's Legacy: Civil War and the Emergence of the Roman Empire*. Cambridge.

Otis, B. (1964) *Virgil: A Study in Civilized Poetry*. Oxford.

Page, T. E. (1894, 1900) *Virgil:* Aeneid. 2 vols. London.

Panoussi, V. (2002) "Vergil's Ajax: Allusion, Tragedy, and Heroic Identity in the *Aeneid*." *Classical Antiquity* 21: 95-134.

———. (2009) *Greek Tragedy in Vergil's* Aeneid: *Ritual, Empire, and Intertext*. Cambridge.

Pavlock, B. (1985) "Epic and Tragedy in Vergil's Nisus and Euryalus Episode." *Transactions of the American Philological Association* 115: 207-24.

Pelling, C. (1996) "The Triumviral Period." In *The Augustan Empire: 43 B.C.-A.D. 69*. 2nd ed., ed. A. Bowman, E. Champlin, and A. Lintott, 1-69. Vol. 10 of *The Cambridge Ancient History*. Cambridge.

Perkell, C. (1989) *The Poet's Truth: A Study of the Poet in Virgil's* Georgics. Berkeley, CA.

———. (1994) "Ambiguity and Irony: The Last Resort?" *Helios* 21: 63-74.

———. (1999) "*Aeneid* 1: An Epic Program." In *Reading Vergil's* Aeneid: *An Interpretative Guide*, ed. C. Perkell, 29-49. Norman, OK.

Petrini, M. (1997) *The Child and the Hero: Coming of Age in Catullus and Vergil*. Ann Arbor, MI.

Pogorzelski, R. (2009) "The Reassurance of Fratricide in the *Aeneid*." *American Journal of Philology* 130: 261-89.

Pöschl, V. (1950) *Die Dichtkunst Vergils: Bild und Symbol in der* Aeneis. Innsbruck.

———. (1962) *The Art of Vergil: Image and Symbol in the* Aeneid, trans. G. Seligson. Ann Arbor, MI.

Powell, A. (ed.) (1992) *Roman Poetry and Propaganda in the Age of Augustus*. Bristol.

Putnam, M. (1965) *The Poetry of the* Aeneid: *Four Studies in Imaginative Unity and Design*. Cambridge, MA.

———. (1979) *Virgil's Poem of the Earth: Studies in the* Georgics. Princeton.

———. (1993) "The Language of Horace's *Odes* 1.24." *Classical Journal* 88: 123-35.

———. (1994) "Virgil's Danaid Ekphrasis." *Illinois Classical Studies* 19: 171-89.

———. (1995) *Virgil's* Aeneid: *Interpretation and Influence*. Chapel Hill, NC.

———. (2011) *The Humanness of Heroes: Studies in the Conclusion of Virgil's* Aeneid. Chicago.

Quint, D. (1993) *Epic and Empire: Politics and Generic Form from Virgil to Milton*. Princeton.

———. (2018) *Virgil's Double Cross: Design and Meaning in the* Aeneid. Princeton.

Reed, J. D. (2007) *Virgil's Gaze: Nation and Poetry in the* Aeneid. Princeton.

Rijser, D. (2011) Afterword to *The Humanness of Heroes: Studies in the Conclusion of Virgil's* Aeneid, by M. Putnam, 135-50. Chicago.

Rosati, G. (2017) "Evander's Curse and the 'Long Death' of Mezentius (Verg. *Aen*. 8.483-488, 10.845-850)." *Harvard Studies in Classical Philology* 109: 377-82.

Ross, D. O. (1987) *Virgil's Elements: Physics and Poetry in the* Georgics. Princeton.

———. (2007) *Virgil's* Aeneid: *A Reader's Guide*. Oxford.

Rossi, A. (2004) *Contexts of War: Manipulation of Genre in Virgilian Battle Narrative*. Ann Arbor, MI.

Sandbach, F. H. (1965-66) "Anti-Antiquarianism in the *Aeneid*." *Proceedings of the Virgil Society* 5: 28-38.

Saunders, C. (1940) "Sources of the Names of Trojans and Latins in Vergil's *Aeneid*." *Transactions and Proceedings of the American Philological Association* 71: 537-55.

Saunders, K. B. (1999) "The Wounds in *Iliad* 13-16." *Classical Quarterly* 49: 345-63.

Saylor, C. F. (1974) "The Magnificent Fifteen: Vergil's Catalogue of the Latin and Etruscan Forces." *Classical Philology* 69: 249-57.

Schmidt, E. (2001) "The Meaning of Vergil's *Aeneid*: American and German Approaches." *Classical World* 94.2: 145-71.

Scullard, H. H. (1982) *From the Gracchi to Nero: A History of Rome from 133 B.C. to A.D. 68*. 5th ed. London.

Shotter, D. (2005) *Augustus Caesar*. 2nd ed. London.

Skutsch, O. (1985) *The Annals of Q. Ennius*. Oxford.

Smith, R. A. (2011) *Virgil*. West Sussex, UK.

Southern, P. (1998) *Augustus*. New York.

Spence, S. (1991) "Cinching the Text: The Danaids and the End of the *Aeneid*." *Vergilius* 37: 11-19.

Stahl, H. P. (1981) "Aeneas an un-Homeric Hero." *Arethusa* 14: 157-75.

———. (ed.) (1998) *Vergil's* Aeneid: *Augustan Epic and Political Context*. London.

———. (2016) *Poetry Underpinning Power: Vergil's* Aeneid; *The Epic for Emperor Augustus*. Wales.

Stover, Tim. (2011) "Aeneas and Lausus: Killing the 'Double,' and Civil War in *Aeneid* 10." *Phoenix* 65: 352-60.

Syme, R. (1939) *The Roman Revolution*. Oxford.

Tarrant, R. (2012) *Virgil*, Aeneid *XII*. Cambridge.

Thibodeau, P. (2011) *Playing the Farmer: Representations of Rural Life in Vergil's* Georgics. Berkeley, CA.

Thomas, R. (1986) "Virgil's *Georgics* and the Art of Reference." *Harvard Studies in Classical Philology* 90: 171-98.

———. (1988) *Virgil: The* Georgics. 2 vols. Cambridge.

———. (1999) *Reading Virgil and His Texts: Studies in Intertextuality*. Ann Arbor, MI.

———. (2001) *Virgil and the Augustan Reception*. Cambridge.

———. (2004-5) "Torn between Jupiter and Saturn: Ideology, Rhetoric and Culture Wars in the *Aeneid*." *Classical Journal* 100: 121-47.

Thomas, R., and J. Ziolkowski (eds.) (2014) *The Virgil Encyclopedia*. 3 vols. Malden, MA.

Trappes-Lomax, J. M. (2005) "Virgil *Aeneid* 10.366-7." *Classical Quarterly* 55.1: 315-17.

Van Sickle, J. (1992) *A Reading of Virgil's Messianic* Eclogue. New York.

Vernant, J.-P., and P. Vidal-Naquet (1988) *Myth and Tragedy in Ancient Greece*, trans. J. Lloyd. New York.

Volk, K. (ed.) (2008a) *Virgil's* Eclogues. Oxford.

———. (ed.) (2008b) *Virgil's* Georgics. Oxford.

Wallace-Hadrill, A. (1993) *Augustan Rome*. London.

———. (2008) *Rome's Cultural Revolution*. Cambridge.

West, D. A. (1969) "Multiple-Correspondence Similes in the *Aeneid*." *Journal of Roman Studies* 59: 40-9.

White, P. (1993) *Promised Verse: Poets in the Society of Augustan Rome*. Cambridge, MA.

———. (2005) "Poets in the New Milieu: Realigning." In *The Cambridge Companion to the Age of Augustus*, ed. K. Galinsky, 321-39. Cambridge.

Wigodsky, M. (1972) *Vergil and Early Latin Poetry*. Wiesbaden.

Wilkinson, L. P. (1969) *The Georgics of Virgil: A Critical Survey.* Cambridge.

Willcock, M. M. (1983) "Battle-Scenes in the *Aeneid.*" *Proceedings of the Cambridge Philological Society* 29: 87-99.

Williams, C. A. (2010) *Roman Homosexuality.* 2nd ed. Oxford.

Williams, G. (1983) *Technique and Ideas in the* Aeneid. London.

Williams, R. D. (1972-3) *Virgil:* Aeneid. 2 vols. London.

Wiltshire, S. F. (1989) *Public and Private in Vergil's* Aeneid. Amherst.

Wlosok, A. (1976) "Vergils Didotragödie: Ein Beitrag zum Problem des Tragischen in der *Aeneis.*" In *Studien zum antiken Epos,* ed. H. Görgemanns and E. A. Schmidt, 228-50. Meisenheim.

———. (1999) "The Dido Tragedy in Virgil: A Contribution to the Question of the Tragic in the *Aeneid.*" In *Virgil: Critical Assessments of Classical Authors,* ed. P. Hardie. Vol. 4, 158-81. London.

Zanker, P. (1988) *The Power of Images in the Age of Augustus,* trans. A. Shapiro. Ann Arbor, MI.

List of Abbreviations

abl.	= ablative	f.	= feminine
acc.	= accusative	gen.	= genitive
adj.	= adjective	i.e.	= id est, that is
adv.	= adverb	nom.	= nominative
cf.	= confer, i.e., compare	sc.	= scilicet, i.e., understand, supply
conj.	= conjunction	sing.	= singular
dat.	= dative	s.v.	= sub verbo, under the word

Vocabulary

(In general, macrons are placed only over long vowels in a metrically indeterminate position, as in the *Oxford Latin Dictionary*.)

A

ā, ab, abs, prep. with abl., *from, by*
Abās, Abantis, m., *Abas*, Etruscan ally of Aeneas, 170
abdūcō, -ere, -dūxī, -ductus, *to take away*
abeō, -īre, -iī, -itum, *to go away/ depart; get away* (800)
abiciō, -ere, -iēcī, -iectus, *to throw down/away*
abnuō, -ere, abnuī, abnuitus, *to refuse, forbid*
abscessus, -ūs, m., *departure*
absum, -esse, āfuī, āfutūrus, *to be away, be absent*
ac, conj., short form of **atque**, only used before consonants, *and*
accēdō, -ere, accessī, accessus, *to approach*
accendō, -ere, accendī, accēnsus, *to kindle, set on fire, stir up*
accipiō, -ere, -cēpī, -ceptus, *to receive, welcome, hear* (675)
acclīnis, -e, adj., *leaning on or against* (with dat.)
accurrō, -ere, -currī (-cucurrī), -cursus, *to run to*
ācer, ācris, ācre, adj., *keen; energetic; sharp*
acerbus, -a, -um, adj., *bitter*
acervus, -ī, m., *heap, pile*
Achātēs, Achātae, m., *Achates*, Aeneas' faithful friend, 332, etc.
Achillēs, -is, m. or Achilleus, -eī, m., *Achilles*, son of Peleus and Thetis. Most famous Greek hero at Troy, 581
Achīvus, -a, -um, adj., *Achaean, Greek* (89)
aciēs, -eī, f., *edge; line of battle; army; battle* (543)
Acmōn, Acmonis, m., *Acmon*, an ally of Aeneas, 128
Ācrōn, Ācrōnis, m., *Acron*, a Greek exile ally of Aeneas, 719, 730
acūtus, -a, -um, adj., *sharp, piercing*
ad, prep. with acc., *to, up to, toward, near*
addēnseō, -ēre, or addēnsō, -āre, *to make compact, to close up*
addō, -ere, addidī, additus, *to give to; add*

addūcō, -ere, -dūxī, -ductus, *to lead to, induce*
adeō, -īre, -īvī/iī, -itus, *to go to*
adfīgō, -ere, -fīxī, -fīxus, *to fasten to*
adfor, -ārī, -fātus sum, *to speak to; address*
adhūc, adv., *thus far, to this point, still, as yet*
adiciō, -ere, -iēcī, -iectus, *to add, contribute*
adigō, -ere, -ēgī, -āctus, *to drive to, force to*
adiuvō, āre, -iūvī, -iūtus, *to help, assist, support*
adlābor, -lāpsus sum, *to glide in, come to*
adlacrimāns, -antis, adj., *weeping*
adloquor, -loquī, -locūtus sum, *to speak to, address, appeal*
admoneō, -ēre, -monuī, -monitus, *to admonish, remind; urge on* (587)
adnuō, -ere, -nuī (-ūtus, -rare), *to nod to* (with dat.)
adōrō, -āre, -āvī, -ātus, *to pray to, venerate*
adsēnsus, -ūs, m., *an assenting; answering sound*
adsimulō, -āre, -āvī, -ātus, *to make like; to counterfeit*
adsistō, -ere, -adstitī, *to stand at, stand by*
adsum, -esse, -fuī, -futūrus, *to be present* (with dat.)
adsurgō, -ere, -surrēxī, -surrēctus, *to rise up; rise*
adulter, -erī, m., *adulterer*
advehō, -ere, -vexī, -vectus, *to carry; convey to*
advena, -ae, m./f., *newcomer, stranger*
adveniō, -īre, -vēnī, -ventus, *to arrive*
adversus, -a, -um, adj., *opposed; opposite; facing; toward*

advertō, -ere, -vertī, -versus, *to turn toward*
advolō, -āre, -āvī, -ātus, *to fly to*
Aegaeōn, Aegaeōnis, m., *Aegaeon, a giant,* 565
aeger, aegra, aegrum, adj., *sick, weak*
aemulus, -a, -um, adj., *striving to equal* (with dat.)
Aeneadēs, Aeneadae, m., *a son or follower of Aeneas. A Trojan,* 120
Aenēās, -ae, m., *Aeneas, son of Venus and Anchises. Mythical ancestor of the Romans,* 25, 48, 65, etc.
Aenēius, -a, -um, adj., *of Aeneas,* 156, 494
Aeolia, -ae, f., *Aeolia, an island N.E. of Sicily, home of the winds,* 38
aequālis, -e, adj., *of the same age*
aequō, -āre, -āvī, -ātus, *to make equal, equalize*
aequor, aequoris, n., *level surface; sea; plain; field of battle* (451, 569)
aequus, -a, -um, adj., *equal*
aerātus, -a, -um, adj., *bronze-plated*
aereus, -a, -um, adj., *made of copper or bronze*
aes, aeris, n., *copper, bronze*
aestās, aestātis, f., *summer*
aestuō, -āre, -āvī, -ātus, *to be very hot, burn; seethe; fret*
aestus, -ūs, m., *tide, flood* (292), *current* (687)
aetās, aetātis, f., *age*
aeternus, -a, -um, adj., *everlasting, eternal*
aethēr, -is, n., *upper air*
aetherius, -a, -um, adj., *heavenly*
Aetōlus (Aetōlius), -a, -um, *Aetolian, of Aetolia,* 28
aevum, -ī, n., *age; life-span*
age, agite, *come on! Let's go!*
ager, agrī, m., *field, land*

agger, -is, m., *mound, rampart*
Āgis, Agidis, m., *Agis,* Lycian ally of Aeneas, 751
agitō, -āre, -āvī, -ātus, *to drive; disturb; pass* (of time)
āgmen, āgminis, n., *army; rank; line of battle*
āgnōscō, -ere, āgnōvī, agnitus, *to recognize*
agō, -ere, ēgī, āctus, *to drive, do, act*
agrestis, agrestis, agreste, adj., *rural, rustic*
agricola, -ae, m., *farmer*
āiō, *to say, affirm, say yes*
alacer, alacris, alacre, adj., *lively, eager*
albus, -a, -um, adj., *white*
Alcānor, -oris, m., *Alcanor,* a Latin, 338
Alcathous, -ī, m., *Alcathous,* a Trojan, 747
Alcīdēs, -ae, m., *a descendant of Alceus,* Hercules, 321, 461, 464
āles, -itis, m./f., *bird*
aliēnus, -a, -um, adj., *strange, unrelated, another's*
aliquis, aliquid, and aliquī, aliqua, aliquod, pron. and adj., *someone, something; anyone, anything*
aliter, adv., *otherwise, differently*
alius, alia, aliud, adj., *other, another*
Allēctō, -ūs, f., *Allecto,* one of the three Furies, 41
almus, -a, -um, adj., *giving nourishment; blessed; kind*
Alpēs, -ium, f., *the Alps* (13)
Alphēus, -a, -um, *of the Alpheus* (river); *Alphean,* a river in Elis, 179
altē, adv., *aloft, on high; deeply*
alter, altera, alterum, adj., *other of two*
altum, -ī, n., *deep sea; height*
altus, -a, -um, adj., *tall, high; noble*
alvus, -ī, f., *belly*

amārus, -a, -um, *bitter; harsh*
Amathūs, Amathūntis, f., *Amathus,* town of Cyprus, 51
ambiō, -īre, -īvī (-iī), -ītus, *to go round; encircle*
ambō, ambae, ambō, adj., *both*
āmēns, āmentis, adj., *mad, insane, distraught*
amīcus, -a, -um, adj., *friendly* (with dat.)
amnis, amnis, m., *river, torrent*
amō, -āre, -āvī, -ātus, *to love*
amor, -ōris, m., *love*
amplector, amplectī, amplexus sum, *to embrace*
Amȳclae, -ārum, f., *Amyclae,* a town in Latium, 564
Amycus, -ī, m., *Amycus,* a Trojan, 704
an, conj. *or?* Introduces second of two questions. The first is sometimes not expressed but implied
an...an, *whether...or* (681)
anceps, adj., *two-headed; balanced; uncertain*
Anchemolus, -ī, m., *Anchemolus,* a Latin, 389
Anchīsēs, -ae, m., *Anchises,* father of Aeneas, 534
Anchīsiadēs, -ae, m., *Anchisiades,* son of Anchises, Aeneas, 250, 822
anhēlō, -āre, -āvī, -ātus, *to pant*
anima, -ae, f., *breath, spirit*
animus, -ī, m., *spirit, mind, heart*
annōsus, -a, -um, adj., *aged, old*
annus, -ī, m., *year*
Antaeus, -ī, m., *Antaeus,* a Latin, 561
ante, adv., *before, sooner* and prep. with acc., *before; in front of* (643)
antīquus, -a, -um, adj., *ancient, old*
Antōrēs, -ae, m., *Antores,* companion of Heracles, 778
Anxur, -is, m., *Anxur,* a Latin, 545

aper, aprī, m., *wild boar*
aperiō, -īre, aperuī, apertus, *to open*
apex, apicis, m., *the point of anything; peak; helmet-crest*
Apollō, Apollinis, m., *Apollo, the god Apollo,* 875. *A ship's figurehead,* 171
appāreō, -ēre, apparuī, apparitus, *to appear, become visible*
apparō, -āre, -āvī, -ātus, *to get ready*
applicō, -āre, -āvī, -ātus, *to apply to, place to/near*
aptō, -āre, -āvī, -ātus, *to make ready*
aqua, -ae, f., *water*
arātor, -ōris, m., *ploughman*
arbor (or arbos), arboris, f., *tree, mast; oar* (207)
arbustum, -ī, n., *growth of trees; grove; thicket*
Arcadia, -ae, f., *Arcadia, region in the Peloponnese, Greece,* 429
Arcadius, -a, -um, *of Arcadia* (425)
Arcas, Arcadis, *Arcadian, an Arcadian,* 239, 364, 397, etc.
arcessō (accersō), -ere, arcessīvī, arcessītus, *to fetch, summon*
arcus, -ūs, m., *bow, arch*
ārdēns, ārdentis, adj., *burning; gleaming*
ārdeō, -ēre, ārsī, ārsus, *to burn, glow*
ārdor, -ōris, m., *burning, heat, eagerness*
arduus, -a, -um, adj., *steep, on high, towering*
argentum, -ī, n., *silver*
Argī, Argōrum, m., *Argos, town in N.E. Peloponnese, Greece,* 779, 782
Argolicus, -a, -um, *of Argolis; Argolic; Greek* (56)
arma, armōrum, n., *arms, weapons; battle* (259); *forces* (150)
armō, -āre, -āvī, -ātus, *to equip, arm*

armus, -ī, m., *shoulder*
Arpī, Arpōrum, *Arpi, a town in Apulia, Southern Italy,* 28
arrigō, -ere, arrēxī, arrēctus, *to raise up; erect; bristle up*
arripiō, -ere, arripuī, arreptus, *to snatch, seize*
ars, artis, f., *skill*
arvum, -ī, n., *field*
arx, arcis, f., *summit, citadel; shelter* (805)
Ascanius, -iī, m., *Ascanius, son of Aeneas,* 47, 236, 605
Asia, -ae, f., *Asia, Asia,* 91
Asīlās, -ae, m., *Asilas, an Etruscan seer, ally of Aeneas,* 175
Āsius, -iī, m., *Asius, a Trojan,* 123
aspectō (adspectō), -āre, -āvī, -ātus, *to look at or upon*
asper, -a, -um, adj., *rough; fierce*
aspiciō, -ere, aspēxī, aspectus, *to look at*
Assaracus, -ī, m., *Assaracus, a Trojan,* 124
ast, conj., *but*
astō, astāre, astitī, *to stand near*
Astur, Asturis, m., *Astur, an Etruscan ally of Aeneas,* 180
astus, -ūs, m., *cunning;* abl. **astū**
at, conj., *but*
āter, atra, atrum, adj., *black; pitchy*
atque or ac, only before consonants, conj., *and, also;* after **secus,** *than* (272)
attingō, -ere, attigī, attāctus, *to touch*
attollō, -ere, *to raise up*
auctor, -ōris, m., *founder; cause; encourager* (67)
audāx, audācis, adj., *bold; reckless*
audeō, -ēre, ausus sum, *to dare*
audiō, -īre, -īvī, -ītus, *to hear*

auferō, auferre, abstulī, ablātus, *to take away, remove*
augurium, -ī(ī), n., *prophecy, omen*
Aulestēs, Aulestis, m., *Aulestes,* an Etruscan, brother of Ocnus and ally of Aeneas, 207
aura, -ae, f., *breeze*
aurātus, -a, -um, adj., *golden*
aureus, -a, -um, adj., *golden*
aurōra, -ae, f., *dawn, aurora*
aurum, -ī, n., *gold*
Auruncus, -a, -um, *Auruncan,* of Aurunca, a town in Campania, 353
Ausonia, -ae, f., *Ausonia,* ancient name for Italy, 54, 356
Ausonidēs, -ae or Ausonidae, -ārum or Ausonidae, -ūm, m., *Ausonides,* people of Ausonia, Italians, 564
Ausonius, -a, -um, adj., *Ausonius,* of Ausonia, Italian (105, 268)
ausum, -ī, n., *daring deed; outrage*
aut; aut...aut, conj., *or; either...or*
autem, conj., *however; moreover*
auxilium, -ī, n., *aid, help; forces*
āvellō, -ere, -vellī (vulsī), -vulsus, *to pluck, tear away*
āvertō, -ere, avertī, aversus, *to turn away; carry off* (78)
avītus, -a, -um, adj., *of a grandfather, ancestral*
avus, avī, m., *grandfather, ancestor*

B

bacchor, bacchārī, bacchātus sum, *to revel, rage as a bacchante*
balteus, -ī, m., *belt*
barba, -ae, f., *beard*
bellātor, -ōris, m., *warrior*
bellum, -ī, n., *war*
Bēnācus, -ī, m., *Benacus,* a lake from which the Mincius flows, 205

biiugus, -a, -um, adj., *of a two-horse team, yoked*
bipatēns, bipatentis, adj., *with double doors*
bonus, -a, -um, adj., *good*
Boreās, -ae, m., *the god of the North Wind* (350)
bracchium, -ī(ī), n., *arm*
brevis, breve, adj., *short, brief; shallow* (289)
breviter, adv., *briefly*
buxus, -ī, f., *box wood*

C

cadō, -ere, cecidī, cāsus, *to fall*
cadūcus, -a, -um, adj., *doomed to fall*
Caeculus, -ī, m., *Caeculus,* son of Vulcan, ally of Turnus, 544
caecus, -a, -um, adj., *blind; unseen; dark*
caedēs, -is, f., *killing; slaughter; dead people* (245)
Caedicus, -ī, m., *Caedicus,* a Latin ally of Turnus, 747
caedō, -ere, cecīdī, caesus, *to kill, strike, cut*
caelicola, -ae, m./f., *an inhabitant of heaven; a god*
caelō, -āre, -āvī, -ātus, *to cut in relief; carve*
caelum, -ī, n., *sky, heaven; air* (899)
Caere, n. (gen. Caeritis f. abl. Caerēte f.), *Caere,* a town in Etruria, 183
caerulus (caeruleus), -a, -um, adj., *dark blue*
calamus, -ī, m., *reed, cane; an arrow*
calidus (caldus), -a, -um, adj., *warm, hot*
calx, calcis, f. and rarely m., *heel; hoof* (892)
Camers, Camertis, m., *Camers,* a Latin ally of Turnus, 562

Campānus, -a, -um, adj., *of Campania,* an Italian region, 145
campus, -ī, m., *plain*
canis, -is, m. or f., *dog*
cānitiēs, -eī, f., *hoariness; white hair; old age*
canō, -ere, cecinī, cantus, *to sing; foretell; ring out* (310)
cantus, -ūs, m., *singing or playing; melody; song*
capillus, -ī, m., *hair*
capiō, -ere, cēpī, captus, *to seize; arrive at* (106)
caprea, -ae, f., *wild goat*
captīvus, -a, -um, adj., *captured, captive*
capulus, -ī, m., *the handle; hilt*
caput, capitis, n., *head, one's life; chief*
Capys, Capyos or -yis, m., *Capys,* ally of Aeneas, 145
carīna, -ae, f., *keel; ship*
cārus, -a, -um, adj., *precious; dear*
Cassandra, -ae, f., *Cassandra,* prophetess daughter of Priam and Hecuba, 68
Castor, -is, m., *Castor,* a Trojan, 124
castra, castrōrum, n. pl., *camp*
cāsus, -ūs, m., *fall, disaster; chance*
caterva, -ae, f., *band (esp. of soldiers); a crowd*
causa, -ae, f., *cause, reason*
cavus, -a, -um, adj., *hollow; convex* (784)
cēdō, -ere, cessī, cessus, *to yield, give way; fail* (276)
celerō, -āre, -āvī, -ātus, *to speed*
cēlō, -āre, -āvī, -ātus, *to hide*
celsus, -a, -um, adj., *high, lofty*
Centaurus, -ī, m., *a Centaur,* a half-man, half-horse monster. The name of a ship (and its figurehead), 195

centēnī, -ae, -a, adj., *one hundred each; one hundred*
centum, num. adj. indecl., *one hundred*
cerebrum, -ī, n., *brain*
cernō, -ere, crēvī, certus, *to discern, see*
cernuus, -a, -um, adj., *with head or face prone downward*
certāmen, certāminis, n., *contest, struggle*
certō, -āre, -āvī, -ātus, *to fight, compete*
certus, -a, -um, adj., *sure, fixed*
cervīx, cervīcis, f., *neck*
cervus, -ī, m., *stag*
ceu, adv., *as, just as*
Chalybes, -um, m., *Chalybes,* a people who lived on the Black Sea coast and were famous for working iron, 174
chorēa, -ae, f., *circling dance*
chorus, -ī, m., *band; troop*
cieō, -ēre, -cīvī, -citus, *to cause; call up, summon*
cingō, -ere, cīnxī, cīnctus, *to surround*
cinis, cineris, m. or f., *ashes*
circulus, -ī, m., *circle, orbit; ring; torque, circlet*
circum or circa, adv., and prep. with acc., *around*
circumdō, -āre, -dedī, -dātus, *to surround*
circumferō, -ferre, -tulī, -lātus, *to bear round; pass around*
circumstō, -stāre, -stetī, *to stand around*
Cissēis, Cisseidis, f., *Cisseis,* daughter of Cisseus. Hecuba, wife of Priam, 705
Cisseus, -ī, m., *Cisseus,* a Latin, ally of Turnus, 317
clāmō, -āre, -āvī, -ātus, *to call, shout*

clāmor, -ōris, m., *outcry, shout*
Clārus, -ī, m., *Clarus,* a Trojan, 126
classis, -is, f., *fleet, ships*
claudō (clūdō or clodō), -ere, clausī, clausus, *to close, enclose*
Clausus, -ī, m., *Clausus,* ally of Turnus, 345
clāva, -ae, f., *club*
clāvus, -ī, m., *tiller; helm*
clipeus, -ī, m. or clipeum, -ī, n., *round shield*
Clonius, -iī, m., *Clonius,* a Trojan, 749
Clonus, -ī, m., *Clonus,* a metalwork artist, 499
Clūsīnus, -a, -um, adj., *of Clusium,* 655
Clūsium, -iī, n., *Clusium,* a town in Etruria, 167
Clytius, -iī, m., *Clytius,* an ally of Aeneas, 129; a Latin, 325
coeō, coīre, coīvī/coiī, coitus, *to come together*
coeptum, -ī, n., *thing begun; an undertaking, attempt*
cōgō, -ere, -ēgī, -āctus, *to compel*
cohors, cohortis, f., *cohort, band, troupe*
colligō, -ere, -lēgī, -lēctus, *to collect*
collum, -ī, m., *neck*
coma, -ae, f., *hair; mane*
comes, comitis, m. or f., *companion*
comētēs (comēta), -ae, m., *comet*
comitor, -ārī, comitātus sum, *to accompany*
commercium, -iī, n., *trade; negotiation*
comminus, adv., *hand to hand*
committō, -ere, -mīsī, -mīssus, *to join, entrust*
cōmō, -ere, cōmpsī, cōmptus, *to arrange, adorn*
compellō, -āre, -āvī, -ātus, *to address*
compōnō, -ere, -posuī, -positus, *to arrange; calm down*

concēdō, -ere, -cessī, -cessus, *to withdraw; allow, concede* (906)
concha, -ae, f., *shellfish; cockle shell*
conciliō, -āre, -āvī, -ātus, *to win over, reconcile*
concilium, -ī(ī), n., *council, meeting*
conclāmō, -āre, -āvī, -ātus, *to shout together*
concrēdō, -ere, -didī, -ditus, *to entrust*
concurrō, -ere, -cucurrī, -cursus, *to clash, meet in battle* (with dat.)
condō, -ere, condidī, conditus, *to hide, bury; form*
cōnferō, -ferre, -tulī, collātus, *to engage in; to engage in battle with*
congredior, -gredī, -gressus sum, *to meet, join in battle*
coniciō, -ere, -iēcī, -iectus, *to hurl; to dive* (with *se*)
cōnītor, -nītī, -nīxus (-nīsus) sum, *to strain, struggle*
coniungō, -ere, -iūnxī, -iūnctus, *to join together; moor* (653)
coniūnx, coniugis, f., *spouse*
conlūceō, -ēre, *to be wholly shining, gleam*
cōnor, -ārī, cōnātus sum, *to try, attempt*
cōnscendō, -ere, -scendī, -scēnsus, *to board (a ship)*
cōnscius, -a, -um, adj., *conscious; knowing, aware* (often with gen.)
cōnsīdō, -ere, -sēdī, -sessus, *to sit down; settle* (780)
cōnsistō, -ere, -stitī, -stitus, *to take position; halt, stand*
cōnsors, -consortis, *having a common lot* (with gen.)
cōnspectus, -ūs, m., *look, sight, view*
cōnspiciō, -ere, -spexī, cōn-spectus, *to catch sight of, behold*

cōnsuēscō, -ere, -suēvī, -suētus, *to accustom oneself; to be accustomed to*
cōnsurgō, -ere, -surrēxī, -surrēctus, *to rise together*
contendō, -ere, -tendī, -tentus, *to strain, exert; hurl* (521)
contiguus, -a, -um, adj., *near, within reach* (with dat.)
contineō, -ēre, -tinuī, -tentus, *to contain, restrain*
contrā, adv., *in reply, against* and prep. with acc., *against, opposite*
contrīstō, -āre, -āvī, -ātus, *to make sad*
convertō, -ere, -vertī, versus, *to turn round, cause to turn, turn back, change*
convexum, -ī, n., *vault; arch* (of the sky)
coorior, -īrī, -ortus sum, *to arise*
cor, cordis, n., *heart; delight* (252)
cornū, -ūs, f., *horn*
corōna, -ae, f., *garland; crown; circle of defenders*
corpus, corporis, n., *body*
corripiō, -ere, -ripuī, -reptus, *to seize, plunder; rebuke*
corruō, -ere, -uī, *to fall completely; fall down, sink*
coruscō, -āre, -āvī, -ātus, *to brandish*
Corythus, -ī, m., *Corythus*, a town in Etruria, 719
Cosa, -ae, or Cosae, -ārum, f., *Cosa*, a town in Etruria, 168
costa, -ae, f., *rib*
crassus, -a, -um, adj., *thick, fat; crass, coarse*
crāstinus, -a, -um, adj., *pertaining to tomorrow*
crēdō, -ere, crēdidī, crēditus, *to trust, believe* (with dat.); *entrust* (with acc. and dat.)

creō, -āre, -āvī, -ātus, *to create, produce*
crepīdō, crepidinis, f., *ledge; quay*
crēscō, -ere, crēvī, crētus, *to grow, increase*
crīmen, crīminis, n., *charge, guilt, crime*
crīnis, crīnis, m., *hair*
crista, -ae, f., *crest; helmet-plume*
crūdēlis, crūdēle, adj., *unfeeling, cruel*
crūdus, -a, -um, adj., *bloody, raw; cruel*
cruentō, -āre, -āvī, -ātus, *to make bloody*
cruentus, -a, -um, adj., *bloody, blood-stained*
cruor, -ōris, m., *blood, bloodshed*
culta, cultōrum, n., *plowed fields*
cum, conj., *when; since; although*
cum, prep. with abl., *with*
Cunarus, -ī, m., *Cunarus*, a Ligurian leader, 186
cūnctor, -ārī, -ātus sum, *to delay; hesitate*
cūnctus, -a, -um, adj., *all*
Cupāvō, Cupavōnis, m., *Cupavo*, a Ligurian leader, 186
Cupīdō, Cupīdinis, m., *Cupid*, son of Venus and god of Love and erotic desire, 93
cupiō, -ere, cupiī/cupīvī, cupītus, *to desire*
cūr, conj., *why*
cūra, -ae, f., *care, concern*
Curēs, -ium, m., *Cures*, chief town of the Sabines, 345
currus, -ūs, m., *chariot*
cursus, -ūs, m., *course, advance*
curvus, -a, -um, *curved, curving*
cuspis, cuspidis, f., *sharp point, spear*
Cybelē (Cybēbē), -ēs or -ae, f., *Cybele*, a Phrygian goddess, 220

Cycnus, -ī, m., *Cycnus,* a Ligurian king, changed into a swan, 189
Cydōn, Cydōnis, m., *Cydon,* a Latin ally of Turnus, 325
Cȳmodocē, -ēs or Cȳmodocēa, -ae, f., *Cymodoce,* a sea nymph, previously one of Aeneas' ships, 225
Cythēra, Cythērōrum, n. or Cythērē, -ēs, f., *Cythera,* island in Southern Greece, sacred to Venus, 51, 86

D

Dardanidēs, -ae, m., *Dardanides,* a descendant of Dardanus, 4, 263, 545
Dardanius, -a, -um, adj., *Dardanian; Trojan* (92, 133, 326, 603, 638, 814)
Daucius, -a, -um, adj., *of Daucus* (391)
Daunus, -ī, m., *Daunus,* father of Turnus, 616, 688
dē, prep. with abl., *down from, about, concerning; according to* (832)
dea, -ae, f., *goddess*
dēbeō, -ēre, dēbuī, dēbitus, *to owe; ought*
decet, decēre, decuīt, impersonal, *it is fitting* (to)
dēcīdō, -ere, -cīdī, -cīsus, *to cut off*
decus, decoris, n., *beauty; ornament; glory; pride*
dēcutiō, -ere, -cussī, -cussus, *to shake off*
dēdecus, dēdecōris, n., *shame, disgrace*
dēdūcō, -ere, -dūxī, -ductus, *to derive*
dēfendō, -ere, dēfendī, dēfensus, *to defend, ward off; shelter* (709)
dēferō, -ferre, -tulī, -lātus, *to carry down*
dēflectō, -ere, -flexī, -flexus, *to turn aside*
dēfodiō, -ere, -fōdī, -fossus, *to bury*
dēfōrmō, -āre, -āvī, -ātus, *to disfigure*

dehīscō, -ere, -hīvī, *to gape*
dēiciō, -ere, -iēcī, -eīctus, *to throw down, hurl down; cut off* (546)
deinde or dein, adv., *then, next*
dēlābor, -lābi, -lāpsus sum, *to glide; fall from, slip from*
dēlūdō, -ere, -lūsī, -lūsus, *to deceive*
dēmēns, dēmentis, adj., *mad, raving*
dēmittō, -ere, -mīsī, -missus, *to send down, drop*
Dēmodocus, -ī, m., *Demodocus,* Arcadian ally of Aeneas, 413
dēmoror, -āri, -ātus sum, *to keep waiting* (30)
dēmum, adv., *finally*
dēnī, -ae, -a, adj., *ten, ten at a time*
dēns, dentis, m., *tooth*
dēnsus, -a, -um, adj., *thick, dense*
dēpendeō, -ēre, *to hang down*
dēprehendō, -ere, -prehendī, -prehensus, *to catch, seize*
dērigō, -ere, -rēxī, -rēctus, *to direct; aim*
dēripiō, -ere, -ripuī, -reptus, *to snatch away, tear down*
dēsaeviō, -īre, -iī, *to rage furiously*
dēserō, -ere, -seruī, -sertus, *to leave, abandon*
dēsiliō, -īre, -siluī, -sultus, *to leap or spring down*
dēsinō, -ere, -siī, -situs, *to leave off, cease*
dēsistō, -ere, -stitī, -stitus, *to cease, desist from* (with dat.)
dēspectō, -āre, -āvī, -ātus, *to look down upon*
dēsum, -esse, -fuī, *to be lacking*
dētegō, -ere, -tēxī, -tēctus, *to uncover*
dētonō, -ere, -tonuī, *to cease to thunder*
dēturbō, -āre, -āvī, -ātus, *to dash down*

deus, deī, m., *god*
dēvincō, -ere, -vīcī, -victus, *to conquer completely*
dextera, -ae, f., *right hand*
diciō, -ōnis, f., *dominion; authority*
dīcō, -ere, dīxī, dictus, *to say, speak*
dictum, -ī, n., *word; saying*
diēs, -ēī, m. or f., *day*
diffugiō, -ere, -fūgī, *to scatter*
diffundo, -ere, -fūdī, -fūsus, *to pour out*
digitus, -ī, m., *finger*
dīgnor, -ārī, -ātus sum, *to deem worthy of* (+ acc. and abl.)
dīgnus, -a, -um, adj., *worthy of* (with abl.)
dīmittō, -ere, -mīsī, -mīssus, *to send away*
Dindyma, Dindymōrum, n. or Dindymus, -ī, m., *Dindyma, a mountain in Mysia*, 252
Diomēdēs, -is, m., *Diomedes, a Greek hero at Troy*, 581
dīruō, -ere, -uī, -utus, *to tear apart*
dīrus, -a, -um, adj., *dreadful*
discēdō, -ere, -cessī, -cessus, *to go away, depart*
discordia, -ae, f., *disagreement, dissension*
discors, discordis, adj., *disagreeing; discordant; opposed*
discrepō, -āre, -crepuī, *to be discordant in sound; differ*
discrīmen, discriminis, n., *difference; division; dividing line* (511)
dispergō, -ere, -spersī, -spersus, *to scatter; smash*
dītissimus, -a, -um, adj., *very rich*
diū, adv., *for a long time*
dīva, -ae, f., *goddess*
dīves, dīvitis, adj., *rich*; as substantive *rich man*
dīvidō, -ere, dīvīsī, dīvīsus, *to divide, separate*
dīvīnus, -a, -um, adj., *divine*
dīvus (dīus), dīvī, m., *god*
dīvus (dīus), -a, -um, adj., *divine*
dō, dare, dedī, datus, *to give*
doctus, -a, -um, adj., *taught, learned, skilled*
Dolichāōn, Dolichāonis, m., *Dolichaon, a Trojan*, 696
dolor, -ōris, m., *pain, grief*
dominus, -ī, m., *master*
domus, -ī, f., *house, home; palace; temple*
dōnec, conj., *until*
dōnō, -āre, -āvī, -ātus, *to give; concede*
dōnum, -ī, n., *gift*
dorsum, -ī, n., *back; reef* (303)
Dryopē, -ēs, f., *Dryope, a nymph*, 551
Dryops, Dryopis, m., *Dryops, ally of Aeneas*, 346
dūcō, -ere, dūxī, ductus, *to lead; derive* (145); *draw over* (192); *consider* (669)
ductor, -is, m., *leader*
dūdum, adv., *not long ago; just now*
dulcis, dulce, adj., *sweet*
dum, conj., *while, until, provided that*
duō, duae, duo, *two*
duplex, duplicis, adj., *double*; pl. *both* (667)
dūrus, -a, -um, *hard, harsh*
dux, ducis, m. or f., *leader, general*

E

ē, ex, prep. with abl., *out of, from*
ebur, eboris, n., *ivory*
ecce, interj., *behold!*
ēdīcō, -ere, ēdīxī, ēdictus, *to make known, proclaim*
ēdō, -ere, ēdidī, ēditus, *to emit, cause*

ēdoceō, -ēre, -docuī, -doctus, *to teach completely; communicate*
ēdūcō, -ere, -dūxī, -ductus, *to lead forth; pull out* (744)
ēducō, -āre, -āvī, -ātus, *to bring up, rear*
efferō, -ferre, extulī, ēlātus, *to carry out or away; raise, lift*
efferus, -a, -um, adj., *savage, frantic*
effingō, -ere, -fīnxī, -fīctus, *to mold out; imitate*
effor, -fārī, -fātus sum, *to speak forth; speak*
effundō, -ere, -fūdī, -fūsus, *to pour out; throw off* (574, 893)
egēnus, -a, -um, adj., *needy, in want*
ego, meī, mihi, mē, mē, personal pron., *I, me*
ēgredior, ēgredī, ēgressus, sum, *to depart; disembark*
ēgregius, -a, -um, adj., *distinguished, uncommon*
ēiciō, ēicere, ēiēcī, ēiectus, *to throw out, expel; dislocate* (894)
ēmētior, ēmētīrī, ēmēnsus sum, *to measure out or off*
ēmineō, -ēre, -uī, *to stand out*
ēminus, adv., *from afar*
ēmittō, -ere, -mīsī, -mīssus, *to send out; throw*
emō, -ere, ēmī, ēmptus, *to buy*
enim, conj., *in fact, for*
ēnsis, is, m., *sword*
eō, īre, iī/īvī, itus, *to go*
eques, equitis, m., *horseman,* collectively *cavalry*
equidem, adv., *indeed, truly*
equīnus, -a, -um, adj., *pertaining to horses*
equitō, -āre, -āvī, -ātus, *to ride*
equus, -ī, m., *horse*
ergō, adv., *therefore*

Erichaetēs, -ae, m., *Ericetes*, a Trojan, 749
ēripiō, -ere, ēripuī, ēreptus, *to tear away, snatch away*
error, -ōris, m., *wandering, error*
ērumpō, -ere, -rūpī, -ruptus, *to break out, burst out*
Erycīnus, -a, -um, adj., *of Eryx*, a mountain in Sicily, 36
et, conj. and adv., *and, even, also*
et...et, *both...and*
etiam, adv., *also*
Etrūscus, -a, -um, adj., *Etrurian*, 148, 180, 238, 429
Eurōpa, -ae, f., *Europa*, Europe, 91
Eurytidēs, -ae, m., *Eurytides*, son of Eurytides, 499
ēvādō, -ere, ēvāsī, ēvāsus, *to go out, evade*
Evander (-drus), Evandrī, m., *Evander*, an Arcadian. Ally of Aeneas and father of Pallas, 148, 370, 420, 492, 515, 780
Evandrius, -a, -um, adj., *of Evander; Evandrian* (394)
Evanthēs, -ae, m., *Evanthes*, a Phrygian ally of Aeneas, 702
ēventus, -ūs, m., *result*
ēvertō, -ere, -vertī, -versus, *to overturn, overthrow*
exanimus, -a, -um or exanimis, -e, adj., *breathless, lifeless*
excidium, -iī, n., *ruins*
exciō (excieō), -īre, -īvī (-iī), -ītus (-itus), *to summon, rouse up or forth; call forth*
excipiō, -ere, -cēpī, -ceptus, *to catch, receive*
excutiō, -ere, -cussī, -cussus, *to shake off;* in pass. *glance from* (777)
exerceō, -ēre, exercuī, exercitus, *to work at; to cultivate; keep busy* (808)

exercitus, exercitūs, m., *army*
exhauriō, -īre, -hausī, -haustus, *to drain, exhaust; endure to the end*
exigō, -ere, -ēgī, -āctus, *to drive out; finish; live out* (53)
exiguus, -a, -um, adj., *small, little*
exilium/exsilium, exiliī/exsiliī, n., *exile, banishment*
exitium, existi(ī), n., *destruction, ruin; death*
exitus, ūs, m., *departure; end*
exōrsum, -ī, n., *thing begun or undertaken; enterprise*
expellō, -ere, -pulī, -pulsus, *to propel, drive out, expel*
expendō, -ere, -pendī, -pēnsus, *to weigh out; pay*
experior, experīrī, expertus sum, *to test, try, experience*
expers, expertis, adj., *lacking* (with gen.)
expōnō, ere, -posuī, -positus, *to land; cast out; put out* (654)
expūgnō, -āre, -āvī, -ātus, *to assault, capture*
exsecō, -āre, -secuī, -sectus or -ecror, -ārī, *to cut out*
exspīrō, -āre, -āvī, -ātus, *to breathe out; die*
exsultō (exultō), -are, -āvī, -ātus, *to leap; dash up; prance*
exsuperō, -āre, -āvī, -ātus, *to be completely above; overcome, surmount*
extendō, -ere, -tendī, -tentus (-tēnsus), *to stretch forth; stretch*
externus, -a, -um, adj., *outside, foreign, strange*
exterreō, -ēre, -uī, -itus, *to frighten; alarm*
extrēmus, -a, -um, *last; in the rear*
exūrō, -ere, -ussī, -ūstus, *to burn out*

exuviae, -ārum, f., *that which has been taken off; spoils*

F

faciēs, facieī, f., *appearance*
faciō, -ere, fēcī, factus, *to do, make*
factum, factī, n., *deed*
factus, -a, -um, adj., *wrought* (527)
fallō, -ere, fefellī, falsus, *to deceive*
falsus, -a, -um, adj., *deceptive, false*
fāma, -ae, f., *rumor, fame*
famēs, famis, f., *hunger, famine*
fātidicus, -a, -um, adj., *prophetic*
fatīgō, -āre, -āvī, -ātus, *to tire, wear out*
fātum, -ī, n. or fātus, -ī, m., *destiny, fate*
Faunus, -ī, m., *Faunus, god of shepherds and agriculture,* 551
fax, facis, f., *torch*
femur, femoris, n. (rarely femen, -inis, n.), *thigh*
feriō, ferīre, *to hit; make a treaty*
ferō, ferre, tulī, lātus, *to bear, carry, report;* **ferunt,** *they say that* (189)
ferōx, ferōcis, adj., *bold; wild*
ferreus, -a, -um, adj., *made of iron*
ferrum, -ī, n., *iron; sword*
ferus, -a, -um, adj., *wild, fierce*
fervidus, -a, -um, adj., *intensely hot, blazing*
fervor, fervōris, m., *fury; heat*
fibra, -ae, f., *fiber; entrails*
fidēs, -eī, f., *trust, faith*
fīdō, -ere, fīsus sum, *to trust, believe* (with dat. or abl.)
fīdūcia, -ae, f., *trust*
fīdus, -a, -um, adj., *faithful, trustworthy*
fīgō, -ere, fīxī, fīxus, *to fix, fasten; pierce* (343, 778)
figūra, -ae, f., *form, shape*

fīlius, -iī, m., *son*
fīlum, -ī, n., *thread, string*
findō, -ere, fidī, fissus, *to split apart; cleave*
fīnis, fīnis, m., *end, boundary*
fīō, fierī, factus sum, *to become; occur*
flāmen, flāminis, n., *gust, blast* (of wind)
flamma, -ae, f., *flame*
flāveō, -ēre, *to be yellow*
flectō, -ere, flexī, flexus, *to bend; wheel*
fleō, -ēre, flēvī, flētus, *to cry*
fluctuō, -āre, -āvī, -ātus, *to waver*
fluctus, -ūs, m., *flood*
fluitō, -āre, -āvī, -ātus, *to float*
flūmen, flūminis, n., *river*
fluxus, -a, -um, adj., *flowing away; perishing, weak, unstable*
foedē, adv., *shamefully, foully*
foedus, foederis, n., *contract, treaty*
for, fārī, fātus sum, *to speak, say*
fōrma, -ae, f., *shape; beauty*
formīdō, formīdinis, f., *fear*
fornix, -icis, m., *arch, vault, overhang*
fōrs, fōrtis, f., *chance, luck*
fortasse or fortassis, adv., *perhaps*
forte, adv., *by chance*
fortis, forte, adj., *brave; strong*
fortūna, -ae, f., *fortune, chance*
fossa, -ae, f., *ditch*
foveō, -ēre, fōvī, fōtus, *to warm; favor, support* (838)
frāgmen, -inis, n., *fracture; piece broken off*
frangō, -ere, frēgī, frāctus, *to break, shatter*
frāter, frātris, m., *brother*
fraus, fraudis, f., *fraud*
fremō, -ere, fremuī, *to rustle; roar* (572)
frēnum, -ī, n, *bridle, reins*
frequēns, frequentis, adj., *in crowds*

fretum, -ī, n., *strait; sea*
frīgidus, -a, -um, adj., *cool, cold*
frōns, frondis, f., *leaf*
frōns, frōntis, f., *forehead*
frūstrā, adv., *in vain*
fuga, -ae, f., *flight*
fugāx, fugācis, adj., *swift in flight*
fugiō, -ere, fūgī, fugitus, *to flee, escape*
fugō, -āre, -āvī, -ātus, *to put to flight*
fulgēns, fulgentis, adj., *gleaming*
fulgeō, -ēre, fulsī, *to shine*
fulmen, -inis, n., *lightning, thunderbolt*
fulvus, -a, -um, adj., *reddish or tawny yellow*
fūmō, -āre, -āvī, -ātus, *to smoke*
fundō, -ere, fūdī, fūsus, *to pour, scatter*
fundus, -ī, m., *foundation, bottom*
fūnis, fūnis, m., *rope, line*
fūnus, fūneris, n., *funeral; death; dead body*
furiae, -ārum, f., *rage; ravings*
furō, furere, *to rage, be mad*
furor, -ōris, m., *madness*
fūrtum, -ī, n., *theft, treachery*
futūrus, -a, -um, adj., *about to be; future*

G

galea, -ae, f., *helmet*
gaudeō, -ēre, gāvīsus sum, *to be glad*
gaudium, -i(ī), n., *joy*
geminus, -a, -um, *twin*
gemitus, -ūs, m., *groaning; groan*
gemma, -ae, f., *jewel, gem*
generōsus, -a, -um, adj., *noble-blooded; high-born*
genetrīx, genetrīcis, f., *she who brings forth; mother*
genitor, -ōris, m., *father*

gēns, gentis, f., *family, clan; offspring* (228)
genū, genūs, n., *knee*
genus, generis, n., *origin; lineage*
germānus, -a, -um, adj., *having the same parents*
gignō, -ere, genuī, genitus, *to bring forth; beget*
gladius, -iī, m. or **gladium, -iī,** n., *sword*
glaucus, -a, -um, adj., *grey, sea-green*
globus, -ī, m., *mass*
glōria, -ae, f., *renown, glory*
gōrȳtus, -ī, m., *quiver*
gradior, gradī, gressus sum, *to step, walk*
Gradīvus, -ī, m., *Gradivus*, a name for Mars, the god of war, 542
Grāī (Grāiī), -ōrum, or **-um,** the Greeks, 81, 334, 430
Grāius, -a, -um, adj., *Greek* (720)
grandō, grandinis, f., *hail*
grātus, -a, -um, adj., *pleasant; grateful*
gravidus, -a, -um, adj., *heavy; pregnant*
gravis, grave, adj., *heavy; serious, grim*
Graviscae, -ārum, f., *Graviscae*, a town in Etruria, 184
graviter, adv., *heavily*
gravō, -āre, -āvī, -ātus, *to burden, load, to refuse* (628)
gremium, -i(ī), n., *lap, bosom*
gressus, -ūs, m., *stepping; step*
grus, gruis, f., *crane*
gurges, gurgitis, m., *whirlpool; water, sea*
guttur, -uris, n., *windpipe, throat*
Gyās, -ae, m., *Gyas*, a Latin, ally of Turnus, 318
gȳrus, -ī, m., *circle*

H

habēna, -ae, f., *rein*
habeō, -ēre, habuī, habitus, *to have, hold; keep* (827)
hāc, adv., *by this way or route*
hāctenus, adv., *thus far, so far, of space and time*
Haemonidēs, -ae, m., *Haemonides*, a Latin, ally of Turnus, 537
haereō, -ēre, haesī, haesus, *to stick to, hang on to* (with dat.)
Halaesus, -ī, m., *Halaesus*, ally of Turnus and chief of the Aurunci, 352, 411, 417, etc.
harundineus, -a, -um, adj., *reedy*
harundō, harundinis, f., *reed, stick*
hasta, -ae, f., *spear*
hastīle, hastilis, n., *the shaft of a spear; a spear*
haud, adv., *not at all, by no means*
hauriō, -īre, hausī, hastus, *to drain, drink in* (648)
Hēbrus, -ī, m., *Hebrus*, a Trojan, 696
Helicōn, Helicōnis, m., *Helicon*, mountain in Beotia, Greece, sacred to the Muses, 163
Herculēs, Herculis, m., *Hercules*, son of Jupiter and Alcmene, deified after his death, 319, 779
hērōs, herōis, m., *demigod; hero*
heu, interj., *alas! oh!*
hīc, adv., *here*
hīc, haec, hōc, dem. pron. and adj., *this, these*
Hicetāonius, -a, -um, adj., *of Hicetaeon*, 123
hiems, hiemis, f., *winter; storm*
hinc, adv., *from here, hence;* **hinc...hinc,** *on one side...on the other*
hiō, -āre, -āvī, -ātus, *to yawn; open the mouth*

hirsūtus, -a, -um, adj., *rough, hairy*
Hisbō, Hisbōnis, m., *Hisbo,* a Latin ally of Turnus, 384
hispidus, -a, -um, adj., *shaggy, hairy*
hodiē, adv., *today*
homō, hominis, m., *human being, man*
honestus, -a, -um, *honorable, decent; lovely*
honor, or **honos, -ōris, m.,** *honor; office*
horrēns, -entis, *bristling*
horreō, -ēre, horruī, *to bristle; shudder at; dread* (880)
horridus, -a, -um, adj., *rough, uncouth*
hortor, -ārī, -hortātus sum, *to urge*
hospitium, hospiti(ī), n., *hospitality*
hostīlis, hostīlis, hostīle, adj., *hostile*
hostis, hostis, m., *(public) enemy*
hūc, adv., *to here, hither*
hūmānus, -a, -um, adj., *human*
humō, -āre, -āvī, -ātus, *to lay earth on anything; bury*
humus, -ī, f., *ground*
Hydaspēs, -is, m., *Hydaspes,* ally of Aeneas, 747
hymenaeus, -ī, m., *marriage*

I

iaceō, -ēre, iacuī, *to lie; lie dead*
iaciō, iacere, iēcī, iactus, *to throw; brandish*
iactō, -āre, -āvī, -ātus, *to throw*
iaculum -ī, n., *thing hurled; spear*
iam, adv., *now; already;* **iam...iam,** *at one moment...at another*
ictus, -ūs, m., *blow, stroke*
Īda, -ae, f., *Mount Ida,* a mountain near Troy. A ship's figurehead, 158
Īdaeus, -a, -um, adj., *of Mount Ida* (230, 252)
Īdalia, -ae, f. or **Īdalium, -iī, n.,** *Idalium,* city in Cyprus sacred to Venus, 52, 86

Īdās, -ae, m., *Idas,* a Thracian father of three allies of Turnus, 351
īdem, eadem, idem, adj. and pron., *same*
ignārus, -a, -um, adj., *ignorant; unaware; a stranger* (706)
ignipotēns, -entis, adj., *having power over fire,* epithet of Vulcan
ignis, -is, m., *fire*
īgnōtus, -a, -um, adj., *unknown*
īlia, -ium, n. pl., *the groin*
Īliacus, -a, -um, adj., *belonging to Ilium; Ilian; Trojan* (62, 335, 635)
ille, illa, illud, dem. pron. and adj., *that; he, she, it*
illūc, adv., *to there*
Īlus, -ī, m., *Ilus,* a Latin ally of Turnus, 400
Ilva, -ae, f., *Ilva,* the island of Elba (in Tuscany), 173
imāgō, imāginis, f., *image, echo; phantom*
Imāōn, Imaonis (acc. Imāona), m., *Imaon,* ally of Turnus, 424
Imbrasidēs, -ae, m., *Imbrasides,* son of Imbrasus, a Trojan, 123
immāne, adv., *wildly, vastly*
immānis, immāne, adj., *huge, monstrous*
immineō, -ēre, *to threaten; overhang* (with dat.)
immisceō, -ēre, -miscuī, -mixtus (-mistus), *to mingle with; usually with dat.*
immittō, -ere, -mīsī, -mīssus, *to cast at; loosen* (229); *launch against*
immolō, -āre, -āvī, -ātus, *to immolate, to slay*
immōtus, -a, -um, adj., *unmoved, unchanged, unrelenting*
impār, imparis, adj., *unequal, in unequal combat*

impāstus, -a, -um, adj., *unfed*
impavidus, -a, -um, adj., *not afraid*
impediō, -īre, impedīvī/impediī, impedītus, *to hinder; entangle*
impellō, -ere, -pulī, -pulsus, *to drive; urge on*
imperditus, -a, -um, adj., *undestroyed*
imperium, -iī, n., *command, power*
imperterritus, -a, -um, adj., *undaunted*
impleō, -ēre, -plēvī, -plētus, *to fill in/up*
implicō, -āre, -āvī (implicuī), implicitus, *to fold in; pin down* (894)
implōrō, -āre, -āvī, -ātus, *to implore*
impōnō, -ere, -pōsuī, -pōsitus, *to put on, impose*
imprimō, -ere, -pressī, -pressus, *to apply with pressure, imprint*
improbus, -a, -um, adj., *bad; remorseless*
īmus, -a, -um, adj., *lowest; bottom of*
in, prep. with acc., *into, to, for*; abl., *in, on*
inānis, inānis, ināne, adj., *empty, void*
incautus, -a, -um, adj., *unguarded, unsuspecting*
incēdō, -ere, -cessī, -cessus, *to go, happen; proceed; walk*
incendium, -i(ī), n., *fire*
incendō, -ere, -cendī, -census, *to set fire to, burn*
incestō, -āre, -āvī, -ātus, *to defile; pollute*
incidō, -ere, -cidī, *to fall in/on; hit* (477)
incipiō, -ere, -cēpī, -ceptus, *to begin*
inclūdō, -ere, -clūsī, -clūsus, *to enclose*
incolumis, incolume, adj., *uninjured*
increpitō, -āre, -āvī, -ātus, *to make a great noise; chide*

increpō, -āre, -āvī/increpuī, -atus/increpitus, *to taunt, reprove*
incumbō, -ere -cubuī -cubitus, *to lean or recline upon* (with dat.)
inde, adv., *from there, from then*
indīgnus, -a, -um, adj., *unworthy (of)*
indiscrētus, -a, -um, adj., *unseparated; indistinguishable*
indoles, -is, f., *that which is bred within; natural disposition; genius*
indulgeō, -ēre, -dulsī, -dultus, *to gratify, indulge in*
induō, -ere, -duī, -dūtus, *to put on, clothe*
inermus, -a, -um, adj., *unarmed*
iners, inertis, adj., *unskilled; helpless* (595)
inexhaustus, -a, -um, adj., *unexhausted*
īnfandus, -a, -um, adj., *not to be uttered*
īnfectus, -a, -um, adj., *not done; unworked; unwrought*
īnfēlīx, īnfēlīcis, adj., *unfortunate, unhappy*
īnfēnsus, -a, -um, adj., *hostile, angry*
īnferiae, īnferiārum, f., *sacrifices/rites in honor of the dead*
īnferō, -ferre, -tulī, -lātus, *to bring upon/against*; with **se**, *go, advance*
īnfestus, -a, -um, adj., *hostile, aggressive*
īnfit, defective verb, *to begin* (to speak)
īnflīgō, -ere, -flīxī, -flīctus, *to strike; dash against*
īnfremō, -ere, -uī, *to bellow; rage*
īnfrendeō, -ēre, or īnfrendō, -ere, *to gnash*
īnfrēnus, -a, -um; also īnfrēnis, -e, adj., *unbridled; riding without bridle*

īnfringō, -ere, -frēgī, -frāctus, *to break in; break*
īnfula, -ae, f., *fillet, band of wool*
ingemō, -ere, -uī, -itus, *to sigh or groan*
ingēns, ingentis, adj., *huge*
inglōrius, -a, -um, adj., *without glory*
ingrātus, -a, -um, adj., *ungrateful for* (with gen.)
ingredior, -gredī, -gressus sum, *to step in, enter*
inguen, inguinis, n., *groin*
inhaereō, -ēre, -haesī, -haesus, *to stick to; cling to*
inhorrēscō, -ere, -horruī, *to be rough; bristle*
iniciō, -ere, -iēcī, -iectus, *to throw, lay hands on*
inimīcus, -a, -um, adj., *unfriendly, hostile*
inīquus, -a, -um, adj., *uneven; hostile*
inligō, -āre, -āvī, -ātus, *to bind on; attach to; impede*
innō, -āre, -āvī, -ātus, *to swim upon, over, or along*
innocuus, -a, -um, adj., *harmless*
inoffēnsus, -a, -um, adj., *unhindered*
inquam, inquit, *to say*
inreparābilis,-e, adj., *irrecoverable*
inrigō, -āre, -āvī, -ātus, *to water*
inrītō (irrītō), -āre, -āvī, -ātus, *to provoke, annoy, vex*
inritus (irritus), -a, -um, adj., *invalid, void*
inruō, -ere, -ruī, *to rush in*
īnsānia, -ae, f., *madness*
īnscius, -a, -um, adj., *not knowing; unaware*
īnsidiae, īnsidiārum, f. pl., *ambush*
īnsidō, -ere, -sēdī, -sessus, *to settle upon*
īnsīgne, īnsīgnis, n., *medal, decoration*
īnsīgnis, īnsīgne, adj., *distinguished*
īnsōns, -sontis, adj., *innocent*
īnstaurō, -āre, -āvī, -ātus, *to renew*
īnstō, -āre, -stitī, *to press hard on* (dat.)
īnsuētus, -a, -um, adj., *unaccustomed*
īnsula, īnsulae, f., *island*
īnsultō, -āre, -āvī, -ātus, *to triumph, exult over*
intāctus, -a, -um, adj., *untouched, unharmed*
intempestus, -a, -um, adj., *unseasonable; unhealthy*
intemptātus, -a, -um, adj., *untried*
intepeō, -ēre, -uī, *to become warm*
inter, prep. with acc., *between, among; during*
intercipiō, -ere, -cēpī, -ceptus, *to catch a thing passing along; intercept*
intereā, adv., *meanwhile*
interimō, -ere, -ēmī, -ēmptus, *to destroy, kill*
interpres, -etis, m./f., *an agent between parties; a mediator*
intexō, -ere, -uī, -tus, *to weave into or in*
intorqueō, -ēre, -torsī, -tortus, *to turn or hurl toward*
intrā, prep. with acc., *within;* adv., *inside, within*
inultus, -a, -um, adj., *unavenged*
inundō, -āre, -āvī, -ātus, *to overflow*
inūtilis, -e, adj., *useless, unserviceable*
invādō, -ere, -vāsī, -vāsus, *to go in, attack*
inveniō, -īre, -vēnī, -ventus, *to find, discover*
invictus, -a, -um, adj., *unconquered*
invidia, -ae, f., *envy, jealousy, ill will*
invītus, -a, -um, adj., *unwilling*

ipse, ipsa, ipsum, intensive pron., *himself, herself, itself*
īra, -ae, f., *anger*
īrāscor, īrāscī, īrātus sum, *to grow angry*
Īris, Īridis, f. (acc. Īrim), *Iris, messenger of the gods,* 73
is, ea, id, dem. pron., *he, she, it; that*
Ismara, -ae, f., *Ismara, city in Thrace,* 351
Ismarus, -ī, m., *Ismarus, a Lydian ally of Aeneas,* 139
iste, ista, istud, pron., *that* (of yours)
istīc, adv., *there*
ita, adv., *thus, so*
Italī, -ōrum, or -um, m., *Italians, inhabitants of Italy,* 41, 74, 109
Italia, -ae, f., *Italy* (8, 32, 67)
Italus, -a, -um, adj., *Italian,* 780
iter, itineris, n., *journey; path*
iterum, adv., *again*
iuba, -ae, f., *the mane of a horse; crest*
lubeō, -ēre, iussī, iussus, *to order*
iugālis, -e, adj., *yoked; nuptial*
iugulum, -ī, n., *throat*
iugum, iugī, n., *yoke; team* (594)
Iūlus, -ī, m., *Julus, another name for Ascanius, son of Aeneas,* 524, 534
iungō, -ere, iūnxī, iūnctus, *to join*
Iūnō, Iūnōnis, f., *Juno, daughter of Saturn, wife and sister of Jupiter,* 62, 73, 96, etc.
Iuppiter, Iovis, m., *Jupiter, the father of the gods, husband of Juno,* 16, 111, 116, etc.
iurgium, -ī, n., *altercation, quarrel*
iūssum, -ī, n., *command, order*
iūstus, -a, -um, adj., *just, fair*
iuvenis, -is, m., *youth, young man*
iuventūs, iuventūtis, f., *youth, young men*
iuvō, -āre, iūvī, iūtus, *to help; please*

K

Karthāgō, Karthāginis, f., *Carthage, a city in North Africa,* 12, 54

L

labō, -āre, -āvī, -ātus, *to totter, waver*
lābor, labī, lapsus sum, *to glide, slip*
labor, -ōris, m., *work, toil; trouble*
lacertus, -ī, m., *the arm, esp. the upper arm*
lacēssō, -ere, lacēssīvī, lacēssītus, *to provoke*
lacrima, -ae, f., *tear*
lacteus, -a, -um, adj., *milky*
Lādōn, Ladōnis, acc. **-ōna, m.,** *Ladon, an Arcadian ally of Aeneas,* 413
laetor, laetārī, laetātus sum, *to rejoice, be glad*
laetus, -a, -um, adj., *happy*
laeva, -ae, f. (sc. manus), *the left hand*
laevus, -a, -um, adj., *left; baneful* (275)
Lagus, -ī, m., *Lagus, a Latin ally of Turnus,* 381
lambō, -ere, -ī, -itus, *to lick*
langueō, -ēre, languī, *to be faint, sink*
lānūgō, -inis, f., *soft hair, down*
lāpsus, -ūs, m., *slipping; gliding; fall*
largior, largīrī, -ītus sum, *to give largely; bestow*
largus, -a, -um, adj., *ample; liberal*
Lārīdēs, Lārīdis, m., *Larides, a Latin ally of Turnus,* 391, 395
Latagus, -ī, m., *Latagus, a Latin ally of Turnus,* 697, 698
lātē, *far and wide*
latebra, -ae, f., *hiding place, concealment*
lateō, -ēre, latuī, *to lie hidden, be hidden*
Latīnī, -ōrum, m., *the Latins, inhabitants of Latium,* 77, 237, 311, 895

Latīnus, -a, -um, adj., *of Latium; Latin* (4, 300, 360)
Latīnus, -ī, m., *Latinus*, king of Latium, father of Lavinia, 66
Latium, -iī, n., *Latium*, a region of Italy where Aeneas built a settlement, 58, 365
latus, latĕris, n., *side, flank*
lātus, -a, -um, adj., *broad, wide*
laudō, -āre, -āvī, -tus, *to praise*
Laurēns, -entis, adj., *Laurentine, of Laurentum*, a Latin town, 671, 706
Laurentius, -a, -um, adj., *of Laurentum; Laurentian* (635, 709)
laus, laudis, f., *praise, glory; noble deeds* (825)
Lausus, -ī, m., *Lausus*, son of Mezentius, killed by Aeneas, 426, 434, 439, etc.
lēctus, -a, -um, adj., *chosen*
legiō, legiōnis, f., *legion*
legō, -ere, lēgī, lēctus, *to gather up; choose, pick*
leō, -ōnis, m., *lion*
lētifer, -era, -erum, adj., *death-bringing*
lētum, -ī, n., *death*
levis, leve, adj., *light; insubstantial*
levō, -āre, -āvī, -ātus, *to relieve; free; rest* (834)
līber, lībera, līberum, adj., *free*
lībrō, -āre, -āvī, -ātus, *to brandish; balance* (480)
licet, licēre, licuit/licitum est, impersonal, *it is permitted*
Lichās, -ae, m., *Lichas*, a Latin ally of Turnus, 315
Liger, -ī, m., *Liger*, a Latin ally of Turnus, 576, 580, 584
Ligus, Liguris, m., *Ligurian*, an inhabitant of Liguria, an Italian region, 185

līmen, -inis, n., *threshold*
līmes, -itis, m., *path*
līneus, -a, -um, adj., *of linen*
lingua, -ae, f., *tongue; speech; cry*
linquō, -ere, līquī, *to leave, relinquish*
liquidus, -a, -um, adj., *clear, liquid*
lītus,-oris, n., *seashore*
locō, -āre, -āvī, -ātus, *to place, put*
locus, locī, m. or loca, locōrum, n. pl., *place; ground; position, station*
longē, adv., *long after; at a distance, from far away*
longum, adv., *for a long time* (740)
longus, -a, -um, adj., *long, far*
loquor, loquī, locūtus sum, *to speak*
lōrīca, -ae, f., *breastplate*
Lūcagus, -ī, m., *Lucagus*, a Latin ally of Turnus, 575, 577, 586, 592
Lūcās, -ae, m., *Lucas*, a Latin ally of Turnus, 561
lūceō, -ēre, lūxī, *to shine*
lūctus, -ūs, m., *mourning, grief*
lūdō, -ere, lūsī, lūsus, *to play; mock*
lūgubris, -e, adj., *baneful*
lūmen, luminis, n., *light; eye* (746)
luō, -ere, luī, *to satisfy, pay for*
lūstrō, -āre, āvī, -ātus, *to move around, circle around; survey, review*
lūx, lūcis, f., *daylight*
Lycāonius, -a, -um, adj., *of Lycaonia* (region); *of or descended from Lycaon*, an Arcadian king, 749
Lycia, -ae, f., *Lycia*, a country in Asia Minor, 126
Lycius, -a, -um, adj., *Lycian, of Lycia*, a country in Asia Minor, 751
Lȳdius, -a, -um, adj., *of Lydia*, a region in Asia Minor; *Lydian* (155)
lympha, -ae, f., *clear spring water; water*
Lyrnēsius, -a, -um, adj., *of Lyrnesus*, a town in Troad; *Lyrnesian* (128)

M

mactō, -āre, -āvī, -ātus, *to punish, reward, kill*
maculō, -āre, -āvī, -ātus, *to spot; stain; defile*
Maeōn, Maeonis, m., *Maeon,* a Latin ally of Turnus, 337
Maeonius, -a, -um, adj., *of Maeonia,* a town in Lydia, Asia Minor, 141
maereō, -ēre, *to be sorrowful*
maestus, -a, -um, adj., *sad*
magis or mage, adv., *more*
magnanimus, -a, -um, adj., *noble-spirited*
māgnus, -a, -um, adj., *great; loud* (873)
Magus, -ī, m., *Magus,* a Latin ally of Turnus, 521
māla, -ae, f., *cheek*
mālō, mālle, māluī, *to prefer*
malum, -ī, n., *evil, calamity*
malus, -a, -um, adj., *bad, evil*
mandātum, -ī, n., *order, commission*
maneō, -ēre, mānsī, mānsus, *to remain; await*
Mānēs, -ium, m., *Manes* (spirits of the dead), 34, 534
Mantō, Mantūs, f., *Manto,* mother of Ocnus, founder of Manua, 199
Mantua, -ae, f., *Mantua,* city on the river Mincius, Virgil's birthplace, 200
manus, -ūs, f., *hand; band of men*
mare, maris, n., *sea*
marmor, -ōris, n., *marble; surface of the sea*
Mārs, Mārtis, m., *Mars,* god of war; *warfare,* 22, 237, 280
Mārsī, -ōrum, m., *Marsi,* a Latin people, 544
Massicus, -ī, m., *Massicus,* Etruscan ally of Aeneas, 166

māter, mātris, f., *mother*
mātūrus, -a, -um, adj., *mature*
maximus, -a, -um, superl. adj. of **magnus,** *greatest; tallest; mighty* (685)
meditor, -ārī, meditātus sum, *to think, rehearse; practice*
medium, medi(ī) n., *middle of, in the middle*
medius, -a, -um, adj., *middle of, in the middle*
Melampus, Melampodis, m., *Melampus,* a companion of Hercules, 320
melior, -ius, comp. adj. of **bonus,** *better*
membrum, -ī, n., *limb*
memor, memoris, adj., *mindful*
memorandus, -a, -um, adj., *worthy of mention; famed*
memorō, -āre, -āvī, -ātus, *to remember; relate; say* (680)
Menestheus, -eī or -eos, m., *Menestheus,* a Trojan, 129
mēns, mentis, f., *mind*
mēnsa, -ae, f., *table; hospitality* (460, 516)
mentum, -ī, n., *chin*
mereō, -ēre, meruī, meritus, *to earn, deserve; serve as a soldier*
mergō, -ere, mersī, mersus, *to dip, sink, plunge*
Messāpus, -ī, m., *Messapus,* son of Neptune, ally of Turnus, 354, 749
mēta, -ae, f., *limit, goal, boundary, turning point*
metallum, -ī, n., *metal, mine* (in the pl.)
metō, -ere, messuī, messus, *to mow down*
metuō, -ere, metuī, *to fear, dread*
metus, metūs, m., *fear, dread, anxiety*
meus, -a, -um, poss. adj., *my, mine*

Mēzentius, -iī, m., *Mezentius,* an exiled Etruscan tyrant, ally of Turnus; father of Lausus, 150, 204, 689, etc.
micō, -āre, micuī, *gleam; flicker; twitch* (396)
mīlia, -ium, *thousands*
mīlle, sing. indecl. adj., *one thousand*
Mimās, Mimāntis, m., *Mimas,* a Trojan, friend of Paris, 702, 706
minae, -ārum, f. pl., *threats*
mināx, minācis, adj., *threatening*
Mincius, -iī, m., *Mincius,* an Italian river, tributary of the Po River; a ship's figurehead, 206
Miniō, Miniōnis, m., *Minio,* a river in Etruria, 183
ministrō, -āre, -āvī, -ātus, *to attend, serve* (with dat.)
minor, -ārī, minātus sum, *to threaten* (with dat.)
minor,-ōris, comp. adj of **parvus,** *smaller, lesser*
minus, adv., *less*
mīrābilis, -e, adj., *wonderful, extraordinary*
mīror, -ārī, mīrātus sum, *to wonder, be astonished*
mīrus, -a, -um, adj., *marvelous, wonderful*
misceō, -ēre, miscuī, mixtus, *to mix; cause confusion in*
miser, misera, miserum, adj., *wretched, pitiable*
miserandus, -a, -um, *to be pitied*
misereor, -ērī, miseritus sum, *to pity* (with gen.)
miserēscō, -ere, *to feel pity* (with gen.)
miseror, -ārī, miserātus sum, *to feel or show pity*
missile,-is, n., *dart; missile*
missilis, -e, adj., *hurled*

mittō, -ere, mīsī, missus, *to send; release, let go, throw*
Mnestheus (Menestheus), -eī or -eos, m., *Mnestheus,* a Trojan, 143
modus, -ī, m., *measure; manner; moderation* (502)
moenia, moenium, n. pl., *walls*
mōlēs, mōlis, f., *mass; bulk* (771)
mōlior, -īrī, mōlītus, *to hurl* (131); *force* (477)
mollis, molle, adj., *soft; pliant*
moneō, -ēre, monuī, monitus, *to warn, advise*
monitum, -ī, n., *admonition; counsel; advice*
monitus, -ūs, m., *admonition*
mōns, montis, m., *mountain*
mōnstrum, -ī, n., *omen; monster; marvel* (637)
mōra, -ae, f., *delay; barrier* (485)
morbus, -ī, m., *sickness, disease*
moribundus, -a, -um, adj., *ready to die*
morior, morī, mortuus sum, *to die*
moror, -ārī, morātus sum, *to delay*
mors, mortis, f., *death*
morsus, -ūs, m., *bite*
mortālis, -e, adj., *mortal*
mōs, mōris, m., *custom; way; manner*
moveō, -ēre, mōvī, mōtus, *to move, rouse, stir up; turn over* (890)
mox, adv., *soon; then*
mūcrō, -ōnis, m., *sharp point or edge; sword-point*
multum, adv., *much; often* (839)
multus, -a, -um, adj., *much; many*
murmur, -uris, n., *rumble, roar; murmur*
murmurō, -āre, -āvī, -ātus, *to murmur*
mūrus, -ī, m., *wall*

Vocabulary

Mūsa, -ae, f., *a Muse,* one of the nine goddesses of the Arts, 191
mūtō, -āre, -āvī, -ātus, *to change*
mūtuus, -a, -um, adj., *mutual; on both sides* (755)

N

nam, conj., *for*
namque, conj., *for in fact*
nāscor, nāscī, nātus sum, *to be born, come into being*
nātūra, -ae, f., *nature*
nātus, -ī, m. (or gnātus), *son*
nauta, -ae, m., *sailor*
nāvis, -is, f., *ship*
nē, particle of negative command, *do not;* conj., *in order that...not; that...not;* **-ne,** *questioning particle*
Nealcēs, -is, m., *Nealces,* a Trojan, 753
nebula, -ae, f., *cloud; mist*
nec or neque, conj., *nor; and not*
nec...nec or neque...neque, *neither...nor*
nefandus, -a, -um, adj., *unutterable; monstruous*
nefās, n., *divinely forbidden* (undeclinable); *sin, crime*
negō, -āre, -āvī, -ātus, *to deny, refuse*
neō, nēre, nēvī, nētus, *to spin; weave, embroider*
nepōs, -ōtis, m., *grandchild; descendant*
Neptūnius, -a, -um, adj., *of Neptune,* the god of the sea; *Neptunian* (353)
nēquīquam, adv., *in vain*
Nēreūs, -eī, or -eos, m., *Nereus,* a sea god, the sea, 764
nervus, -ī, m., *tendon; cord, bowstring*
nescius, -a, -um, adj., *ignorant* (with gen.)
neu or neve, conj., *and lest, and that not*
ni, conj., *if not; unless*
nihil or nīl, n., *nothing*
nimbus, -ī, m., *rain cloud, downpour*
Niphaeus, -ī, m., *Niphaeus,* a Latin ally of Turnus, 570
nisi or nī, conj., *if...not; unless*
nītor, nītī, nīxus sum, *to press/lean upon* (with abl.)
nō, nāre, nāvī, *to swim*
noctivagus, -a, -um, adj., *night-wandering*
nōdus, -ī, m., *knot*
nōmen, -inis, n., *name*
nōn, adv., *not*
nōnne, interrogative part., *is not?*
nōs, nostrum/nostrī, personal pron., first pers.pl., *we; us*
noster, nostra, nostrum, poss. adj., *our, ours*
nōtus, -a, -um, adj., *well-known*
Notus, -ī, m., *the South Wind* (266)
noverca, -ae, f., *stepmother*
novus, -a, -um, adj., *new; strange*
nox, noctis, f., *night*
nūbēs, nūbis, f., *cloud*
nūbilum, -ī, n., *cloud*
nūllus, -a, -um, adj., *not any, no*
num, interrogative part., *surely...not?* In indirect questions *whether*
Numa, -ae, m., *Numa,* a Latin ally of Turnus, 562
nūmen, -inis, n., *divine will, god*
numerus, -ī, m., *number, amount*
Numitor, -ōris, m., *Numitor,* a Latin ally of Turnus, 342
numquam, adv., *never*
nunc, adv., *now*
nusquam, adv., *nowhere*
nūtus, -ūs, m., *nod, will*
nympha, -ae (nymphē, -ēs), f., *bride; nymph*

O

ō, interj., *oh!*
ob, prep. with acc., *on account of*
obdūcō, -ere, -dūxī, -ductus, *to draw over*
obeō, -īre, -iī/īvī, -itus, *to face; survey* (447); *cover* (483); with **mortem**, *die*
ōbex, obicis, m./f., *obstacle; barrier*
obiciō, -ere, -iēcī, -iectus, *to throw in the way of*
oblīviscor, oblīvisci, oblītus sum, *to forget* (with gen.)
obnītor, -niti, -nīxus (-nīsus) sum, *to press* (with dat.); *strive, strain*
oborior, -orīri, -ortus sum, *to rise*
obruō, -ruere, -ruī, -rutus, *to cover; overwhelm*
obsideō, -sidēre, -sēdī, -sessus, *to blockade*
obsidiō, -ōnis, f., *siege, blockade*
obstō, -stāre, -stitī, -stātus, *to stand before, stand in the way* (with dat.)
obtendō, -ere, -tendī, -tentus, *to stretch before; draw*
obtestor, -ārī, -testātus sum, *to call to witness; implore*
obtruncō, -āre, -āvī, -ātus, *to lop off; cut down; cut to pieces*
obvius, obvia, obvium, adj., *in the way; to meet* (552, 877); *facing* with dat. (694); **obvius ire**, *to meet* (with dat.)
occidō, -ere, -cidī, -cāsus, *to go down; fall; perish*
occīdō, -ere, -cīdī, -cīsus, *to knock down, kill*
occubō, -āre, -āvī, -ātus, *to lie*
occumbō, -ere, -cubuī, -cubitus, *to sink*
occupō, -āre, -āvī, -ātus, *to anticipate; attack first* (699)

occurrō, -ere, -currī, -cursus, *to run to meet* (with dat.)
ōcior, -ius, comp. adj., *swifter*
Ocnus, -ī, m., *Ocnus*, an Etruscan, founder of Mantua, 198
oculus, -ī, m., *eye*
ōdī, ōdisse, *to hate*
odium, -iī, n., *hatred*
offerō, -ferre, -tulī, -lātus, *to offer; go toward;* with **se**, *go forward*
olim, adv., *formerly; in the future*
olōrīnus, -a, -um, adj., *of the swan*
Olympus, -ī, m., *Olympus*, a mountain in Thessaly, the abode of the gods, 1, 115, 216, etc.
ōmen, ōminis, n., *omen*
omnipotēns, -entis, adj., *all-powerful*
omnis, omne, adj., *every; all*
onerō, -āre, -āvī, -ātus, *to load, burden*
onus, oneris, n., *load, burden*
opācus, -a, -um, adj., *shady, dark*
opīmus, -a, -um, adj., *rich, fertile*
opperior, -perīrī, oppertus/opperitus sum, *to wait, expect*
oppōnō, -ere, -posuī, -positus, *to place opposite*
ops, opis, f., *resource*
optimus, -a, -um, superlative adj. of **bonus**, *best, excellent*
optō, -āre, -āvī, -ātus, *to desire; choose*
opus, operis, n., *work; deed*
ōra, -ae, f., *shore, coast; rim* (243)
orbis, -is, m., *circle, orb*
Ōricius, -a, -um, adj., *of Oricus or Oricum*, city in Illyria, 136
orīgō, originis, f., *origin, lineage*
Ōrīōn, Ōrīōnis, m., *Orion*, a famous hunter. After his death, he became a constellation in the sky, 763

ōrnō, -āre, -āvī, -ātus, *to equip, decorate*
ornus, -ī, f., *ash-tree*
ōrō, -āre, -āvī, -ātus, *to pray, to speak*
Orōdēs, Orōdis, m., *Orodes, a Trojan*, 732, 737
ōrsa, -ōrum, n., *beginnings; intentions* (632)
Orsēs, -ae, m., *Orses, a Trojan*, 748
ōs, ōris, n., *mouth, face*
os, ossis, n., *bone*
Osīnius, -iī, m., *Osinius, king of Clusium, ally of Aeneas*, 655
ostrum, -ī, n., *purple dye*
ovō, -āre, -āvī, -ātus, *to shout, celebrate an ovation (a lesser triumph)*

P

pacīscor, pacīscī, pactus sum, *to agree*
pacta, -ae, f., *one contracted for; a bride*
Pactōlus, -ī, m., *Pactolus, river in Lydia, said to carry down golden sand*, 142
paeān, paeānis, m. (acc. paeāna and -em), *shout of triumph*
Pallās, Pallantis, m., *Pallas, son of Evander, ally of Aeneas. Killed by Turnus*, 160, 365, 374, etc.
palleō, -ēre, palluī, *to be pale*
pallidus, -a, -um, adj., *pale, ghastly*
palma, -ae, f., *hand, palm*
Palmus, -ī, m., *Palmus, ally of Aeneas*, 697, 699
pālor, -ārī, -ātus sum, *to wander about*
palūs, -ūdis, f., *marsh*
pandō, -ere, pandī, passus, *to spread out, open wide*
pangō, -ere, pepigī, pactus, *to agree upon, to make a compact*

Paphos (-us), -ī, f., *Paphos (-us), town of the island of Cyprus where there was a temple of Venus*, 51, 86
pār, paris, adj., *equal, like* (with dat.)
Parca, -ae, f., *Parca, one of the three Fates*, 419, 815
parcō, -ere, pepercī, parsus, *to spare* (with dat.); *have regard for* (880)
parēns, parentis, m. or f., *parent*
pāreō, -ēre, pāruī, pāritus, *to obey* (with dat.)
Paris, Paridis, m., *Paris, son of Priam and Hecuba, carried off Helen from Sparta*, 702, 705
pariter, adv., *equally; together* (865)
parma, -ae, f., *small round shield or buckler*
parō, -āre, -āvī, -ātus, *to prepare*
pars, partis, f., *part, portion*
Parthenius, -iī, m., *Parthenius, a Trojan*, 748
partim, adv., *partly*
parvus, -a, um, adj., *small, young*
pāscō, -ere, pāvī, pāstus, *to feed*
pāstor, pāstōris, m., *shepherd*
pater, patris, m., *father*
paternus, -a, -um, adj., *paternal*
patiens, patientis, adj., *long-suffering, patient; hardy; able to bear* (with gen.)
patior, patī, passus sum, *to suffer, endure; allow*
patria, -ae, f., *country*
patrius, -a, -um, adj., *paternal*
paucus, -a, -um, sing., *small*; pl., *a few*
pāx, pācis, f., *peace; favor; approval* (31)
peccātum, -ī, n., *fault; sin*
pectus, pectoris, n., *chest, breast; heart*
pecus, pecudis, f., *one animal of a flock or herd; an animal*
pedes, peditis, m., *foot soldier*

pedester, pedestris, pedestre, adj., *pedestrian, unmounted*
pelagus, -ī, m., *sea*
pellis, pellis, f., *skin, hide*
pellō, -ere, pepulī, pulsus, *to strike; drive away*
pendeō, -ēre, pependī, *to hang; bend* (586)
penetrābilis, -e, adj., *piercing*
penitus, or penitē, adv., *internally, deep within*
penna, -ae, f., *wing, feather*
per, prep. with acc., *through;* in oaths or entreaties, *by, in the name of*
peragrō, -āre, -āvī, -ātus, *to travel through fields or lands; to roam*
perdō, -ere, -didī, -ditus, *to destroy*
pereō, -īre, periī, peritūs, *to perish*
perferō, -ferre, -tulī, -lātus, *to endure*
perfidus, -a, -um, adj., *faithless, treacherous, false*
perforō, -āre, -āvī, -ātus, *to bore or pierce through*
perfringō, -ere, -frēgī, -frāctus, *to break*
perfundō, -ere, -fūdī, -fūsus, *to pour over or along; wash*
Pergama, -ōrum, n. or Pergamum, -ī, n. and Pergamus (-os), -ī, f., *Pergamon, the citatel of Troy, Troy,* 58
perīculum, ī, n., *danger*
perimō (peremō), -ere, perēmī, perēmptus, *to take away completely; annihilate, kill*
permisceō, -ēre, -miscuī, -mistus (-mixtus), *to mix completely*
persequor, -sequī, -secūtus sum, *to pursue*
perstringō, -ere, -strīnxī, -strīctus, *to graze*
perterreō, -ēre, -terruī, -territus, *to terrify*

perveniō, -īre, -vēnī, -ventus, *to reach*
pēs, pedis, m., *foot*
pestis, pestis, f., *plague, curse, bane*
petō, -ere, petiī/petīvī, petītus, *to seek, go toward*
Phaëthōn, Phaëthontis, m., *Phaëthon, son of the Sun god. Killed by Jupiter's thunderbolt,* 189
Pharus, -ī, m., *Pharus, a Latin ally of Turnus,* 322
Pherēs, Pherētis, m., *Pheres, an Arcadian ally of Aeneas,* 413
Phoebē, Phoebēs, f., *Phoebe, the Moon goddess, Diana,* 216
Phoebus, -ī, m., *Phoebus, the radiant one, a name for the god Apollo as god of sunlight,* 316, 537
Phorcus, -ī, m., *Phorcus, a Latin ally of Turnus,* 328
Phryges, -um, m., *Phryges, Phrygians, Trojans,* 255
Phrygia, -ae, f., *Phrygia, a region in Asia Minor country,* 88, 582
Phrygius, -a, -um, adj., *Phrygian; of Phrygia, a territory in Asia minor; Trojan,* 157, 702
pietās, pietātis, f., *devotion, loyalty*
Pīlumnus, -ī, m., *Pilumnus, a Latin diety, ancestor of Turnus,* 76, 619
pinguis, pingue, adj., *fat; rich, fertile*
pīnifer, -era, -erum, adj., *pine-bearing*
pinna, -ae, f., *feather, wing*
pīnus, -ūs or -ī, f., *pine tree; ship*
Pīsae, -ārum, f., *Pisae, name of two towns, one in Etruria and one in Elis, Greece,* 179
piscis, piscis, m., *fish*
pistris, -is, f., *sea-monster*
pius, -a, -um, adj., *dutiful*
pix, picis, f., *pitch*
placeo, -ēre, *to please* (with dat.)
placet, impersonal, *it pleases*

placidus, -a, -um, adj., *pleasant*
placitus, -a, -um, adj., *resolved, pleased*
plāga, -ae, f., *blow*
pluit, pluere, pluit, *it rains*
plūma, -ae, f., *feather, down*
plūres, -a, comp. adj. of **multus**, *more*
plūs, adv., *more*
poena, -ae, f., *punishment*
pondus, ponderis, n., *weight*
pōne, adv., *behind, after*
pōnō, pōnere, posuī, positus, *to place; ordain* (623); *abate* (103)
pōns, pontis, m., *bridge, gangway*
pontus, -ī, m., *the open sea*
poples, -itis, m., *the hinder part of the knee; hamstring*
pōpuleus, -a, -um, adj., *of the poplar tree*
Populōnia, -ae, f., *Populonia,* a town in Etruria, 172
populus, -ī, m., *people*
porta, -ae, f., *gate*
portō, -āre, -āvī, -ātus, *to carry a load*
poscō, -ere, poposcī, *to demand*
possum, posse, potuī, *to be able*
post, prep. with acc., *after, behind*
postquam, conj., *after, when*
potentia, -ae, f., *power*
potestās, potestātis, f., *power; ruler*
potior, potīrī, potītus sum, *to obtain* (with gen. or abl.)
potius, neuter adj. comp. of **potis** used as adv., *rather, more*
praebeō, -ēre, praebuī, praebitus, *to supply*
praeceps, praecipitis, adj., *headlong*
praecipiō, -ere, -cēpī, -ceptus, *to anticipate; seize first*
praecipitō, -āre, -āvī, -ātus, *to rush down*
praeclārus, -a, -um, adj., *very clear; famous*

praecordia, praecordiōrum, n., *the diaphragm or midriff; the vital parts; the heart*
praeda, -ae, f., *booty, prey*
praedō, -ōnis, m., *robber*
praedūrus, -a, -um, adj., *very hard, very strong*
praeferō, -ferre, -tulī, -lātus, *to prefer; show, display*
praefīgō, -ere, -fīxī, -fīxus, *to fasten before*
praegnāns, praegnantis, adj., *pregnant*
praesāgus, -a, -um, adj., *prophetic*
praesēns, -entis, adj., *present*
praeter, adv., *past*
praeterea, adv., *moreover; besides*
prātum, -ī, n., *meadow*
precor, -ārī, precātus sum, *to beg, pray*
premō, -ere, pressī, pressus, *to press, crush*
prex, precis, f., *prayer*
prīmaevus, -a, -um, adj., *youthful*
prīmum, adv., *first*
prīmus, -a, -um, adj., *first*
prīnceps, principis, adj., *chief, first;* as a substantive *leader*
principiō, adv., *first of all*
prīncipium, -i(ī), n., *beginning*
prior, priōris, comp. adj., *former, previous, prior, first; superior to* (+ abl. of comparison)
prīstinus, -a, -um, adj., *former*
pristis, pristis, f., *a sea monster*
prius, adv., *earlier, preceding, before; first* (882)
prō, prep. with abl., *in front of, for, instead of, in accordance with*
prōcēdō, -ere, -cessī, -cessus, *to advance*
procer, -eris, m., *chief*
procul, adv., *at a distance, hard by*
prōdeō, -īre, -iī, -itus, *to go; run forward*

prōdō, -ere, -didī, -ditus, *to put forth, betray; give warning* (99)
proelium, -iī, n., *battle*
profugus, -a, -um, adj., *fugitive, exiled*
prōgeniēs, prōgenieī, f., *offspring*
prōiciō, -ere, iēcī, -iectus, *to cast forth, throw out, fling to the ground*
prōlēs, prōlis, f., *offspring*
prōmittō, -ere, -mīsī, -missus, *to promise*
prōmoveō, -ēre, -mōvī, -mōtus, *to move forward; push forward*
prōnus, -a, -um, adj., *sloping; bending forward*
prōpexus, -a, -um, adj., *hanging down*
propinquō, -āre, -āvī, -ātus, *to bring near; approach*
propius, comp. adv., of **prope,** *nearer*
prōra, -ae, f., *the extreme forward part of a ship; the prow*
prōripiō, -ere, -ripuī, -reptus, *to snatch forth, rush forth*
prōrumpō, -ere, -rūpī, -ruptus, *to cause to burst forth; cast forth*
prōspectō, -āre, -āvī, -ātus, *to look forward; expect*
prōtegō, -ere, -texī, -tectus, *to cover, conceal; protect*
prōtinus or **prōtenus,** adv., *at once*
prōturbō, -āre, -āvī, -ātus, *to drive away*
prōvolvō, -ere, -volvī, -volūtus, *to roll forward or along*
proximus, -a, -um, adj. used as superl. of **propior,** *nearest*
pudor, -is, m., *decency, shame*
puer, -ī, m., *boy, slave*
pugna, -ae, f., *battle, fight*
pulcher, pulchra, pulchrum, adj., *beautiful*
pulmō, -ōnis, m., *lung; lungs*
pulsō, -āre, -āvī, -ātus, *to hit*
pulvis, -eris, m., *dust*
puppis, -is, f., *stern of a ship, ship*
purpureus, -a -um, adj., *purple*
putō, -āre, -āvī, -ātus, *to think, consider*
Pyrgī, Pyrgōrum, m., *Pyrgi,* a town in Etruria, 184

Q

quā, adv., *where; how; by any way*
quadriiugis, -e, adj., *four-yoked*
quadrupēs (quadripēs), quadupedis, adj., *four-footed, on all fours; a horse*
quaerō, -ere, quaesiī/quaesīvī, quaesītus, *to seek*
quālis, quāle, adj., *what sort, such as, like*
quam, conj., with correlative **tam,** *as* (763)
quamquam, conj., *although*
quandō, conj., *since;* adv., *at any time*
quandōquidem, conj., *since*
quantus, -a, -um, adj., *how great; how much*
quartus,-a, -um, adj., *fourth*
quaternī, -ae, -a, adj., *four each*
quatiō, -ere, quassī, quassus, *to shake*
quattuor, *four*
-que, enclitic conj., *and;* **que...que,** *both...and*
queō, quīre, quīvī/quiī, quitus, *to be able*
quercus, -ūs, f., *an oak tree*
querēla, -ae, f., *complaint*
quī, quae, quod, relative pron., *who, which;* interrogative adj., *who? what?;* indefinite adj. (without **ali**), *any*
quianam, conj., *why?*
quīcumque, quaecumque, quodcumque, relative pron., *whoever, whatever*

quidem, adv., *moreover, indeed*
quiēs, quiētis, f., *sleep, rest*
quiēscō, -ere, quiēvī, quiētus, *to sleep, keep quiet*
quiētus, -a, -um, adj., *at rest, free from exertion, inactive, in repose*
quīn, conj., *in fact;* after verbs of hindering, *but that* (615)
quīngentī, -ae, -a, adj., *five hundred*
quīnquāgintā, *fifty*
quinque, *five*
quis, quae, quid, interrogative pron., *who?, what?* **quid,** adv. *why*
quis, quae, quid after **sī nisī ne** or **num,** indefinite pron., *anyone/thing, someone/thing*
quisquam, quicquam (or quidnam), indefinite pron. (after a negative expression), *someone, anyone, anything*
quisque, quaeque, quodque or, as a substantive **quidque/quīcque,** indefinite pron., *each, every*
quisquis, quidquid or quicquid, indefinite pron., *whoever, whichever*
quō, adv., *where; to what purpose, in order that*
quod, conj., *because*
quondam, adv., *formerly, at times, sometimes*
quoque, adv., *also*
quot, num. adj., indecl., *how many, as many as*

R

rāmus, -ī, m., *branch*
rapidus, -a, -um, adj., *swift*
rapiō, -ere, rapuī, raptus, *to seize, carry off; hasten along*
Rapō, Rapōnis, m., *Rapo,* a Latin ally of Turnus, 748

rārus, -a, -um, adj., *loose, thin*
ratis, ratis, f., *ship*
receptō, -āre, -āvī, -ātus, *to take back or out; recover*
recidīvus, -a, -um, adj., *returning; rebuilt*
recipiō, -ere, -cēpī, -ceptus, *to take back*
reclūdō, -ere, -clūsī, -clūsus, *to unclose; to open*
recondō, -ere, -condidī, -conditus, *to thrust; bury* (816)
recursus, -ūs, m., *running back; return; retreat*
recūsō, -āre, -āvī, -ātus, *to shrink from*
reddō, -ere, -didī, -ditus, *to return, reply*
redeō, -īre, -iī, -itus, *to go back*
redimio, -īre, -iī, -itus, *to encircle* (with a garland)
reditus, -ūs, m., *return, revenue*
redūcō, -ere, -duxī, -ductus, *to bring back, recall, reply*
referō, -ferre, rettulī relātus, *to bring back*
reficiō, -ere, -fēcī, -fectus, *to repair, restore*
reflectō, -ere, -flexī, -flexus, *to bend back*
rēgīna, -ae, f., *queen*
regiō, -ōnis, f., *region*
rēgius, -a, -um, adj., *royal*
rēgnātor, -ōris, m., *one who reigns; sovereign*
rēgnō, āre, -āvī, -ātus, *to rule*
regō, -ere, rēxī, rēctus, *to rule*
reiciō, -ere, -iēcī, -reiectus, *to turn away*
relābor, relābī, -lāpsus sum, *to retreat; flow back*

relinquō, -ere, -līquī, -lictus, *to abandon*
reminīscor, reminīscī, *to call to mind; recall*
remittō, -ere, -mīsī, -missus, *to send back*
remurmurō, -āre, -āvī, -rātus, *to murmur back*
rēmus, -ī, m., *oar*
reor, rērī, ratus sum, *to think*
repente or repens, adv., *suddenly*
repetō, -ere, -petīvī, -petītus, *to demand back; recall, mention again*
reposcō, -ere, *to ask again, claim*
reprimō, -ere, -pressī, -pressus, *to restrain, hold back*
rēs, reī, f., *matter, affair, thing, property*
respiciō, -ere, -spexī, -spectus, *to look back*
respōnsum, -ī, n., *answer*
restō, -āre, restitī, *to remain; be in store*
resultō, -āre, *to leap back or again*
rēte, rētis, n., *net, trap*
retineō, -ēre, -tinuī, -tentus, *to hold back*
retrāctō, -āre, -āvī, -ātus, *to handle again; gripe or grasp again*
retrahō, -ere, -trāxī, -tractus, *to draw back*
retrō, adv., *backward*
revocō, -āre, -āvī, -ātus, *to call back*
revolvō, -ere, -volvī, -volūtus, *to roll back, ebb* (660)
rēx, rēgis, m., *king*
Rhaebus, -ī, m., *Rhaebus,* Mezentius' horse, 861
Rhoeteus, Rhoeteos, m., *Rhoeteus,* a Latin ally of Turnus, 399, 402
Rhoetus, -ī, m., *Rhoetus,* king of the Marsi, 388
rigidus, -a, -um, adj., *hard, rigid, stiff*

rīpa, -ae, f., *bank*
rīte, adv., *with the proper rites; duly, correctly*
rōbur, -oris, n., *oak; spear* (479)
rogitō, -āre, -āvī, -ātus, *to ask frequently*
rogus, -ī, m., *funeral pyre*
Rōmānus, -a, -um, adj., *Roman* (12)
rōstrum, -ī, n., *beak, prow, speaker's platform*
rota, -ae, f., *wheel; chariot* (pl.)
rotō, -āre, -āvī, -ātus, *to move like a wheel; whirl about*
rubeō, -ēre, rubuī, *to be red*
rudēns, rudentis, m., *rope; cord*
rumpō, -ere, rūpī, ruptus, *to break*
ruō, ruere, ruī, rūtus, *to rush; fall* (338, 756)
rūpēs, -is, f., *rock*
Rutulī, -ōrum, m., *Rutuli,* a Latin tribe whose leader was Turnus, 20, 84, 111, etc.
Rutulus, -a, -um, adj., *Rutulian* (108, 232, 245, etc.)

S

sacer, sacra, sacrum, adj., *holy*
sacerdōs, -ōtis, m. or f., *priest, priestess*
Sacrātor, -ōris, m., *Sacrator,* a Latin ally of Turnus, 747
sacrō, -āre, -āvī, -ātus, *to consecrate*
saepe, adv., *often*
saeviō, -īre, saeviī, saevitus, *to rage*
saevus, -a, -um, adj., *savage*
sagitta, -ae, f., *arrow*
sāl, salis, m., *salt; sea*
saliō, -īre, saluī, saltus, *to leap*
Salius, -iī, m., *Salius,* a Latin ally of Turnus, 753
saltus, -ūs, m., *jump*
salūs, -ūtis, f., *health; safety*
sānē, adv., *reasonably; by all means*

sanguineus, -a, -um, adj., *bloody, bloodshot*
sanguis, -inis, m., *blood*
Sarpēdōn, Sarpedonis, m., *Sarpedon, son of Jupiter, killed by Patroclus in the Trojan War,* 125, 471
satis or sat (comp. satius), adv., *enough;* comp. *better*
Sāturnius, -a, -um, adj., *belonging to Saturn; Saturnian* (659, 760)
satus, -a, -um, adj., *begotten of*
saxum, -ī, n., *rock, boulder, stone*
scālae, -ārum, f., *ladder; scaling ladder*
scēptrum, -ī, n., *royal staff; scepter*
scindō, -ere, scidī, scissus, *to cut, rend, cleave*
sciō, -īre, scīvī/sciī, scītus, *to know*
scūtum, -ī, n., *shield*
secō, -āre, secuī, sectus, *to cut, cleave, mark out* (107)
secundus, -a, -um, adj., *favorable; exultant* (266)
secūrus, -a, -um, adj., *free from care; untroubled*
secus, adv., *otherwise, differently, not so, the contrary*
sed, conj., *but*
sedeō, -ēre, sēdī, sessus, *to sit; settle down; stay fixed* (785)
sēdēs, sēdis, f., *seat; home*
sēgnis, -e, adj., *slow; cowardly*
semel, adv., *once*
sēmianimis (in hexam. poetry pron. semyanimis), -e, adj., *half-alive*
sēmifer, -fera, -ferum, adj., *half-wild*
sēminex (nom. not in use), sēminecis, adj., *half dead*
semper, adv., *always*
senecta, -ae, f., *old age*
senex, senis, adj., *old, aged*
senior, -ōris, subst., *old man;* adj., *older*

sēnsus, -ūs, m., *feeling*
sententia, -ae, f., *opinion; decision*
sentiō, -īre, sēnsī, sēnsus, *to perceive; feel; understand*
septem, *seven*
septēnī, -ae, -a, adj., *seven each*
sepulcrum, -ī, n., *tomb, grave*
sequāx, -ācis, adj., *following, pursuing*
sequor, sequī, secūtus sum, *to follow; pay heed to* (258)
Serestus, -ī, m., *Serestus, a Trojan,* 541
sērus, -a, -um, adj., *(too) late*
servō, -āre, -āvī, -ātus, *to save; watch for* (288)
sescentī, -ae, -a, adj., *six hundred*
seu, conj., *whether; or if;* **seu...seu,** *whether...or*
sī, conj., *if*
sīc, adv., *thus*
siccō, -āre, -āvī, -ātus, *to make dry*
siccus, -a, -um, adj., *dry*
sīdereus, -a, -um, adj., *starry*
sīdus, -eris, n., *star*
signum, -ī, n., *sign, standard* (258)
silentium, -i(ī), n., *silence*
sileō, -ēre, siluī, *to be silent*
silēscō, -ere, siluī, *to become silent*
silva, -ae, f., *forest*
silvicola, -ae, m./f., *an inhabitant of the woods*
similis, -e, adj., *similar*
Simoīs, Simoentis, m., *Simois, a river near Troy,* 60
simul, adv., *at the same time*
sīn, conj., *but if*
sine, prep. with abl., *without*
sinister, -a, -um, adj., *left; unfavorable*
sinistra, -ae, f. (sc. manus), *the left hand*
sinō, -ere, sīvī, situs, *to allow; let be*
sinus, -ūs, m., *fold, pocket, chest*

Sīrius, -a, -um, adj., *of the Dog Star* (273)
sistō, -ere, stitī, status, *to set up; place, plant*
sitis, sitis, f., *thirst*
sīve or seu, conj., *whether; or if*
socer, -ī, m., *father-in-law*
socius, -iī, m., *ally, comrade*
sodālis, sodālis, m., *comrade*
sōl, sōlis, m., *sun*
sōlāmen, -inis, n., *means of consoling; solace*
solium, -iī, n., *seat; throne*
sollicitō, -āre, -āvī, -ātus, *to stir up; taunt* (612)
sōlor, -ārī, sōlātus sum, *to console*
solum, -ī, n., *bottom, native territory*
sōlus, -a, -um, adj., *alone, only*
solvō, -ere, solvī, solūtus, *to release, loosen; break; absolve*
somnium, -i(ī), n., *dream*
somnus, -ī, m., *sleep*
sonitus, -ūs, m., *sounding; noise*
sōns, sontis, adj., *hurtful; guilty*
sonus, -ī, m., *sound*
sōpiō, -īre, sōpīvī, sōpītus, *to put to sleep, lull to sleep*
soror, -ōris, f., *sister*
sors, sortis, f., *fate*
Sparta, -ae, f., *Sparta*, capital of Laconia. Home of Menelaus and Helen, 92
spatium, -i(ī), n., *space; extent*
spectātor, -is, m., *beholder*
spectō, -āre, -āvī, -ātus, *to look at*
specula, -ae, f., *lookout; watchtower*
speculor, -ārī, speculātus sum, *to watch, examine*
spērō, -āre, -āvī, -ātus, *to hope*
spēs, speī, f., *hope; ambition*
spīculum, -ī, n., *sharp point, sting, arrow*

spīna, -ae, f., *spine*
spīrō, -āre, -āvī, -ātus, *to breathe; surge; heave*
spolia, spoliōrum, n., *plunder*
spūmeus, -a, -um, adj., *foamy, frothy*
spūmō, -āre, -āvī, -ātus, *to foam*
squāleō, -ēre, -uī, *to be stiff*
stabulum, -ī, n., *stable*
stagnum, -ī, n., *standing water, pool*
statiō, -ōnis, f., *anchorage*
sternō, -ere, strāvī, strātus, *to lay low, strike down*
Sthenius, -iī, m., *Sthenius*, a Latin ally of Turnus, 388
stīpō, -āre, -āvī, -ātus, *to crowd together, mass*
stirps, stirpis, f., *stem, stalk; family tree*
stō, -āre, stetī, status, *to stand; be fixed; cost* (with dat. and abl.)
strepō, -ere, -uī, -itus, *to make a noise; murmur*
strīdeō, -ēre or strīdō, -ere, strīdī, *to produce a grating or shrill sound; to creak*
stringō, -ere, strīnxī, strictus, *to draw tight; graze*
Strȳmonius, -a, -um, adj., *Strymonian; of the Strymon* (river), 265
Strȳmonius, -iī, m., *Strymonius*, an Arcadian, 414
stupeō, -ēre, stupuī, *to be amazed or dazed; to be bewildered*
Stygius, -a, -um, adj., *Stygian; pertaining to Styx* (river of the Underworld), 113
suādeō, -ēre, suāsī, suāsus, *to recommend, urge, advise*
sub, prep. with acc. and abl., *under, down to, under cover of*
subdūcō, -ere, -dūxī, -ductus, *to take away by stealth* (with acc. and abl.)

subeō, -īre, subīvī/subiī, subitus, *to go under; to approach from under; to approach* (877); *advance* (371); *come to help* (338)
subigō, -ere, -ēgī, -āctus, *to compel*
subitō, adv., *suddenly*
subiungō, -ere, -iūnxī, -iūnctus, *to join under or to; fasten*
sublevō, -āre, -āvī, -ātus, *to lift from beneath; uplift*
sublīme, adv., *loftily, on high*
sublīmis, -e, adj., *elevated, lofty, heroic, noble*
subnectō, -ere, -nexuī, -nexus, *to tie beneath; to bind*
subrēmigō, -āre, -āvī, -ātus, *to row lightly, paddle*
subrīdeō, -ere, -rīsī, -rīsus, *to smile (down) upon*
subsidium, -i(ī), n., *help*
subsistō, -ere, -stitī, *to stand after; halt*
succēdo, -ere, -cessi, -cessus, *to follow; take the place of; enter* (with dat.)
succīdō, -ere, -cīdī, -cīsus, *to cut beneath; cut*
succingō, -ere, -cīnxī, -cīnctus, *to gird beneath; gird up; wrap*
succurrō, -ere, -currī, -cursus, *to help, rescue*
suggerō, -ere, -gessī, -gestus, *to bring or put under or up to; supply; to collect*
suī, sibi, sē, sē, reflexive pron., *himself, herself, itself* (reflexive)
sulcō, -āre, -āvī, -ātus, *to plow*
sulcus, -ī, m., *furrow*
Sulmō, -ōnis, m., *Sulmo,* a follower of Turnus, 517
sum, esse, fuī, futūrus, *to be*

summa, -ae, f., *peak, sum; chief command*
summittō (submittō), -ere, -mīsī, -missus, *to place under; to be humbled*
summus, -a, -um, adj., used as superl. of **superus,** *highest; supreme*
suō, -ere, suī, sūtus, *to sew*
super, adv., *further;* prep. with acc. and abl., *over, about*
superbus, -a, -um, adj., *arrogant*
superēmineō, -ēre, *to rise above*
superī, -ōrum, m., *those above,* i.e., *the gods*
superstō, -āre, *to stand over*
supersum, -esse, -fuī, -futūrus, *to be left over; survive*
superus, -a, -um, adj., *above; upper*
supervolō, -āre, -āvī, -ātus, *to fly over or above*
supplex, -icis, *suppliant*
suprēmus, -a, -um, adj. *highest; greatest; last*
surgō, -ere, -surrēxī, surrēctus, *to rise; grow* (524)
suscitō, -āre, -āvī, -ātus, *to stir up*
suspiciō, -ere, -pexī, -pectus, *to look up at*
sustentō, -āre, -āvī, -ātus, *to support*
sustineō, -ēre, -tinuī, -tentus, *to sustain, be able to, endure*
sūta, sūtōrum, n., *coat of mail*
suus, -a, -um, poss. adj., *his/her/its own*
syrtis, syrtis, f., *sandbank or shoal in the sea; sandbank off N. African coast*

T

tacitus, -a, -um, adj., *silent*
taedet, taedēre, taesum est, *it makes (one) tired*

taeter, taetra, taetrum, adj., *disagreeable, vile*
talentum, -ī, n., *a talent*
tālis, tāle, adj., *such*
tam, adv., *so*
tamen, adv., *nevertheless, however*
tandem, adv., *finally*
tantum, adv., *so much*
tantus, -a, -um, adj., *so much; so great*
Tarchōn, Tarchōnis (-ontis), m., *Tarcho,* an Etruscan ally of Aeneas, 153, 290, 299, etc.
tardō, -āre, -āvī, -ātus, *to make slow;* intr., *to fail*
Tarquitus, -ī, m., *Tarquitus,* a Latin ally of Turnus, 550
taurus, -ī, m., *bull; bull's hide*
tēctum, -ī, n., *roof; house*
tegmen (tegumen), tegmenis, n., *means of covering; skin; shield* (887)
tegō, -ere, tēxī, tēctus, *to cover; bury* (904)
tellūs, tellūris, f., *earth*
tēlum, -ī, n., *spear*
temnō, -ere, tempsī, temptus, *to despise*
tempestās, tempestātis, f., *storm*
tempto, -āre, -āvī, -ātus, *to try; excite; disturb*
tempus, temporis, n., *time; the side of the forehead* (538, 891)
tendō, -ere, tetendī, tentus, *to stretch; strive; make for*
teneō, -ēre, tenuī, tentus, *to hold*
tenor, -ōris, m., *course, direction*
tenuis, -e, adj., *thin*
tenus, prep. with gen. and abl., *down to, as far as*
tepeō, -ēre, *to be moderately warm; to reek*
ter, adv., *three times*

terebinthus, -ī, f., *the turpentine tree;* a kind of ebony
tergum, -ī, n. or tergus, -oris, n., *the back of men or animals; shield* (718)
terra, -ae, f., *land*
terreō, -ēre, terruī, territus, to terrify
tertius, -a, -um, adj., *third*
Teucrī, -ōrum, m., *Teucri, Trojans,* 8, 22, 28, etc.
Teuthrās, Teuthrantis, m., *Teuthras,* ally of Aeneas, 402
Thaemōn, Thaemōnis, m., *Thaemon,* Lycian, ally of Aeneas, 126
thalamus, -ī, m., marriage bed; bedchamber
Theānō, Theānūs, f., *Theano,* wife of Amycus, 703
Thērōn, -ōnis, m., *Theron,* a Latin ally of Turnus, 312
Thoās, Thoantis, m., *Thoas,* an Arcadian, ally of Aeneas, 415
thōrāx, -ācis, m., *corselet*
Thrēicius, -a, -um, adj., *Thracian; northern* (350)
Thronius, -iī, m., *Thronius,* a Trojan, 753
Thȳbris, Thȳbridis, m., *Thybris,* the Tiber River, 421
Thymber, Thymbrī, m., *Thymber,* a Latin ally of Turnus, 391, 394
Thymbris, Thymbridis, m., *Thymbris,* a Trojan, 124
Thymoetēs, -ae, m., *Thymoetes,* a Trojan, 123
Tiberīnus (Thȳbrinus), -a, -um, adj., *pertaining to the Tiber* (833)
tigris, -idis, m. or f., *tigress; a ship's figurehead* (166)
timeō, -ēre, timuī, *to fear*
Tīsiphonē, Tīsiphonēs, f., *Tisiphone,* one of the three Furies, 761

tollō, -ere, sustulī, sublātus, *to raise; destroy, remove*
tōnsa, -ae, f., *oar*
torqueō, -ēre, torsī, tortus, *to twist, hurl*
torrens, -entis, m., *a rushing stream, torrent*
torreō, -ēre, -uī, tostus, *to burn*
torvus, -a, -um, adj., *stern; grim*
tot, num. adj. indecl., *so many*
totidem, num. adj., indecl., *just as many*
totiēns, adv., *so often*
tōtus, -a, -um, adj., *whole*
trahō, -ere, trāxī, tractus, *to drag*
trāiciō, -ere, -iēcī, -iectus, *to pierce*
trānō, -āre, -āvī, -ātus, *to swim or sail across*
trānseō, -īre, -īvī/iī, -itus, *to go across, pass through*
trānsiliō, -īre, silīvī (-iī or -uī), *to leap over; pass over*
trānstrum, -ī, n., *cross-timber; thwart*
trānsverberō, -āre, -āvī, -ātus, *to beat or strike through; pierce through*
trecentī, -ae, -a, adj., *three hundred*
tremebundus, -a, -um, adj., *quivering*
tremefaciō, -ere, -fēcī, -factus, *to cause to tremble*
trepidō, -āre, -āvī, -ātus, *to be agitated*
trepidus, -a, -um, adj., *agitated*
trēs, tria, *three*
triplex, -icis, adj., *threefold*
trīstis, trīstis, trīste, adj., *sad*
Trītōn, -ōnis, m., *Triton, a sea god; a ship's figurehead,* 209
Trivia, -ae, f., *Trivia, goddess of the three ways, an epithet of Hecate or Diana,* 537
Trōes, Trōum, m. pl., *Trojans* (31, 895)
Troia, -ae, f., *Troy* (27, 45, 60, etc.)

Trōiānus, -a, -um, adj., *Trojan* (77, 360, 598, etc.)
Trōius, -a, -um, adj., *of Troy; Trojan* (584, 886)
tropaeum, -ī, n., *trophy*
Trōs, Trōis, m., *a Trojan* (108, 250)
truncus, -ī, m., *trunk*
trux, trucis, adj., *savage*
tū, tuī, tibi, tē, tē, personal pron., *you*
tueor, tuērī, tūtus sum, *to look at*
tum, adv., *then, at that time*
tumidus, -a, -um, adj., *swollen; proud*
tumulus, -ī, m., *mound; grave*
tunc, adv., *then*
tundō, -ere, tutudī, tūnsus, *to beat*
tunica, -ae, f., *tunic*
turba, -ae, f., *crowd*
turbidus, -a, -um, adj., *confused, wild*
turbō, -inis, f., *whirlwind*
turma, -ae, f., *troop*
Turnus, -ī, m., *Turnus, king of the Rutuli, enemy of Aeneas,* 20, 75, 143, etc.
turpō, -āre, -āvī, -ātus, *to make indecent; to soil*
turriger, -gera, -gerum, adj., *tower-crowned*
turris, turris, f., *tower*
Tuscus, -a, -um, adj., *Etrurian; Tuscan* (164, 199, 203, etc.)
tūtus, -a, -um, adj., *safe*
tuus, -a, -um, poss. adj., *your*
Tȳdīdēs, -ae, m., *the son of Tydeus; Diomedes* (29)
tyrannus, -ī, m., *tyrant*
Tyrēs, -ae, m., *Tyres, ally of Aeneas,* 403
Tyrius, -a, -um, adj., *of Tyre; Tyrian or Phoenician* (55)
Tyrrhēnus, -a, -um, adj., *Tyrrhenian; Etruscan; Tuscan* (71, 691, 787, etc.)

U

ubī, adv., *where, when*
Ūfēns, Ūfentis, m., *Ufens*, a Latin ally of Turnus, 518
ūllus, -a, -um, adj., *any*
ultor, -ōris, m., *avenger, punisher*
ultrā, adv. *farther* and prep. with acc., *beyond*
ultrō, adv., *furthermore, beyond; voluntarily*
umbō, -ōnis, m., *the boss (of a shield)*
umbra, -ae, f., *shadow*
Umbrō, -ōnis, m., *Umbro*, leader of the Marsi, ally of Turnus, 544
umerus, -ī, m., *shoulder*
ūnā, adv., *together*
unda, -ae, f., *wave*
unde, adv., *from where, whence*
undique, adv., *from all sides*
undō, -āre, -āvī, -ātus, *to flow, stream*
ūnus, -a, -um, adj., *one*
urbs, urbis, f., *city*
urgeō, -ēre, ursī, *to press forward*
usquam, adv., *anywhere*
ūsque, adv., *continuously, ever*
ut or utī, conj., *so that; as* (454), *when* (441, 570); *would that* (631); *how?* (20)
uterque, utraque, utrumque, pron., *each of two*

V

vacō, -āre, -āvī, -ātus, *to be empty;* **vacat,** impersonal *it is allowed, there is time for*
vadum, -ī, n., *ford; shallow; water*
vāgīna, -ae, f., *scabbard*
valeō, -ēre, valuī, valitus, *to be strong, be worth*
Valerus, -ī, m., *Valerus*, a Latin ally of Turnus, 752

validus, -a, -um, adj., *strong*
vallus, -ī, m., *stake; stockade*
vānus, -a, -um, adj., *empty; devoid of*
varius, -a, -um, adj., *varied*
vāstus, -a, -um, adj., *vast, enormous*
ve, postpositive enclitic, *or;* **ve...ve,** *either...or*
vehō, -ere, vēxī, vectus, *to carry*
vel, conj., *or*
vellō, -ere, vulsī/vellī, vulsus, *to pluck out, pull*
vēlō, -āre, -āvī, -ātus, *to cover, veil*
vēlum, -ī, n., *sail, awning*
velut or velutī, conj., *just as*
venēnum, -ī, n., *poison*
venia, -ae, f., *pardon*
Venīlia, -ae, f., *Venilia*, mother of Turnus, 76
veniō, -īre, vēnī, ventus, *to come*
ventus, -ī, m., *wind*
Venus, Veneris, f., *Venus*, goddess of Love, mother of Aeneas, 16, 132, 332, etc.
verber, verberis, n., *whip; a beating or blow with a whip*
verberō, -āre, -āvī, -ātus, *to whip, flog, beat*
verbum, -ī, n., *word*
vērō, adv., *certainly*
versicolor, -ōris, adj., *of various colors*
versō, -āre, -āvī, -ātus, *to keep turning; debate*
vertex, verticis, m., *peak, summit, head*
vertō, -ere, vertī, versus, *to turn*
vērum, -ī, n., *that which is true; truth*
vēsānus, -a, -um, adj., *insane; furious*
vester, vestra, vestrum, poss. adj., *your*
vestīgium, -i(ī), n., *footstep*
vestis, vestis, f., *clothing*
Vesulus, -ī, m., *Vesulus*, a mountain in Liguria, 708

vetitum, -ī, n., *that which is forbidden; a prohibition*
vetus, veteris, adj., *old*
vetustās, -ātis, f., *antiquity*
vetustus, -a, -um, adj., *old*
via, -ae, f., *street*
viātor, -ōris, m., *traveler, wayfarer*
vibrō, -āre, -āvī, -ātus, *to shake*
victor, -ōris, m., *conqueror*
victōria, -ae, f., *victory*
videō, -ēre, vidī, vīsus, *to see; decide* (pass.) *to seem*
vigilō, -āre, -āvī, -ātus, *to be awake*
vincō, -ere, vīcī, victus, *to conquer*
vinculum, -ī, n., *bond*
violentus, -a, -um, adj., *violent, savage*
vir, -ī, m., *man*
virtūs, -ūtis, f., *manliness; courage*
vīs, vis, f., *force; violence;* (pl.) *strength*
vīscus, vīsceris, n., *innards*
vīsus, -ūs, m., *sight; glance*
vīta, -ae, f., *life*
vitta, -ae, f., *ribbon*
vīvidus, -a, -um, adj., *lively, vigorous*
vīvō, -ere, vīxī, vīctus, *to live*
vix, adv., *scarcely*
vōciferor, -ārī, -ātus sum, *to raise the voice; cry out*
vocō, -āre, -āvī, -ātus, *to call; summon*
Volcānius, -a, -um, adj., *pertaining to Vulcan* (408)
Volcānus, -ī, m., *Vulcan, the Roman god of fire,* 543

Volcēns, Volcentis, m., *Volcens, father of Camers, an ally of Turnus,* 563
volēns, volentis, adj., *willing*
volitō, -āre, -āvī, -ātus, *to fly around*
volō, -āre, -āvī, -ātus, *to fly*
volō, velle, voluī, *to wish*
volucer, volucris, volucre, adj., *flying; winged*
volucris, volucris, m. or f., *bird*
voluptās, -ātis, f., *pleasure*
volūtō, -āre, -āvī, -ātus, *to roll about; ponder over* (159)
volvō, ere, voluī, volūtus, *to roll*
vomō, -ere, vomuī, vomitus, *to vomit; belch*
vorāgō, vorāginis, f., *chasm; whirlpool*
vōs, vestrum/vestrī, personal pron., *you*
vōtum, -ī, n., *vow; wish; prayer*
voveō, -ēre, vōvī, vōtus, *to vow*
vōx, vōcis, f., *voice; word*
vulgō, -āre, -āvī, -ātus, *to publish, circulate; lay open*
vulnus, vulneris, n., *wound*
vultus, -ūs, m., *expression*

X

Xanthus, -ī, m., *Xanthus,* a river near Troy, 60

Z

Zephyrus, -ī, m., *Zephyr,* the West Wind, 103

Index

This index lists grammatical, metrical, and stylistic items mentioned in the commentary; numbers refer to line numbers in the commentary. Terms with an asterisk are defined in Appendix 2.

ablative: absolute, 52, 101, 208, 241, 298, 312, 339-41, 342, 347-8, 366-7, 405-9, 449, 533, 535-6, 552-3, 586-8, 641, 646, 699-700, 733, 739, 803, 807-8, 878, 893-4; attendant circumstance, 31, 445; comparison, 129, 248, 811; degree of difference, 226-27, 765; manner, 97,107-8, 356-7, 447, 459, 466, 505, 556, 578, 654, 742; material,137-8, 499, 636, 783-4, 784-5, 817-18; motion away from, 38, 143-4, 215-16, 330-2, 349, 473, 717-8, 766; origin, 141, 205-6, 345, 388, 517, 543, 563-4, 618, 703-6; place where (locative), 5, 23-4, 98-9, 104, 118-19, 138, 165, 169, 181, 236, 270-1, 356-7, 418, 540, 559, 563-4, 566-8, 648, 680, 701, 750, 780, 804-5, 806, 836, 845, 887, 901, 906; price, 494-5, 503-4; quality, 178, 381, 511-12, 538, 550-2; separation, 25, 315, 363, 444, 624, 774-6; specification, 20-2, 87, 174, 185-6, 201, 329, 354-5, 411, 435, 609-10, 722, 734-5, 748, 754; time, 147, 272-3, 405-9

accusative: adverbial, 319-20, 740-1; cognate, 84, 572; duration, 708; Greek form; 65, 89, 163, 264-6, 315, 316-17, 337, 373-4, 403, 413, 424, 442, 459, 702, 732, 738, 747, 749, 873; respect, 631-2; specification, 132-3, 157-8, 324-5, 699, 711, 869

Aegaeon: and Aeneas, 543-74, 755-68; and Gigantomachy, 543-74

Aeneas: as Achilles, 272-3, 308-908, 510-605, 513, 530, 559, 600, 606-88, 755-832, 832, 833-908, 904-5; as Aegaeon, 543-74; anger (rage), 510-605, 513, 603, 604, 802, 813-14; *aristeia** of, 308-44, 510-605; as Augustus, 260-75, 261, 270-1, 271, 272-3, 510-605; behavior toward Lausus, 794-832; difference of

Index

behavior with Turnus, 439-509, 443, 490, 491, 492, 496, 824; duel with Mezentius, 755-832, 873-908; good general, 159; as Hector, 755-832; human sacrifice, 510-605, 519; *impietas*, 521, 523, 534, 591, 600, 783-4; as Paris, 79, 90-1; as Patroclus, 510-605, 591; phantom of, 606-88; as Pyrrhus, 555
affective vocabulary, 45-6, 121, 172, 380, 386, 392, 393, 394, 395, 411, 800, 821-2, 833
Alexandrian footnote, 189, 565-6
Allecto, 39-41
alliteration*, 99, 103, 212, 246, 393, 555, 590, 672, 677, 802, 821-2, 842, 864
anachronism, 120, 157-8, 258-9, 310
anaphora*, 36-7, 46, 67-8, 280-2, 358-9, 429, 442, 672, 677, 804-5, 861-2
antithesis*, 737
apostrophe*, 139, 185-6, 200, 324-5, 326-7, 390, 394, 411, 509, 514, 557, 791-3
archaism*, 2, 4, 6, 53, 65, 97, 107-8, 168, 228-9, 261, 312, 445, 470, 481, 531-2, 538, 631-2, 677, 681-3, 743-4, 745-6, 755, 874
arsis, lengthening*, 720
Ascanius: beauty, 118-45, 137-8; and Marcellus, 47; as *puer*, 47
assembly, of the gods, 1-117; *deductio*, 117
assonance*, 212, 572, 734-5, 873, 900
asyndeton*, 46, 203, 295-6, 429, 515-16, 677
baldric, of Pallas, 479-509. *See also* Danaids
beauty: erotic, 137-8; heroic, 180-1, 435
brevity, in speech, 16-17

caesura*, 103; hiatus at, 136; lengthening before, 382-3, 394, 432-3, 487
catalogue, 163-214
chiasmus*, 137-8, 267-8, 360, 372-3, 756
cinematic technique, 147
Cymodocea: deceptive prophecy, 245; speech 228-245
Danaids, 479-509, 497
dative: advantage, 400-1, 525, 531-2, 616, 622-3; agent, 6, 430; double, 252; ethical, 88; motion forward, 148, 507, 546; possession, 76, 86, 100, 145, 152-3, 168, 182, 201, 202, 239-40, 326-7, 375-6, 414, 468, 527-8, 565-6, 613, 619-20, 712, 759; purpose, 214, 252, 586-8, 714-15; reference, 6, 111-12, 135, 137-8, 170-1, 203, 210-11, 270-1, 283, 313-14, 322-3, 366-7, 392, 414, 452, 467, 503-4, 525, 538, 551, 583-4, 628-9, 676, 745-6, 813-14, 849, 858-9, 861-2, 902, 903; separation, 50, 81-2, 276-8, 462-3
deixis*, 198, 234, 354-5, 373-4, 707, 862
diaeresis* (bucolic), 830
dicolon abundans, 9-10, 31, 47, 104, 258-9, 442, 558, 622-3, 819-20, 850, 855
dum clause, 43, 58, 321, 800, 807-8
ecphrasis*, 653
elision, 691-2
ellipsis*, 599, 672
enallage*, 113-15, 230-1, 426-7, 444, 662, 791, 898-9
enjambment*, 28-9, 89, 122, 150-1
epanalepsis*, 180-1, 200, 400-1, 691-2, 821-2

epithet*, 1, 16-17, 87, 184, 219-21, 253, 276-8, 324-5, 373-4, 425, 439-40, 541-2, 591, 615-6, 685, 783-4, 825-6
euphemism*, 352
focalization* (point of view), 445, 514, 781-2
Furies, 67-8, 761
genitive: Greek, 199; objective, 100, 143-4, 189, 280-2, 326-7, 426-7, 501, 524, 609-10, 789, 843, 863; partitive, 312, 400-1, 478, 563-4; possessive, 125; quality, 714-5; respect, 563-4; separation, 154, 326-7, 441, 630, 752; subjective, 426-7, 853-4, 863, 904-5
gerund, 116, 182, 225, 493, 681-3, 797-8, 846
gerundive, 557, 793
gladiatorial allusion, 873-908, 907
half-lines, 17, 284, 490
hendiadys*, 460, 698
Hercules: prayer to, 439-509, 460, 461, 462-3; tears of, 464-78; 464-5
hiatus*, 18, 136, 141, 156
homosexuality, 324-5
hyperbaton*, 326-7, 681-3
hypermetric line*, 781-2, 895
ictus and accent (coincidence), 95, 245; clash 258-9, 505
Ida, Mount, 157-8, 230-1, 252
immature death, 439-509
imperative, 15, 61-2, 241, 598, 600, 743-4, 881; future, 53, 67-8, 280-2; negative, 11, 372-3
infinitive: complementary, 118-19, 130, 354-5; historical, 267-8, 288, 299, 301, 457-8; of purpose, 9-10, 61-2, 64, 66, 67-8, 366-7, 701
interlocking word order*, 99

interrogative adjective, 9-10, 90-1, 150-1, 152-3, 164, 675
interrogative pronoun, 9-10, 72, 285-6
irony*, 67-8, 81-2, 89, 109-10, 245, 305, 402, 494-5, 534, 592, 607, 689, 783-4, 825-6, 882
Juno: compassion of, 633-4, 686; and the phantom of Aeneas, 606-88; and power over weather, 633-4; and *Saturnia*, 659
Jupiter: and ambiguity, 15, 96-117; and fate, 15, 34-5, 63, 464-78; intervention in human affairs, 96-117, 107-8, 436-7, 689
Juturna, 439-509, 439-40, 675
Latinus, king of Latium, 79, 80, 118-307, 551, 659, 671, 693-6, 821-2, 870-1
Lausus: as Adonis, 794-832, 832; as Antilochus, 794-832; *aristeia** of, 362-438, 426-438; beauty of, 426-38, 435, 794-832; death of, 755-832; filial devotion of, 362-438, 800; as Hector, 755-832, 832; as paradigm of *pietas*, 362-438, 783-4, 812, 824, 825-6; and parallelism with death of Pallas, 439-509; as Patroclus, 362-438, 755-832; as Sarpedon, 362-438; as Scipio Africanus, 794-832; young age, 426-38, 433-4, 800, 816
line-end: with monosyllabic word, 2, 107-8, 258-9, 734-5, 771, 802, 843, 864; with quadrisyllabic word, 136, 505; with three disyllables, 302, 400-1, 442, 772
litotes*, 185-6, 247, 272-3, 297, 657, 737, 907
locative, 558, 696-7

Mars, as abstract spirit of war, 20-2, 237, 280, 755

metaphor*, 57, 58, 61-2, 78, 87, 88, 107-8, 147, 166, 214, 226-7, 264-6, 291, 296, 395, 492, 503-4, 513, 524, 680, 764-5, 813-14, 870-1, 887

metonymy*, 174, 191, 207, 208, 231-2, 237, 479, 549, 764-5, 900

Mezentius: as Achilles, 689-754, 738, 742, 833-908, 844; 858-72; as Anchises, 821-2; *aristeia** of, 689-754; death of, 873-908; and duel with Aeneas, 755-832, 873-908; as epicurean, 689-754, 880; as Hector, 689-754, 833-908, 904-5; heroic ethic of, 732; as Orion, 755-68, 763, 764-5, 766, 768; as Patroclus 689-754; as Polyphemus; 755-68, 766, 767, 768, 771, 858-72, 864; as Sarpedon, 689-754; 755-832;

Muses, invocation to the, 163-5, 163

nam(que), postponed, 400-1, 584-5, 614, 815

-ne, interrogative, 673

Pallas: and Aeneas, 160-2; *aristeia** of, 362-438; baldric of (*see* baldric); beauty of, 426-38, 435; and Dido, 160-2; duel with Turnus, 439-509; erotic fallen body of, 479-509; as Hector, 439-509, 479-509; introduced to the iron age, 160-2; and Marcellus, 326-7; parallelism with death of Lausus, 439-509; as Patroclus, 308-908, 362-438, 439-509, 479-509; prayer to Hercules, 457-63, 460, 461, 462-3; rivaling the deeds of his father, 371, 373-4; as Sarpedon, 308-908, 362-438, 362-79, 439-509; young age, 326-7, 362-438, 426-38, 433-4

parataxis*, 80, 659

participle: concessive, 385; passive, used as active, 403; passive, used as middle, 256-7, 573; as substantive, 79, 111-12, 141

patronymic*, 4, 123, 250, 263, 321, 461, 464-5, 499, 545, 659, 703-6, 821-2

personification*, 172, 364-5, 395, 396, 508, 556, 740-1, 904-5

plural, instead of singular, 54-6, 69, 79, 113-15, 389, 476-7, 524, 586-8, 731

polyptoton*, 149, 361, 375-6, 619-20, 839

praeteritio*, 36-7

prolepsis*, 103, 231-2, 379

quid, used adverbially, 87, 611, 878, 900

relative clause: characteristic, 44-5; concessive, 482-4; purpose, 19, 519, 679, 840, 879

Rhaebus, silence of, 858-72

Silver Line*, 245

simile*, 97, 134-7, 248, 264-6, 272-3, 356-7, 405-9, 454-6, 565-6, 642, 693-6, 708, 723-8, 763, 803-8; trespassing, 717-18, 808-9

singular, collective, 207, 238, 333-4

subjunctive: deliberative, 36-7, 378; disjunctive, indirect questions, 107-8, 681-3, 684; indirect command, 54-6, 258-9; indirect question, 20-2, 150, 150-1, 152-3, 160-2, 164, 285-6, 481, 772; jussive, 32-3, 43, 46, 85, 254-5, 280-2, 296, 617, 853-4, 875; optative, 50, 443, 461, 462-3, 631-2, 774-6, 853-4; potential, 19, 185-6, 675; purpose, 239-40, 679, 807-8; result, 847

super, preposition (instead of *de*), 42, 839

supine, 637
synchysis*. *See* interlocking word order*
syncope*, 244, 693-6, 609-10
synecdoche*, 5, 140, 205-6, 223, 271, 399, 570, 594, 639, 733, 784-5
synizesis*, 116, 129, 378, 396, 487, 496, 764-5
Tarchon: and Brasidas, 287-307; and the Tarquins, 152-3, 287-307
tmesis*, 794
transferred epithet. *See* enallage*
tricolon*, 430, 482-4
Trojan camp, as new Troy, 26-27, 74-5

Turnus: as Achilles, 653-88; difference of behavior with Aeneas, 439-509, 443, 490, 491, 492, 496, 824; duel with Pallas, 439-509; as good general, 285-6, 308; as Hector, 439-509; 479-509, 606-88, 653-88; helmet of, 271; heroic physique, 446; as Iliadic Aeneas, 606-88; impetuosity, 20-2, 150-1, 276-8; lack of restraint, 479-509, 490, 501; and mother Venilia, 76; as Patroclus, 439-509; as proto-Roman, 74-5; as Pyrrhus, 443, 491
Venus: *aurea*, 16-17; loquacity of, 16-17; cities worshipping Venus, 51, 52, 86
wordplay, 211, 225, 318, 454-6, 572, 575, 737, 825-6
zeugma*, 12-13, 87, 667